Scale-Up in Education
Volume I

Scale-Up in Education
Volume I

Ideas in Principle

Edited by Barbara Schneider
and Sarah-Kathryn McDonald

ROWMAN & LITTLEFIELD PUBLISHERS, INC.
Lanham • Boulder • New York • Toronto • Plymouth, UK

ROWMAN & LITTLEFIELD PUBLISHERS, INC.

Published in the United States of America
by Rowman & Littlefield Publishers, Inc.
A wholly owned subsidary of The Rowman & Littlefield Publishing Group, Inc.
4501 Forbes Boulevard, Suite 200, Lanham, Maryland 20706
www.rowmanlittlefield.com

Estover Road
Plymouth PL6 7PY
United Kingdom

Preparation of this publication was funded, in part, by the National Science
Foundation under grant no. 0129365. Any opinions, finding, conclusions, or
recommendations expressed in this publication are those of the authors and do
not necessarily reflect the views of the National Science Foundation.

British Library Cataloguing in Publication Information Available

Library of Congress Cataloging-in-Publication Data

Scale-up in education / edited by Barbara Schneider and Sarah-Kathryn McDonald.
   2 v. ; cm.
  Includes bibliographical references and index.
  Contents: v. 1. Ideas in principle — v. 2. Issues in practice.
  ISBN-13: 978-0-7425-4730-8 (v. 1 : cloth : alk. paper)
  ISBN-10: 0-7425-4730-2 (v. 1 : cloth : alk. paper)
  ISBN-13: 978-0-7425-4731-5 (v. 1 : pbk. : alk. paper)
  ISBN-10: 0-7425-4731-0 (v. 1 : pbk. : alk. paper)
  1. School improvement programs—United States. 2. Educational change—
United States. I. Schneider, Barbara L. II. McDonald, Sarah-Kathryn. III. Title.
LB2822.82.S295 2007
371.200973—dc22   2006016982

Printed in the United States of America

♾™ The paper used in this publication meets the minimum requirements of
American National Standard for Information Sciences—Permanence of Paper
for Printed Library Materials, ANSI/NISO Z39.48-1992.

Contents

List of Figures

List of Tables

Acknowledgments

The two volumes comprising *Scale-Up in Education* are the product of many people. First and foremost a thank-you must go to the Interagency Education Research Initiative (IERI) community in its effort to develop, understand the impacts of, and learn the conditions under which exemplary educational interventions improve student learning outcomes in reading, mathematics, and science. We would like to thank the National Science Foundation (NSF), the Institute of Education Sciences (IES), and the National Institute of Child Health and Human Development (NICHD) for supporting and sponsoring the valuable contributions of the IERI community.

The interdisciplinary community at the University of Chicago facilitated our efforts. A special thanks to Craig Coelen, president of NORC, who generously housed and supported the Data Research and Development Center (DRDC). Richard Saller, provost, and Mark Hansen, dean of the Social Sciences Division, provided us with support for graduate students, workshops, and conferences. We also need to thank Kai Jackson, Grants and Contracts administrator, for providing budget oversight and reimbursements.

The Data Research and Development Center needs to be acknowledged for being the driving force behind these volumes. Kevin Brown, research scientist at DRDC, took on the role of principal project manager in supervising this collaborative contribution to the field of research and education. Lisa Hoogstra also provided invaluable editorial assistance to these volumes.

We must also acknowledge the efforts of countless research assistants and support staff, including Katie Bennett, Malkah Bressler, Eric Hedberg, Michelle Llosa, Zack Kertcher, Elizabeth McGhee-Hassrick, Daniel Menchik, Ann Owens, Jessica Pan, Lara Perez-Longobardo, Demetria Proutsos, Justin

Rosenthal, Rafael Santana, Sara Van Hoose, and Sam Yount. We appreciate their hard work in formatting chapters, entering editorial corrections, proofreading, checking references, indexing, contacting contributors, and planning and coordinating the scale-up conference.

A very special thank-you to all those who participated in the conference, "Conceptualizing Scale-Up: Multidisciplinary Perspectives." These edited volumes are based on the conference proceedings, which explored how the educational community's efforts to research scale-up can be enriched with theories, traditions, models, and practices found in other fields that routinely extend successful innovations to society at large. Last but not least, we need to thank Janice Earle, program director at NSF, for her unwavering support of the IERI community. Thank you all!

Introduction

Barbara Schneider and Sarah-Kathryn McDonald

For the past decade U.S. education policy has supported a variety of activities designed to enhance the quality of educational research. One such activity was the establishment of the Interagency Education Research Initiative (IERI), a collaborative venture of the National Science Foundation, the U.S. Department of Education, and the National Institute for Child Health and Human Development in the National Institutes of Health. A primary objective of the IERI program is "to identify the conditions under which effective, evidence-based interventions to improve preK–12 student learning and achievement succeed when applied on a large scale" (National Science Foundation 2005). In 2002, the National Science Foundation (NSF) established the Data Research and Development Center (DRDC), a research and technical center designed to support and advance knowledge generated by the IERI projects throughout the United States. One of the major goals of the DRDC is to build a science of scale-up based on insights from other disciplines and the results of original research conducted within and outside the IERI community.

Initial examinations of the scientific work on scale-up seemed to suggest that investigators designing and implementing promising educational interventions would benefit from interactions with individuals in other disciplines who regularly use principles of scale-up in their work. Researchers in fields outside of education have been tackling issues of scale-up for quite some time, and many have developed practical means for addressing some of the fundamental challenges of scale-up.[1] The classic example of scaling through straightforward replication or with modifications developed through intermediate trials was first developed in chemical engineering more than a century ago (Zlokarnik 2002; Levin 2001; Palakodaty et al.

2000; Royal Society of Chemistry 1999). Today, engineers continue to work on scale-up issues. For example, industrial engineers have developed procedures to scale up from prototypes to mass production (see Hopp and Spearman 2001), and software engineers turn working computing code into software compatible with numerous machine configurations that can be used in a variety of contexts by people other than its developers (see Brooks 1995).

Issues of scale-up are certainly not limited—historically or currently—to engineering or health fields; scaling is a long-standing and current challenge in fields ranging from international development, economics, and social welfare policy to strategic management in a wide range of institutional organizations. In international development, governments, activists, and not-for-profit organizations have long pursued their policy objectives through the replication of models that "work" in multiple locations (see Uvin and Miller 1996), and struggled to identify critical success factors that, properly adhered to, would ensure replicability of impacts across contexts (e.g., positive impacts of agroecological initiatives on the economic viability of small farming communities; see Altieri 2005; Altieri et al. n.d.). Economic models of scale-up, with their "ambition to provide a general model of individual choice behavior," are increasingly applied "to broader sets of outcomes and issues," including in education (see Moffitt in this volume). Cutting across policy domains are questions regarding how to mobilize resources and partnerships to ensure the viability and sustainability of successful scale-up including in response to the HIV/AIDS epidemic, in development planning, and in conflict resolution (see, e.g., World Health Organization 2004, 2005; Mukerjee 1988; Howard-Grabman and Snetro 2003; Maiese 2005).

Although conceptualizations of scale-up and methods used in these and other disciplines may not be directly applicable to scale-up in education, it is reasonable to expect that they can provide models that are likely to broaden our thinking and stimulate us to conceive of the challenges of scale-up—and their solutions—in new ways. In November 2003 DRDC hosted an invitational conference to provide members of the IERI research community with an opportunity to explore how educational research on scale-up might be enriched with theories, traditions, models, and practices found in other fields that routinely extend successful innovations into products and practices in different types of organizations. Participants heard from scholars who identified, compared, and contrasted the concepts and methods commonly used to scale up programs and processes in chemical engineering, manufacturing, software engineering, management and organization theory, public health, economics, sociology, and other disciplines and fields of practice. Education and measurement experts considered the implications of these different views of scale-up for researchers and practitioners working to understand the challenges and impacts of implementing exemplary interventions in varied school settings with diverse student populations. Together they explored critical questions, including:

- What are the prevailing conceptualizations of scale-up in social science research today?
- What models have the most potential regarding transference to the scale-up of educational interventions?
- How do the features that characterize and distinguish conceptualizations of scale-up affect the selection of appropriate research designs to assess intervention effects?
- To what extent does scale affect the identification of patterns?
- What approaches are particularly effective in generalizing theoretical propositions derived about phenomena at one level on a spatial, temporal, or quantitative scale to other levels?
- What design components, benchmarks, or preexisting conditions should be considered before bringing an intervention to scale?
- What factors are emerging as major impediments to achieving sustainable results when exemplary interventions are scaled up from prototype or pilot to a wider context?

This volume and its companion, *Scale-Up in Education: Issues in Practice*, are products of both that conference and subsequent advances in scale-up research in education and other disciplines. They include specially commissioned manuscripts and commentaries prepared by conference program members who frequently elaborated and enriched their remarks with the participants' comments and questions in mind. They present new and updated reports on the ongoing work of the IERI community, including in *Scale-Up in Education: Issues in Practice* chapters from six IERI projects that have developed effective designs for scale-up and have begun to evaluate the impact of implementing promising educational interventions as they are brought to scale at various sites and with various populations of students across the United States.[2] This volume includes chapters from members of seven additional IERI project teams.[3] Together these volumes focus on how scale-up is most productively conceptualized and accomplished in multiple disciplines. While each stands alone, read together *Scale-Up in Education: Ideas in Principle* and *Scale-Up in Education: Issues in Practice* are designed to be both thought provoking and of practical value to researchers, practitioners, and policy makers interested in scale-up research design and the dissemination and utilization of scale-up research findings in education.

CONCEPTUALIZING SCALE-UP:
AN EDUCATIONAL PERSPECTIVE

Scale-up is the enactment of interventions whose efficacy has already been established in new contexts with the goal of producing similarly positive impacts in larger, frequently more diverse populations. Efforts to scale up educational innovations are not new; the drive to roll out proven curricular materials and pedagogical approaches across the country is long-standing, historical local controls of community-based educational systems notwithstanding. What is innovative in more recent approaches to scaling is the effort to bring conceptual and analytic rigor to studies of and prescriptions for successful scale-up. From an educational perspective, scale-up investigations encompass two of the most fundamental challenges facing educational researchers today: how to ensure the quality of the evidence base available to inform policy decisions, instructional practices, and school choices, and how to resolve common obstacles to the timely dissemination and appropriate use of research findings as a basis for decisions made by a wide range of individuals and organizations with a stake in the performance of our educational institutions. Scale-up research is research on the cusp, with the promise if not the expectation of bridging philosophical and methodological questions regarding standards of evidence, and organizational, sociological, and technological questions regarding the communication, accumulation, and utilization of knowledge by individuals within and across institutional boundaries.

The first four chapters of this volume succinctly frame three fundamental theoretical and associated methodological questions that guide and reflect conceptualizations of scale-up in education: What do we mean by *scale*? What research designs are most appropriate for generating the evidence of efficacy that is a prerequisite for scale-up? How likely is it that a given set of findings is context dependent, and what are the implications for our ability to generalize treatment effects? The answers to these three questions are critically important in establishing standards for evidence to warrant scale-up.

In chapter 1, "Educational Innovation and the Problem of Scale," David K. Cohen and Deborah Loewenberg Ball relate scale to expectations, prompting us to reflect on what we should expect from educational interventions—in particular, whether it is "reasonable to expect innovations to be adopted widely and well." Against a backdrop of "no discussions of what might reasonably be expected from innovation in education, let alone what might be expected, given the nature of schooling in the U.S."; limited research on "what or who adopts innovations" and why; differences in implementation associated with the relationships between innovators and adopters, and the environments in which educational change occurs; and incomplete understanding of the processes by which innovations are transferred from one place to another, the authors address a range of pressing questions, including: How likely is it that innovations devised in schools and classrooms will be adopted at any scale? Are more broadly sponsored innovations likely to be more widely adopted? How likely are innovations to be implemented with integrity versus reinterpreted by educators who "make their own sense of others' innovations"? Are innovations "more likely to succeed when they do not call for serious departures for teaching and learning"? What are the prospects for policies and programs pressing "more aggressive and ambitious innovation on schools" and "how researchers might best frame inquiry about them"? When does it make sense for innovators to attempt to "supply what is missing in the environment," when to try to "change the environment," and when to "accommodate to environments"? And what are the implications of the answers to all of the above questions—and many others that Cohen and Ball address—for the merits of conceptualizing scale-up as a quantitative versus a qualitative problem?

In "Principles for Scaling Up: Choosing, Measuring Effects, and Promoting the Widespread Use of Educational Innovation" (chapter 2), Eva L. Baker considers the evidence required to support scaling up "scientifically vetted innovations" (i.e., "new ideas that are built on the findings of quality research and development"). Baker describes seven principles for producing evidence to warrant claims that particular research-based interventions merit scale-up (i.e., the adaptation of innovations for "widespread and supported use"). These principles, drawn from extensive experience using true experiments to assess intervention outcomes and multiple methods to generate evidence in support of intervention designs and implementation plans, suggest that decisions to scale up research-based educational innovations should be predicated upon satisfactory answers to such questions as: How appropriate is the evidence base? Does the preponderance of evidence—not just the most recently completed study—document the superiority of the intervention over alternatives? Was the development process itself enriched with well-designed and well-executed formative evaluation (results-redesign) research employing a wide range of measures of the intended (and other potential) outcomes? "How, in what order, and with what schedule of support" can users "begin to take on responsibility for renewing the intervention on their own"? Importantly, Baker's discussion provides valuable insights for crafting research that answers these and other pressing questions. Her concluding thoughts on scalability, sustainability, and the future of scale-up research raise questions regarding the commercialization of proven interventions and "the relationship between researchers and the private sector" to which later contributors return—including Conley and Wolcott in this, and Foorman, Santi, and Berger in the companion volume.

The last two chapters in part I are concerned with how to estimate the effects of interventions and how to judge how likely it is that these findings are context dependent. Larry V. Hedges takes a quantitative approach to the latter question in his exploration of the "Generalizability of Treatment Effects: Psychometrics and Education" (chapter 3). Hedges draws an analogy to psychometric theory to advance methods that could both "provide an empirical basis for" and "lead to more widespread use of" designs "better suited to providing evidence" of effects' generalizability. Like Cohen, Ball, and Baker, Hedges emphasizes the importance of context on effects, thus the prospect that generalizability will be affected by interactions (e.g., treatment by school, treatment by class, or treatment by school by class). He suggests that researchers consider how reproducibility is affected by (depends on) "the conceptual entities one is considering generalizing about," and the implications for the development of measurement strategies, the estimation of reproducibility coefficients, and the generalization of "an index of quantitative reproducibility that acknowledges" the effects of specific contexts on the reproducibility of treatment effects.

The methods Hedges describes can be used to resolve questions regarding the generalizability of evidence of intervention effects—a task that assumes the evidence of effectiveness is valid. How to select the design features best suited to provide such evidence is the subject of Charles S. Reichardt's contribution to this volume. In "Estimating the Effects of Educational Interventions" (chapter 4), Reichardt presents seven "prototypical research comparisons" which, combined with various design "embellishments" (e.g., additional measurement occasions or outcome measures) "produces the full spectrum of possible research designs." Reichardt encourages us to ask which prototypical comparisons of "what happened after the intervention was implemented with what would have happened if it had not been implemented" most closely align with four criteria for assessing validity, with an emphasis on minimizing threats to internal validity by ruling out factors other than the intervention that could plausibly account for variations in the outcome variable. Taking as his starting point the position that "the ideal comparison for estimating an effect cannot be obtained in practice," Reichardt underscores the importance of carefully considering—and provides guidance to help answer—questions including: How are particular comparisons "flawed in ways that could lead to biased estimates of treatment effects"? What are the potential threats to validity associated with given designs? Which designs are most likely to "produce the most credible and useful results under the constraints of the research setting"? Which "design elaborations can best be implemented to rule out the most plausible threats to validity"? A fundamental point that Reichardt highlights is a recognizable theme in all four of these considerations of scale-up from an educational perspective: evidence from single trials or program evaluation studies is context dependent; accumulating a body of knowledge that can inform decisions regarding the prospects of success when interventions are scaled across contexts is critically important in leveraging research resources and findings to guide educational policymaking and practice.

MODELING SCALE-UP: LESSONS FROM OTHER FIELDS

Scale-up in education (particularly educational policy) often seems conceived as broadly similar to scale-up as it is commonly understood to be approached in commercial organizations and medicine. Prototype products and treatments are developed, and if they prove effective for their intended (or other) uses (i.e., satisfy particular markets' needs and wants at prices the markets can afford), they are presumably rolled out for consumption by a mass market. The reality is often quite different, as the first two chapters in this part underscore. Prototypes that "work" for one audience often do not work equally well for others, and even when an innovation's generalizability is supported by sound evidence of efficacy, such evidence all too frequently fails to bring about the idealized changes in decisions that are expected to result in widespread adoption. The realities of scale-up from the perspective of industrial engineers, managers, and the health professions are, consequently, both more similar and more instructive to scale-up in education than skeptics might assume.

A key similarity, which James G. Conley and Robert C. Wolcott highlight in chapter 5, "Scaling from Prototype to Production: A Managed Process for Commercial Offerings," is the extent to which recognizable differences in use contexts argue in favor of early, planned innovation adaptations. Such adaptations are typically designed to engineer from prototypes solutions that take maximum advantage of the efficiencies of scale with minimal customization to key market characteristics. What can educational researchers take from Conley and Wolcott's review of methodologies that "seek to manage risk in production"? Certainly the methodologies resonate in thought-provoking ways with Baker's observations regarding the merits of results-redesign intervention improvement cycles—but are there practical implications for scaling educational interventions? If educational innovations are developed by academic researchers, not new product development units in commercial organizations with profit-seeking motives, what are the incentives to develop the "closely managed" "process monitoring and measurement tools" that Conley and Wolcott credit with ensuring successful scale-up from prototype to production in manufacturing industries? Is it feasible for educational innovators to emulate the "Design for X" methodologies that enhance the prospects of successful scale-up by "explicitly integrat[ing] production and scale-up issues into the design and development processes, before products even make it to production planning"? Can the strategies and the specific practices managers in for-profit firms have developed to bring innovations to scale be translated into managed processes for the development of scalable educational interventions? Should a paradigm of scaling through replication of educational innovations be replaced with one of scale-up through mass customization of core instructional practices? Is scale-up in education, like scale-up in industrial engineering and management, "fundamentally a question of information management, effective decision making, and accurate execution," and, if so, what are the implications for district administrators and school-based personnel charged with scaling innovations adopted by—rather than developed within—their organizations?

A related, critical question concerns the factors that enhance (and impede) knowledge utilization. Under what conditions and to what extent is scientific evidence of efficacy "translated," through effective communication of findings and their implications, to not only influence individual practitioners' decision making, but ultimately result in the pervasive, accurate applications of revised standards of practice? This is the central question James J. Dignam addresses in chapter 6, "From Efficacy to Effectiveness: Translating Randomized Controlled Trial Findings into Treatment Standards." Dignam reminds us that even in medicine, where RCTs are "established as the gold standard for evaluation and evidence generation," the practice of random assignment to treatment conditions, on its own, is not sufficient to ensure trials will yield credible findings. If the RCT kitemark of approval is insufficient to ensure unquestioned acceptance of a study's findings, what other criteria do critical consumers look to researchers to satisfy? What "additional design requirements" must RCTs meet "to provide credible information"? How do we reassure practitioners that our findings are unequivocal? That they are not tainted by biased, inaccurate assessments of outcomes? Dignam also reminds us that even when these methodological (and associated practical) challenges are overcome, it is by no means a foregone conclusion that the hard-won scientific evidence will influence standards of practice. He advances a variety of explanations for this phenomenon, prompting us to consider questions that include: How can we encourage the development of consensus around educational research findings? What lessons does medicine hold regarding the steps necessary to ensure that scientifically based education research influences policy and practice appropriately, and in a timely manner? What feedback mechanisms should we provide to ensure that subsequent trials are designed to better influence policy and practice?

The third chapter in part II, "Linking Program Implementation and Effectiveness: Lessons from a Pooled Sample of Welfare-to-Work Experiments" by Howard S. Bloom, Carolyn J. Hill, and James A. Riccio, addresses a central theme in Dignam's and Hedges's chapters: how to build and generalize appropriately from a persuasive body of evidence about the effectiveness of an intervention—or, in this case, a class of social programs. In treating this theme, Bloom, Hill, and Riccio take up two key issues addressed by Baker in this volume and by numerous contributors in the companion volume: What does it mean to enact interventions with integrity? What evidence can usefully be accumulated from enactments with varying degrees of fidelity of implementation? Bloom and his colleagues pool data from three "large-scale, multisite random assignment experiments" and examine "the relationship between program implementation and effects" (in this case, effects of welfare-to-work experiments on short-term client earnings). The analysis described here and the authors' discussion of it speaks powerfully to the extra traction that can be obtained in grappling with the policy implications of implementation studies when an adequate supply of such studies (e.g., multiple random assignment experiments with comparable measures and methods) is envisaged and supported by those who develop and those with access to the funds required to sustain long-term research agendas.

Chapter 8 by Robert A. Moffitt concludes this part by examining from an economics perspective the problem of "forecasting the effects of interventions at a larger scale than that for which their estimated effects were originally obtained." While acknowledging a dearth of economic research and models addressing "certain types of scale-up effects, particularly those concerning the change in the nature of the intervention itself," Moffitt provides compelling evidence of the contributions economics brings to conceptualizing and addressing the challenges of scaling. Moffitt argues that "purely statistical models alone" are not likely to prove adequate as the basis of a conceptual model to guide our thinking about scale-up, including our thoughts on the most appropriate interpretations of the data available to us, as such models "will most likely not adequately separate the different confounding factors and individual effects that are at work." Moffitt employs an "economic model of production processes" to answer questions including: How can we explain "one of the most common findings in the scale-up literature, namely, that effects at larger scales always seem to be weaker than at smaller scales"? How can scale-up effects be measured "by nonexperimental means using natural variation"? Like Cohen and Ball, Baker, Hedges, and Conley and Wolcott, Moffitt emphasizes the significance of accounting for the contextual factors that shape the impacts of classroom-based interventions, and other confounds, in accurately assessing their effects. The emphasis here is not, however, on these contextual factors—or what happens to interventions when they change—but rather on the challenges of generalizing to larger numbers of similar population elements.

The authors in this part highlight the challenges to generalizability that context imposes—in all disciplines and fields of practice—on even the most rigorous evidence of efficacy. In doing so the authors encourage us to think about the institutional arrangements that create barriers to scale-up—and the mechanisms that may overcome them. Examples of the former include the relative independence of local educational systems, which can make it difficult for administrators and instructors to share craft knowledge regarding procedural adaptations that enable them to implement innovations with fidelity to their essential characteristics, if not precise replication of each of their features in subsequent enactments. Examples of the latter include the development of new social relations and domains—developments with the potential to achieve deeper organizational and environmental adaptations, facilitating the successful implementation of innovations at increasingly larger scales.

BREAKING BOUNDARIES: SUCCESSFUL SCALE-UP IN TRANSFORMING ORGANIZATIONS

The chapters in part III fall outside a "random assignment to generate evidence" model of thinking about scale-up to consider how scale-up is achieved operationally. Of particular interest are the prospects that organizational and technological obstacles and facilitators may not only affect the way educational interventions are brought to larger audiences, but also call for continued innovations in the methods we employ to monitor their efficacy over time. How is information disseminated to achieve scale-up in organizations that are not formally structured, and/or which require information flows across traditional knowledge domains and institutional boundaries? How do technological innovators and sociologists on the cutting edge think about scale-up within and across organizations that themselves are not clearly defined? What are the implications for education?

Chapter 9, "Breaking Boundaries: Scaling Collaboration in Time and Space" by Ian Foster and Carl Kesselman, and chapter 10, "Sociodigital Formations: Constructing an Object of Study" by Saskia Sassen, are both concerned with how technological advances make it possible to redraw—and rescale—networks across the boundaries of institutional organizational structures. Foster and Kesselman "introduce some of the concepts and approaches that are being used to enable effective collaboration beyond" these boundaries. In doing so they raise the possibility (still constrained by entrenched disciplinary norms and social conventions—in particular those that identify trustworthy from other prospective collaborators) that common interests rather than common institutional affiliations will increasingly come to define and join practitioner and researcher communities.

These possibilities raise a number of provocative questions for education, including: How might new and evolving technologies "allow innovative researchers [or practitioners] to explore new problem-solving approaches"? How might the extension of collaborative groups or the development of professional communities "beyond the confines of a single physical institution" enrich or challenge our conceptions and approaches to resolving entrenched problems in education? How might grid and other technologies, by making it possible for virtual student communities to flourish, over time effectively alter the context within which instruction occurs—a context we have only recently developed methodologies and tools (e.g., hierarchical linear modeling) to better understand?

Sassen similarly prompts us to consider such questions as: How might new technologies (notably, "computer-centered interactive technology" and "interactive electronic information and communication structures") contribute to the construction of "whole new domains of interaction" among teachers, parents, administrators, and students in elementary and secondary education? How can the interconnectivity and simultaneity that these technologies support combine "to produce significant qualitative transformations in communication and information structures" among educators, those who train and provide professional development services to them, public policy makers, administrators, parents and other taxpayers, and our children? How might technology transform the deeply embedded patterns of designing and delivering educational interventions and instruction associated with the U.S. public education system? Sassen reminds us that the social science implications of these technology-enabled "sociodigital" formations have not yet been fully articulated as an object of inquiry in their own right. Doing so is a goal of a 2000 Social Science Research Council initiative that she describes here and with Latham in *Digital Formations: Information Technologies and New Architectures in the Global Realm*. Enough is known about the mechanisms and capabilities by which these technologies affect social relations, however, to suggest their power to transform key facets of the educational system and the institutional structures that until now have flourished within it.

The organization-intervention interface is frequently referenced in discussions of the limits or obstacles to scale-up in education. Interestingly, the relationship is often portrayed as asymmetrical—that is, a particular organizational structure or set of characteristics is assumed to be essentially fixed, with relatively minor changes in the cast of characters occupying key positions and incremental adjustments as a result of organizational learning and/or adaptation to exogenous forces. The prevailing view of change similarly imagines interventions adapted to "fit" organizations—one-time adjustments to match or tailor innovations to particular contexts. In chapter 11, "Measuring and Managing Successful Organizational Scale-Up," Eric G.

Flamholtz and Yvonne Randle remind us that organizations themselves are dynamic, and periodically must realign ("scale up") in fundamental ways if they are to grow/develop—in some cases, remain viable—over time. Flamholtz and Randle use a life cycle approach to address questions including: At what points should "specific scale-ups to the business enterprise" occur? "What needs to be done for successful scale-up"? What goes wrong when "an organization fails to develop and implement the systems, structures, and processes needed to support its growth/development"? What external and internal factors provide incentives for organizations to adapt—or adopt new—forms, processes, and structures? Flamholtz and Randle's consideration of organizational change and scaling is particularly useful for the contrast it provides to scale-up as replication; here, scale-up is explicitly, unashamedly an adaptive process. "What works" is not what worked best in the past, but what it emerges will best "fit" the ever-changing organizational environment. Taken together, the three chapters here raise the possibility that a contingency approach will perhaps increasingly become the hallmark of scale-up in multiple domains if technology fulfills its promise to shorten the life cycle of specific social networks and organizational structures.

SYNTHESIZING CONCEPTS OF SCALE-UP FOR EDUCATION

What are the implications of these different disciplinary and programmatic perspectives on the challenges and imperatives of scale-up for educational research? What are the prospects of developing more general theoretical and methodological approaches to scaling? What are the lessons for organizations less interested in understanding, more interested in developing institutional mechanisms that accomplish scale-up? How might the evolution and growth of new social structures challenge us to reconceptualize the contexts in which learning takes place, and reconsider the permeability of level-2 and level-3 structures that we have come to take for granted as circumscribing individual students' instructional experiences? These are the questions posed and addressed in the final three chapters of this volume.

In chapter 12, "Toward a Program of Research on Scale-Up: Analytical Requirements and Theoretical Possibilities," Mark A. Constas and Kevin L. Brown ask how the "two different approaches to establishing a conceptual base for scale-up research in education" described in part I can be used to "inform our thinking about how best to develop a [theoretical] framework for scale-up research." Do they suggest a definition of scale-up that can be "operationalized in a way that is methodologically sound"? Do they identify "an empirically justifiable set of variables and measures" that can be "used to define and investigate scale-up"? Can the "scaling-up dimensions and variables," identified by the authors here as well as by other empirical research, be organized to specify a "clearly articulated prediction model"? Constas and Brown address these questions in turn, then present a model capturing key hypothesized relations that can be used to develop an "empirically based body of knowledge on scale-up" based on the guidelines suggested by the contributors to this volume.

Chapter 13, "Successful Scale-Up in Three Stages: Insights and Challenges for Educational Research and Practice" by Paul Horwitz, highlights lessons educational researchers and practitioners can take from other fields' attempts to model scale-up and break the boundaries that can impede organizational change as described in parts II and III. Horwitz addresses a number of provocative issues, including: "What obstacles to using control groups" are particularly challenging if not unique to education research? What are the implications of the decreased likelihood educational research can adhere to "double-blind" procedures? What resource implications and constraints arise when achieving adequate statistical power requires large-scale longitudinal effectiveness studies? What are the prospects of developing common understandings of and sharing instruments that adequately capture, "at the appropriate level of granularity," the multifaceted nature of many educational innovations' outcomes? Once developed, what are the prospects such measures will be administered to sufficiently large numbers of subjects repeatedly over time to establish the sustainability and secondary and unanticipated impacts of innovations? What are the prospects of establishing, supporting, and institutionalizing consensus development processes and procedures in education? How are the futures of proven interventions associated with the interests and success of the commercial organizations that may be best placed to carry them to market? And how can individual scale-up research projects use technology to address such challenges?

The final chapter in this volume, "Technology and Scale-Up: Implications for Research and Practice," considers the impact transformative technologies may—and potentially should—have on research regarding scale-up and its practice. Individual classrooms, schools, districts, and governmental departments and colleges of education are all acknowledged to be dynamic organizations, shifting in response to and in anticipation of a wide range of internal and external environmental forces. Arguably, changes in the nature of these organizations—including those that are the objectives of certain educational reforms—are often not factored into our conceptions of or designs for researching scaling in theoretically meaningful ways. Changing classroom compositions and teacher rosters—even evidence that students and instructors are increasingly using information and computer technologies to build new, often transient, communities of practice and knowledge—are often acknowledged (e.g., for the difficulties they pose to collecting data over time), but we have yet to tackle their implications for the development of a science of scale-up. Organizational change is not always the sort of incremental adjustment that effectively produces only background noise in the medium term. Organizational, like individual, development often occurs in somewhat uncomfortable and dramatic spurts. Effective interventions may prompt, even when they are not designed primarily to induce, such dramatic shifts in organizational structures, processes, and strategic plans. Transformative technologies have the power to accelerate the pace of such changes, or to promote other social-structural changes in opposition to them. The potential scenarios, and their implications for how we conceptualize "successful" scale-up—(must it be sustainable? Or is it inappropriate to associate longevity with success?)—and design research both to provide evidence in support of scaling and to evaluate it, merit increased attention. How should we conceptualize scale-up in environments with fluid boundaries and dynamic contexts? When new instructional tools and curricular materials are offered online, how do we account for home-schooled children in our samples and observation protocols? How does the creation of virtual communities of teachers, who are joint (if not concurrent) participants in web-based teacher professional development programs, impact the teachers' sense of community and the groups with which they most closely identify? What are the implications of technology that can lead groups of science teachers across the country to feel more closely connected than teachers within the same school building? Clearly, technology holds great promise; scale-up researchers have used it to develop new pedagogical tools, assessments, and tutors, and to deliver interventions not only more widely but with more quality control and automated monitoring than could previously be engineered into them. Technology also holds the promise—and the challenge—of (re)aligning the participants in the educational, especially the instructional, system in ways that may introduce new confounds and require us to rethink our research designs and the principles of scale-up.

NOTES

1. See Hedges 2004; McDonald, Keesler, Kaufmann, and Schneider, 2006.
2. These include chapters by Barbara Foorman, Kristi Santi, and Larry Berger, "Scaling Assessment-Driven Instruction Using the Internet and Handheld Computers"; Sharon Lynch, Michael Szesze, Curtis Pyke, and Joel Kuipers, "Scaling Up Highly Rated Middle Science Curriculum Units for Diverse Student Populations: Features That Affect Collaborative Research and Vice-Versa"; James McPartland, Robert Balfanz, and Nettie Legters, "Scaling Up High School Reforms: Model Specificity and Local Decision Making"; Nancy Butler Songer, "Rethinking Sustainability of Curricular Innovations: Notes from Urban Detroit"; Jack Mostow and Joseph Beck, "When the Rubber Meets the Road: Lessons from the In-School Adventures of

an Automated Reading Tutor That Listens"; and Robert Slavin and Nancy Madden, "Scaling Up Success for All: The First Sixteen Years."

3. These include Eva Baker (IERI: Assessments to Support the Transition to Complex Learning in Science, and IERI: Collaborative Research: Automating Early Assessment of Academic Standards for Very Young Native and Non-Native Speakers of American English), Deborah Loewenberg Ball and David Cohen (Developing Measures of Instructional Improvement, and IERI: Scaling Up Instructional Improvement), Larry Hedges (Academic Achievement and Teacher Development in Science, and the Data Research and Development Center), Paul Horwitz (Modeling Across the Curriculum), and also Kevin Brown, Michelle Llosa, Sarah-Kathryn McDonald, and Barbara Schneider from the Data Research and Development Center.

I

CONCEPTUALIZING SCALE-UP: AN EDUCATIONAL PERSPECTIVE

1

Educational Innovation and the Problem of Scale[1]

David K. Cohen and Deborah Loewenberg Ball

The United States has had five decades of increasing pressure for school reform, beginning before the Soviet Sputniks and continuing today. Researchers appear to believe that none of these reforms were implemented at scale—that is, widely and well.[2] Despite this view, most authors write as though it was reasonable to expect innovations to be adopted widely and well; when studies report innovation failure, they usually do so in a disappointed tone (Stake and Easley 1987; Welch 1979). Yet, like love affairs, many innovations consist more of ideas and hopes than of the carefully designed details of daily operations that often are required to make appreciable change. Our scrutiny of the literature revealed no discussions of what might reasonably be expected from innovation in education, given the nature of schooling in the United States. We found only three studies that sought to discern broad patterns of innovation, adoption, or implementation.[3]

The contemporary pressure for major national improvement of student learning has created an appetite for better knowledge about innovation. We sketch what is known and believed about innovation and scale, offer some conjectures that merit investigation, and consider strategies for successful innovation.

SOME KEY IDEAS

Begin at the beginning: What is an innovation? It is a departure from current practice—deliberate or not, originating in or outside of practice, which is novel. Innovations include novel practices, tools or technologies, and knowledge and ideas. In some cases there are clear distinctions between "designers" and "users" of innovations, as when a textbook publisher markets a new text to a state, and teachers and students use the books. In other cases, designers and users are one and the same, as when teachers devise their own innovations. On this inclusive view there are several sorts of innovators, including practitioners, agencies that sponsor and govern schools, and organizations external to practice that urge, design, and market changes. These innovators often are associated with different sorts of innovations, but all have two things in common: they urge a departure from conventional practice, and both design and use require accommodation with the environment. When designers consider what sort of innovation may appeal, or work, or help, they weigh such accommodation among many other things. If practitioners decide to use an innovation, they are likely to consider and take advantage of such accommodations.

What is scale? The answer depends partly on the innovation, and partly on how we judge scale. One could judge it in terms of adoption, or in terms of use, or in terms of intended use. Adoption is always a different matter from use, but as innovations become more complex, the difference grows. In some cases—texts, curricula, and tests, for instance—one might plausibly contend that the extent of scale can be decided quantitatively, by the number of schools that adopt it. To require a new textbook series in New York City, and get it to all teachers, is to achieve a sort of scale, since all or nearly all of the texts will be used somehow. But that tells us little about use, because it depends on many factors besides adoption. In other cases—Comprehensive School Reform Designs (CSRD), for instance—adoption is a much weaker proxy for assessing the extent of scale, because these designs cannot be used in any meaningful sense unless there is extensive qualitative change in the schools that adopt them.

In the latter case, the very meaning of scale is distinctive, because its qualitative elements can be as important as, or more important than, quantitative elements. How deeply an innovation permeates practice may be as important to an assessment of its success at scale as how many sites adopt it, and innovations differ in how much is needed for them to deeply affect practice. For instance, many whole school designs require building school infrastructure for professional education, supervision, and leadership that will enable use. Success for All and other CSRD designs contain such infrastructure as key elements of the designs, and the designs are accompanied by unprecedented external assistance. In contrast, though textbooks contain directions for their use by teachers, most are designed to be used with little direction or external assistance. Whole school reforms, in contrast, contain elaborate and often carefully staged guidance for use; so central are these directions that they often are indistinguishable from "the innovation."

If this analysis is roughly correct, there can be no single definition of scale, nor any single metric to judge it, for the tasks and problems of implementation vary with types of innovation.

EXPLAINING FAILURE

We take up these explanations because they have been the focus of much prominent research on innovation, and thus offer a quick view of the terrain. There are at least four schools of thought.

Innovations fail because they were badly designed. For some researchers, this means that innovations fit poorly with practice (Cuban 1993). Others argue that they do not make room for practitioners to adapt them to practice (Berman and McLaughlin 1979). Still others argue that the key design flaw in innovations is that they do not make room for teachers to learn how to use them. In these lines of work, innovations are the villains and schools are the victims, for the problems arise in the poor design of innovations.[4]

In a second sort of work, schools are the villains and innovations the victims. Researchers argue that innovations fail because schools and school systems offer few or no incentives to change practice (Hanushek 1989; Friedman and Friedman 1962), or that educators resist change (Lortie 1975), or that schools are so rigidly organized that they leave no room for innovation (Sarason 1971; Lortie 1975), or that schools are institutionalized organizations that effectively buffer the technical core from environmental pressures (Meyer and Rowan 1977).

In a third way of framing the issues, researchers claim that few innovations succeed because few were robust treatments that addressed problems that seriously concerned practitioners. When robust designs that addressed serious problems of practice were tried, they reached scale (Cohen and Ball 2003).

In a fourth set of views, the problems of innovation center in environments. One argument focuses on the complexity and fragmentation of educational environments, which promote openness to proposals for change at the same time as they inhibit consistency of adoption and implementation among units and over time (Cohen and Spillane 1993). Another argument holds that the openness of U.S. educational environments enables the emergence of many educational innovations at all levels, but the school improvement industry tends to inhibit the growth, maturation, and institutionalization of organizations that develop and sponsor innovations (Rowan 2002).

KNOWLEDGE ABOUT INNOVATION

All the accounts have some appeal, but how might we judge their relative merits? We begin to explore that by asking what we know about three rudimentary matters. Who adopts innovations? What sorts of innovations do we consider? In what environments do they occur? The answers to these questions will shed a bit of light on the answers to another: what can reasonably be expected concerning the scale of innovation? The answer to that could help us to evaluate the explanations of presumed innovation failure, sketched above. It might also suggest some conjectures about innovation and the scale of change that researchers could test.

Adopters

Though there has been little research on what or who adopts innovations, we do know a few important things. One is that the size and organization of the adopting units vary. Adopters include individual professionals, individual schools, districts, states, and federal agencies. Some adoptions bridge these units. The most commonly studied adopters are teachers and schools; there are fewer studies of districts, states, or federal education agencies. Yet the very considerable differences among adopters suggest a question: Would explanations for the actions of one sort of adopter be likely to hold for others—that is, would we expect explanations for the adoption of teacher-initiated innovations to be similar to explanations for the adoption of state-sponsored innovations? That seems unlikely. In addition, it seems likely that innovations that are to be adopted and used by individual teachers would have greater difficulty spreading than innovations that must be adopted by states. We found no studies that probe these issues.

The relations between innovators and adopters also vary quite dramatically. In an appreciable number of cases, the adopter also is the designer, as in the case of many teacher-devised innovations, and for some innovations devised by local educational authorities (LEAs) and states. In such cases, the meaning of "adoption" is different than when we consider innovations that are designed by people and organizations that are external to the intended adopters. For when adopters and users are not also the innovation designers, a variety of personal, professional, and organizational differences are likely to come into play around adoption and use. It also seems likely that implementation would differ between the two types. We found no analysis of these matters.

Adopters' resources vary. The United States is distinctive among developed nations for great inequalities in the educational, human, and fiscal resources to which adopters have access. That is true among states, LEAs within states, and among teachers within LEAs. If schools, LEAs, and states are at all like other organizations, we would expect such resource differences to influence the design, adoption, and use of innovations. We would not expect teachers in Mississippi Delta schools to either initiate or adopt innovations at the same rate or with the same facility as teachers in Evanston, Illinois, or Shaker Heights, Ohio. Moreover, we would not expect explanations for innovation to be the same across those differences. These variations suggest differences in the potential for scale, and in the requirements for achieving it. Studies of innovation infrequently mention these matters.

Whether devised by practitioners or external agents, the idea of "scaling up" an innovation brings with it the problem of "transfer": getting the innovation from one place to another. Researchers conceptualized that in different ways. Some portrayed it as agentless "diffusion." Others saw it as a matter of unidirectional "broadcasting." Still others represented it as a fairly straightforward process of bilateral communication. When considering scale-up, the challenges of both framing the processes of transfer and of devising ways to deal with it hold for the practitioner-designer who seeks to spread the innovation to others, and for the external designer who seeks the same. As research and experience accumulated, these earlier conceptualizations of "transfer" turned out to be weak, to be focused on not-so-complex innovations, and thus made "scaling up" appear to be pretty transparent. There also was little attention to the use of innovations and their implementation.

Innovations

One source of variation is sponsorship: some innovations are created and sponsored by individual practitioners, some by LEAs, others by state and federal governments, and still others by agencies outside of schools or government, including publishers, civic leaders, advocacy groups, and professional associations. Some are multiply sponsored, as with privately published texts that gain state adoption. Such differences are likely to create variation in the comparative advantage for scale of some innovations. We found no studies that probe these differences.

Another difference among innovations concerns the sector of schooling at which they aim: Do they concern finance, instruction, budgeting, assessment, professional licensing, or hiring? Each is a distinct operational domain, with distinctive constraints and opportunities. Each bears on others, but none is overarching. It seems reasonable to expect that the adoption and use of innovations in some of these domains would be explained differently than in others. For instance, the influences on innovations in budgeting are likely to differ, at least in part, from those in professional licensing and hiring. We found no studies that investigate these differences.

Still another difference among innovations centers on whether they occur as the result of standard operating procedures. If they do, they are more likely to be routinely adopted at a large scale. Examples include state-approved textbooks, state academic standards, and state test programs. In these cases, adoption is either compulsory or very nearly so. Many other innovations are not due to standard operating procedures. Adoption thus is more voluntary, and typically there are no penalties for nonadoption. Innovations of the first type are more likely to achieve some version of scale broadly and quickly, while those of the second type are less likely to do so. Teacher-made innovations would face rather different problems of scale-up—including communication, resources, and authority—than state-made innovations. We found no studies that investigate these matters.

Most research on innovation concerns instruction, and a substantial fraction concerns efforts to promote ambitious instruction, including NSF-sponsored and other curricula, some state standards-based reforms, and Progressive education. These are a distinctive sort of innovation, for they pertain to what many researchers refer to as the "technical core" of schooling, a domain that, until very recently, has been little managed by extra-classroom authorities. It is difficult to imagine why patterns of or explanations for the creation, adoption, and use of instructional innovations would resemble patterns of or explanations for the creation, adoption, and use of changes in school schedules or school finance, for the phenomena to be described and explained, and the units of analysis, are quite different. We found no research that addresses these differences.

One of the most distinctive differences among instructional innovations is in their ambitions for academic work, and thus the demands that they make on practice. Some call for sharp departures from conventional practice, because they seek fundamental reorientation of teaching and learning. Others have more modest aims. As Eugene Bardach pointed out in a different context, innovation creates incompetence by proposing to retire familiar practices in favor of novel and less-familiar practices.[5] More ambitious innovations cause or imply more incompetence among practitioners.

Innovation at scale—or implementation—is a function of design, adoption, and use. Two features of innovation design can affect implementation by influencing practitioners' capability to learn new practices and thus overcome incompetence. One, which we call "elaboration," concerns the detail with which a reform is developed; the second, "scaffolding," is the degree to which the innovation includes a design for and other means of learning to carry it out. We consider these in turn, beginning with elaboration: innovation designs are plans for what is to be done, and those plans can be more or less rich and detailed.[6] Every innovation is elaborated to some degree. Some consist primarily of goals, principles, and visions that suggest broad directions. Others include curriculum, examples of intended learning and teaching, and tests. Full elaboration is impossible, since even modest departures from conventional practice are too complex to exhaustively plan, and even routine classes include unpredictable events.

Even very elaborated designs leave room for much invention, as implementers reorganize practice around them. Some things are best worked out in practice, and much elaboration can occur only in practice. Elaborating a design is more or less of a beginning, and always entails trade-offs between designers' view of what is essential, and limits on what can be spelled out. Given the inevitable incompleteness of any innovation, what is elaborated matters, for that influences both the quality of implementation and the distribution of work between designers and implementers.

Elaboration is sometimes treated as a matter of preference; some say that innovations should not constrain autonomy and invention, while others contend that little would happen without detailed direction. But to elaborate innovation designs is not necessarily to constrain, for different sorts of elaboration are possible. An intellectually ambitious elementary mathematics curriculum that was designed to encourage students' active engagement in mathematical reasoning and problem solving might be elaborated only in terms of its broad objectives. Or it could be further elaborated in terms both of its objectives and its main mathematical themes. Or it could be more elaborated in terms of its objectives, main mathematical themes, and the specific types of instructional activities. It could be even more elaborated in terms of all those things, and extensive examples of desired student performance. Or it could be differently elaborated in lists of topics, the order of coverage, suggested tasks for each topic, and even examples of teacher-student interactions. Each of these elaborations of the innovation offers users different information, detail, and guidance. More elaboration in this case offers users more resources, thus enabling—not constraining—them.

From one angle, extensive elaboration seems essential to illuminate an innovation's requirements for use, to alert designers and implementers to work to be done, and to reveal potential problems. Less-elaborated designs would be not only less useful but even self-defeating, for they tacitly delegate large amounts of invention to implementers, increasing the probability that the implementers would interpret interventions as versions of conventional practice, since the designs offer little guidance for anything else, and conventional practice is both familiar to and understood by implementers. Limiting instructional designs to general principles does not reveal much about their operation to designers or users. It is likely to increase the chances of confusion, the load on implementers to invent the design, and to yield generally weak and variable implementation. That, in turn, would be likely to erode the coherence and identity of innovations. From this perspective, less-elaborated innovations constrain implementers more, for they limit the implementers' capacity for real change.

Other things being equal, more elaborated designs are likely to improve implementation by providing operating information about innovations. But other things are not equal, for more elaboration takes more time, forethought, and knowledge, and increases work, time, and cost. Designs that are thinly elaborated require less of innovators, and leave more to implementers' choices. Many educators may prefer such designs, for they intrude less. Despite their greater usefulness, more elaborated designs may discourage or turn away adopters. In addition, greater elaboration would almost certainly require more of designers as well, for elaboration depends on greater experience with and learning from implementing an innovation, in order to make sound decisions about what and how to elaborate. That implies a recursive process of innovation design and development, systematic formative research in the development process, and more time, human resources, and money. Extensive elaboration can turn innovation into a very complex enterprise, partly because it tends to expand the innovator's role, pushing it toward more involvement with and responsibility for implementation.

Another feature of innovation design that can influence the quality of implementation, by influencing the capability to learn new practices, is how well scaffolded they are. By *scaffolding* we mean the materials and social processes that can support, or scaffold, learning. Innovations can be implemented only as they are apprehended and used by teachers and learners; all influences on instruction are mediated through their ideas, norms, and practices. The more innovations depart from conventional practice, the more new ideas, beliefs, norms, and practices teachers and students would have to learn, and the more implementation would depend on that learning.

All innovations are scaffolded to some degree, for all include some means to acquaint implementers with new practices. These may include brief or extended professional education, parent education, examples of adoption processes, and video materials that depict the knowledge and skills required for use.[7] The extent of scaffolding varies greatly among innovators: some leave it to implementers to devise their own opportunities to learn, while others devise and offer extensive opportunities. Scaffolding can offer rich guidance with few constraints on invention and autonomy, or be quite structured and relatively constraining, with many combinations in between. An intellectually ambitious elementary mathematics curriculum could be scaffolded in several different ways, which parallel the options for elaboration. If it were elaborated only in terms of its objectives, scaffolding would likely be restricted to creating opportunities to learn about those objectives. If it were elaborated in terms of its objectives and the main mathematical themes of representing, reasoning, communicating, and solving problems, scaffolding could include opportunities to learn about the themes and how they compared with those in other mathematics curricula. If the innovation were elaborated in terms of its objectives, main mathematical themes, and types of activities, scaffolding could match this, adding opportunities to probe examples of the activities, objectives, and themes.[8]

The first sort of scaffolding offers implementers modest opportunities to learn, and would impose only modest burdens on innovators; nearly everything would be left to implementers. The second offers slightly more opportunities to learn and comparably increased burden for innovators, and the third a bit more. Still, all three delegate most learning to implementers, and do not greatly burden innovators. Most teachers would not learn much, either about the innovation's aims and designs, or about how to extend and adapt the designs.

Other things being equal, more scaffolded designs would improve implementation by providing more opportunities for adopters to learn how to use the innovation. But other things are not equal, for more scaffolding takes more time, forethought, and money, and increases work, time, and costs. Extensive scaffolding would require extensive elaboration, and the combination would turn innovation into an even more complex enterprise and place greater demands on designers. Greater scaffolding also would depend on greater experience with and learning from implementation, to inform decisions about what to scaffold, and how. That implies a recursive process of innovation development, more systematic formative research in the process of development, and more time, human resources, and money. Work of this sort would also revise the innovator's role, pushing it toward more involvement with and responsibility for implementation.

At the same time, more-scaffolded interventions complicate potential implementers' decisions about adoption, since the interventions would make plain the need for extended relations with innovators or a third party, to teach and learn the intervention. Less-scaffolded designs leave more to adopters' interpretation and choice. Many educators prefer that approach, partly because it intrudes less. Hence, more-scaffolded designs could discourage adopters, and this in turn could deter designers. Because they demand so much more capability and effort, more-scaffolded designs also may not appeal to some designers.

This discussion reveals that our analysis of innovation design, use, and implementation stands in sharp contrast to several earlier approaches. To the extent that innovations require substantial elaboration and scaffolding, simpler notions of "diffusion" and "broadcasting" would not be helpful in understanding the requirements of scale. In addition, the differences among innovations reveal a curious pattern: there is little or no descriptive evidence on the most rudimentary patterns of innovation, or how these might influence implementation, yet researchers have offered broad explanations for why innovation fails. How can such sweeping explanations be valid if we know rather little about the most elementary patterns of innovation?

Environments

The environments in which innovation, adoption, and implementation occur also vary. Consider the difference between California, which has relatively weak state standards and accountability, and Texas, which has relatively strong standards and accountability. These and other features of the environment seem likely to bear on the formation, spread, and implementation of innovations, in part because they would be likely to shape the incentives for innovation design, adoption, and implementation. Yet we found only one study of what these features of the environment may be, or how they exert influence (Grissmer et al. 2000). We do, however, know a few important things about the environments in which educational change occurs.

States, LEAs, schools, and teachers work in a sector in which, until very recently, neither professionals nor schools or school systems could fail and go out of business, unless the student population vanished. Whatever incentives for change there were, they were not tied to the success of schools or professionals working in them; whether students learned or not had no influence on whether schools existed or teachers held their jobs. If there were incentives to innovate, they could not have been linked to the educational success of the organization or the professionals in it.

Until very recently there also have been weak standards of professional performance in schools. The extant standards concerned teachers' coursetaking, their experience, and their students' decorum. These things aside, there was no common basis for professionals to judge their academic work. There also was very weak knowledge about teaching and learning that was grounded in common academic standards. If there were any incentives or standards for innovation, they could not have been strongly and generally related to commonly held criteria for professional academic work.

If practitioners wished to change teaching or learning, then, it was likely to be for personal and somewhat idiosyncratic reasons, or for local political reasons. It was not likely to occur because there were strong and broad professional or organizational incentives to change, or because there were strong and salient standards against which performance was judged and the need for change estimated. At the same time, the issue-attention cycle in education policy grew increasingly short in the last five decades; there were many more innovations, but many came and went quite quickly, as they often lacked the features necessary for implementation, and educators learned that they had few incentives to take most innovations seriously.

Until very recently, most authority for instruction in the United States was devolved to classroom teachers. State and local school agencies had very modest strengths in teaching, learning, curriculum, and school improvement. Following Jefferson, Jackson, and classical liberal economic ideas, state governments were loath to build their own strengths, and eager to delegate problem solving to localities or the private sector. Local educational authorities also were reluctant to build central capability. State and local education agencies did not develop deep capability in the technical core, and were thinly staffed in those domains. For instance, when California began a very ambitious set of innovations in mathematics teaching in the middle and late 1980s, the state education agency employed fewer than three full-time professionals concerned with mathematics to monitor and support all the schools and districts in that huge state. Test and text publishers often have had more capability in curriculum than most state or local school agencies. Managers in schools and central offices, and governing boards, took only very general responsibility for instruction, had little knowledge of it, and had no common criteria with which to review or change it. This offered classroom teachers less guidance than in most nations, and more room for personal idiosyncrasies with respect to teachers' practice and changes in it.

The education professions have not taken a deep interest in the quality of professional work. Teacher unions are politically influential on bread and butter issues, but until the recent history of the American Federation of Teachers (AFT), no organizations that represented education professionals sought to define good practice, to investigate practice, or to improve practice. Or rather, their conception of practice improvement consisted of more spending and more professional education. The higher education institutions that offer professional education likewise took little or no responsibility for defining standards of practice, took little or no role in trying to improve it, and took a similarly weak role in regulating or informing practice with research. Researchers did studies, and some were informative, but neither professional organizations nor higher education institutions attempted to use research or professional knowledge to set standards for practice, to judge its quality, or to improve practice or education for practice.

Public education thus lacked anything approaching strong internal standards for the quality of practice, strong professional pressure to align practice with such standards, or substantial capability, in government or education, to evaluate or improve practice. The environments of public education offered little support for the implementation of innovations that made even moderately serious demands on practitioners. The innovations most likely to be widely adopted and sustained in these circumstances were those that made few demands on users, for the greater the demands, the less likely that users or innovators could find resources to support improvement in practice. The lack of connection between the political and professional environment, on the one hand, and educational innovation on the other, does not create resources for improvement, and thus impedes reform.

The preceding discussion deals mainly with the way that environments bear on innovation users, yet those same environments bear on innovators. As they developed new products, they had to choose. They could accommodate to the environment either by developing modest innovations that required little capability to be used effectively, or they could develop more ambitious innovations that required appreciable capability, but delegate that problem to users or some other agents. The first course of action would increase the chances for adoption and effective use. Though the second might yield broad adoption, it would reduce the chances of effective use. The burdens of development would be greater in the second case, but neither would saddle developers with the task of designing and operating systems to scaffold use. Alternatively, innovators could challenge the environment by developing more ambitious innovations that required appreciable capability, and by designing and operating systems to scaffold use. Until very recently, there have been few cases of the third sort, at least in part because the tasks of development and support are so formidable.

CONJECTURES

Several conjectures follow from this analysis. They derive from research, but we offer them as suggestions for further research. First, under the circumstances sketched above, it would be quite unlikely for innovations that were devised in schools and classrooms to be adopted at any scale. Practitioners devise many innovations, but extensively devolved authority for instruction, the lack of common standards of practice, and the lack of incentives for substantial change inhibit their diffusion. Even if such innovations were well designed, and many educators wanted to change, the incentives, communications networks, common standards of practice and vocabulary that would support diffusion, adoption, and use are absent. There is no social system that could turn practitioners' inventiveness to educational advantage.

Innovations that were more broadly sponsored—that is, by state education agencies, commercial publishers, or national and regional professional groups—would be more likely to be widely adopted. Judgments about the quality of use would depend on the nature of the innovation. For some, including commercial texts, fidelity in use seems a questionable concept, because there is little evidence that faithful use is intended. For many texts have been increasingly stuffed with material, on the assumption that teachers would pick and choose. For others, like CSR designs, for which fidelity was intended, implementation with fidelity to the developers' design and intentions would be quite difficult, because devolved authority for instruction and the lack of common standards of practice and incentives for substantial change would discourage high-quality use, even if innovations were well designed and educators wanted to change.

Second, one would expect innovation design to accommodate to the circumstances that we sketched above. One such accommodation is a broad menu of choices, from which adopters could select according to their inclinations; textbooks and other curriculum materials have developed in this direction, including greater and greater amounts of material. Another accommodation would be to define innovation in rather spare terms—that is, as a set of "principles"—that offer implementers room to redefine them to suit their situations and inclinations. Several widely adopted innovations, including school restructuring and the Coalition of Essential Schools, among others, took this path. Still another accommodation would be to tacitly delegate to users most or all responsibility for implementation, with little guidance about use. Many innovative curricula and several whole school designs (Core Knowledge is a leading candidate), have taken this path. Such accommodation tends to blur the nature of the innovation, making it difficult to identify what fidelity might mean. That would have survival value in public education, for it fits with the absence of standards of practice, and fragmented school governance.

Third, we expect innovative activity at every level of education, but typically sketchy implementation. Decentralized decision making, the absence of much extended professional learning, and the lack of strong professions all offer educators great latitude to make their own innovations, and to make their own sense of others' innovations. The environment offers many points of access, there is little overarching direction, there are many weak priorities, and there is little institutional memory. These conditions offer entrepreneurial innovators and educators many opportunities to design products that deal very partially with instruction, to do little to anticipate implementation, and thus, even when there is broad adoption, to expect variable and often weak use in practice.

At the same time (fourth), we expect that innovations that arise from social and cultural rather than educational changes could achieve broad adoption and use. For weak professionalism, popular governance and strong nongovernment agencies mean that schools are quite permeable to their environments. One example is the effects that prosperity and antipoverty programs appear to have on the school achievement of Hispanic and African American students: there was a dramatic reduction of racial differences in average achievement in reading and math on the NAEP between the early-to-middle 1970s and the mid-1980s (O'Day and Smith 1993). Another example is the simultaneous spread of more relaxed classroom conduct and organization and the demise of strict discipline and formal recitation. These changes spread widely and rapidly between the 1920s and the early 1970s, beginning in primary schools between the world wars and spreading in secondary schools in the 1960s. The change arose partly from the growing popularity of child-centered family life, and a growing aversion to strict discipline, rigid feeding schedules, early toilet training, and the view that children should be seen and not heard. Broad social change outside schools provided most of the infrastructure needed for broad change in schools, as teachers and students arrived with the new values and behavior already in hand, in schools that had habits but few strong professional norms.

Several researchers argue that innovations are more likely to succeed when they do not call for serious departures from teaching and learning.[9] But we have found several examples of substantial innovation in instruction that were adopted quickly and broadly. They suggest a fifth conjecture— namely that instructional innovations that depart sharply from conventional practice can reach impressive scale if they fit with the circumstances identified above. If innovations promise to solve problems that educators see as urgent, are relatively usable, and require only modest professional learning, they have a good chance of broad adoption and use. Graded elementary schools and graded texts were sharp departures from established practice in the 1880s and 1890s, but a flood of students made it increasingly difficult for teachers to manage with the existing nongraded materials and classes. These innovations helped schools to accommodate unprecedented waves of students, in schools that had meager funding. Schools and school systems could retool themselves for an age of batch processing.

Just a few decades later, standardized tests, elementary school ability grouping, and differentiated secondary curricula offered ways for the newly graded elementary schools and rapidly growing high schools to accommodate a continuing avalanche of students. They differentiated instruction, screened seemingly weak students out of many classes, and defended these changes with science. In the 1950s, secondary schools invented and adopted several demanding academic curricula and courses in response to continued enrollment growth from working-class and disadvantaged students and rising pressure to improve academic content. The Soviet Sputniks provided a stimulus and a rationale for sweeping changes in secondary curricula (Powell, Farrar, and Cohen 1985, chapter 5). These were conditions in which dramatic innovation in instruction could scale up rapidly.

These conjectures suggest a remarkably open and active system of schooling, in which substantial innovation in instruction can occur, either when external social change infiltrates schools or when innovations satisfy specific conditions in and around schools. A final conjecture, then, is that broad adoption and quality implementation of instructional innovations become increasingly less likely as innovations depart further from conventional practice. The "normal" state of affairs has been frequent but modest innovation, accompanied by variable but generally weak implementation.

STRATEGIES FOR INNOVATION

The last twenty years have seen escalating ambitions for instruction: state standards-based reform, Goals 2000, Bill Clinton's Improving America's Schools Act, the Comprehensive School Reform Designs program, and George W. Bush's No Child Left Behind all urge higher academic standards and more school improvement. Whatever their differences and difficulties, these policies and programs press more aggressive and ambitious innovation on schools. Our analysis implies a few things about the prospects for such innovation, and how researchers might frame inquiry about them.

Public education is currently the scene of a collision between rapidly rising expectations for school performance on the one hand, and modest capability for the use of innovations on the other. Academically ambitious innovations are unlikely to succeed on any scale unless they deal with the sources of that collision. There are three general strategies that innovation designers and implementers could use to do that. One is to attempt to supply what is missing in the environment—that is, to design and implement innovations so as to compensate for the problems sketched earlier in this paper. That would mean designing innovations that would: (a) offer powerful and continuing guidance for instruction; (b) compensate for weakness in the schools and professions; (c) support the formation of new professional norms, so that those at work in schools could not only orient their work to more ambitious standards, but could do so on their own; (d) include potent incentives, built into instructional guidance and professional norms, for more demanding and difficult teaching and learning, to increase the chances that the work would be engaging enough to bear the greater load of effort; and (e) reorganize instruction, school organization, and leadership to enable these changes. Innovations that included these elements would be more likely to be implemented by schools and professionals that have modest capability to improve instruction on their own. They also would hold more promise for use in environments in which only weak support for change from government and private agencies can be expected, and under conditions in which educational and political priorities often change rapidly. Such designs also would be more likely to cope with the lack of commonly accepted and understood standards concerning ambitious instruction, and in an inherited culture of innovation that offers potent incentives for quick and superficial action.

Since the best innovation design would be of little use if it could not be implemented widely and well, this approach probably would require implementation strategies that made it more likely that innovations could become self-sustaining at scale. One element of any such strategy would be intensive, sustained support for implementation. Given limitations in the environment, the designer would be the most likely source of that support, but because that would place a considerable burden on designers, other sources of support probably would have to be devised. One possibility would be the construction, by designers and implementers, of new educational subsystems. If they could be created and sustained, these could build social and professional solidarity, support the innovation's ambitious educational and professional values, and, by offering mutual aid, increase social capital. Such subsystems would be situated in the larger school system and its environment, but would include means to both support improved professional performance and to buffer, or insulate, schools from that environment. One example might be networks of continuing technical and professional assistance, including tools, networks for the exchange of usable knowledge for practice, and troubleshooting. Another might be digital archives of resources for practice. Still another might be new organizations, like some of the CSR designs, or networks of charter schools, that elaborate and scaffold responsible professional performance.

A second alternative would be for innovators and practitioners to change the environment, to make it less disruptive for ambitious efforts to improve instruction. The creation of state standards could be a step in this direction, and in some jurisdictions it seems to have had that effect. But even if the standards were exemplary, and written in ways that could be useful, they would be only a first step toward more coherent instructional guidance. It would remain to devise tests that were consistent with the standards and validly measured students' academic progress, to invent or adapt curriculum that could be turned into appropriate academic tasks, and to change professional education so that it focused on the standards, curriculum, and tests.

This is an incomplete account of the required changes, but it is an enormous set of tasks. It would require great change in federal, state, and local government, in private organizations, and in public expectations of schools and government. The changes would be desirable, but innovators have not had much influence on them in the past, and we can see no reason to expect that to change in the near future.

That leaves a third alternative, which is for innovation designers to accommodate to environments. This implies designs that conflict little with environments, and have survival value in them. It also implies a sharp trade-off between detail of design and fidelity of implementation. In the environments of U.S. schooling, more open and less elaborated designs are likely to have more survival value. These trade-offs grow steeper as innovation designs depart further from conventional practice. It is difficult to imagine that weakly elaborated designs for academically ambitious instruction would be either effectively or consistently implemented in very many schools, or, if they were implemented well, that they could be sustained for long. In the circumstances that we sketched in this paper, the designs that would best adapt to the environments of U.S. education are those that would be most likely to be weakly implemented.

THE SCALE OF SCALE

Most discussions of "scaling up" treat it as a quantitative problem, a matter of broad adoption and implementation.[10] Our analysis suggests instead that scale is as much a qualitative as a quantitative problem. All of the barriers to effective implementation that we discussed are qualitative. They include the difficulty of designing innovations that are usable for teachers who have modest professional knowledge and few common professional standards, the difficulty of addressing weaknesses of capability, and the difficulty of devising means to manage the environment and support implementation. These are qualitative because they refer to the attributes of innovations. They do have quantitative implications, for these barriers could be much less substantial if innovators were working with ten implementers than if they were working with five hundred. To solve the problem of "scaling up" requires "scaling in"—by this we mean developing the designs and infrastructure needed to support effective use of an innovation. That, in turn, requires consideration of the problems that have made some sorts of innovation difficult, and taking these into account in deciding what to change and how to design the means to do so. It also requires significant attention to designing the use of innovations by practitioners in the environments in which the practitioners work.

Given the difficulty of doing such work, it is worth considering what "large scale," or "scale-up" might mean. Most accounts reference scale to the number of schools. From this angle, implementation in 10 percent of schools in New York City would seem small. But if innovation designs and schools have been as weak, and environments as unruly, as we claim, effective implementation of even a modestly complex intervention in 10 percent of New York City schools would be an enormous achievement. Scale is relative not just to the universe of possible implementers, but to the scope and depth of what must be done to devise and sustain change. The idea of scale thus means both less and more than has been imagined.

NOTES

1. An earlier draft of this chapter was presented at a 2003 meeting ("Conceptualizing Scale-Up: Multidisciplinary Perspectives"), sponsored by the Data Research and Development Center of the University of Chicago, and supported by the National Science Foundation, in connection with the Interagency Research Initiative (IERI). The ideas in the paper owe a good deal to our work with Karen Gates, Joshua Glazer, Simona Goldin, and Donald Peurach, all colleagues in the Study of Instructional Improvement at the University of Michigan. We owe special thanks to Donald Peurach and Simona Goldin for the improvements that they made to this draft.

2. Michael Fullan, who has done the most extensive work in this field, argues that view in *The Meaning of Educational Change* (1982).

3. The longest-running study is Everett Rogers's *Diffusion of Innovations* (2003), which deals, even in its later editions, only glancingly with implementation. The

most comprehensive is Fullan (1982). The other study is by Paul Berman and Milbrey McLaughlin (1979); it considered several federally sponsored programs.

4. Seymour Sarason was the first to write about this problem, in 1971. Cohen and Levinthal (1990) offer a more general version of this perspective.

5. Bardach (1977) writes: "Incompetence is not, of course, a trait like having brown eyes. It is a description of a relationship between a task or function in the situation up to a given, though ultimately arbitrary, standard of some sort . . . it may not in any meaningful sense be 'his fault' that he is incompetent to perform certain tasks—it may well be the fault of the people who assigned him the task in the first place" (126).

6. Elaboration modifies design; it refers to specificity of detail in design.

7. Scaffolding is not the flip side of elaboration. For example, a direct instruction scheme could be extensively elaborated, but have thin and mechanistic materials for professionals to learn to use the approach.

8. Elaboration with little scaffolding leaves it to implementers to learn how to bring the intervention to reality. Scaffolding with little elaboration provides implementers with resources for improvement without much guidance as to how the resources could be used or toward what ends.

9. One of us included; see Cohen (1987).

10. A notable exception is Corbett and Wilson (1998).

2

Principles for Scaling Up: Choosing, Measuring Effects, and Promoting the Widespread Use of Educational Innovation[1]

Eva L. Baker

The goal of scaling up educational innovations is to produce robust, effective, replicable outcomes. This chapter addresses requirements to support scale-up of scientifically vetted innovation (or new ideas that are built on the findings of quality research and development). Scaling up—that is, adapting innovation for widespread and supported use—is a laudable goal, but one clearly not appropriate for all research-based innovations. Documented effectiveness and feasibility are especially important for innovations that involve children, who in schools have little or no option to agree to the services provided to them. Despite the enthusiasm of designers and early users, many innovations need an extended period of time to develop in order to meet feasibility requirements and to gain the credibility conferred by a strong base of evidence. In this chapter, a number of issues will be considered, including: (1) the context of evidence of effectiveness; (2) definitions of scaling up; (3) how to measure implementation and effects; and (4) areas in need of continuing work, from the research point of view. The ultimate goals are the articulation of usable principles for scale-up and a contribution to the definition of this slippery concept.

EVIDENCE FOR INNOVATION—A BRIEF PERSONAL HISTORY

No discussion of scaling up research can stray far from current federal policy preferences for certain types of scientific evidence, as prerequisites for broader implementation. To begin this analysis, I will draw on my own scientific training, the evolution of thinking in the field as I experienced it, and, where relevant, the work of my colleagues at the Center for Research on Evaluation, Standards, and Student Testing (CRESST).

Experimental Design Beliefs and Realities

Few of the readers will have any reason to know that I was mentored by an experimentally oriented learning psychologist and statistician (A. A. Lumsdaine). Lumsdaine worked with a very small number of graduate students, and was both revered and feared mostly because he gave backbreaking assignments and detailed, public feedback. For instance, every week he required an original, full, complete (long) proposal for a significant instructional, true experiment, including a (pre-Google) review of the literature, and a formal oral defense of the merit of the work. In addition, we were to select one of these proposals (with his guidance) and conduct at least one true experiment with a reasonable treatment time each term. Apart from garnering an early publication record, and steeled acceptance for public criticism, we were taught by him about programmatic efforts that should build and accumulate knowledge—knowledge from the work of other scholars and our own line of effort. His interests were in making a difference in the real world. My studies with him lasted two years, including summers, prior to his assuming the chair of the psychology department at the University of Washington. In abbreviated form, the following ten precepts can be synthesized from my experience:

1. The gold standard for research design and analysis was randomization—which meant, in addition to randomly assigned treatments, randomized selection of subjects and order of dependent measures, or else probability estimates were inappropriate.
2. The situations and learners to which one intended to generalize necessarily defined the subjects and domains from which one sampled.
3. Comparing treatment X with present practice was not research, but an imprecise approach to evaluation. Research required manipulable, independent variables compared at different intensities.
4. Satisfactory research findings required generalization and replication.
5. Fidelity of treatments delivered had to be adequately verified.
6. Treatments should be of sufficient duration to have an impact.
7. The unit of analysis should be based upon the unit of randomization and generalization—that is, students, classrooms, or schools.
8. Obtained effects should be robust over stringent or lax criteria and across multiple dependent measures and time.
9. Never say "proven" or "was significant," because we are operating in a probabilistic world with many unmeasured variables. The best we can do is say we "found" given results.
10. If you can't do it right, don't do it.

The precepts taught by Lumsdaine in the form of intense, project-based learning were not original. We read R. A. Fisher's *The Design of Experiments* (1951), a seminal volume that made the point that the use of inferential statistics was logically legitimated by introducing chance into the experiment through randomization, a point that is no doubt still news to an occasional student. We replicated Fisher's findings in simulations. We studied the evaluations of the *Why We Fight* series and other experiments in instruction (Hovland, Lumsdaine, and Sheffield 1949). We analyzed the eloquent expansion of Fisher by Campbell and Stanley (1963) in a chapter in the *Handbook of Research on Teaching* (Gage 1963), the details of which decades of my own graduate students can no doubt still recite. We also consumed *The Conduct of Inquiry* (Kaplan 1964) to understand logic and evidence from the perspective of the philosophy of science. I was happily schooled in analysis of variance methods (my mentor preferred plots, with the goal to "see" whether differences were important rather than "significant"). We calculated effect sizes and plotted power curves. All were pathetically heady experiences for me—a literature graduate student with history and anthropology minors. I was sure I was objectively and technically prepared to fix American education, or at least to know when it happened. Cookbooks were used only for cooking dinner.

In fact, thirty years ago at the annual AERA meeting, as a fledgling professor I took my learning into the professional realm. I presented a paper on the topic of the use of true experiments during the development of instructional interventions, and modestly suggested that, in the absence of scientific knowledge on which to base design decisions, instructional developers should conduct applied experiments to choose the components most effective empirically for potential interventions. I was ripped by the discussant. Undaunted, I continued to apply experimental approaches in my early work in teacher education and in developing primary-age reading curricula, using true experiments to investigate theoretically based options or seemingly arbitrary choices. Early on I was concerned with the sensitivity of measures to detect change, so I also employed the newly formulated criteria for designing achievement tests suggested by Wells Hively and his colleagues (Hively, Patterson, and Page 1968).

The Context: From Then to Now

Note that the gold standard I was trained on does not much exist today—partly because methodologies have been invented to compensate for experimental controls, partly because of unintended burdens placed on researchers by human subjects' protection requirements, and last, and most obviously, because the complexities and options of educational delivery of instructional alternatives rely on agreements, acceptance, and actions by multiple players.

But twenty years ago (or more) I was hardly alone in my beliefs. At that time, it was widely believed that schools ought not to use interventions (curricula or instructional products) unless experimental studies supported the superiority of the proposed treatments against some criterion. The Educational Product Information Exchange (EPIE), at Columbia University, had a proponent of this view in its director, Ken Komoski. Lumsdaine (1965, chap. 7) argued that effectiveness was a defining characteristic of the term "instructional program"; one did not really have an educational program unless one could document that at least two criteria had been met: that the program processes could be *essentially reproduced* from occasion to occasion, and that the program's effects were also *reproducible or replicable*. In fact, California passed a law stating that before curricular materials could be used in public schools, commercial publishers were required to present experimental data documenting the intervention's effectiveness. The law was never enforced. Somewhat later, the National Diffusion Network, an arm of the U.S. Office of Education, required that experimental data be presented to obtain federal support in delivering interventions to Title 1 schools. At that time, evaluation studies followed the paradigm of experimental research, a view advocated variously by Freeman and Sherwood (1970), Cook and Campbell (1979), Boruch (1976), and of course, Campbell and Stanley (1963).

For the most part, the procedures of experimental research on learning and instruction continued to be divorced from the large-scale implementation of educational curricula. With some notable exceptions, including a few products of some of the Regional Educational Laboratories and a scattering of technology-based interventions, most of the curricula and instruction headed for schools were not convincingly evaluated. Written by one or more university professors or classroom teachers, these curricula (texts, workbooks, etc.) were published and distributed by commercial firms. The marketing cycles and profit margins associated with these enterprises were, respectively, too frequent and too thin for serious scholarly inquiry about the premarket effects of their products. When advertisements referenced "demonstrated effectiveness," they more than likely referred to reviews and tryouts of lessons by a handful of teachers prior to the development of a teachers' manual in the curriculum of interest.

Methodology Expands

So what happened to true experiments? The utility of standard experimental features as essential to the evaluation of broad-based education programs was countered in the 1970s and 1980s with writings by Glass (1977b), Cronbach et al. (1981), Bloom, Madaus, and Hastings (1981), Stake (1967), Scriven (1967), House (1974), Patton (1978), Weiss (1977), and Alkin (1985). Many argued for decision-theoretic studies—for studies of whether the program met identified needs, and whether comparisons, if any, were sensible. These writers variously identified multiple purposes for the use of such data. They also focused on the valuing of findings and the ability to understand what happened, including both intended and unintended consequences for all the participants in the studies. They were concerned with "merit," not simply numbers.

Their thoughts may have been influenced by a well-developed conceptual document by Cronbach and Suppes (1969) that identified criteria for distinguishing research from evaluation studies—between knowledge-producing and decision-related studies. This push-back on experimentation was bolstered by the creation of a large number of methodological innovations made to permit the study of real schools, that is, environments putatively unsuitable for true experimentation.

The difference between those positions and Lumsdaine's view resides in the difference between the positions' conceptions of the entity *program*. For the most part, *programs* to be evaluated referred to complex state or federal policy interventions rather than tightly conceived instructional treatments or products. Considerable scholarship on the topic of the relationship of evidence to decisions of policy makers (for instance, Lindblom and Cohen 1979; Weiss 1977; and Wildavsky 1993) has continued across the realm of social science, rather than from an exclusively psychological perspective (e.g., Lumsdaine 1965, excluding Fisher 1951). Such analyses credited a wide range of approaches to obtaining legitimate evidence. As a result, there grew a less literal view of research, development, and evaluation than one that inevitably follows a clean left-to-right chronology and logic. Differing points of entry into the research and development (R&D) process and the influence of political and social factors were provided as explanations for seeing the R&D situation as vastly more complex than choosing between two or more options.

A simple summary is that most policy makers use the best evidence they can obtain *to bolster their own preferences within their political context*, rather than using the evidence as the basis for forming their original opinion. The inference to be drawn, of course, is that there were more powerful incentives operating to influence decisions than documented effectiveness, such as beliefs, political power, and cost. Furthermore, studies of program implementation documented the enormous variation in application of policy and program features, which resulted in great diversity of uses and effects. Nonetheless, the evaluation industry continued to the mid-1980s. Both interpretive and true experimental designs were applied to ill-defined and partially implemented educational programs; outcome measures logically insensitive to treatments were routinely employed, with an avalanche of no-difference findings as a result. The predictable inference was that—if the data were correct—educators did not know what they were doing in classrooms. Thus began the steady public drumbeat of concern.

Another factor that shifted methods was the simultaneous redesign of schools of education and of scholarly education faculties. Faculties diversified and expanded well beyond the dominance of psychologists and philosophers, to include anthropologists, political scientists, historians, and sociologists. These scholars brought with them a wider set of methods, a penchant for focusing on close-up interpretative analyses, and clear goals to explore the *why* as well as the *what*. New faculty shifted the norms of research, so that what had previously been rewarded—for example, conducting lots of brief, treatment-true experiments (still the norm in some psychology departments)—was no longer of high value. Serious redefinitions of "scholarship" occurred at top-tier schools of education.

Why dwell on the past? And why these fascinating snippets of yore? They are directed to the young among the readers, who may believe that the present federal focus on scientific evidence is a wholly new concept. Now let's turn to the crux of the discussion.

SCIENTIFIC EVIDENCE

Although I recommend a highly readable volume from the National Research Council (Shavelson and Towne 2002) for a recent treatment of scientific evidence, let me make some brief remarks on the topic. Scientific evidence is a matter of degree. We in social science understand that there is no single scientific method that produces sufficient evidence for every purpose. We acknowledge, almost revel in, the reality that there is a range of legitimate forms of inquiry, and that quality criteria exist for each of the different methods and strategies.

Yet, for the most part, the lay public and most policy makers do not get the idea. They think that we do the best science when it is large-scale and objective (read *quantitative*), and that we can *prove* for all time (or for four years) that one alternative is better than all other choices. The public now may be encouraged to believe that one method should always be used to determine educational value. If we could help people understand the difference between the production of knowledge and the making of decisions (Cronbach and Suppes 1969; Clark 1985), we would be mightily advantaged. However, the differences between theory development, inductive logic, and ad hoc evaluation may well never be learned by our broadest constituencies, so let us focus our sights on the Interagency Education Research Initiative (IERI) and other programs.

Principle 1: Understand the Appropriateness of the Evidence for the Innovation.
Scientific evidence may be inferred by many to mean experimental and con-

trolled studies of the effectiveness of a proposed intervention. Yet, the minimum requirements for true experiments are rarely met in educational situations, especially those in urban settings. For instance, volunteer populations of districts or teachers may be used because of bargaining agreements, extant policy, or penchants for collaboration. Thus, generalizing results to nonvolunteers is always problematic. Second, there is great volatility in the stability of some urban school sites, where students, teachers, and leadership may change substantially within a treatment period such as one year. Students are mobile. Substitute teachers may be a regular feature of instruction. There is also often a climate of distrust that has implications for methodology. For example, relying on self-report approaches—logs, surveys, notes, or diaries—in order to verify treatments is likely to yield overstatements of activities and result in inferences about large process differences where they may be very slight. Because affecting the course of education requires attention to a number of socially connected practices (as opposed to the difficult, but more simple, matter of patient compliance, to regularly swallow a dose of Lipitor in the privacy of one's bathroom), social context and trust among players matter.

Furthermore, the embedding of schools themselves in broader political and economic contexts suggests that influences far stronger than classroom events and the considered treatments may vitiate or exaggerate impact of the treatment. For example, changing state policy requirements for language of instruction, reducing or raising class size or the amount of money available for school spending, and altering the incentive structures implied by different accountability systems are intended to be "big ticket" interventions that may swamp other treatment effects. Contamination is also an issue. For instance, my colleagues and I valiantly tried to conduct true experiments over multiple years with real control groups and known interventions (see Baker, Herman, and Gearhart 1996). We found, however, that when an intervention was perceived to be effective or even desirable by teachers, administrators, or parents, the leadership of the district or school was placed under pressure to find a way to compensate for the control groups' experience. To the extent possible, the administrators and teachers rapidly provided approximations of experimental treatment to the original control students, and naturally reduced the functional differences in teachers' and children's experience between control and treatment groups.

Principle 2: Document the Scientific Evidence in Support of the Design of the Intervention. There are two related aspects to the scaling up of an innovation: its design and implementation. Evidence is required in support of both of these features. Unfortunately, a trend has been to credit evidence for full implementations of innovation. As a result, there is a misconception that the last in, or the most recent, study matters most. This view has led a few practitioners and policy makers to support the idea of the "grand finale" study, the one that *proves once and for all* the superiority of X instead of Y. A more legitimate and scientific approach is to look at the cumulative impact of scholarship, analysis, interpretative studies, and experimental verifications. One should judge the quality of the whole stream of evidence rather than look only at the findings of the latest study. It is true that more recent work may incorporate remedies to earlier research flaws, but the full range of studies should be addressed. Although standard meta-analytic approaches may be crude, they give a starting point to identify studies that have comparable goals and quality-dependent measures. Furthermore, the evidence sources should not be parochial and reference exclusively the work of a particular research team. Instead, they should include those completed by the research team, but also must include a wide swath of scholarship, especially those studies conducted by intellectual competitors.

CRESST Assessment Models Scale-Up: Example 1

How did we argue the scientific base of our Model Assessment approach in CRESST (Baker, Freeman, and Clayton 1991; Baker and Mayer 1999; Wittrock and Baker 1991)? Our first effort was to consolidate research evidence in the area of knowledge comprehension. There were two main approaches in this literature. One held that all knowledge domains were idiographic and required specialized domain knowledge for expertise. The other held that there were some general principles of knowledge comprehension (Bransford and Johnson 1972; Wittrock 1974) and of developing expertise (Chi, Glaser, and Farr 1988; Larkin et al. 1980). We chose to combine both approaches, adopting the argument that generalization of learning did occur and that attributes of expertise had common elements.

The integration of the literature suggested that deep understanding of content or subject matter required the following components:

- Distinguishing the main principles or themes of the topic
- Understanding the relationship among principles
- Connecting concrete examples and nonexamples to the structure of knowledge

After many false starts, we converted these features into a scoring rubric. We asked students to write about various primary sources of knowledge— letters, speeches, experiments, graphical representations—and to explain their meaning and importance (and, in those cases where contrasting material was presented, their differences). The scoring rubric was applied to writing of students in history at a number of different grade levels. We then asked history experts, that is, professors and advanced graduate students, to answer the identical history questions, presented with the same materials. We contrasted their performance with that of the students. Using methods derived from the expert-novice literature, we were able to document that experts did write principled, concrete, related pieces as responses. Moreover, their work included references to their prior knowledge in the area. In contrast, we found that students tended to miss the principle, relational and prior knowledge, and rather used such concrete knowledge as was available in the testing materials. They also wrote flat, relatively undifferentiated prose, with numerous misconceptions (Baker 1994). Building on the literature in learning and in expertise, as well as our own series of studies, we refined the scoring rubric so that it generated a two-factor solution: an expert factor—principles, prior knowledge—and a novice factor—dependence on the text presented and misconceptions. The expert factor repeatedly predicted overall scores. Furthermore, the use of this scoring scheme gave teachers guidance for teaching students ways to learn types of material (rather than a particular text). Our own studies contrasted students who were in ability-tracked classrooms, students with different language backgrounds, students given multiple readings of the materials, students given support in prompts, and students given tests first in background knowledge. Much of our attention was spent on getting score-reliable (agreeing with each other) and content-valid (agreeing with the intended expert scoring scheme) measures, as well as on experimenting with response mode. Our results showed *predicted* relationships with other extant measures, such as standardized tests of knowledge, standardized writing measures, grades, and so forth. Relationships varied as we would have predicted.

We decided to scale up after more than thirty such studies and conducted studies on a sampling basis statewide in Hawaii with fourth-, fifth-, seventh-, and tenth-grade students; but more on that later. Note that before we began modest scale-up in Hawaii (about 1,000 students per grade and different curricula), we had assembled data from the literature, from multiple trials of teachers, from classrooms at grades seven through twelve, and in studies ranging from 60 to 400 students (Baker et al. 1996).

Principle 3: Embrace Design and Development. One of the persistent biases of psychologically oriented research has been its dependence on short treatment times, artificial situations, and a limited, volunteer subject pool. Scale-up is not just bigger research. For research to become a usable innovation, it must go through a development process. This process (described in Baker 1973) involves the statement of goals, creation of procedures (replicable, à la Lumsdaine), and measured results that are subject to improvement by modified design and testing. It should sound a lot like No Child Left Behind (NCLB), which has adopted a systems approach to improvement, with only little control over the system elements. Nonetheless, in the more tractable area of a single innovation, it is possible to use this kind of engineering (horrors!). But engineering is theory made real. The resulting comparison of the innovation to an alternative (spare us the unverifiable "conventional practice" as the option) is not strictly research to create new knowledge, but is decision-oriented investigation, what is commonly known as evaluation. The label in this case is important because it distinguishes between what types of inferences can be legitimately drawn, or the validity of the findings of the study.

There are tested approaches for the design and implementation of large-scale, research-based interventions that focus on the formative evaluation, or results-redesign, improvement cycle, that determine what research elements can be "saved" in a complex, messy environment, and at what cost and risk. Researchers themselves are rarely prepared to anticipate users' needs in a volatile policy and social environment. Let me return to the CRESST example to drive the point home.

In our Hawaii studies, we were interested in a series of research questions: Did the models and templates we used for performance assessment generalize across grade levels (fourth, fifth, seventh, and tenth)? Did the approach to measurement work across topics within subject areas (ten topics within each of the elementary, middle school, and high school environments), and were similar patterns found among subject matters (Hawaiian history—where the research team had paltry levels of expertise—and high school American history from colonial times to World War II)? In addition, we were interested in multilevel models that might predict performance (e.g., students' reading comprehension and teachers' self-reported topic-by-topic subject matter expertise). We also investigated the opportunity to learn and group differences in performance. All of these questions were related to the general validity and instructional utility of the assessments. With respect to scale-up issues, we were interested in teacher reactions, complexity of administration directions, time, and central office efficiency in distributing, collecting, and transferring data. For scoring, our concerns again were validity with the expert scale, level of scorer agreement, time and cost per student paper scored, training and retraining requirements for raters, and methods of clear reporting. In the second year, our interest focused not only on change in performance, but also on teachers' reactions and initiatives to share instructional knowledge, and most importantly, whether the system could train raters by themselves and obtain usable results (it could).

All of this effort was based on the assumption that CRESST would "transfer its technology" to an entity external to the university, such as a state, school district, or commercial enterprise, and get out of the continued scale-up business. Why? Because our organization is focused on the R&D needed for quality models and tools, and our expertise does not lie with packaging, marketing, distribution, and massive technical support. It is clear that, under any transition, expert advice is needed during the scale-up phase to sustain and adapt the interventions.

Principle 4: Measure a Broad Range of Variables in Formative Evaluation. The credibility and ultimate success of any innovation will depend upon its motivated and practical use on the ground. We recommend that any intervention or indicator be subject to empirical tests using a broad base of dependent measures and the fastest cycle time possible, to enable multiple iterations of trial and revision.

Multiple measures need to be selected to address the range of potential outcomes or the value of the innovation. Here are some precepts for multiple measures in the formative evaluation of scale-up.

- Multiple measures of the desired outcome, divided into those that measure the construct in ways similar to the intervention's goals, and those that measure it through different formats and item pools
- Criteria for success, tested under different conditions of stringency— that is, does it work when criteria are high and rigid as well as when they are flexible and variable
- Measures of short-term effect and retention
- Measures of transfer—performance on similar tasks and formats; performance with varying prompts (much versus little information; timed and untimed; changed stimulus situations)
- Measures of implementation—observations, self-reports, student data, records, technology evidence
- Measures of user reaction
- Cost and efficiency data

CRESST Assessment Models Scale-Up: Example 2

CRESST's venture with the Los Angeles United School District (LAUSD) scale-up (reported in depth in Niemi et al., in press) was extraordinary and replete with opportunities for us to learn. LAUSD educates approximately 780,000 students, more than most states, in an area of approximately 500 square miles. During our involvement, California moved from frameworks, to no-standards-no-test, to standardized-test-no-standards, to variations of standards and test development, and now, to a steady state of standards and an evolution to quality standards-based assessment. In this period, the laws about bilingual education and testing in multiple languages changed, five superintendents were in office, class size reduction required massive day-to-day changes, and NCLB came into being. LAUSD went from believing it needed to have its own standards and measures to comply with the Improving America's Schools Act (1994) to full compliance with the state. LAUSD also was keen at the outset to develop assessments that could be used in classrooms in order to communicate clearly to teachers and the public the expectations that they should hold for their students. The highlights of the scale-up involved the following:

- Obtaining and maintaining political support for multiyear trials, involving school board, union, legislature, and administrative leadership
- Developing standards in conjunction with the district and the Council for Basic Education
- Mediating ideological differences in curriculum and content
- Developing content-focused assessments and trying them out in multiple classrooms at three grade levels (elementary, middle, and high school) in history, science, language arts, and mathematics in Spanish and in English
- Reducing focus to math and English, dropping Spanish versions, adding grade levels, and retaining performance and open-ended focus
- Changing the purpose of the assessments from classroom improvement and system monitoring to promotion
- Changing the number of test occasions per child and the total number of minutes allowed
- Moving to literacy testing for 450,000 students a year
- Working with 6,000 teachers to help them design and score assessments according to our models, and conducting appropriate studies of training effectiveness
- Transitioning from CRESST-trained to trainer-of-trainers scoring models, with varying levels of monitoring
- Interacting with six different points of contact, many of whom were shifted as a result of changing superintendents
- Preparing camera-ready versions of the tests and overseeing scoring and data entry
- Conducting series of technical quality studies, involving modifications for different subgroups of learners, multiple formats, and experimental contrasts among instructional variations
- Monitoring cost per student
- Maintaining support of the teachers' union and board, with the help of our "idea champion" in the district
- Briefing new superintendents and their staffs on progress
- Being involved in presentations that the district wanted, providing advice on other technical matters
- Developing validity evidence using external examinations, for example, pass rates on the California High School Exit Examination, generalizability studies, and evidence that domain-independent components could be embedded in different subject matter. This finding is of

great importance as it reduces the cost of renewal and also supports the ability of teachers and students to engage in transfer

- Navigating bureaucratic issues, such as span of control, review of materials by the public and various committees, planning far out into the future, and coping with real scale. For example, I was asked to meet with the lead teachers to explain the progress of our work; as an afterthought, I asked how many I would be seeing, imagining about seventy-five people at the outside. Ultimately, 1,000 lead teachers came to my presentation, a fact that rapidly changed my plans for an informal discussion and information-gathering session.

What happened, in a nutshell, is that for a small amount of money, we tested the scale-up of our research and Hawaii experience under conditions far more volatile and with far less control than we expected. It was hard and frustrating, with times of great satisfaction and crashing dismay. We learned that our assessment models were robust across varying levels of design and scoring. We learned, from an independent study (The Achievement Council, n.d.), that our assessments did in fact change teacher understanding of goals and promoted collaboration and the development of relevant performance tasks. We developed strong support among teachers and staff, some of whom were more invested than we were in the efforts. When the latest superintendent was appointed, he began the process anew with a different provider. So we scratched our heads and moved on. The timing for us was excellent given that we were ready to commercialize and take the next step with technology.

Principle 5: Design the Best Study Possible. So what might count as evidence of an effective intervention? Here are three options and some caveats.

1. The single, high-quality evaluation study. The most obvious option is to conduct an evaluation study of an intervention, sampling settings and teachers and learners to which the findings should generalize. Here the unit of analysis should be the classroom average (of subgroups).

But—consider the trade-off between sufficient treatment exposure and the need to disseminate something useful rapidly. How long should an evaluation last to show immediate and long-term impact? At a minimum, one should expect data to show that the intervention led to desired results compared to a criterion, or to well-defined alternatives, using dependent measures that are likely to be *sensitive* to change over the period of the study. A big flaw in the current application of experiments is the relative lack of credible, technically adequate, and appropriate dependent measure(s). Testing treatment and controls on poorly executed outcome measures yields no information. If appropriate measures are available, then niceties such as treatment verification, randomization, and so on should be observed, and mixed methods, including intensive substudies of groups or individuals, are desirable. Thus, this kind of study serves as an existence-proof—the intervention "worked" somewhere.

2. Extrapolating from cumulative results of scientific knowledge. One might analyze the *design* of the intervention to note the degree to which it is composed of elements that exemplify best knowledge in a field (see principle 2). Were teachers prepared with a range of examples to use? Were opportunities to engage in significant intellectual activity provided in the program? Was useful feedback given? In this instance, one is using the history of stable scientific findings from series of studies to generalize to the new setting.

But—the analysis of instruction would have to be carefully conducted, by collecting information on use, as well as structure of materials. The view should be from the learner's eye. It is possible that the particular combination or the actual instantiation of heretofore effective variables might yield weaker-than-expected results. Nonetheless, this example emphasizes interventions built on application of accumulated knowledge rather than those dependent on a single, go/no-go study.

3. A good, one-shot case study with internal variations. A third option would be a carefully implemented study that shows the differential effects of implementation conditions of the treatment (program) on multiple dependent measures. First, a range of implementations must be used so internal comparisons (conditional differences, or even contrasts between strong and weak implementers) can be made against the dependent measures of choice. Dependent measures (to harp on a theme) must minimally document that (a) they are sensitive to the highest strength of instruction; (b) effects systematically show up on direct, transfer, and retention measures; and (c) the implementation supports (or has no negative impact on) measures of social capital (e.g., sense of efficacy of teachers and students, effort, teamwork, trust), as well as intellectual and skill outcomes. Longitudinal findings are always desired.

But—the comparisons on dependent measures assume that previous performance increments or trajectories (e.g., 2 percent a year) are known. Measures of instructional process (still not well formulated after all these years) would need to be obtained. This is not real theory building but rule-of-thumb guidance for practice. In any case, the cost of such studies is an issue. Many researchers do not have the funds to translate their ideas into practical interventions, and many commercial entities have neither the inclination nor the funds to defer marketing until a high-quality, perhaps multiyear study can be conducted. Our studies must recognize that effectiveness differences are necessary but not sufficient. The stability of impact and the acceptability of acquisition and maintenance costs (for material, required updates, and continuous training) will make a difference in the long-term impact of an intervention.

Principle 6: Support Flexibility and Local Innovation. The interesting tension in the adoption of innovation comes between the prestige, credibility, and cost of branded product lines and the "not invented here" (NIH, no federal relation) idea. While prestige, ease of use, and policy may push adoption of a particular approach, tradition and cost constraints operate to maintain current practices. My onetime mentor Susan Meyer Markle shared a rule of implementation, just at the time when people were first trying to design programmed instructional materials that were "teacher-proof," a time fast approaching from some directions again. Dr. Markle's advice was to encourage participants to "add their egg" to the mix, referring to cake mixes that required the cook to add a fresh egg (despite the fact that better effects were maintained by using a known amount of powdered egg). The reason was to help the cook feel more like a cook by offering up an essential component. Similarly, in interventions, it is important to preserve avenues for local contribution and innovation. For the most part, these will not undermine the already effective programs. And more often than one realizes, the "egg addition" turns into a terrific recipe augmentation, much like the Pillsbury Bake-Off competition. With little effort and expense, through websites and Internet boards, it is possible to share interventions among users, and for the developer or marketer to identify potential variations for the next version. Holding a place for local innovation and contribution shows more than tolerance of teachers' "messing" with the intervention. It creates an ambience of welcomed exploration.

One place where local flexibility may best be shown is the manner in which the users move to "hands-off" practice by the R&D team. Assuming that we intend to promote independence and accountability, it is important to learn from users how, in what order, and with what schedule of support they can begin to take on the responsibility for renewing the intervention on their own. In the CRESST Assessment Models area, we began this work in two places: at the administrative level, cooperating with the leadership to internalize the policies needed to use the system, such as how to train and vet raters and defining what data flow should look like; and at the teacher level, working so that teams of teachers could design new assessments that met our specifications and could share with one another positive instructional experience and help for those having difficulty.

Principle 7: Define Minimums for Scalability and Sustainability. As an enterprise emphasizing multidisciplinary approaches and technology, IERI more recently has focused on the scalability and sustainability of the R&D theme. There is a series of questions that can be directed to scalable and sustainable education innovations (and who should implement them), but let me start by defining *scalable* and *sustainable* in my own terms.

Scalable:

- Multiple sites (districts) with full implementation
- Predicted effects across diverse settings at known cost
- Cost-sensitive and fully available training and technical support

Sustainable:

- Robust
- Survives without halo effect or incentives
- Needs minimal cheerleading
- Good results without the oversight of the developer
- Pliant and adaptive while maintaining key attributes and effects

But who should be responsible for such functions and for documenting their empirical studies? The school user who wishes to adopt the intervention? The researcher who wishes to explore, refine, and promote it? The commercial entity that wishes to do good, and to make money from it?

On a train to Lyon, a venture capitalist illustrated to me a now-obvious truth—that the surest way to fail with the scale-up of an intervention is to let the inventor or research team continue to guide the implementation and marketing of the enterprise. Simplification and robustness are not always compatible with the particular vision a researcher brings to an application. What if we posited that commercial enterprises or specially conceived organizations—rather than the originating developer—should be responsible for evaluation, scale-up, and sustenance? If we believed that such organizations have distribution capacity, help, training, marketing capacity, and general savvy not usually shared by researchers, how would that change our view of IERI's program direction?

Here are some propositions:

It is not possible for IERI to stimulate sensible between-project comparisons of ways to scale up. Developing a theory of scale-up is best done by studying like enterprises in other fields. Theories of dissemination, too, come and go, and come and go again (e.g., remember the agricultural extension agent), and their adequate testing conflicts with demand for solutions to the educational problems addressed. IERI projects have not adopted outcome measures that can be aggregated to enable one to make between-project comparisons.

Furthermore, cycles of change—political, ideological, substantive, and, particularly, technological—set the limits for scale-up and sustainability. An important question is, what is the shelf life of the intervention? We are in an era of very rapid change. Good things, even the glimmer of good things, need to get out into the market.

THE FUTURE OF SCALE-UP RESEARCH

If IERI wishes to support the development of private enterprise versions of funded work, it need only fund Small Business Innovation Research (SBIR) projects with existing procurement mechanisms. Another option is to review the policies of other agencies, for instance, the Office of Naval Research (ONR). ONR requires for the funding of its applied research projects that a sponsor (a particular part of the navy, like the submarine service) will agree to take on and pay for the intervention once the research period is over and effects are demonstrated. ONR researchers and managers must spend time lining up these potential, serious, ultimately paying users or else the funding priority for project continuation is lowered. In education, we might think of commercial companies or states or districts as the target partner users.

In such cases, no doubt, the relationship between researchers and the private sector needs consideration, to avoid much of the messiness attendant in the science or medical areas about ownership, research credibility, and conflict of interest. But it is clear that if broad-scale sustainability is desired, such concerns must be designed-in early. We cannot grow research projects forward, in tiny steps, from pilot to larger trials to big trials as we usually complete transfer from the laboratory to practice. If practice is the goal, then the improvement of practice should be the aim. What implication does this backward-chaining view have for research? Theoretically oriented research must continue, and a good proportion of it needs to occur in settings of potential use. But scale-up and sustainability are criteria that are applicable not to most research, but to development and engineering. And they need continued expertise to survive. Research dollars cannot be justified exclusively by whether current applications are scalable and effective. Such an approach is not future oriented and does not take into account the real intellectual basis of research—exploring, hypothesizing, and developing potential for the future.

One approach for IERI is to support both theoretically oriented studies and integrated applications. It could explore how expertise is used to sustain and expand potential successes. Greater emphasis in the research/evaluation phases should be given to studying differences among various dependent measures, with different types of students and with volunteer and nonvolunteer educators. Scale-up and sustainability should be built into those projects with the appropriate "track record" by using partnerships with existing or developing commercial entities. Scale-up, to be serious, must involve the early participation of both users and potential commercial partners. I have suggested that there are seven principles that should guide scale-up efforts in education: (1) Understand the appropriateness of the evidence for the innovation; (2) document the scientific evidence in support of the design of the intervention; (3) embrace design and development; (4) measure a broad range of variables in formative evaluation; (5) design the best study possible; (6) support flexibility and local innovation; (7) define minimums for scalability and sustainability. Future efforts can be improved if we adhere to—or strengthen—such criteria.

NOTE

1. The work reported herein was partially supported under the Educational Research and Development Centers Program, PR/Award Number R305B960002, as administered by the Institute of Education Sciences, U.S. Department of Education. The findings and opinions expressed in this report do not reflect the positions or policies of the National Center for Education Research, the Institute of Education Sciences, or the U.S. Department of Education.

Excerpts of this paper have been taken from "Evidence-Based Interventions: What Then and Now What?" presented at the 2003 annual meeting of the American Educational Research Association. In M. Constas, session 48.010 PRES-59, *Advancing the Scientific Investigation of Large-Scale Interventions: The Interagency Education Research Initiative* (Presidential Invited Session), Chicago.

3

Generalizability of Treatment Effects: Psychometrics and Education

Larry V. Hedges

One way to conceptualize scale-up is in terms of generalizability of treatment effects. The key generalizability question is, if an intervention is found to produce effects of a certain magnitude in a particular intervention study carried out in a particular context, how applicable are those findings about treatment effects to other implementations carried out in other contexts? We might frame this question as, given what we know about the effectiveness of this intervention, how dependable are those findings of intervention's effects when applied elsewhere?

Many authors have written about the notion of generalizability of research findings. Campbell and Stanley (1963) and Bracht and Glass (1968) introduced the concept of external validity to capture the idea of the degree to which research findings would transfer to other settings. Cook and Campbell (1979) incorporated external validity as one of their four fundamental validity considerations in social research. Shadish, Cook, and Campbell (2002) substantially elaborated on the concept of external validity in their treatment of causal generalization. While much has been written about external validity, these writings have often taken a somewhat broader view than is required for research about scale-up. The discussion of external validity and generalization has typically been in qualitative rather than quantitative terms. The purpose of this chapter is to provide a quantitative approach to generalizability of treatment effects.

In order to provide a quantitative analysis of generalization, it is necessary to be more precise about at least three things. The first thing requiring more precise specification is the original evidence on which the generalization is based, particularly the research design. The nature of the research design constrains the evidence it can provide about generalizability of the findings.

In fact, certain research designs can provide very limited information about generalizability without strong assumptions that may be implausible.

The second thing requiring more precise specification is the target of generalization, including the level of analysis about which generalizations are desired. Most research designs permit estimates of *average* treatment effects in the group of individuals that is assigned to treatment conditions (such as a classroom or school). While it is natural to consider the generalizability of treatment effects to other *single* classrooms or schools, this is not the only level of analysis that may be important in education. Many policies are applied at the level of whole schools, districts, or states. If we are interested in generalizations that may inform such policies, generalization at the level of schools, districts, or states may be more relevant than generalization at the level of individual classrooms. In other words, the question "Will this treatment effect generalize to every classroom?" may be less relevant than the question "Will this treatment effect generalize to the school or district (on the average)?" Because treatment effects will likely vary somewhat across groups (e.g., classrooms) as a function of context or other factors, the generalizability of school mean treatment effects will typically be greater than the generalizability of treatment effects at the classroom level, and the generalizability at the district level will be even greater.

The third consideration requiring more precise specification is the meaning of generalization itself. The notion of dependability, reproducibility, or generalizability of treatment effects must be specified precisely enough to be quantified in an explicit index. This makes it possible to determine which research designs permit estimation of this index of generalizability, and at what levels of analysis. Intervention (scale-up) studies can then provide estimates of generalizability indexes—a quantitative description of the degree to which intervention effects "scale up."

This analysis of generalization of treatment effects draws heavily on an analogy to psychometrics. In psychometric theory, the quantity being measured (conventionally called *ability*) is assumed to have a constant, but unknown, value for each individual being measured. This constant value for each individual is called that individual's *true score* or *universe score*. If actual measurements (or observed test scores) differ from the true score for an individual, the measurements exhibit measurement error. To say that measurements for the same individual are highly consistent is the same as saying that the measurement errors are generally small. The problem of psychometrics is to provide a coherent theory of the degree to which measurements made on different occasions and in different contexts are consistent with one another (and therefore with the true score). This can be conceived as a problem of generalization, consistency, or dependability of test scores across measurements made on different occasions, in different contexts, and under different conditions. It is desirable that measurement devices such as tests produce scores for the same individual that are highly consistent (that is, highly generalizable) across occasions of measurement.

The analogy with treatment effects is striking. We conceive a treatment as having a constant, but unknown (average), effect (which is analogous to the true score). The treatment effect we observe in any *particular* implementation in any particular context is analogous to an actual measurement (an observed test score). If the effects we observe in a particular implementation of the treatment differ from the average effect, that particular effect is subject to a "measurement error." Treatments whose effects are highly generalizable are therefore those that exhibit high consistency across implementations (or generally small "measurement errors"). It might seem more conventional (at least using analysis of variance terminology) to regard differences in treatment effects as a function of context as interactions of treatment with context, rather than "measurement errors." However, this is a matter of which terms are used to label concepts. In psychometric generalizability, interactions with context *are* measurement errors.

In both psychometric theory and in the theory of generalizability of treatment effects proposed here, the specific effects of contexts and other features specific to an implementation are treated as unsystematic—they are identified as "measurement errors." It is important to recognize that treating them as unsystematic, for the purposes of the model, does not imply that they cannot be understood as having reproducible components. In fact, Cronbach (1957) eloquently noted that what was conceived as "error" in models used in experimental psychology was often exactly what was conceived as systematic in the psychology of individual differences, and vice versa. Moreover, Cronbach and others (1972) point out that in modern psychometrics, "the error formerly seen as amorphous is now attributed to multiple sources, and a suitable experiment can estimate how much variation arises from each controllable source" (1).

Psychometric theory (true score theory) is an account of how to describe the generalizability of measurements, provide meaningful quantitative indexes of generalizability, and estimate those indexes from feasible data collections. This chapter draws on the analogy with generalization of measurements to provide an account of generalization of treatment effects. This theory of generalization of treatment effects includes the definition of quantitative indexes of generalizability, a logic for interpreting them, and a description of how these indexes of generalizability might be estimated from feasible experiments.

PSYCHOMETRIC THEORY

It is useful to begin by briefly explicating the theory of reproducibility (reliability and generalizability) in psychometrics (for more comprehensive discussions of psychometric theory see Lord and Novick 1968 and Cronbach et al. 1972). This treatment of psychometric concepts makes it possible to develop the analogy with the generalizability of treatment effects developed in later sections. Using that analogy, coefficients of reproducibility of treatment effects that are analogous to those of reliability and generalizability of behavioral measurements in psychometrics are developed. I then consider the implications of possible research designs for estimation of these generalizability coefficients.

Reliability Theory in Psychometrics

Classical test theory posits that the observed test score X for a particular unit (such as a person) can be decomposed into two (unobservable) components, a true score (T) and a measurement error (E), so that

$X = T + E.$

The true score T is assumed to be a constant characteristic of the individual being measured. If we imagine replications of the measurement process so that we obtain several observed test scores X_1, X_2, and so on on the same individual, all of these observed scores would have the same true score, and any difference among them would be due to measurement error, that is $X_1 = T + E_1$, $X_2 = T + E_2$, and so forth. Classical test theory does not posit the details of the process leading to measurement error. Instead it describes measurement error as a random process subject to certain simplifying assumptions. The four key assumptions are:

1. The measurement errors of different measurements (measurements on different people or the same people at different times) are statistically independent.
2. The measurement errors are statistically independent of true scores.
3. The measurement errors of all measurements have mean (expected values) of zero across repeated measurements (of different people or of the same people at different times).
4. The variances of the measurement errors are the same across different measurements (of different people or of the same people at different times).

In this framework, the reproducibility of a measurement is determined by the magnitude of measurement errors in comparison to true scores. Loosely, if measurement errors are small in magnitude compared to the magnitude of the true scores, observed scores (X values) will be rather consistent (reproducible) across repeated measurements. On the other hand, if measurement errors are typically large compared to true scores, observed scores will not be very reproducible. Both measurement errors (across different people or of the same people at different times) and true scores (across people) are random quantities. Thus the concept of "typically large (or small)" needs to be operationalized in some way to make use of this characterization of reproducibility.

One way to operationalize the "typical size" of a random quantity is to use the concept of *variance*. The variance of the measurement errors, σ_E^2, is the average size of the squared measurement error (since the mean of the measurement errors is zero). The variance of the true scores, σ_T^2, can be conceived as the average size of the squared deviation of the true score from the mean. In situations where the measurements are not on a ratio scale (or when the measurement model is norm referenced), no information is lost by setting the mean of the true score scale to zero, so the interpretation of the true score variance as the mean of the square of the magnitude can be applied to both true scores and measurement errors.

The reliability $\rho_{XX'}$ of a measurement process (e.g., a test) is defined as the proportion of the variance of the observed score explained by the true score

$$\rho_{XX'} = \rho^2_{TX} = \frac{\sigma^2_T}{\sigma^2_T + \sigma^2_E} = \frac{\sigma^2_T}{\sigma^2_X}.$$

Because true scores and measurement errors are independent, it follows that

$$\sigma^2_X = \sigma^2_T + \sigma^2_E$$

and therefore an alternative expression for the reliability is

$$\rho_{XX'} = \frac{\sigma^2_X + \sigma^2_E}{\sigma^2_T + \sigma^2_E} = \frac{\sigma^2_X + \sigma^2_E}{\sigma^2_X}.$$

The reliability coefficient ranges from zero (indicating no reproducibility of test scores) to one (indicating perfect reproducibility of test scores).

Psychometric Generalizability Theory

Psychometric generalizability theory is a generalization of classical test theory that acknowledges that measurements may be affected by many specific factors and that understanding the specific impact of these factors leads to a more sophisticated understanding of the reproducibility of behavioral measurements. In principle, generalizability theory can accommodate any number of factors that might influence measurement. However, most applications of generalizability theory have focused on the effects of observers and occasions of measurement, as well as individual differences among persons or units measured.

Consider an application of generalizability theory to a measurement model involving measured units, observers, and occasions of observation. The structural model for X_{ijk}, the measurement of the ith person by the jth observer on the kth occasion, would be

$$X_{ijk} = \mu + \alpha_i + \beta_j + \gamma_k + \alpha\beta_{ij} + \alpha\gamma_{ik} + \beta\gamma_{jk} + \alpha\beta\gamma_{ijk} + \epsilon_{ijk}$$

where each of these structural components has implications for measurement. In this model μ is the average value of the measurement across persons, observers, and occasions and α_i is the effect of the ith person: the degree to which the average of that person's measurements, averaged across occasions and observers, is different from the grand mean μ. The ith person's universe score (the analogue in generalizability theory to a true score) is $\mu + \alpha_i$. The main effects β_j and γ_k, are the effects of the jth observer and the kth occasion of observation, respectively—the degree to which the average of that observer's measurements, averaged across persons and occasions, is different from the grand mean μ or the degree to which the average of that occasion's measurements, averaged across persons and observers, is different from the grand mean μ.

The interactions $\alpha\beta_{ij}$ and $\alpha\gamma_{ik}$ represent the degree to which the measurement of the ith person depends on the jth observer and the kth occasion of observation, respectively. These interactions have important implications for measurement because they represent differential effects on a particular person's measurement of the observer or occasion of measurement. That is, $\alpha\beta_{ij}$ reflects the extent to which measurements of the same person are not reproducible across observers and $\alpha\gamma_{ik}$ reflects the extent to which measurements of the same person are not reproducible across different occasions of observation. The three-way interaction $\alpha\beta\gamma_{ijk}$ also has important implications for measurement. It can be explained in either of two (mathematically equivalent) ways. The three-way interaction represents the extent to which the observer j's effect on measurements of person i itself depends on occasion k. Alternatively, we might say that the three-way interaction $\alpha\beta\gamma_{ijk}$ represents the extent to which the effect of occasion k on person i's measurement itself depends on observer j. Regardless of how one chooses to explain it, the interaction $\alpha\beta\gamma_{ijk}$ characterizes the extent to which measurements are not reproducible across particular combinations of observers and occasions. The term ϵ_{ijk} reflects a residual measurement error not otherwise specified in the model. Finally, the term $\beta\gamma_{jk}$ reflects the extent to which the effect of the jth observer depends on the kth occasion.

In this structural model all of the parameters are random effects and each has an associated component of variance. The variance of the observed measurements depends on each of these variance component parameters. However, the exact *form* of the relation of the variance components to the variance of measurements depends on the design of the measurement scheme. This consideration is one of the great strengths of generalizability theory; it provides a basis for the design of measurement schemes that will produce measurements with high reproducibility.

In classical test theory the measure of reproducibility is the reliability coefficient. The analogue to the reliability coefficient in generalizability theory is the *generalizability coefficient*: the proportion of variance of the measurement explained by the universe score. Like reliability coefficients, generalizability coefficients are between zero (indicating essentially no reproducibility) and one (indicating perfect reproducibility), inclusive. Because the variance of the observations depends on the variance components and the particular measurement model, the generalizability coefficient depends on these same variance components and the measurement model.

For example, suppose that we randomly choose an observer and an occasion from a population of observers and occasions. All measurements will be made on that occasion with that observer. Because we are conditioning on (holding constant) j and k, the effects β_j, γ_k, and $\beta\gamma_{jk}$ are constants. Because they depend on the person, the effects α_i, $\alpha\beta_{ij}$, $\alpha\gamma_{ik}$, and $\alpha\beta\gamma_{ijk}$ are still random effects even after conditioning on j and k. Thus the variance of the observations conditional on the choice of observer j and occasion k would be

$$\sigma_\alpha^2 + \sigma_{\alpha\beta}^2 + \sigma_{\alpha\gamma}^2 + \sigma_{\alpha\beta\gamma}^2 + \sigma_\epsilon^2$$

where σ_α^2, $\sigma_{\alpha\beta}^2$, $\sigma_{\alpha\gamma}^2$, $\sigma_{\alpha\beta\gamma}^2$, and σ_ϵ^2 are the variance components associated with α_i (the person effect), $\alpha\beta_{ij}$ (the person by observer interaction), $\alpha\gamma_{ik}$ (the person by occasion interaction), $\alpha\beta\gamma_{ijk}$ (the person by observer by occasion interaction), and ϵ (the residual measurement error). Because the variance of the universe scores is σ_α^2, the generalizability coefficient of measurements made by this measurement scheme is

$$g_1 = \sigma_\alpha^2 / \{\sigma_\alpha^2 + \sigma_{\alpha\beta}^2 + \sigma_{\alpha\gamma}^2 + \sigma_{\alpha\beta\gamma}^2 + \sigma_\epsilon^2\}.$$

The generalizability coefficient g_1 will be large if all of the interactions (and σ_ϵ^2) in the denominator are small. This corresponds to the intuition that if measurements of an individual are not differentially influenced much by observers or occasions, or combinations thereof, and if residual measurement error is small, measurements will be reproducible. If any of the interactions in the denominator are large, this generalizability coefficient cannot be large. This corresponds to the intuition that if measurements are of individuals differentially influenced by an observer or an occasion, measurements will not be highly reproducible.

Now consider a different measurement scheme, one in which not one, but n observers are chosen (at random) to observe the same persons on one occasion. All measurements will be made on that occasion with those n observers. The new measure is the average of the n measures made by the individual observers. Because we are conditioning on (several values of) j and (one value of) k, the effects β_j, γ_k, and $\beta\gamma_{jk}$ are constants. Because they depend on the person, the effects α_i, the n $\alpha\beta_{ij}$, $\alpha\gamma_{ik}$, and the n $\alpha\beta\gamma_{ijk}$ are still random effects even after conditioning on j and k. However, averaging over observers changes the variance of the observations. In this case the variance of the observations conditional on the choice of observer j and occasion k would be

$$\sigma_\alpha^2 + \sigma_{\alpha\beta}^2/n + \sigma_{\alpha\gamma}^2 + \sigma_{\alpha\beta\gamma}^2/n + \sigma_\epsilon^2/n.$$

Because the variance of the universe scores is still σ_α^2, the generalizability coefficient of measurements made by this measurement scheme is

$$g_2 = \sigma_\alpha^2/\{\sigma_\alpha^2 + \sigma_{\alpha\beta}^2/n + \sigma_{\alpha\gamma}^2 + \sigma_{\alpha\beta\gamma}^2/n + \sigma_\epsilon^2/n\},$$

which will be larger than g_1 because the denominator of g_2 is smaller than that of g_1.

This example illustrates the fact that reproducibility (the generalizability coefficient) depends on the design of measurement schemes. To put it another way, reproducibility depends on the conceptual entities one is considering generalizing about (e.g., one measurement by one observer versus an average of measurements by several observers). In the case of psychometric generalizability theory, components of variance estimated in a methodological study (a generalizability study) are used to determine how to organize a measurement strategy (e.g., how many observers, how many occasions, etc.) that will provide sufficiently reproducible measurements for a study used to test substantive hypotheses (a decision study).

Estimating Generalizability Coefficients

To make practical use of generalizability theory, it is essential to estimate the components of variance that determine generalizability coefficients. Such a study is called a *generalizability study*. The most informative design for estimating variance components used in generalizability theory is what is called in the experimental design literature a *completely crossed factorial design* (see, e.g., Kirk 1995). Such a design involves obtaining measurements in all possible combinations of factors in the measurement model (e.g., all observers observing all persons on all occasions). Note that if the persons, observers, and occasions are all random samples, the variance components relevant to generalizability calculations can be estimated even if the particular persons, observers, and occasions used are not the same as those that will be used in the eventual measurement of interest. Completely crossed designs are desirable because they permit estimation of all of the variance components (except perhaps σ_ϵ^2, which may be confounded with $\sigma_{\alpha\beta\gamma}^2$).

Whatever their theoretical merits, completely crossed designs are sometimes practically impossible, even for a sample of persons, observers, and occasions. In such cases other designs may be used, but they will not permit unambiguous estimation of all variance components. That is, estimates of some variance components will be confounded with others. In such cases, it may not be possible to estimate precise generalizability coefficients for all measurement designs, but bounds on generalizability coefficients are often possible (see, e. g., Cronbach et al. 1972).

THEORY OF GENERALIZATION OF TREATMENT EFFECTS

Now consider the case of the effects of a particular treatment on a specified unit (such as classrooms or schools). The treatment effect is defined as a contrast between the mean outcome score that a unit would have had *if* it *did* receive the treatment and the mean outcome it would have had if it *did not* receive the treatment. This is estimated in experiments by creating two randomly equivalent sets of units and giving one set the treatment and the other the control condition. The treatment effect becomes the difference between the means of these two sets (see Rubin 1974). The specification of *which* units (units at which level of analysis) are made randomly equivalent is important, as we will see later.

Consider a model in which we have n sites with pairs of units that are equivalent (e.g., made so by random assignment) except that one receives the treatment of interest and the other receives the control condition. These units could be classrooms or schools. Each site is a replication of the treatment and control condition and the collection of sites is therefore a set of repeated implementations. We may have treatment effect parameters (true treatment effects, free of estimation errors) δ_1, δ_2, and so on that are defined as mean differences (the mean difference *parameters*) between the units in each site, that is, the treatment effect in various implementations of the treatment. Let μ_δ be the average treatment effect across all (conceptual) implementations. Let $\epsilon_1 = \delta_1 - \mu_\delta$ and $\epsilon_2 = \delta_2 - \mu_\delta$ be deviations of each particular treatment effect parameter from the average treatment effect. To generalize classical measurement theory to the situation of treatment effects, draw the analogy of the treatment effect in a given situation to the observed score T, the mean treatment effect (μ_δ) to the true score, and $\epsilon = \delta - \mu_\delta$ to the measurement error. That is:

Reliability of Measurements		Reliability of Treatment Effects
X	$\leftrightarrow$	δ
T	$\leftrightarrow$	μ_δ
E	$\leftrightarrow$	ϵ

If we imagine that treatment effects vary across sites (implementations) for a particular treatment, this model is similar to that for variations of measurements across replications. It is also possible to imagine that the independence assumptions of classical measurement theory might apply.

Note that there are two conceptual differences between the psychometric model and the treatment effect model proposed here. One is that, while the corresponding quantities T and μ_δ, and E and ϵ, are all unobserved, the quantity X (observed score) is directly observed in psychometrics, but the corresponding quantity δ (the treatment effect) is an unobserved parameter in the treatment effect model.

The second conceptual difference is that, unlike the situation of classical measurement theory, there is only one treatment effect (true score) for each treatment. To put it another way, treatment is a fixed effect, not a random effect. One strategy for dealing with this difference is to regard the treatment effect as a random effect. That is, we suppose that there is a population of treatment effects, and the effect of the observed treatment is a sample. One way of making this precise is to impose a linear model on the population means of the units involved as follows. If μ_{1j} is the mean of the treatment group in the jth pair and μ_{2j} is the mean of the control group in the jth pair, let

$$\mu_{ij} = \mu_\bullet + \alpha_i + \beta_j + \alpha\beta_{ij}$$

where $\mu_\bullet$ is the grand mean of the outcome across both treatment conditions and all replications, $\alpha_1 - \alpha_2 = \mu_\delta$ is the average treatment effect across replications, β_j is the average across treatments in each replication, and $\alpha\beta_{ij}$ is the interaction of the ith treatment with the jth replication, so that $\epsilon_j = \alpha\beta_{1j} - \alpha\beta_{2j}$, and $\delta_j = \alpha_1 - \alpha_2 + \alpha\beta_{1j} - \alpha\beta_{2j}$.

Just as in the case of measurements, reproducibility of treatment effects implies that the ϵ's, the deviations of the treatment effect from the average, μ_δ, are small. Large deviations of the treatment effect from the average, μ_δ, imply that the treatment effect is not reproducible.

In this setting we can define an analogue to the reliability by the reproducibility coefficient

$$\rho_{\delta\delta'} = \frac{\sigma_\alpha^2}{\sigma_\alpha^2 + \sigma_\epsilon^2},$$

where σ_α^2 is the variance of the average treatment effects. One way of interpreting this coefficient is in terms of variation of treatment effects about zero. Under the assumption of independence of the α_i's and the ϵ_i's (or alternatively, the δ_i's from μ_δ), the "variance" of the treatment effect parameters around zero is $\sigma_\alpha^2 + \sigma_\epsilon^2$. Therefore, this coefficient is essentially the proportion of the "variance" of treatment effects about zero that is accounted for by the average (main) effect of the treatment.

Because there are only two values of α (α_1 and α_2) with an equal probability of occurrence, it follows that the variance of α is

$$\sigma_\alpha^2 = (\alpha_1 - \alpha_2)^2/4 = \mu_\delta^2/4.$$

Thus

$$\rho_{\delta\delta'} = \frac{\mu_\alpha^2}{\mu_\alpha^2 + 4\sigma_\epsilon^2} = \frac{1}{1 + 4v}$$

where $v = \sigma_\epsilon/\mu_\delta$ is the coefficient of variation of the treatment effect parameters. The reproducibility coefficient $\rho_{\delta\delta'}$ is a kind of generalizability measure that quantifies how a treatment effect "scales up" across implementations in the sense that the treatment effect is consistent.

This definition has many desirable features. It is consistent with an existing concept, reliability, and therefore captures an intuition about reproducibility that is widely understood: reproducibility is the fraction of variance in treatment effects about zero that is explained by the main effect of treatment. Like psychometric reliability, it has a range of zero to one with zero indicating no reproducibility and one indicating perfect reproducibility across replications. It is also estimable from feasible research designs.

This definition also has features that might be regarded as undesirable. One is that reproducibility is a function of the size of the mean (main) effect of the treatment, not just the variation of treatment effects across implementations. Thus two treatments that exhibited the same variation in effects across implementations could have different reproducibility coefficients if they had different mean treatment effects.

This is similar to the situation with measurement reliability, where the reliability does not depend only on the magnitude of the measurement error, but also on the variability of true scores. Thus if two measurement procedures had measurement errors of exactly the same magnitude (as measured

by their variance), these measurement procedures would have different re-
liabilities if the magnitude of the true scores (measured by their variance)
were different. This idea is widely understood in measurement, where it is
well known that reliability depends on the population to which the measurement is applied (in particular, the variance of true scores in that population).

Estimation of the Reproducibility Coefficient

The reproducibility coefficient $\rho_{\delta\delta'}$ could be estimated from replicated
data on the treatment effects (mean differences) in a set of implementations. Suppose that classrooms are randomly assigned within n schools to
receive treatment or the control conditions so that each school has at least
one treatment and at least one control classroom. This design is often called
the *generalized randomized block design* (see, e.g., Kirk 1995). The Tennessee
class size experiment, for example, has essentially this design (see, e.g., Nye,
Hedges, and Konstantopoulos 2000). The units that are assigned to treatment or control within each school are classrooms. The schools are the sites
and the data could be a two treatments-by-n sites design analyzed by the
corresponding random effects analysis of variance, yielding estimates of
variance components for treatment (σ_α^2), sites (σ_β^2), and the site-by-treat-
ment interaction $(\sigma_{\alpha\beta}^2)$. Since $\epsilon_j = \alpha\beta_{1j} - \alpha\beta_{2j'}$ it follows that

$$r_{\delta\delta'} = \frac{\hat{\sigma}_\alpha^2}{\hat{\sigma}_\alpha^2 + \hat{\sigma}_{\alpha\beta}^2}$$

is an estimate $r_{\delta\delta'}$ of $\rho_{\delta\delta'}$.

An Index of Qualitative Reproducibility

The previous development stresses quantitative reproducibility of treatment effects. A different strategy for developing a coefficient of reproducibility is to utilize a feature of treatment effect data that is not available
in psychometric data. Most psychometric models are designed for measurement data that is on an interval scale, meaning that there is no natural,
meaningful zero point. Data on treatments *does* have a natural zero point.
A treatment effect of zero is not only meaningful, but consequential—it
means that the treatment had no effect relative to the control condition. It
is natural and conventional to categorize treatments into conditions according to the direction of their effect: positive or negative (ignoring the category of exactly zero effect). Treatment effects that have the same direction
are often said to be in *qualitative agreement* and when the effects of a treat-

ment in different replications have different signs there is said to be *no qualitative interaction.*

It is therefore natural to develop a measure of reproducibility that emphasizes *qualitative* reproducibility: How often are different replications of the treatment in qualitative agreement? Perhaps the most obvious place to start in creating an index of qualitative agreement is based on the proportion of replications that have a positive treatment effect, which (assuming a negligible proportion of exactly zero effects) also determines the proportion of replications with negative effects.

We would like to define an index of qualitative reproducibility that takes its maximum value if either all (100 percent) of the replications had positive treatment effects *or* all (100 percent) of the replications had negative treatment effects. In this logic, the situation reflecting the least qualitative reproducibility would be if exactly one-half of the treatment effects were positive and one-half were negative. Thus we would like to define an index of qualitative reproducibility so that it takes its minimal value in the later situation.

If treatment effect parameters are normally distributed, the probability that a replication will have a positive effect is just

$$P\{\delta > 0\} = P\{(\delta - \mu_\delta)/\sigma_\epsilon > -\mu_\delta/\sigma_\epsilon\} = 1 - \Phi(-\mu_\delta/\sigma_\epsilon) = \Phi(\mu_\delta/\sigma_\epsilon)$$

where $P\{X\}$ is the probability of X and $\Phi(x)$ is the standard normal cumulative distribution function. However, a treatment in which replications consistently find negative effects is just as qualitatively reproducible as one for which replications consistently find positive effects. Therefore, we define the index of qualitative reproducibility as

$$r_Q = 2[P\{|\delta| > 0\} - 0.5] = 2[\Phi(-|\mu_\delta|/\sigma_\epsilon) - 0.5].$$

Like the quantitative index of reproducibility $r\delta\delta_{,\prime}$, r_Q has a range of zero to one. The index r_Q takes the value zero, indicating minimal reproducibility, when $\mu_\delta = 0$ or when σ_ϵ is very large so that exactly one-half of the treatment effects are positive and half are negative. The index r_Q takes the value one when $\sigma_\epsilon = 0$ or when $|\mu_\delta|$ is very large, indicating 100 percent of the treatment effects have the same sign. Because r_Q depends only on μ_δ and σ_ϵ, it is also possible to estimate r_Q from the same research designs that permit estimation of $\rho_{\delta\delta'}$.

Generalizability Theory Applied to Treatment Effects

Psychometric generalizability theory can be employed to create a generalization of the index of quantitative reproducibility that acknowledges that treatment effects may be affected by many specific factors and that understanding the specific impact of these factors leads to a more sophisticated understanding of the reproducibility of treatment effects. In principle, this theory can accommodate any number of factors that might influence treatment effects. However, the most obvious applications focus on the effects of classrooms and schools on treatment effects, although one can easily imagine incorporating larger units such as districts or states into the model.

Consider an application of generalizability theory to a measurement model involving two levels of treatment (the treatment and a control) in schools and classrooms. Following the development of psychometric generalizability theory, the conceptual structural model for μ_{ijk}, the mean of the ith treatment group in the kth class in the jth school, would be

$$\mu_{ijk} = \mu_{\bullet\bullet\bullet} + \alpha_i + \beta_j + \gamma_k + \alpha\beta_{ij} + \alpha\gamma_{ik} + \beta\gamma_{jk} + \alpha\beta\gamma_{ijk}$$

where each of these structural components has implications for reproducibility of the treatment effect. In this model $\mu_{\bullet\bullet\bullet}$ is the average value of the outcome variable across treatments, schools, and classes, and α_i is the main effect of the ith treatment condition, so that $\alpha_1 - \alpha_2 = \mu_\delta$ is the average treatment effect across schools and classrooms. The main effects β_j and γ_k are the effects of the jth school and the kth classroom, respectively—the degree to which the average of that school's outcome, averaged across treatments and classes, is different from the grand mean $\mu_{\bullet\bullet\bullet}$ or the degree to which the average of that class's measurements, averaged across treatments and schools, is different from the grand mean $\mu_{\bullet\bullet\bullet}$.

The interactions $\alpha\beta_{ij}$ and $\alpha\gamma_{ik}$ represent the degree to which the ith treatment effect depends on the jth school and the kth class, respectively. These interactions have important implications for measurement because they represent differential effects on a particular treatment effect of the school or class. That is, $\alpha\beta_{ij}$ reflects the extent to which the effect of the ith treatment is not reproducible across schools and $\alpha\gamma_{ik}$ reflects the extent to which the effect of the ith treatment is not reproducible across different classrooms. The three-way interaction $\alpha\beta\gamma_{ijk}$ also has important implications for reproducibility of treatment effects.

The three-way interaction can be explained in either of two mathematically equivalent ways. The three-way interaction represents the extent to which the school j's effect on treatment i itself depends on class k. Alternatively, we might say that the three-way interaction $\alpha\beta\gamma_{ijk}$ represents the extent to which the effect of class k on the effect of treatment i itself depends on school j. Regardless of how one chooses to explain it, the interaction $\alpha\beta\gamma_{ijk}$ characterizes the extent to which measurements are not reproducible across particular combinations of schools and classes. Finally, the term $\beta\gamma_{jk}$ reflects the extent to which the effect of the jth school depends on the kth class. Note that there is no residual term in this model because it is the model for population means.

In this structural model all of the parameters are random effects; thus, each has an associated component of variance. The variance of the treatment effects depends on each of these parameter variance components. However, the exact *form* of the relation of the variance components to the variance of treatment effects depends on the level of the units being considered, that is, at which level of aggregation we are interested in treatment effects' being reproducible. This consideration, like its analogue in psychometric generalizability theory, is useful because it permits us to compute from the variance components the reproducibility of treatment effects at any level of aggregation in which we may be interested.

I propose an analogue to the quantitative reproducibility coefficient described above. I will call this analogue a *generalizability coefficient*: the proportion of variance (about zero) of the treatment effect explained by the main effect of treatment μ_δ. Like the previous reproducibility coefficients, this generalizability coefficient is between zero (indicating essentially no reproducibility) and one (indicating perfect reproducibility), inclusive. Because the variance of the observations depends on the variance components and the particular measurement model, the generalizability coefficient depends on these same variance components and the level of aggregation of interest.

Suppose that we are interested in the degree to which the treatment effect generalizes to any classroom in any school. We randomly choose a school and a classroom from a population of schools and classes. We start by computing the variance of the treatment effect in a single classroom (which is exactly the variance of the treatment effect across classrooms). The treatment effect in the kth classroom is

$$\delta_{jk} = \mu_{1jk} - \mu_{2jk} = (\alpha_1 - \alpha_2) + (\alpha\beta_{1j} - \alpha\beta_{2j}) + (\alpha\gamma_{1j} - \alpha\gamma_{2j}) + (\alpha\beta\gamma_{1jk} - \alpha\beta\gamma_{2jk}),$$

which has variance

$$V\{\delta_{jk}\} = 2\sigma_\alpha^2 + 2\sigma_{\alpha\beta}^2 + 2\sigma_{\alpha\gamma}^2 + 2\sigma_{\alpha\beta\gamma}^2$$

where σ_α^2, $\sigma_{\alpha\beta}^2$, $\sigma_{\alpha\gamma}^2$, and $\sigma_{\alpha\beta\gamma}^2$ are the variance components associated with α_i (the treatment effect), $\alpha\beta_{ij}$ (the treatment by school interaction), $\alpha\gamma_{ik}$ (the treatment by class interaction), and $\alpha\beta\gamma_{ijk}$ (the treatment by school by class interaction). Note that the residual variance is not involved because the variance of δ_{jk} is the variance of the treatment effect parameters (not sample estimates). The effects α_i, $\alpha\beta_{ij}$, $\alpha\gamma_{ik}$, and $\alpha\beta\gamma_{ijk}$, which depend on the classroom and school, are still random effects.

Because the variance of the main effect of treatment is σ_α^2, the generalizability coefficient of measurements made by this measurement scheme is

$$g_1 = \sigma_\alpha^2 / \{\sigma_\alpha^2 + \sigma_{\alpha\beta}^2 + \sigma_{\alpha\gamma}^2 + \sigma_{\alpha\beta\gamma}^2\}.$$

The generalizability coefficient g_1 will be large if all of the interactions in the denominator are small. This corresponds to the intuition that if treatment effects are not differentially influenced much by schools, classrooms, or combinations thereof, and if the residual is small, treatment effects will be reproducible. If any of the interactions in the denominator are large, this generalizability coefficient cannot be large. This corresponds to the intuition that if treatment effects are differentially influenced by schools or classes, treatment effects will not be highly reproducible.

Now consider a different measurement scheme, one in which not one, but n classes (e.g., all of the classes in an entire school at a given grade level) are chosen and we wish to compute the generalizability of the mean treatment effect in these n classes (e.g., the school mean treatment effect). The aggregate treatment effect is the average of the n treatment effects for the individual classes, that is, the average of the treatment effect for one value of j (one school) over several values of k (several classrooms). Averaging over classrooms in school j yields the average treatment effect $\delta_{j\bullet}$ given by

$$\delta_{j\bullet} = \frac{1}{n}\sum_{k=1}^{n} \mu_{1jk} - \mu_{2jk}$$

$$\frac{1}{n}[n(\alpha_1 - \alpha_2) + n(\alpha\beta_{1j} - \alpha\beta_{2j}) + \sum_{k=1}^{n}\alpha\gamma_{1k} - \alpha\gamma_{2k} + \sum_{k=1}^{n}\alpha\beta\gamma_{1jk} - \alpha\beta\gamma_{2jk}].$$

The variance of the mean treatment effect of the n classes (the school mean treatment effect in the jth school) is

$$V\{\delta_{j\bullet}\} = 2\sigma_\alpha^2 + 2\sigma_{\alpha\beta}^2 + 2\sigma_{\alpha\gamma}^2/n + 2\sigma_{\alpha\beta\gamma}^2/n.$$

Because the variance of the mean treatment effect is still σ_α^2, the generalizability coefficient of mean treatment effects in this scheme is

$$g_2 = \sigma_\alpha^2 / \{\sigma_\alpha^2 + \sigma_{\alpha\beta}^2 + \sigma_{\alpha\gamma}^2/n + \sigma_{\alpha\beta\gamma}^2/n\},$$

which will be larger than g_1 because the denominator of g_2 is smaller than that of g_1, and (depending on the pattern of variance components) g_2 may be much larger than g_1.

Now consider a third measurement scheme, one in which not one school, but m schools, each with n classes (e.g., all of the schools in an entire school district at a given grade level) are chosen and we wish to compute the generalizability of the mean treatment effect in these m schools and mn classes (e.g., the district mean treatment effect). The aggregate treatment effect is the average of the mn treatment effects for the individual classes, that is, the average of the treatment effect for m values of j (m schools) over n values of k per school (n classrooms in each school). Averaging over classrooms and schools yields the average treatment effect $\delta_{\bullet\bullet}$ given by

$$\delta_{\bullet\bullet} = \frac{1}{mn} \sum_{j=1}^{m} \sum_{k=1}^{n} \mu_{1jk} - \mu_{2jk}$$

$$= \frac{1}{mn} [mn(\alpha_1 - \alpha_2) + n \sum_{j=1}^{m} \alpha\beta_{1j} - \alpha\beta_{2j} + m \sum_{k=1}^{n} \alpha\gamma_{1k} - \alpha\gamma_{2k} +$$

$$\sum_{j=1}^{m} \sum_{k=1}^{n} \alpha\beta\gamma_{1jk} - \alpha\beta\gamma_{2jk}].$$

The variance of the mean treatment effect of the m schools (the district mean treatment effect) is

$$V\{\delta_{\bullet\bullet}\} = 2\sigma_\alpha^2 + 2\sigma_{\alpha\beta}^2/m + 2\sigma_{\alpha\gamma}^2/n + 2\sigma_{\alpha\beta\gamma}^2/mn.$$

Because the variance of the mean treatment effect is still σ_α^2, the generalizability coefficient of mean treatment effects in this scheme is

$$g_3 = \sigma_\alpha^2 / \{ \sigma_\alpha^2 + \sigma_{\alpha\beta}^2/m + \sigma_{\alpha\gamma}^2/n + \sigma_{\alpha\beta\gamma}^2/mn \},$$

which will be larger than g_1 or g_2 because the denominator of g_3 is smaller than that of g_1 and g_2, and (depending on the pattern of variance components) g_3 may be much larger than g_1 and g_2.

These examples illustrate the fact that reproducibility (the generalizability coefficient) depends on the objects (e.g., the level of aggregation) about which generalizations are made. To put it another way, reproducibility depends on the conceptual entities one is considering generalizing about (e.g., treatment effect in one class versus the mean effect across all classes in a school or a district). All else being equal, the higher the level of aggregation, the larger the generalizability coefficient will be.

Estimating Generalizability Coefficients of Treatment Effects

The theoretical analysis above describes generalizability in terms of variance components for treatments, classes, and schools as crossed factors. However, due to the inherent nesting of classrooms within schools, not all of these variance components can be estimated independently. Therefore, it is possible only to think of the effect of classroom paired with the school in which it is nested and not paired with any other school. Exactly how variance components are affected depends on how the treatments are assigned.

If treatments are crossed with schools (that is, every school has both treatment and control conditions, as when classes are assigned to treatments within schools), then the class effect is confounded with the school effect. The variance components for treatment, school, and their interactions (σ_α^2, σ_β^2, and $\sigma_{\alpha\beta}^2$) can be estimated independently, but the effects involving the class effect can be estimated only as a variance component of classes within schools and treatment:

$$\sigma^2_{\gamma(\alpha\beta)} = \sigma_\gamma^2 + \sigma_{\alpha\gamma}^2 + \sigma_{\beta\gamma}^2 + \sigma_{\alpha\beta\gamma}^2.$$

Thus substituting $\sigma^2_{\gamma(\alpha\beta)}$ for the sum of any subset of the variance components it contains provides a conservative overestimate of the value of those components.

While we cannot estimate the generalizability coefficient, g_1, we can estimate a generalizability coefficient g_1', which is defined by replacing the denominator of g_1 with an overestimate of that denominator and therefore underestimating the generalizability coefficient yielding

$$g_1' = \sigma_\alpha^2/\{\sigma_\alpha^2 + \sigma_{\alpha\beta}^2 + \sigma_{\gamma(\alpha\beta)}^2\}.$$

It should be emphasized that this is not the generalizability coefficient of the treatment effect, but a biased underestimate of it, a lower bound on the estimate of generalizability (albeit the only estimate possible from the design being used).

Similarly, we can estimate a lower bound on the generalizability of aggregates such as school means, g_2', which is defined by replacing the denominator of g_2 with an overestimate of that denominator. Note, however, that the denominator involves ($\sigma^2_{\alpha\gamma} + \sigma^2_{\alpha\beta\gamma}/n$). In order to assure an overestimate, we must replace ($\sigma^2_{\alpha\gamma} + \sigma^2_{\alpha\beta\gamma}/n$) with $\sigma^2_{\gamma(\alpha\beta)}$ (not $\sigma^2_{\gamma(\alpha\beta)}/n$). Therefore the generalizability coefficient that we can estimate, but which is a conservative value (less than the actual generalizability coefficient), is

$$g_2' = \sigma_\alpha^2/\{\sigma_\alpha^2 + \sigma_{\alpha\beta}^2/n + \sigma_{\gamma(\alpha\beta)}^2\}.$$

Note that g_2' will be larger than g_1' whenever $\sigma_{\alpha\beta}^2 > 0$ and $n > 1$, illustrating the fact that the generalizability of school mean treatment effects is generally larger than that of classroom level treatment effects. However, the term $\sigma_{\gamma(\alpha\beta)}^2$ in the denominator means that there is an upper limit to the generalizability of school means, regardless of the number of classes, namely

$$g_2' \leq \sigma_\alpha^2/\{\sigma_\alpha^2 + \sigma_{\gamma(\alpha\beta)}^2\}$$

for any number of classrooms. Therefore, if $g_2' = \sigma_{\gamma(\alpha\beta)}^2$ is large, g_2' can never be large.

Note: While programs for the analysis of variance are well suited to the estimation of variance components in nested designs when the design is completely balanced, analyses of variance methods are much more complicated when designs are unbalanced (as they almost always are in real educational data). Consequently, the variance components in nested designs like those considered here (where students are nested within classes, nested within schools) can be most easily estimated using specialized programs for the analysis of hierarchical linear models (like Raudenbush and Bryk's HLM program or SAS Proc Mixed) rather than programs designed for analysis of variance.

Generalizability Theory and Qualitative Agreement

The variance components derived in generalizability theory can be used to refine coefficients of qualitative agreement. If treatment effect parameters are normally distributed, the probability that a replication will have a positive effect is just

$$P\{\delta > 0\} = P\left\{\frac{\delta - \mu_\delta}{\sqrt{\sigma_{\alpha\beta}^2 + \sigma_{\alpha\gamma}^2 + \sigma_{\alpha\beta\gamma}^2}} > \frac{-\mu_\delta}{\sqrt{\sigma_{\alpha\beta}^2 + \sigma_{\alpha\gamma}^2 + \sigma_{\alpha\beta\gamma}^2}}\right\}$$

$$= \Phi\left(\frac{\mu_\delta}{\sqrt{\sigma_{\alpha\beta}^2 + \sigma_{\alpha\gamma}^2 + \sigma_{\alpha\beta\gamma}^2}}\right)$$

where $P\{X\}$ is the probability of X and $\Phi(x)$ is the standard normal cumulative distribution function. Using the logic of the qualitative reproducibility index created earlier, we define the index of qualitative reproducibility as

$$g_Q = 2\left(P\{|\delta| > 0\} - 0.5\right) = 2\left[\Phi\left(\frac{|\mu_\delta|}{\sqrt{\sigma_{\alpha\beta}^2 + \sigma_{\alpha\gamma}^2 + \sigma_{\alpha\beta\gamma}^2}}\right) - 0.5\right].$$

Like the quantitative indices of reproducibility $r_{\delta\delta'}$ and g and the previous index of qualitative reproducibility r_Q, g_Q has a range of zero to one, with zero indicating no reproducibility and one indicating perfect reproducibility across replications. It is also possible to obtain at least conservative estimates of g_Q feasible research designs.

Like the indexes of quantitative generalizability, indexes of qualitative generalizability can be defined at different levels of aggregation. For example, consider a measurement scheme in which not one, but n classes (e.g., all of the classes in an entire school at a given grade level) are chosen and we wish to compute the qualitative generalizability of the mean treatment effect in these n classes (e.g., the school mean treatment effect). We have already computed the average treatment effect for the n in school j, $\delta_{j\bullet}$, and its variance. The index of qualitative generalizability at the school level is

$$g_{Q2} = 2\left(P\{|\delta|>0\}-0.5\right) = 2\left[\Phi\left(\frac{|\mu_\delta|}{\sqrt{\sigma_{\alpha\beta}^2 + \sigma_{\alpha\gamma}^2/n + \sigma_{\alpha\beta\gamma}^2/n}}\right)-0.5\right].$$

A third measurement scheme is one in which not one school, but m schools, each with n classes (e.g., all of the schools in an entire school district at a given grade level) are chosen and we wish to compute the qualitative generalizability of the mean treatment effect in these m schools and mn classes (e.g., the district mean treatment effect). The aggregate treatment effect is the average of the mn treatment effects for the individual classes, that is, the average of the treatment effect for m values of j (m schools) over n values of k per school (n classrooms in each school). Averaging over classrooms and schools yields the average treatment effect $\delta_{\bullet\bullet}$ and its variance. The index of qualitative generalizability at the district level is

$$g_{Q3} = 2\left(P\{|\delta|>0\}-0.5\right) = 2\left[\Phi\left(\frac{|\mu_\delta|}{\sqrt{\sigma_{\alpha\beta}^2/m + \sigma_{\alpha\gamma}^2/n + \sigma_{\alpha\beta\gamma}^2/mn}}\right)-0.5\right].$$

The qualitative reproducibility index at the level of a single class can be estimated by

$$g_{Q1}' = 2\left\{\Phi\left(\frac{|\hat{\mu}_\delta|}{\sqrt{\hat{\sigma}_{\alpha\beta}^2 + \hat{\sigma}_{\gamma(\alpha\beta)}^2}}\right)-0.5\right\}.$$

The qualitative reproducibility index at the level of n classes (e.g., a school) can be estimated by

$$g_{Q1}' = 2\left\{\Phi\left(\frac{|\hat{\mu}_\delta|}{\sqrt{\hat{\sigma}_{\alpha\beta}^2/n + \hat{\sigma}_{\gamma(\alpha\beta)}^2}}\right)-0.5\right\}.$$

As in the case of the indexes of quantitative generalizability, g_{Q2}' will be larger than g_{Q1}' whenever $\sigma_{\alpha\beta}^2 > 0$.

IMPLICATIONS FOR RESEARCH DESIGN

If we are designing studies to estimate the generalizability of treatment effects, different research designs will permit us to estimate different variance components that may be used to estimate generalizability coefficients. Most feasible designs will confound some components of variance. The greater the number of components that are confounded, the more likely it will be that the design can yield only a very crude underestimate of the generalizability of treatment effects.

Consider the case of a design in which treatments are crossed with schools (both treatments occur in every school) but there is only one classroom per treatment condition in each school. In this case it will not be possible to estimate $\sigma_{\gamma(\alpha\beta)}^2$, the variance of classes within schools within treatment conditions. In this case, the only alternative to obtain a (liberal) estimate is to use $\sigma_{\alpha\beta}^2$ (which is confounded with $\sigma_{\gamma(\alpha\beta)}^2$ in this design). In this case, since $\sigma_{\alpha\beta}^2$ cannot be estimated separately from $\sigma_{\gamma(\alpha\beta)}^2$, the generalizability coefficient estimable is

$$g_4 = \sigma_\alpha^2 / \{\sigma_\alpha^2 + \sigma_{\gamma(\alpha\beta)}^2\}$$

which in this design is an estimate of

$$\sigma_\alpha^2 / \{\sigma_\alpha^2 + \sigma_\gamma^2 + \sigma_{\alpha\beta}^2 + \sigma_{\alpha\gamma}^2 + \sigma_{\alpha\beta\gamma}^2\}$$

because here $\sigma_{\alpha\beta}^2$ is confounded with $\sigma_{\gamma(\alpha\beta)}^2$. Thus it will not be possible to estimate the increase in generalizability at the school level that is associated with the larger number of classes (n) per school.

Consider the design in which the treatments are administered to whole schools. In this design, we can estimate σ_α^2 but not $\sigma_{\alpha\beta}^2$, which is confounded with σ_β^2. That is, we can estimate only $\sigma_{\beta(\alpha)}^2 = \sigma_\beta^2 + \sigma_{\gamma(\alpha\beta)}^2$. Therefore, the generalizability coefficient estimable from this design is

$$g_5 = \sigma_\alpha^2 / \{\sigma_\alpha^2 + \sigma_{\beta(\alpha)}^2\},$$

but because $\sigma_{\beta(\alpha)}^2$ is confounded with σ_β^2 and $\sigma_{\gamma(\alpha\beta)}^2$, this coefficient is really estimating

$$\sigma_\alpha^2 / \{\sigma_\alpha^2 + \sigma_\beta^2 + \sigma_\gamma^2 + \sigma_{\alpha\beta}^2 + \sigma_{\alpha\gamma}^2 + \sigma_{\alpha\beta\gamma}^2\}.$$

It is clear that designs that permit estimation of the most variance components yield the most nuanced (and accurate) estimates of generalizability coefficients.

Table 3.1.   Variance Component Estimates
from the Tennessee Class Size Experiment:
Kindergarten Mathematics and Reading
Achievement

Effect	Mathematics Estimate	Reading Estimate
μ_δ	0.225	0.231
σ_β^2	0.196	0.182
$\sigma_{\alpha\beta}^2$	0.002	0.019

EXAMPLE

The Tennessee class size experiment (Nye, Hedges, and Konstantopoulos 2000) is a large-scale randomized experiment in which students were randomized within schools to different class size conditions; thus, treatment (class size) was crossed with schools, and classrooms were nested within treatments and schools. Although this study was not designed to assess the generalizability of the treatment effect, the design permits us to estimate the variance components to make that assessment. The estimated effect of the treatment (μ_δ), the variance components for schools (σ_β^2), and the treatment by school interaction ($\sigma_{\alpha\beta}^2$) are given in table 3.1.

The quantitative generalizability of classroom treatment effects on mathematics achievement can be estimated as

$$g_1 = \mu_\alpha^2 / \{\mu_\alpha^2 + 4\sigma_{\alpha\beta}^2\} = (0.225)^2 / \{(0.225)^2 + 4(0.002)\} = 0.86.$$

This value suggests that 86 percent of the variance of treatment effects about zero (at the classroom level) is due to the average treatment effect. Because the treatment by school interaction is larger in reading achievement than in mathematics, the generalizability of the treatment effect on reading achievement is somewhat smaller:

$$g_1 = \mu_\alpha^2 / \{\mu_\alpha^2 + 4\sigma_{\alpha\beta}^2\} = (0.231)^2 / \{(0.231)^2 + 4(0.019)\} = 0.41.$$

This value suggests that 41 percent of the variance of treatment effects about zero (at the classroom level) is due to the average treatment effect. The qualitative generalizability index for mathematics achievement is

$$g_{QI} = 2\{\Phi(|\mu_\delta|/\sqrt{\hat{\sigma}^2_{\alpha\beta}}) - 0.5\}$$

$$= 2\{\Phi(|0.225|/\sqrt{0.002}) - 0.5\} = 1.00.$$

The qualitative generalizability index for reading achievement is

$$g_{QI} = 2\{\Phi(|\mu_\delta|/\sqrt{\hat{\sigma}^2_{\alpha\beta}}) - 0.5\}$$

$$= 2\{\Phi(|0.231|/\sqrt{0.019}) - 0.5\} = .091.$$

CONCLUSIONS

This chapter explicates a theory of generalizability of treatment effects that draws from an analogy with concepts of reliability and generalizability in test theory. The theory makes clear that the generalizability of treatment effects depends on the level of aggregation to which one wishes to generalize. Two generic classes of generalizability measures are provided, one of which (the quantitative generalizability coefficients) is a direct analogy to coefficients of reliability and generalizability in psychometrics. The second (the coefficients of qualitative generalizability) has no exact analogue in psychometric theory. Descriptions of how to estimate these coefficients of generalizability from feasible research designs, illustrated with data from a real experiment, are included; I hope that researchers will be tempted to use them.

Although this chapter uses the analogy of psychometric theory, other— and somewhat different—analogies could also be employed to develop a quantitative theory of generalization of treatment effects. For example, Cronbach's (1982) theory of construct generalization in program evaluation is very similar in spirit but lacks a developed mathematical basis. Work on total survey error (e.g., Kish 1965) draws on some of the same principles (and adds a concern for bias), as does work on total causal inference error (e.g., Hedges 1997). Quantitative research synthesis provides yet another way of approaching issues of generalizability of research findings (see, e.g., Cooper and Hedges 1994). However, I believe that the analogy to measurement illuminates the essential features of the problem and draws on the best-developed body of theory and empirical work.

This chapter does not discuss the issue of research designs involving co-variates and their potential effects on generalizability. It is clear that concepts of generalizability could be developed in a manner parallel to that described here, but which would take covariate adjustment into account. The major modification of concepts would be that the variance components defining generalizability coefficients would need to be adjusted for covariate effects. This is clearly an area that merits further consideration.

The development provided in this chapter assumes that generalizations are possible from the sample of districts, schools, classrooms, and students involved in the intervention study. In the best of all possible worlds, the intervention study would be based on a probability sample of districts, schools, and classrooms. This is analogous to the idea, in psychometric generalizability studies, of probability sampling of observers, occasions, and so on. This assumption is rarely met in psychometric generalizability studies, where the studies are usually carried out with the observers available, on the occasions it is possible to measure.

In the case of intervention studies, a few experiments actually do use probability samples (e.g., Myers and Schirm 1999) and many other studies obtain samples that are intended to be representative (e.g., Ridgeway et al. 2002). If the actual variation in the districts, schools, and classrooms sampled does not mirror those in the larger population of interest, generalizability will be compromised. However, the problem of inference about treatment effects in larger populations also arises in interpreting point estimates of treatment effects as well as their consistency. It seems unlikely that accurate estimates of either level or consistency of treatment effects can be inferred from intervention studies that are unrepresentative of the target population in important respects.

Empirical evidence about the generalizability of treatment effects is badly needed. There is an expanding body of experimental evidence that might be exploited to guide educational policy. Yet there is considerable controversy about how generalizable this evidence about treatment effects may be. Some respectable quantitative researchers have argued that we should not expect treatment effects to be highly generalizable (e.g., Cronbach 1975). Others (such as Guba and Lincoln) even question generalizability as a valid aspiration for educational research findings. In any event, concerns about generalizability surely constrain the use of available empirical evidence. The methods described in this chapter could be used to provide an empirical basis for determining the generalizability of treatment effects. They could also lead to more widespread use of research designs that are better suited to providing evidence about the generalizability of treatment effects.

4

Estimating the Effects of Educational Interventions

Charles S. Reichardt

The purpose of the present chapter is to explain how to estimate the effect of an educational intervention. Estimating the effect of an educational intervention requires comparing what happened after the intervention was implemented with what would have happened if it had not been implemented. A comparison of this type can be drawn in many different ways. Which is the best way depends greatly on the circumstances of the research setting. My goal is to present the many different types of comparisons that can be used to tailor a comparison to best fit the given circumstances.

The present chapter is divided into three sections. The first section introduces the notion of *threats to validity*, which are criteria that can be used to choose an appropriate comparison from among the many possibilities. The second section describes seven prototypical research comparisons: between-participant randomized experiment, within-participant randomized experiment, nonequivalent group design, regression-discontinuity design, correlational design, before-after design, and interrupted time-series design. The third section describes design features that can be used to embellish any of the prototypical comparisons. Combining each of the prototypical comparisons with the many different embellishments produces the full spectrum of possible research designs.

The educational intervention that is under investigation will be called a *treatment*. In assessing its effects, we could compare a treatment to either an alternative intervention or to the absence of an intervention. For example, a researcher might want to estimate a treatment effect by comparing faculty who receive an innovative training program either to faculty who receive a standard training program or to faculty who receive no training program. In either case, the alternative or no-intervention condition is referred to as the "comparison" condition. Also note that the protocols that comprise the treatment and comparison conditions can be administered to either individuals or to groups of individuals such as classrooms, schools, or communities. For convenience, the label "participants" is used to refer interchangeably to either individuals or groups, whichever is the focus of the study.

Research designs are often categorized along two dimensions, both of which address how the participants are assigned to the treatment and comparison conditions. Table 4.1 portrays the two dimensions and reveals where each of the seven prototypical research designs falls along them. The first dimension distinguishes between "randomized" and "nonrandomized" (or "quasi-experimental") comparisons. In randomized comparisons, the treatment and comparison protocols are assigned at random to the participants. When the treatment and comparison protocols are not assigned at random, the design is called a *quasi experiment*. The second dimension distinguishes "between-participant" from "within-participant" comparisons. In between-participant comparisons, each participant receives either the treatment or comparison protocol, but not both. As a result, the effect of the intervention is assessed by drawing a comparison between those participants who receive the treatment and those who receive the comparison condition. In within-participant comparisons, each participant receives both the treatment and comparison protocols. As a result, the effect of the treatment is assessed by comparing each participant's performance under the treatment condition with the same participant's performance under the comparison condition (i.e., by drawing a comparison "within" the participants). As table 4.1 reveals, the two dimensions are crossed. That is, a randomized experiment can be either a between-participant or within-participant comparison and the same holds for quasi experiments. The relative advantages and disadvantages of randomized experiments compared to quasi experiments and of between-participant designs compared to within-participant designs are described below.

Table 4.1.   Seven Prototypical Research Designs Categorized by Treatment (Randomized vs. Quasi Experiments) and Comparison (Between- vs. Within-Participant) Conditions

	Randomized Experiment	*Quasi Experiment*
Between-Participant	• Between-Participant Randomized Experiment	• Nonequivalent Group Design • Regression-Discontinuity Design • Correlational Design
Within-Participant	• Within-Participant Randomized Experiment	• Before-After Design • Interrupted Time-Series Design

THREATS TO VALIDITY

From among the variety of comparisons that could be used to estimate a treatment effect, a researcher selects the research design to be implemented based on several criteria such as cost, informativeness, and credibility. Although it is impossible to consider in the present chapter all relevant selection criteria, it is important to emphasize four criteria for assessing validity because they have become accepted as focal concerns in the social and behavioral sciences (Shadish, Cook, and Campbell 2002).

Internal Validity

Estimating a treatment effect requires a comparison; however, any comparison that can be obtained in practice will be imperfect. It is important to understand why this is the case and what the implications for biasing results are. The effect of an intervention is the difference between what happens after the intervention is implemented and what would have happened if the intervention had not been implemented but everything else had been the same. Ideally, the treatment and control conditions would differ only with respect to the treatment itself. In practice, however, it is impossible to hold everything the same across the treatment conditions, and whatever is not the same could introduce a bias in the estimate of the treatment effect. For example, consider a design that can be implemented in practice, such as a between-participant comparison. In such a comparison, everything is not the same between the treatment conditions because the participants who receive the treatment and those who receive the comparison condition are different. As a result, differences between the participants could account for some or all of the observed outcome differences between the treatment conditions. Initial differences between the participants in the different treatment conditions are called *selection differences* and are always a potential source of error in between-participant designs.

In any comparison that is drawn in practice, whatever is not held the same across the treatment conditions (besides the treatment itself) is called a threat to internal validity. For example, selection differences are a threat to internal validity in between-participant comparisons. When estimating a treatment effect, researchers must try to recognize the threats to internal validity that are present in the comparison that is being drawn and take these threats into account so that their potentially biasing effects are avoided or removed.

Statistical Conclusion Validity

Drawing an incorrect conclusion about a treatment effect because of a mistake in the application of statistical procedures is called a threat to statistical conclusion validity. Such threats include capitalizing on chance, type I errors, inadequate statistical power, and violations in the assumptions of statistical procedures. It is important to note here that the analysis of data from quasi experiments tends to be far more demanding and tenuous than from randomized experiments.

Construct Validity

Construct validity comes in two varieties: cause and effect. A threat to the construct validity of the cause arises when the active ingredients in the treatment are misidentified. An example is a reading program thought to be effective because it improves teachers' skills when, in fact, it is effective simply because it provides reading materials that are more engaging for students. Thus what is actually being measured is the effect of the different reading materials rather than changes in teachers' behaviors. A threat to the construct validity of the cause would also arise if a program were judged to be ineffective when in fact it had not been implemented with reasonable strength and fidelity. Other threats arise when the effects of a program are either diluted or enhanced because the program is surreptitiously adopted by the comparison group (diffusion of the treatment); teachers and students simply expect the program to be effective (placebo effect); or the act of withholding the program from the participants in the comparison group leads to either resentful demoralization or compensatory rivalry (Shadish, Cook, and Campbell 2002).

A threat to the construct validity of the effect arises when the outcome variable that reflects the true effect is misidentified. For example, a researcher might conclude that a program improved students' critical thinking when in fact only a narrow and mundane form of test-taking ability actually was assessed.

External Validity

External validity concerns the degree to which the results of a study can be generalized to other settings, participants, and times. For example, the results of an assessment of a teaching innovation for elementary grade students might not work in the same manner if applied to middle school students. The question of external validity also arises when a policy maker wishes to know how the results of a study conducted using participants who volunteered for the treatment would generalize if the treatment were imposed on participants involuntarily.

Trade-Offs among the Four Types of Threats

The best research design would be robust to threats to validity of all four types. In practice, however, designs that tend to increase one type of validity often tend to diminish another type. For example, internal validity can often be maximized in a laboratory setting, but such designs often reduce a researcher's confidence that the results can be generalized to nonlaboratory settings, which is a question of external validity.

Statistical conclusion validity, construct validity, and external validity are relevant to many types of studies and not just studies that assess treatment effects. On the other hand, internal validity is unique to studies that assess treatment effects. This chapter, therefore, focuses primarily on internal validity, particularly the threats to internal validity that are most plausible for different designs and design features and means for taking these threats into account.

RANDOMIZED EXPERIMENTS

For estimating treatment effects, randomized experiments have often been described as the "gold standard" of research design. But their advantages are accompanied by limitations.

Between-Participant Randomized Experiment

In a between-participant randomized experiment, participants are assigned randomly to receive either the treatment or comparison condition. Following participants' assignment to the treatment conditions, the different treatment protocols are administered and, at some later point, the participants are assessed on an outcome measure. The effect of the treatment is estimated by comparing the outcomes of the two groups. For example, twenty classrooms might be assigned randomly at the beginning of the school year so that ten receive a novel reading program while the other ten receive the standard reading curriculum, and the reading abilities of the two groups are compared at the end of the year.

Because participants in the treatment condition are not the same as the participants in the comparison condition, initial selection differences are a threat to internal validity. That is, a difference between the treatment conditions on the outcome measure might, in part or whole, be due to differences in the initial characteristics of the participants in the two groups rather than to the differential effects of the treatments. However, the plausibility that selection differences account for outcome differences between the groups is easily evaluated using a statistical significance test. If the difference between the treatment groups on the outcome measure is statistically significant, it is unlikely that the difference is due primarily to selection bias. If the results of a test are statistically insignificant, it means the outcome difference could reasonably be due to selection bias alone. In other words, selection differences are a threat to the internal validity of between-participant randomized experiments, but these differences can be taken into account easily using statistical procedures.

A more pernicious threat to internal validity is "differential attrition." Differential attrition arises when some of the enrolled participants fail to complete the study and those who drop out from one of the treatment groups tend to differ systematically from those who drop out from the other treatment group. The result is that the estimate of the treatment effect can be biased. Strategies such as offering monetary rewards for completing the study, making concerted efforts to locate and engage the participants in the study, and restricting the study to those who promise to fulfill their obligation to finish the study (though this can limit the generalizability of the results to other types of participants) can often reduce differential attrition.

Lam, Hartwell, and Jekel (1994) and Fetterman (1982) document instances where resentful demoralization undermined the credibility of the results of a between-participants randomized experiment because the disappointment of not being assigned to the treatment protocol degraded the performance of those who received the comparison protocol. A related problem is the compensatory equalization of treatment conditions. This problem arises when the participants in the comparison condition seek out and obtain services from sources outside the study that are similar to those provided in the treatment condition. These as well as other difficulties can sometimes be avoided by promising to provide the full set of treatment services to all participants once the study is completed. Alternatively, eligibility to participate in the study could be restricted to those who are willing to accept random assignment to either of the treatment protocols, though this could limit the generalizability of the results to other types of participants.

In spite of these difficulties, the between-participant randomized experiment often provides the most credible estimates of a treatment effect because threats to the validity of alternative designs are even more severe. Nonetheless, administrators are sometimes reluctant to sanction the use of randomized experiments, preferring to allocate services based on other criteria such as perceived need or merit, rather than at random. Sometimes the concerns of administrators can be allayed by arguments that a lottery is the fairest means of allocation of beneficial goods, especially when resources do not allow everyone to be served, and when it is important to obtain a highly credible assessment of the effects of the treatment.

Within-Participant Randomized Experiment

Imagine that an educational television show like *Sesame Street* is being introduced with the purpose, among other things, of teaching children the letters of the alphabet. To assess the effectiveness of the program, half the letters could be chosen at random to be taught on the show (one per week), and a group of preschool children could be enticed to watch the show every day during its inaugural thirteen-week season. At the end of the season, the children would be tested for their knowledge of all the letters in the alphabet. The program would be judged effective to the extent that the children performed better on the random half of the letters that were taught on the show compared to the random half of the letters that were not taught on the show. Such a design is a within-participant randomized experiment because the treatment effect is assessed by comparing the performance of each child under both treatment conditions (i.e., performance on letters that were taught on the show and performance on letters not taught on the show).

In the preceding design, a threat to internal validity is present because the letters in the two treatment conditions are not the same. For example, letters in one group might be more familiar to the children even before the program was shown. However, because the letters were assigned to the two treatment groups at random, this threat to internal validity is easily assessed using a statistical significance test. A statistically significant result means that the difference is not likely due entirely to initial differences between the groups of letters but is most likely due at least in part to something else, such as the effect of the program.

Within-participant randomized experiments can often produce more precise estimates of treatment effects than between-participant randomized experiments. This is because each participant serves in both treatment conditions in a within-participant design; this setup eliminates differences in participant characteristics between groups. As a result, a within-participant randomized experiment can often be implemented with a smaller number of participants than can between-participant randomized experiments. Indeed, it may be possible with this type of design to obtain estimates of treatment effects separately for individual participants, rather than groups of participants. And because the treatment is not withheld from any participants in the study, the within-participant experiment also avoids problems such as differential attrition and resentful demoralization.

A serious drawback to the within-participant design is that it can be implemented only when it makes sense for participants to receive repeated treatments and where the repeated treatments do not have carryover effects. In essence, this means that the treatment protocol must not alter how a participant responds to the comparison protocol, and vice versa. For example, it would not make sense to use a within-participant design to assess different methods for teaching how to ride a bicycle because once you learn by using any one method you cannot go back to not knowing how to ride a bicycle.

Within-participant randomized experiments are far more common in the laboratory than in field studies, and often have superior credibility and power to nonrandomized comparisons.

QUASI EXPERIMENTS

Quasi experiments are often easier to implement than randomized experiments, especially in field settings. The drawback is that quasi experiments tend to be compromised more severely by threats to internal validity.

Nonequivalent Group Design

The nonequivalent group design is a between-participant comparison. It is identical to the between-participant randomized experiment except that the participants are not assigned to the treatment conditions at random. Instead of undergoing random assignment, participants self-select the treatments they receive or are assigned based on administrator preference or convenience or some other nonrandom basis.

As with all between-participant designs, selection differences between the participants in the treatment groups are an inevitable threat to internal validity. But unlike in the randomized design, selection differences in the nonequivalent group design can introduce huge biases, a lesson that we have learned repeatedly. For example, in fifty-one studies of the portacaval shunt surgical procedure, the majority of the studies with nonrandomized comparisons showed marked success while none of the randomized studies did (Chalmers et al. 1983; Freedman et al. 1991). Similarly, in multiple studies involving a total of 27,151 patients, nonrandomized comparisons found a 20 percentage point increase in survival rates (from 71 percent to 91 percent) due to coronary bypass surgery while randomized comparisons found only a 5 percentage point improvement (from 83 percent to 88 percent) (Freeman, Pisani, and Purves 1983). The reason for these biases appears to be that the innovative medical treatments were given to those who were the healthiest at the start. In educational research, selection differences can arise because the treatment condition enrolls participants whose initial abilities tend to be either better or worse than the initial abilities of the participants in the comparison condition, and hence biases due to selection difference could make a treatment look either more or less effective than it really is.

Unfortunately, it can be difficult to remove the biases caused by selection differences in the nonequivalent group design. A wide variety of statistical procedures have been proposed for taking into account the effects of selection differences, including analysis of change scores, analysis of covariance, structural equation modeling, analysis of propensity scores, and selection modeling (Reichardt 1979; Winship and Morgan 1999). All of these procedures require that one or more measures on the participants be collected before the treatment protocols are implemented. Often it is best if these pretreatment (or "pretest") measures are operationally identical to the outcome (or "posttest") measures. But even then, no procedure is guaranteed to make the correct adjustment for the effects of selection differences, and it is usually impossible to know with confidence which, if any, procedure is best suited for the given circumstances (Lord 1967; Cochran and Rubin 1973). Whether or not the results are interpretable will often depend on the pattern of the outcomes and how similar the groups are initially. A pattern of results where the treatment group starts (on the pretest) worse off than the comparison group but surpasses the comparison group on the posttest is often the most robust to reinterpretation as due to selection differences (Cook and Campbell 1979). But this pattern of outcomes usually requires a particularly powerful treatment effect. Minimizing the size of initial selection differences (such as by assigning the treatment conditions to very similar cohorts of participants) can also increase the credibility of results from the nonequivalent group design.

The great appeal of the nonequivalent group design compared to the between-group randomized experiment is that it is far easier to assign participants to treatment conditions nonrandomly than randomly. But without random assignment, the results are often far less credible.

Regression-Discontinuity Design

The regression-discontinuity design is a form of between-participant quasi experiment. Although participants are not assigned to treatment conditions at random, the assignment of participants to treatment conditions is controlled strictly on the basis of a specified cutoff score on a quantitative assignment variable (QAV). The QAV can be any measure (but most often is a measure of need or merit), and the cutoff score can be specified by either the researcher or administrative fiat. All participants are assessed on the QAV, and participants with scores on the QAV below the cutoff score are assigned to one of the treatment conditions while participants with scores above the cutoff score are assigned to the other treatment condition. In this way, an ameliorative program, for example, could be assigned to the neediest students, or a program for gifted and talented students could be assigned to the most meritorious. After the treatment and comparison conditions are administered and given time to have their effects, participants in both groups are assessed on an outcome measure.

The effect of the treatment is estimated by comparing two regression lines. In essence, the outcome scores are regressed onto the QAV scores separately in each group. Figures 4.1 and 4.2 present scatterplots of hypothetical data from two regression-discontinuity designs. In both figures, the QAV is plotted on the horizontal axis and the outcome variable is plotted on the vertical axis. The cutoff score on the QAV is denoted by the vertical dashed line. Participants with scores on the QAV below the cutoff were assigned to

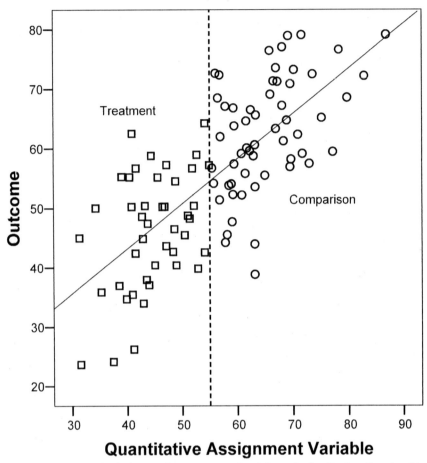

Figure 4.1. Hypothetical Data from a Regression-Discontinuity Design Showing No Treatment Effect

the treatment condition, and their scores in the scatterplot are denoted by squares. Participants with scores above the cutoff were assigned to the comparison condition, and their scores in the scatterplot are denoted by circles. The slanted lines that run through the scatterplots were derived from the regressions of the outcome scores onto the QAV scores.

The results in figure 4.1 are what would be expected if there were no treatment effect. The regression lines in the treatment and comparison groups coincide. In contrast, the results in figure 4.2 are what would be expected if there were a treatment effect. The higher regression line for the treatment group indicates that the treatment improves performance, on average. The shallower slope of the regression line for the treatment group reveals an in-

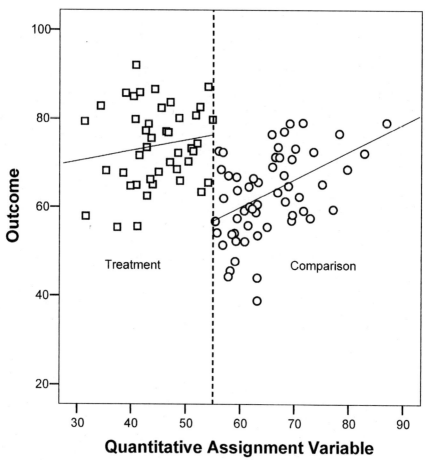

Figure 4.2. Hypothetical Data from a Regression-Discontinuity Design Showing a Treatment Effect

teraction: the treatment has a larger effect on participants who have lower QAV scores.

Estimating the effects of the treatment without bias in the regression-discontinuity design requires fitting the correct shape to the regression surfaces in the two treatment groups. In the examples in figures 4.1 and 4.2, the data were created to have regression surfaces that were properly fit by straight lines, as are drawn in the figures. However, it is possible that the regression surfaces are curvilinear, in which case fitting straight lines could result in biased estimates of the treatment effect. If the true regression surfaces are curvilinear, the correct curvilinear models must be used. The most common ways to model curvilinearity are by adding polynomial terms to the regression equation or using data transformations (Reichardt, Trochim, and Cappelleri 1995; Trochim 1984). To the extent that there is uncertainty about the degree of curvilinearity and how to model it (and there always is such uncertainty), the regression-discontinuity design tends to produce less-credible results than the between-group randomized experiment where the presence of curvilinearity is not nearly as debilitating.

The regression-discontinuity design is also at a disadvantage compared to a between-groups randomized experiment because it is less powerful statistically. Even under ideal conditions, a regression-discontinuity design would need 270 participants to have as much statistical power and precision as a between-groups randomized experiment with only 100 participants (Cappelleri, Darlington, and Trochim 1994). However, the regression-discontinuity design will often provide more credible results than either the nonequivalent group design or correlational design (see below). The drawback is that it is usually far easier to implement either a nonequivalent group design or a correlational design than a regression-discontinuity design.

Correlational Design

A correlational design is similar to a nonequivalent group design. The difference has largely to do with whether the treatment variable is discrete or continuous. To understand the difference, consider an example involving the effect of instruction in phonics on reading performance. One approach to assessing the effect would be to devise a phonics curriculum, implement it in all the classrooms in a school, and compare the subsequent reading performance of students in that school to the performance of students in a comparison school where the phonics curriculum was not implemented. This would be a nonequivalent group design because the treatment variable was discrete; either the phonics instruction was present or it was not. Alternatively, rather than interjecting phonics instruction into a set of classrooms, a researcher could rely on the natural variation in phonics instruction that was already present in classrooms. In this case, the researcher would obtain access to a sample of classrooms, measure the amount of phonics instruction that naturally took place, and then look at the relation between amount of phonics instruction and subsequent reading performance. To the degree there were substantial gradations in the amount of phonics instruction across classrooms, the treatment variable would be continuous rather than discrete, in which case the design would be classified as a correlational design rather than a nonequivalent group design.

As a result of the difference between discrete and continuous treatment variables, the statistical analyses of the data from nonequivalent group and correlational designs differ as well. While the estimate of the treatment effect in the nonequivalent group design is derived essentially from a difference between mean outcomes, the estimate of the treatment effect in correlational designs is derived essentially from regression coefficients. In spite of this analytic difference, the primary threat to internal validity is the same in the two designs. In both designs, one needs to take account of initial differences between the participants who receive different amounts of the treatment. In the correlational design, this is accomplished by adding measures of initial differences to the regression models so as to control for the effects of the initial differences. The problem, as in the nonequivalent group design, is that the researcher has to identify all the sources of initial differences and measure them; neither task is easy. Biases can be introduced if the variables are measured with error, which is almost always the case. Regression models (called *latent variable structural equation models*) have been developed to take account of measurement errors, but these models require that each characteristic be measured in more than one way. But most problematic is the concern that the researcher has simply overlooked important sources of initial differences and therefore not included them in the statistical model. The reason why randomized experiments are so respected is that random assignment eliminates having to worry about including all the necessary variables in the statistical model so as to take account of initial selection differences.

Before-After Design

A before-after design is the simplest version of a within-participant comparison. In such designs, an observation is taken before the treatment is implemented, the treatment is implemented, and then another observation is collected. The difference between the before and the after observations is used as an estimate of the effect of the treatment. Unfortunately, quite a few threats to internal validity are possible, as the following example illustrates.

Imagine that a program designed to increase students' self-esteem is introduced during the fall term in a high school. To assess the effects of the program, the self-esteem of the student participants is assessed before the program is implemented at the start of school in the fall and at the end of the program, which is right before the Christmas holiday. If the self-esteem enhancing program is effective, the average of the self-esteem assessments should increase between the time of the before and after measurements. But the following seven threats to internal validity could also cause a shift in the level of self-esteem, making it difficult to determine how much—if any—of the change was due to the program.

First, the threat to validity of "history" would arise if some other event that influenced self-esteem occurred during the fall term. For example, perhaps the school had a particularly rewarding football season because it won the district or state championship; this accomplishment could have increased self-esteem even in the absence of the program. Second, "seasonality" would be a threat to validity if students' self-esteem was higher in December than in September simply because the start of the school year tends to correspond to a reduction in self-esteem, and the onset of a school break tends to correspond to an increase in self-esteem. Third, "maturation" is a threat to validity if self-esteem increases over time because students get older, more knowledgeable, or more comfortable with school, and so on. Fourth, a threat to validity of "testing" would arise if the process of assessing self-esteem altered the level of self-esteem. For example, perhaps the "before" measurement prompted the students to think about self-esteem more than they had before, and this induced either an improvement or decrement that would have occurred even in the absence of the program. Fifth, "instrumentation" would be a threat to validity if the manner in which the students' level of self-esteem was assessed differed for the before and after measurements. Sixth, "attrition" would be a threat to validity if some of the students dropped out of the program so that the participants who were assessed on the before measure were different from the participants who were assessed on the after measurement. Seventh, "statistical regression" is a threat to validity when the before measurement is either extremely high or low and returns to more typical levels on the after measurement whether or not there is an intervention. For example, students' levels of self-esteem might vary naturally over time, so that if a program were introduced when self-esteem was particularly low, a subsequent measure of self-esteem would likely be higher simply because there would be more room for natural fluctuations to lead to an improvement than to a further decrement.

A before-after comparison can lead to credible estimates of treatment effects under circumstances where none of the above threats to internal validity is plausible (Eckert 2000). This situation is most likely to occur in educational settings when the treatment has a fast-acting effect, so the time interval between the before and after measurements can be brief, and when the outcome being assessed is unlikely to be change due to anything other than the treatment. Such circumstances would arise, for example, if the program were created to convey information that the participants would not plausibly obtain in any other way and the outcome measure were tailored to assess whether the students obtained only that specific knowledge. However, in cases where one or more of the seven threats to internal validity is sufficiently plausible, an estimate of a treatment effect derived from a before-after comparison will typically have little credibility.

Interrupted Time-Series Design

In the elementary interrupted time-series (ITS) design, multiple observations are collected at regular intervals both before and after the treatment is

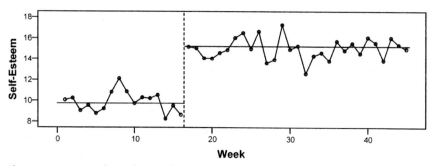

Figure 4.3.   Hypothetical Data from an Interrupted Time-Series Design Showing a Treatment Effect

implemented. The effect of the treatment is estimated by separately model-ing the trend over time in the pretreatment and posttreatment observations. The trend in the pretreatment observations is projected forward in time and compared to the actual trend in the posttreatment observations. Statistically significant discrepancies are attributed to the effect of the treatment. For ex-ample, figure 4.3 presents a schematized version of the results of an assess-ment of the Outward Bound program on self-esteem (based on Smith et al. 1976). The average level of the participants' self-esteem for each week is plotted over a period of forty-five weeks. The vertical line at week 16 de-notes the start of the two-week Outward Bound program. The pretreatment and posttreatment trends are plotted as regression lines. The higher post-treatment trend line suggests that the Outward Bound program improved self-esteem. The break or interruption in the regression lines at the point in time that the treatment was introduced is the source of the name for the in-terrupted time-series design.

Clearly, the elementary ITS design is a within-participant comparison. Like the within-participant randomized experiment, the ITS potentially could be used to assess the effect of a treatment for a single research partic-ipant (rather than for a large group of participants, as is the case for be-tween-participant designs). Another advantage of the ITS design is that it can be used to trace the temporal pattern of the treatment effect. That is, the multiple posttreatment observations can be used to assess whether the size of the treatment effect increases, stays stable, or diminishes over the course of time.

One of the primary threats to the internal validity of the ITS design is that some other historical event occurred at the same time as the intervention and produced the observed changes in the outcomes. For example, a threat to in-ternal validity would be present if the Outward Bound program had begun at the same time as the academic term ended and the summer break began. One of the suggested ways to cope with such a "history" threat to validity is to add a comparison time-series of observations collected on a second set of participants. In this way, an "experimental" time-series of observations would be collected from a group of participants who received the treatment, while a "comparison" time-series of observations would be collected at the same time from a group of participants who did not receive the treatment but who were subject to the same historical events (or other threats to validity). The data analyst would conclude that the treatment had an effect to the extent that the interruption in the trend in the experimental time-series of observations at the point of the intervention was larger than the interruption in the trend in the comparison time-series of observations at that same point in time.

Another issue to keep in mind is that the analysis of the data from an ITS design can be somewhat more complex than the analysis of data from other designs because of the presence of autocorrelation. *Autocorrelation* means that observations close together in time are more highly related than observations separated in time. The presence of autocorrelation violates an assumption in classical regression analyses and requires the use of special procedures such as ARIMA models (Shadish, Cook, and Campbell 2002; Mark, Reichardt, and Sanna 2000).

DESIGN ELABORATIONS

The seven prototypical designs described in the preceding sections reveal some of the elementary variations in comparisons that are possible in research designs used to assess treatment effects. But elaborations can be added to any of the prototypical designs to create an immense diversity of types of comparisons. Four types of elaborations are described which involve adding either measurement occasions, comparison conditions, outcome measures, or treatment conditions. The addition of each of these design features can be used to address threats to internal validity and thereby strengthen the research design.

Adding Measurement Occasions

Using Campbell and Stanley's (1963) classic notation, the before-after design can be denoted as:

$$O_1 \ X \ O_2$$

where an O represents an observation, an X signifies the implementation of a treatment, time proceeds from left to right, and subscripts denote the time at which an observation is obtained. So read from left to right, the notation for the before-after design means that first the O_1 observation was collected, then the treatment (X) was introduced, and finally the O_2 observation was collected.

Using the same notation, the elementary ITS design is diagrammed as:

$$O_1 \quad O_2 \quad O_3 \quad O_4 \quad O_5 \; X \; O_6 \quad O_7 \quad O_8 \quad O_9 \quad O_{10}$$

The obvious difference between the two designs is that the ITS design has measurements collected on many more occasions both before and after the treatment is introduced. Adding measurements at additional time points (or occasions) can greatly increase the credibility of a design because the additions can reduce threats to validity. Consider how this works with the before-after and the ITS designs.

One of the threats to internal validity in the before-after design is maturation, which means that performance may change over time not because of the effect of the treatment but because the participants grow older, gain more experience, get tired or hungry, and the like. This threat to internal validity is addressed in the ITS design using the additional pretreatment observations. These observations are used to model the maturational trend that is occurring in the participants so that the effect of the treatment is estimated based only on changes that deviate from this trend. In this way, the effect of maturation is estimated and removed.

Adding measurement occasions can also increase the credibility of the nonequivalent group design. The simplest nonequivalent group design is diagrammed as follows:

$$X \qquad O_2$$
$$\text{-------}$$
$$\qquad O_2$$

Each row in the diagram denotes a different treatment group, and the dashed line means that participants are assigned to the treatment groups nonrandomly. The problem with this design is that it provides no way to assess the presence and consequent effects of initial selection differences. A slightly more elaborate nonequivalent group design would add a pretreatment measurement:

$$O_1 \quad X \quad O_2$$
$$\text{----------}$$
$$O_1 \qquad O_2$$

Adding the pretreatment observations greatly strengthens the design because it provides data with which to assess the degree of initial selection differences and take them into account. Often the nonequivalent group design could be strengthened even more by adding an additional pretreatment observation to create the following design:

$$O_1 \quad O_2 \quad X \quad O_3$$
- - - - - - - - - - - - - -
$$O_1 \quad O_2 \qquad O_3$$

The additional (O_1) pretest measurement could be used in at least two different ways. First, it could be used to predict the trend in the differences between the treatment and comparison groups over time. For example, one could use the two pretreatment observations $(O_1$ and $O_2)$ to see if the effects of initial selection differences were increasing or decreasing over time. Second, the additional pretreatment observation could be used to conduct a "dry-run" experiment (Boruch and Gomez 1977). In the dry-run experiment, the same analyses that would be used to estimate the treatment effect based on the O_2 and O_3 data would be run using the O_1 and O_2 data. Because there is no treatment difference between the treatment and comparison groups between O_1 and O_2, all analysis strategies should give null results. Such a finding adds credibility to the results when the same analyses are applied to the O_2 and O_3 data where a treatment effect should be evidenced.

Adding an additional pretreatment measurement to a between-participant randomized experiment can also improve that design. Many laboratory studies use a between-participant randomized experiment without any pretreatment measurement. Such a design is diagrammed as:

$$R \quad X \quad O_2$$
$$R \qquad O_2$$

where the R denotes random assignment. Adding a pretreatment observation to create the following design,

$$R \quad O_1 \quad X \quad O_2$$
$$R \quad O_1 \qquad O_{2'}$$

can have three advantages. First, the pretreatment measure can be included in the analytical model as a covariate, and this inclusion can increase the statistical power and precision of the results. Second, adding the pretreatment measure allows the researcher to assess treatment-effect interactions wherein the size of the effect of the treatment varies with a participant's pretreatment score. Third, the pretreatment measure can be used to help take account of any selection differences that are introduced because of differential attrition.

Adding Comparison Groups

Adding a comparison time-series to the elementary ITS design produces the following design:

$$O_1 \quad O_2 \quad O_3 \quad O_4 \quad O_5 \; X \; O_6 \quad O_7 \quad O_8 \quad O_9 \quad O_{10}$$
$$O_1 \quad O_2 \quad O_3 \quad O_4 \quad O_5 \quad O_6 \quad O_7 \quad O_8 \quad O_9 \quad O_{10}$$

As previously noted, adding the comparison time-series allows the researcher to take account of threats to internal validity due to history effects. This is an example of how adding data from a comparison group can strengthen the research design. Another example is the original study of the effectiveness of the Salk vaccine for polio (Meier 1972), which used two designs: a between-participant randomized experiment and a nonequivalent group design. It is the nonequivalent group design that is of interest here because it used two comparison groups rather than just one. In that study, second graders were given the vaccine (and hence served as the treatment group) while both first and third graders, who did not receive the vaccine, served as comparison groups. The design is diagrammed below.

$$O_{grade\;1}$$
- - - - - - - - -
$$X \quad O_{grade\;2}$$
- - - - - - - - -
$$O_{grade\;3}$$

The results showed that the rate of polio was far lower for the second graders (who received the vaccine) than for either the first or third graders (who did not receive the vaccine). If only one of the comparison groups had been used, it would have been easier to argue that the differences were simply due to age, with older or younger children being either more or less likely to contract polio. Because both the younger and older groups experienced more polio than the treatment group, such an explanation is far less plausible.

Adding Outcome Measures

Outcome measures can sometimes be added to a design to reduce the plausibility of threats to validity, especially when the treatment has an effect across a narrow—rather than broad—content area. For example, imagine a before-after study that was designed to assess outcomes in two related content areas: A and B. The credibility of the results would be increased if: (1) there was a large change in scores in content area A, which was the content upon which the intervention was intended to have an effect; (2) there was no change in the scores in content area B, upon which the intervention was not expected to have an effect; and (3) content areas A and B were likely to be influenced by the same threats to internal validity such as testing, history, maturation, statistical regression, and so on. In this case, finding no change in the scores in content area B suggests that the threats to validity were not present and, therefore, that the changes in content area A were due solely to the effect of the intervention.

Adding Treatment Conditions

Larger doses of an intervention often produce larger effects than do smaller doses. As a result, a variety of doses of an intervention could be implemented so as to create a pattern of results that could be used to assess threats to validity. For example, behavioral assessment studies often implement increasing doses of an intervention over time followed by decreasing doses. A corresponding increasing and then decreasing pattern of outcomes is usually not plausibly explained as due to threats to validity, but only as due to the effect of the treatment.

SUMMARY AND CONCLUSIONS

Estimating the effect of a treatment requires comparing what happened after the treatment was implemented to what would have happened if the effect had not been implemented. The ideal comparison for estimating an effect cannot be obtained in practice. Any comparison that can be obtained in practice (and many different types are obtainable) is flawed in ways that could lead to biased estimates of the treatment effect. Sources of bias are called threats to validity. In designing a study, the task is to recognize the variety of designs that are possible under the given circumstances, think through the potential threats to validity for each design, and select the design that would likely produce the most credible and useful results under the constraints of the research setting. This chapter has described seven prototypical research designs and four ways in which each of these prototypes could be elaborated. Researchers should consider all seven of the prototypes and, for each one, consider how design elaborations can best be implemented to rule out the most plausible threats to validity. Combining all the prototypes with all the possible elaborations produces an abundant array of possible designs. Choosing among them becomes easier as you understand more about the relative strengths and weaknesses of each prototype and how the design features can address threats to validity.

In many instances, randomized experiments are superior to quasi experiments because it is easier to rule out some of the most critical threats to internal validity with randomization. For example, selection differences are always a threat to the internal validity of between-participant comparisons. Randomized between-participant designs make initial selection differences random, which means their effects can be easily and confidently assessed with straightforward statistical procedures. Without random assignment, the effects of selection differences can be very difficult to control; this means that the results of a study will often have correspondingly low credibility. However, randomized experiments are not a panacea. Between-participant randomized experiments can be difficult to implement administratively, and their benefits can be vitiated by differential attrition (Boruch 1997). Within-participant randomized experiments can be used only when carryover effects are not present (i.e., when the effect of one treatment protocol does not affect the response to any other treatment protocols).

Because of the benefits of randomized experiments, researchers should consider using them, rather than quasi experiments, whenever feasible. When randomized experiments cannot be reasonably implemented or when their disadvantages outweigh their advantages, researchers need to consider the full range of quasi-experimental designs that are possible and appreciate both their shortcomings and strengths. Compared to randomized experiments, the analysis of data from quasi experiments can be far more demanding. Taking account of the effects of selection differences in either nonequivalent group designs or correlational designs can require advanced statistical analyses. Interrupted–time-series designs can require sophisticated software to cope with the effects of autocorrelation among the observations. But most important, biases due to threats to internal validity are likely to remain even when using the most sophisticated statistical techniques. Such threats are usually best addressed via study design rather than statistical analysis (Shadish and Cook 1999). More elementary, prototypical designs can always be embellished with additional features such as measurement occasions, comparison conditions, outcome measures, and treatment conditions. Choosing a suitable prototypical design and embellishing it with design features crafted to address the most plausible threats to validity is the best way to obtain credible results.

II

MODELING SCALE-UP:
LESSONS FROM OTHER FIELDS

5

Scaling from Prototype to Production: A Managed Process for Commercial Offerings

James G. Conley and Robert C. Wolcott

This chapter addresses "scale-up" questions from the point of view of industrial engineers and managers. Our exploration refers to production models in the context of commercial innovations—for example, those whose success or failure is determined by a competitive market and those who invest in the innovation.

THE APPLIED BIRTHPLACE OF THEORY

We begin by taking a cursory look at the evolution of scale-up practices within industry throughout the twentieth century. While the methodologies and practices described here have been examined and enhanced by academic research and theory, nearly all of the dominant industrial scale-up methodologies and practices arose within an applied context. Practice informed theory.

Figure 5.1 presents a table of critical methodologies from the realm of industrial engineering, from Frederick Taylor's pioneering development of "scientific management" to Motorola's development of Six Sigma. Nearly all of these methodologies seek to manage risk in production, not limited to but certainly including scale-up, by increasing the effectiveness of metrics, measurement, and requisite adjustments. The story of twentieth-century manufacturing has been one of increasingly rigorous and effective approaches to measurement and control, enabling higher quality, more market-responsive production, and ever-increasing productivity. Statistical tools enable highly accurate control regimes, while just-in-time inventory

Taylor Methods (1900)
Build to Gauge, H. Ford (1910–1930)
Shewhart's Control Charts ('20s)
Juran, Romig, et al. Sampling Plans ('20s–'50s)   Increasing
Deming, Juran, JIT, et al. ('40s–'70s)   efficacy and
Statistical Process Control ('80s)   efficiency of
Taguchi Methods, ANOVA, DOE ('80s–'90s)   scale-up
Total Quality Management ('80s–'90s)   operation
ISO 9000 and WCM, DfX ('80s–'90s)
Six Sigma Management, ppsm defects ('90s)

Nearly all sought to control risks in scale-up investment
by measuring and managing inputs to influence efficacy
of production outputs.

Figure 5.1.   History of "Scale-Up" Related Risk Management in Industrial Engineering and Management

and production increase the firm's ability to respond more accurately to demand (Lochner and Matar 1990).

Whether developed by practitioners or researchers—and most of the luminaries of the field were practicing managers and/or consultants rather than academics—the critical insights and subsequent trial and error that led to new, more effective new-product development and scale-up knowledge arose inductively within an applied context for applied purposes. The pioneers were in most cases attempting to solve real problems. Their laboratories were manufacturing plants, industrial research facilities, and even entire manufacturing sectors, in the case of Deming's impact on Japanese postwar industrial development. Purely academic research has made important contributions and continues to serve as a rigorous arbiter and developer of practice; nonetheless, practice typically leads theory, *particularly in those cases where theory has made a substantial impact on the marketplace.*

Manufacturing Firms, Innovation, and Scale-Up

Our background and research interests focus on commercial innovations. Successful innovations in this context are usually required to produce a measure of profit margin that is a net wealth generator for the enterprise.

Commercial innovations are important sources of differentiation that firms seek in order to build competitive advantage (Porter 1996). Nearly all of the innovation constructs, metrics, methodologies, practices, and so on employed by firms are driven by the firm-level imperative to differentiate, to build profit margins associated with competitive advantage, and to sustain that advantage whenever possible.

In nearly all cases, innovations involve capital investments. When a firm makes a financial bet on the scale-up of an innovation, it is standard practice and quite advisable to hedge the bet (i.e., invest resources at a controlled rate), thus minimizing risk exposure. Risk can occur from many factors affecting both demand (e.g., market demand fails to materialize or develop sufficiently) and supply (e.g., production fails to provide proper supply for realized demand).

Many manufacturing industries, such as pharmaceuticals, automotive, aerospace, consumer durables, and food products, require substantial capital investments. These investments and how they create future competitive advantage for the firm are regularly scrutinized by the market analysts, a reality that makes attention to innovation process efficacy a top-level management imperative (CSFB 2002).

As such, the scale-up of an innovation from prototype to production is typically closely managed. Most of these management practices are not new. Modern project management methods and practices trace their origins back more than one hundred years to the planning required to achieve mass production in the moving assembly lines of the Ford Model T.

There is a significant number of process monitoring and measurement tools that have been used over the years in multiple industries (Lochner and Matar 1990). Most of these tools require thoughtful planning and periodic measures of process or product attributes in order to track variability from a predetermined standard. Measurement discipline and attention to detail are prerequisite to the application of such tools. Anytime something is explicitly measured and the metrics determine organizational performance, the organization attempts to optimize in terms of the metric. As such, effective performance metric selection critically influences overall success.

As management scholars and practitioners become more experienced with a specific metric and how it influences behavior, they tend to modify what is measured to align organizational behaviors with firm strategy. A similar phenomenon appears to be at work when teachers in the public school system have an incentive to "teach to the test," due to the fact that they are evaluated (measured) based on their students' performance on standardized tests.

Over the years the disciplines of engineering and management have produced considerable scholarship regarding new-product "scale-up" and closely related subjects (Ulrich and Eppinger 2004). Selecting from disparate sources, this chapter describes processes for managing the scale-up of commercial innovations from prototype to production and, where appropriate, offers some experiential perspective.

Most notably, researchers and managers have found over the course of the century that the decisions made during a product's development affect the requirements and constraints of production scale-up, often radically.

More recent approaches, in particular "Design for X" (DfX) methodologies, explicitly integrate production and scale-up issues into the design and development processes, before products even make it to production planning. We examine DfX methodologies below.

Ironically, focusing on scale-up processes and practices alone will fail to illuminate successful scale-up. The next section expands our aperture to consider preproduction-stage decisions and practices, and relates these insights to achieving effective scale production and marketplace diffusion.

Before Launch: Foundations for Successful Scale-Up

Four key insights of industrial practitioners and researchers over the past few decades appear particularly relevant to constructing an effective foundation for scale-up:

1. Scale-up challenges often arise as a result of decisions made earlier in the development process.
2. Customers, suppliers, and other important stakeholders must be integrated sufficiently early into the new-offering innovation process.
3. Product (or "offering") platforms can confer strategic and tactical advantages.
4. Project cancellation processes are critical to success—and very few firms do a great job of effective project termination.

Each of these insights must be incorporated into management processes and decision making well prior to production; otherwise, the horse will be out of the proverbial barn. We consider each of these insights in turn.

Scale-up challenges often arise as a result of decisions made earlier in the development process. Industrial firms have often developed products without sufficient involvement of manufacturing, marketing, finance, suppliers, customers, and other downstream functions (McGrath 1996). The absence of input from downstream functions results in a range of problems, including delayed product introduction, higher manufacturing costs, issues with suppliers, and lack of market acceptance.

For instance, engineers can, and sometimes do, design products perfectly suited to design and performance specifications without adequately considering how and at what cost the product will be manufactured on a large scale (figure 5.2). This often results in delays in manufacturing scale-up and significantly higher production costs. Products must be developed in order to maximize the value of the product for the firm marketwide, not simply the value of the individual product. Accomplishing this *requires* integrating scale manufacturing and marketing issues directly into the definition stages of product development.

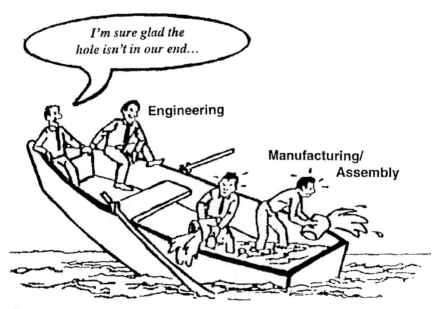

Figure 5.2. The Result of Improper Planning and Integration for Scale-Up

The pharmaceutical industry in particular faces this challenge with the development and production of new biotechnology-based drugs. These drugs tend to be more difficult to produce in volume than traditional, synthetic drugs. Biotech drugs are produced via living organisms (mammalian cell cultures and microorganisms are two typical production methods). Such living "factories" prove much more difficult to manage than the more deterministic chemical reactions used to produce drugs via synthetic chemistry. Living organisms respond to conditions, inputs, and modifications in much more complex ways than synthetic chemical reactions. While production in a lab on a small scale during development can be challenging, full-scale production presents a significantly more complex and difficult proposition. Moreover, lab researchers often spend relatively little time considering eventual production scale-up issues, thus increasing the issues faced during "handoff" to production engineering and planning.[1] Even the most sophisticated and well-capitalized firms such as Merck, Lilly, and Bayer have encountered costly challenges in scaling up manufacture for commercialization of biotech drugs (Brown 2002).

In one critical case, the publicly traded biotech firm Immunex collapsed in market value from a peak of around $45 billion to an acquisition price of $11 billion by competitor Amgen within one year. Immunex's arthritis therapeutic, Enbrel, promised to be one of the most successful blockbuster drugs of all time, with potential annual revenues and early demand much higher than the company had anticipated. Unfortunately, the company failed to plan and invest sufficiently in advance for production scale-up, failed to come close to meeting market demand, and was acquired at a fraction of its potential value. All of this occurred by the end of 2001, despite Immunex's enviable cash position of more than $1 *billion* in 2000. Some of these issues could have been mitigated by more manufacturing involvement earlier in the product development and drug trials stages. There is evidence that some insiders had been advocating for a substantial plant expansion as early as 1997, over three years before crisis ensued. In many ways, scale-up failure had been determined before production had even begun (Acumen 2003).

The proliferation of new-product development processes and rigor within industrial entities over the past two decades has enabled best-practices firms to dramatically increase the rate and success of new-product introductions, from idea all the way to manufacturing scale-up and market introduction. In response to this insight, a number of processes and methodologies have proliferated, most notably including so-called phase-gate development processes, cross-functional teams, and "Design for X" methodologies, to be explained later in this chapter.

Customers, suppliers, and other important stakeholders must be integrated sufficiently early into the New Product Development (NPD) process. Product life cycles have decreased dramatically over the past decade. Firms typically have less time to profit from the products they bring to market; thus, firms must increase the rate at which they introduce new products (Pringle, Drucker, and Ramstad 2003). This suggests that the first insight explored above becomes even more critical. Moving faster requires more thoughtful up-front planning and informed decision making throughout the process.

Firms are under increasing pressure to respond quickly and precisely to market demands. This objective presents particular challenges for innovative products, since by definition such products have not been "tried and tested" in the marketplace. With so many firms bringing new products to market, managers cannot afford to wait until the end of the new-product development process, or even *after* market introduction (which is not at all an atypical practice!) to integrate substantial customer insight into product design and development (see, in particular, Sawhney and Prandelli 2001; von Hippel 1988).

In the past, some best-practice firms tended to wait until a product was at least in the beta prototype stage before soliciting substantial customer input. Today, some leading firms are actually integrating existing and potential customers into the earliest stages of the NPD processes—as early as the "ideation," or idea creation stage. Diesel, the hip European apparel marketer, has built an elaborate online and physical community of lead Diesel trend-setting customers worldwide. The company engages with this invitation-only group to mine for new-offering ideas and trial products before market introduction. Many of these customers enjoy their role with Diesel and believe participation confers prestige (Sawhney and Prandelli 2001).

eBay goes a step further. eBay closely tracks the behavior of its market participants as a significant component of how the company determines new market offerings. The company closely monitors the behavior of buyers, sellers, and service providers within their marketplaces to identify behavior that indicates demand for a new or modified offering. In an intriguing example, eBay determined in 2000 through rigorous market research that users did *not* want to buy and sell used cars on eBay. Then, within a year of making the decision not to offer a used-car marketplace on eBay, management recognized that people were indeed buying and selling used cars on the website through the die-cast car model collectibles site. As a result, eBay changed course and created a used-car trading site, which now represents a significant profitable niche for the company. With the exception of wholesale car markets, more cars were bought and sold on eBay than through any other single source in the United States. eBay also integrates users—particularly "power sellers," who are high-volume, independent eBay users—directly into the new-offering development process.[2]

Integrating customers, suppliers, and other stakeholders into the NPD process should also be accompanied by the integration of business development and marketing expertise. Introducing a solid marketing competency into the NPD organization makes sense, but continues to pose significant challenges for many firms. Development tends to be dominated by R&D, engineering, and eventually by manufacturing, organizations that operate with a very different language and mind-set from the marketing function. Even today, leading-edge firms such as Herman Miller, Motorola, General Motors, and Microsoft continue focusing significant resources on addressing this challenge.

Product (or "offering") platforms can confer strategic and tactical advantages. Product platforms leverage common, modular components and subsystems, thereby enabling firms to more quickly and cost effectively design new offerings for varied market segments (Wolcott, Tibrewal, and Saxena 2004; Gawer and Cusumano 2002). For instance, one product platform can support an offering for a low-price, low-performance customer, and reuse various components as part of a higher-performance, higher-price product for the luxury market. A well-known example would be the model platforms of the automobile industry. Firms such as Volkswagen and Audi and Chevrolet, and Buick and Cadillac share components and subsystems from the low-priced through the luxury segments, adding performance and amenities as required.

Platforms convey substantial advantages during manufacturing scale-up. Platforms by definition include a common architectural foundation and common components and subsystems. New products based on a platform architecture can be:

1. Created more quickly and at lower cost by the addition of new components or the reconfiguration of modular components
2. Manufactured more efficiently, by the higher-volume manufacturing of common foundation, subsystems, and components (more efficient physical plant utilization), or by the facilitation of scale-up
3. Supplied and often even distributed in ways similar to that of other products based on the same platform.

Management must determine to what extent a platform must offer flexibility (which generally comes at a cost), and to what extent a platform should focus on cost savings (which tends to compromise flexibility).

Most literature on platforms focuses exclusively on products (Baldwin and Clark 2000; Pine 1999; Meyer and Lehnerd 1997). Other research suggests that an emerging, broader vision of "offering" platforms, which includes the entire "ecosystem" of suppliers, users, complementors, and partners, provides insight for business systems as platforms (Wolcott, Tibrewal and Saxena 2004). This approach has particular relevance for approaching educational systems attempting to scale up new educational offerings. For instance, the University of Phoenix has built an infrastructure and methodology for creating, marketing, and executing online courses and degree programs. They are able to apply this platform for an ever-wider range of offerings. The company's marketplace success validates their model from a commercial perspective.

Project-cancellation processes are critical to success—and very few firms do a sufficient job of effective project termination. Once development projects have entered the product pipeline (more on this below), many firms find it difficult to cancel heavily vested projects that, if viewed rationally, should be canceled. Likewise, firms have difficulty selecting the projects most likely to support firm success. Many other, noneconomic factors enter the selection process, from the NIH ("not invented here") affliction and managerial fiat or "pet projects," to simple momentum and neglect. Firms even end up making continued investment decisions based on sunk costs; this is clearly a suboptimal practice (Keil and Montealegre 2000).

Most generally, management must effectively separate hopeful people from hopeless projects. Talented human capital must be focused on projects with the highest likelihood to fulfill the objectives of the organization. Inadequate cancellation regimes do a disservice to everyone, not least the people who continue to expend good effort.

The implications for moving from prototype to scale-up phases are considerable. Once a product enters scale-up, costs rapidly multiply. If an otherwise unworthy project fails to be cancelled before the scale-up phase, good dollars continue to follow bad, with increasing magnitude. Additionally, failure to cancel projects crowds out investment in otherwise worthy projects.

Organizational factors make cancellation particularly difficult. Teams driving projects tend to work to find reasons to keep a project going, even in cases where they find an Achilles' heel that guarantees the best action for the firm is to discontinue investment. This happens for reasons of prestige, job security, fear, pride, or even myopia and rationalization. Often, incentive programs are to blame. If a team incentive is based on the "success" of a project, then a team will attempt to keep the project alive. If, however, a team is evaluated based on the contributions it makes to helping the firm make the best possible development and investment decisions, its members are more likely to surface critical problems, determine if a reasonable solution exists, and, if not, recommend cancellation. Improving the project-cancellation process can be accomplished by rewarding teams for accomplishing "milestones" rather than project acceptance. Succeeding at a milestone can include successfully recommending project cancellation if that appears to be the best decision. One technology firm that applies such discipline, XL Tech Group of Melbourne, Florida, uses a practice affectionately entitled "Rejoice in Rejection" to stress the central role of project cancellation in the company's innovation processes (www.xltg.com). Effective, business-case-supported project-cancellation methodologies remain one of the most important and poorly executed disciplines in Innovation Process Management.

Each of the four preceding insights into production success helps an organization to develop offerings prepared to succeed during market introduction and diffusion. Next, we consider the contributions these and other approaches to scale-up in manufacturing can make to the development of a science of scale-up.

DEVELOPING A MULTIDISCIPLINARY PERSPECTIVE ON SCALE-UP: INSIGHT FROM EFFORTS TO SCALE FROM PROTOTYPE TO PRODUCTION

Preexisting Conditions for Scale-Up

For-profit entities should be in the business of wealth generation, not reallocation. Due diligence is the foundation of fiduciary responsibility. Translated into common language, this means that the officers and directors of an enterprise are responsible for investment and allocation of resources in a manner that optimizes shareholder value within the guidelines of ethics and the law. Wise investments in innovation bring a bountiful future harvest.

Mismanaged investments in innovation may lead to prolonged famine (undifferentiated products and commodity pricing) or even corporate death.

The preexisting conditions for investment that must be met are context dependent but typically include a demonstrably profitable product life cycle, manageable costs (direct and indirect, primary and secondary), and alignment with overall corporate strategy. Benchmarks from both the firm's own past experience and that of other firms provide insight regarding how stages of scale-up have behaved in the past under varied conditions. Design tools can be employed to capture elements of life cycle cost in the physical design so as to realize optimal product performance, both within the marketplace and its ecosystem.

Timing and Scale-Up

Many of the decisions and the tools employed to address them relate to timing. Timing plays a critical role in managing scale-up for any innovation project, as described in various forms thus far. "Market readiness" poses a particularly challenging timing issue. Managers enjoy more control over the timing of internal activities; however, the market makes its own decisions that are often obscure until an offering has reached the market.

Questions that confront an innovation's "market readiness" relative to a particular firm's conditions include:

1. How will scaling this innovation provide competitive advantage? Can we sustain this competitive advantage?
2. How much will it cost? How much will the investment return (e.g., net present value), and over what period of time? How confident are you in these projections?
3. How new is "new"? How much of the "old" can we use in the new to minimize additional investment (financial risk) and still achieve the desired degree of differentiation? What existing firm assets will this leverage?
4. How will this help our firm grow? Does the offering match our long-term goals?
5. Is market demand ready for scale production? Who will be our lead customers? Are we ready if demand expands much more quickly than anticipated?

THE DESIGN FUNCTION AND SCALE-UP

The design function and its agents (engineers, product designers, etc.) fulfill the time-honored role of defining and determining what the offering is and how it will perform. Design tools, integral elements of the phase gate regimes discussed below, are often used by the creative community to make product definition-related decisions and manage design attributes over the life cycle. Therefore, design tools play a central role in bringing the constraints of the life cycle onto the decision radar of designers during product definition.

Design for X methodologies, where the X represents any number of important considerations in the life cycle performance and/or cost of a commercial innovation, and closely related disciplines, include:

- Design for Assembly (Boothroyd and Dewhurst 1983)
- Design for Damage Tolerance (Nichols and Conley 2000)
- Design for Inspection (Conley, Moran, and Gray 1998)
- Design for Manufacture (Stoll 1999)
- Design for Mass Customization (Gilmore and Pine 2000)
- Design for Quality (Lochner and Matar 1990)
- Design for Securability (Conley and Wolcott 2004)
- Design for the LifeCycle (Ishii 1995)
- Empathic Design (Buchenau and Fulton-Surrey 2000)
- Modular Design (Baldwin and Clark 2000)
- User Centered Design (Landauer 1995)
- Mechanical Design Axioms (Suh 2001)

At a more fundamental level, *Axiomatic Design* represents a leading philosophy among mechanical engineers and designers (Suh 2001). The axioms are self-evident truths that capture the essence of good design, formerly craft knowledge. Two guiding imperatives underlie this philosophy:

1. **The First Design Axiom**: *Maintain the independence of the functional requirements.*
   For example, this rule states that the functional requirements of an automobile's tires should be independent of the function of the car radio, and, ideally, of every other subsystem in the automobile. Hence, failure of the tire simply requires changing the tire and no other dependent system. Conversely, failure of the radio does not impact the function of the tires.
2. **The Second Design Axiom**: *Minimize the information content of the manufacturing system.*
   In other words, the complexity of an offering and the associated means of production should be minimized. This suggests rationalization and standardization of parts, interfaces to achieve modularity, and suppliers and all associated supporting roles and personnel.

Relative to the Second Axiom, the advent of materials resource planning (MRP) in the 1970s and 1980s was an attempt to bring information technology to bear on the management of production complexity for the extended enterprise. More recently, Enterprise Resource Planning (ERP) systems have extended this control to many functions beyond manufacturing.

It is our personal experience that good design, knowingly or unknowingly, embraces these axioms, thus anticipating many issues related to scale-up.

MANAGING THE PROCESS OF SCALE-UP

Innovations are typically new products or services and/or combinations of the same embodied in an offering. In order for the offering to achieve market appeal, there must be some form of value proposition, implicit or explicit, associated with the offering. In business-to-business markets, the value proposition should be quantitative (e.g., how much money do I save/revenue do I garner as a result of adopting this offering?). In consumer markets, the value proposition is often less quantitative and more subjective (e.g., I absolutely *must* have that Armani suit, or   everyone's favorite—the Pet Rock).

Scale-up to production includes all of the phases, tasks, and activities involved in enabling volume production of an offering. These include industrial design and engineering, public certification (e.g., FDA approval), compliance with government and industry standards, preparation and ramp-up of the pilot and physical plants, market testing, launch, and life-cycle maintenance. Design decisions during scale-up should reflect the "life cycle" idiosyncrasies of the target market for the offering. In the fashion industry, nearly the entire inventory of a business changes in a year or less. In the market for classic motorcycles, the models remain essentially constant for ten to twenty years (Conley et al. 2002).

In markets for high-tech products, the life-cycle curve shows a familiar pattern of customer behavior and sales volume over time (Moore 1995). While innovative new products that make it to market might be quite successful with a limited set of early customers, reaching the mass market poses a unique challenge. In Moore's terminology, "crossing the chasm" refers to this well-documented challenge of making the leap from success with less risk-averse early customers to the broader market. Planning for and managing scale-up under such uncertainty requires not only manufacturing flexibility but also high-quality sales, marketing, finance capabilities, and overall strategic coordination.

Phase Gate Systems: Managing Resource Allocation and Coordinating Activities

While each market and/or industry exhibits its own peculiarities, common management-process attributes exist to achieve scale-up. These common process attributes transcend industries, because the fundamental need to manage resource allocation (thus, risk) for scale-up transcends all economic organizations. The challenge of scaling is essentially one of expanding and filtering knowledge (inputs), comprehending multiple interrelated factors, and gaining acceptance ("buy in") among all those agents of the enterprise that contribute to the sales, end production, distribution, and service of the offering (outputs).

Current state-of-the-art processes for managing new-offering development, market introduction, and scale-up are typically referred to as *phase gate systems* or *regimes*. An example of one such process is known as *Product and Cycle Time Excellence*, or PACE (McGrath 1996). Many firms have instituted variations of phase gate regimes, such as Motorola's "M-Gate" process, which embraces Six Sigma philosophy. The fundamental tool set and processes remain consistent across firms, however.[3] Generally speaking, these processes seek to plan and track all of the phases/tasks/activities associated with a particular project, lay them out along a time line, account for human and capital resources, and create accountability at multiple corporate levels during all phases of the offering's development. These processes require thoughtful, premeditated, up-front planning and the flexibility and confidence to change the plan when necessary. Effective phase gate regimes rationalize resource requirements across multiple projects (the portfolio), proactively balancing resource requirements in order to avoid the disruptions and cultural challenges associated with firefighting and to achieve allocations that come as close possible to optimal levels (Repenning 2002; Repenning 2001).

These processes have multiple components classified as either project-specific or cross-project management elements that are used to reconcile a firm's portfolio of projects. Project-specific process-management elements include core teams, phase gate systems, structured methodologies, and design tools. Cross-project elements include product strategy, pipeline management, and technology management (figures 5.3 and 5.4).

Project-Specific Elements of Phase Gate Management Regimes

Core teams: The core team is the nuclear organizational unit responsible for the successful scale-up of the innovation. Membership of the core team is cross-functional with representation from the pertinent parties within the

How does PACE view the product development process?

PACE is a total product development methodology addressing both project and cross-project management

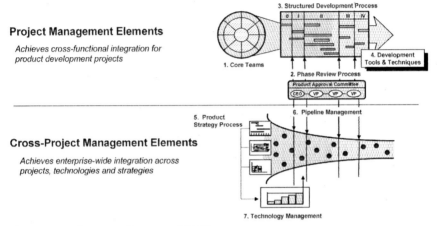

Project Management Elements

Achieves cross-functional integration for product development projects

Cross-Project Management Elements

Achieves enterprise-wide integration across projects, technologies and strategies

Figure 5.3.   The Seven Elements of PACE

firm that contribute to the successful production of the end innovation. Membership in the core team evolves over the duration of the scale-up, typically expanding over time. The team starts small and scales to include more downstream functions as the offering scales and moves closer to launch or market introduction. A strong contingent factor in core team efficacy is the ability of the team leader to plan, anticipate, and manage the personalities and day-to-day challenges of bringing a new offering to market. Specifically, this leader needs to be skilled at navigating the milestone gate reviews at the end of each phase described below.

Phase gate systems: These planning constructs help organize and raise awareness/urgency of development and scale-up activities during a series of phases. Scale-up process performance is subsequently evaluated by senior management at a corresponding milestone, or "gate." Phase duration, objectives, and resource allocations are validated and/or renegotiated at each gate. If all parties (core team and senior management) can agree on core team progress to date and ongoing viability of the future offering, the project proceeds to the next phase of activities and eventually the next gate. While determining a project's fate is always a judgment call, failure to sufficiently meet evaluation criteria at any of the phase gates suggests a project should be reconsidered or canceled. Through this rational, evaluative process, managers can help distinguish hopeful people and projects from hopeless boondoggles.

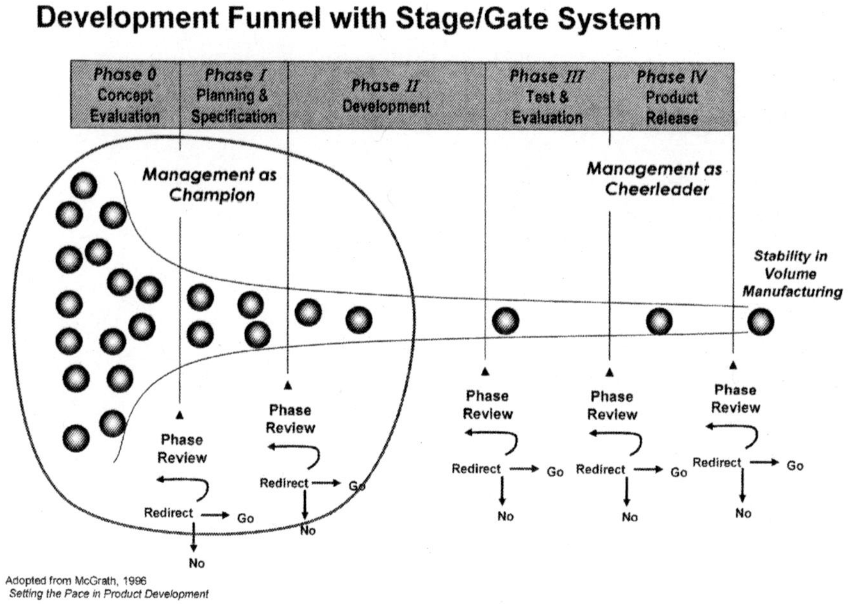

Development Funnel with Stage/Gate System

Phase 0 Concept Evaluation	Phase I Planning & Specification	Phase II Development	Phase III Test & Evaluation	Phase IV Product Release

Management as Champion

Management as Cheerleader

Stability in Volume Manufacturing

Phase Review

Redirect → Go

No

Adopted from McGrath, 1996
Setting the Pace in Product Development

Figure 5.4. Product Development Funnel with Phase Gates to Manage Innovations

Structured methodologies (e.g., GANNT charts): These tools give expression to what needs to be accomplished and when. They help make all core team members and management aware of the time sensitivity of project-related phases, tasks, and activities. They also enable managers to examine issues such as whether certain activities must be accomplished in serial or in parallel fashion. The complexity and level of detail of the structured methodologies can be exhaustive. How exhaustive is usually a function of the nature of the innovation. Something truly new (such as Toyota's hybrid car, the Prius) requires more thorough planning than a simple modification of an existing offering (such as the next model year of the Toyota Camry).

Cross-Project Elements of Phase Gate Management Regimes

Product strategy: The logic and reasoning behind a firm's desire to prototype and scale an innovation should be synchronized with the overall business strategy and competencies of the firm. Product strategy is the innovation process management component that reconciles the logic of the offering with the logic of the business. Though apparent, devising and effecting a successful product strategy can be a complex, uncertain endeavor.

Pipeline management: The pipeline is a management mnemonic that illustrates all innovation projects of the firm across all phases. In an environment with limited resources for engineering and development, it is not uncommon for resources to be assigned to multiple innovations in various stages of scale-up. Pipeline management seeks to balance supply and demand of development resources against risk and return scenarios.

Technology management: Often a firm must decide when to adopt a particular technology and/or incorporate an alternative. Technology management assesses the maturity of evolving technologies and helps determine when and if they are suitable for adoption.

Many firms have innovation project management systems with the elements described above; however, few follow and execute the process guidelines without facing substantial challenges. Contingent internal management factors that impact success during development include timely involvement of the top management, skillful core team leadership, and team empowerment.

The considerable body of knowledge on such processes suggests that simply having a process is not enough to ensure successful scaling. Thoughtful leadership and process discipline are often fleeting when market pressures and other influences compromise the resources required for a project (Conley 2002; Conley et al. 2002). Further, understanding of phenomena such as adoption, diffusion, and product life cycles helps to anticipate when, where, and how an innovation should be scaled to meet the demand of mainstream markets (Moore 1995).

THE IMPACT OF INFORMATION AND
COMMUNICATION TECHNOLOGIES ON SCALE-UP

The adoption and effective use of new offering-related information technologies are a matter of survival (Iansiti and MacCormack 1997). The speed and agility of many firms are measured by how quickly the firms act or react to a market threat or achieve the first-mover advantage in a new market opportunity. As a result, the integration of information technology to facilitate scale-up is ubiquitous in most industries.

Information technology changes the boundaries of the enterprise, thus facilitating a number of efficiencies and interesting new marketplace behaviors. The PACE process, for example, is now entirely web based (see the website of Integrated Development Enterprise, www.ide.com). What was once called *product development* is now referred to by such monikers as *development chain management* or *collaborative product development*. These new IT-enabled management capabilities attain much deeper and more effective synchronization between suppliers, internal and external collaborators, channels, and customers in the development and provision of new offerings. Dell Computer's revolutionary redesign of the computer industry would have been impossible without such IT-driven transformation (Dell and Magretta 1998).

Examples of IT's Influencing Scale-Up to Production

The Boeing 777: Boeing developed this commercial airliner almost entirely with electronic tools such as Computer Aided Design (CAD) and Computer Aided Engineering (CAE). Prototypes were virtual and robust, facilitating everything from numerous virtual prototypes (many more than would have been possible with physical prototypes, and at a much faster rate) and detailed design for maintenance trials. For example, before a single physical prototype was constructed, Boeing simulated a virtual mechanic climbing through all spaces where such maneuvering would be required in maintenance of the airship. Moreover, the 777 was the first commercial aircraft designed in multiple global locations through virtual integration of the dispersed team's efforts. The reliable performance modeling and effective integration of global teams saved *billions* of dollars in prototyping cost and led to more accurate scale-up and production (Petroski 1998).

Digital music distribution: Kazaa and other peer-to-peer networking tools are changing the way music is distributed and delivered to the customer. The rapid replication and direct delivery capabilities enabled by IT represent poignant examples of how IT's impact on production and scale-up can radically transform industries. It is now possible for an increasingly diverse community of small, "off-label" performers to market their music directly to the consumer, even *through* other consumers, avoiding the old label establishment. The music industry is being transformed largely as a result of the flexibility and scalability afforded by digital music distribution capabilities (Mann 2003).

Benetton: The grand challenge of fashion retailing is determining and producing what the public wants before they know they want it. Issues such as color selection can make a critical difference between inventory that sells quickly and inventory that ends up in deep discount. The fashion retailer Benetton delays a few important manufacturing steps such as fabric dyeing until just before delivery to its stores. Through IT-enabled instant feedback from the retail stores (what is selling and what is not) and this delay in finishing, Benetton closely synchronizes on-shelf coloring with emerging demand. Delaying production decisions until better demand information becomes available represents a highly adaptable strategy that can be transmitted to numerous environments.

Even the organizational forms involved in production scale-up have been transformed by information and communications technologies. In the early part of the last century, Henry Ford set the standard for industrialization with his River Rouge plant, a vertically integrated facility that turned raw materials (silica sand, iron ore, rubber, etc.) into automobiles. Today, the automotive industry has moved to what might be known as an *orchestrator* model. Scale-up each year is undertaken by coordinating the arrival of new components/tooling at an assembly plant. The raw materials and subsystem operations (and associated capital risk) that were undertaken by a single firm are today carried out by subcontractors and suppliers. Today, Ford maintains design authority but is really in the assembly business; this is an operating model similar to all other large automotive firms worldwide.

DISCUSSION

Engineers and scientists are often taught to find or form an equation that models the system and "turn the crank until you get a reasonable answer." Largely as a result, the academic industrial engineering and management science approach to the scale-up question has often been overly deterministic. Unfortunately, in scaling from prototype to production, the number of tasks that must be considered, planned, resourced, managed, and executed is one of exponential complexity (Scherpereel 2001). There is no equation or relation (at least not to our knowledge) that solves the challenges of scaling innovation for market.

Fortunately, the associated management practices of scaling involve a broad range of engineering and management knowledge. Many more relativistic disciplines such as marketing, organizational behavior, and customer service provide insights complementary to the engineering sciences toward the effective management of scale-up.

Generally speaking, the processes, design tools, and information technologies described above seek to achieve transparency and manage all elements of project risk. While many of the laws of nature underlying a particular engineering challenge may be deterministic, the process-management tools for bringing a product to market are relativistic and, at times, probabilistic.

Throughout the twentieth century, practitioners and researchers have developed and applied ever more sophisticated NPD and production management methodologies, balancing the benefits of deterministic scientific and engineering knowledge with the more stochastic, potentially chaotic and often perplexing behaviors of humans, firms, and markets (particularly the first!). The push toward Total Quality Management, ISO9000, Six Sigma, and other such initiatives represents ever more detailed efforts to use recorded measurement of system outputs to thoughtfully manage the allocation of resources. So guided, the production function should operate with minimal disruptions, at least in theory.

Unfortunately, even the best-laid plans and analyses cannot reliably anticipate the vagaries of customer adoption, especially in the realm of consumer products. Fortunately, many well-considered actions can encourage success. Addressing the right issues early in any development process—before scale-up even appears on the horizon—limits risk and increases potential reward. Canceling unworthy or less-than-worthy projects fortifies the firm's investment portfolio, and directs execution toward the most likely winners. Introducing rigor and discipline with such methodologies as phase gate regimes and DfX methodologies manages risk through more informed decisions and focuses scarce talent on the right development challenges.

Scale-up is fundamentally a question of information management, effective decision making, and accurate execution. Metrics, measurement, process discipline, and timely thinking regarding the right objectives enable any organization to come as close to optimal outcomes as possible, though consistent success will always present a challenging objective.

NOTES

1. To some extent, this is to be expected. Biotech researchers are routinely pushing the limits of current science, so it stands to reason that they would be less likely to consider manufacturing issues in such an environment. Nonetheless, the disconnect between lab and production presents significant obstacles for firms attempting to profit from biologics.

2. Interview with Gil Penchina, vice president, International, eBay, August 2002.

3. There exist numerous references to Six Sigma processes implemented in firms ranging from GE and Motorola to 3M. Author and Six Sigma pioneer Praveen Gupta provides a number of effective discussions of Six Sigma philosophy and implementation.

6

From Efficacy to Effectiveness: Translating Randomized Controlled Trial Findings into Treatment Standards

James J. Dignam

Modern medicine has largely embraced the scientific method in pursuit of progress toward treating and managing disease, and in recent times has even codified this approach in the concept of *evidence-based medicine*. In that portion of medical research oriented toward developing and testing new therapies, the randomized controlled trial (RCT) has been established as the gold standard for evaluation and evidence generation. The dominance of the RCT in the evidence-based medicine paradigm and its central role in drug regulation and approval by the U.S. Food and Drug Administration stems from its hallmark characteristic of providing an unbiased assessment of the effects (positive and negative) of a therapeutic intervention. The appeal perhaps stems also from its simplicity and logic, in that the majority of RCTs are designed to determine through a direct comparison which treatment option is better.

Because of these attributes, RCTs also fit into a larger framework of evidence generation, synthesis, and summary that results in the evolution of standards of treatment interventions over time. However, for a variety of reasons RCT results often do not translate into changes in medical practice as readily as those conducting and sponsoring trials would hope. First, effective dissemination and communication of broader implications of the findings remains an elusive goal. Second, when results reach practitioners, there is often the perception that RCTs reflect results in a narrow, highly selected patients cohort that does not reflect medicine in practice, and that questions in need of answers go unaddressed in clinical trials due to forces that drive this costly, time-intensive enterprise. Finally, when developments from RCTs are carried forward into routine practice, results may fall short of previously realized benefits, or new risks may be revealed. Nonetheless,

RCTs have been the predominant means by which treatments have been discovered and improved for many conditions.

In this chapter, we discuss the role of RCTs in the development of medical care standards. Described is the process of transition from efficacy demonstration in RCTs to changes in therapeutic standards that ideally will lead to reduced morbidity and mortality from disease. This process is in part quantitative, but also draws heavily on structured review of evidence, expert opinion, and consensus building both within the research community and in a larger constituency, including patients. Also discussed are barriers and challenges to this process, and how an increased desire for RCTs to change treatment policy may be influencing trial design and the types of trials that are being conducted.

THE RISE OF RANDOMIZED CONTROLLED TRIALS IN MEDICAL RESEARCH

Brief History of Clinical Trials and Randomized Controlled Trials

For purposes of this discussion, a *clinical trial* is defined as a prospective experiment involving human subjects and an intervention undertaken for the purpose of disease alleviation or prevention. Experiments that fit this description have a very long history, with some colorful early historical examples including the biblical book of Daniel (1:11–16), which reported on a comparison of the king's rich food to vegetables and water among servants. There is also the account of the French battlefield surgeon Paré (1537), who described in vivid detail the comparison of boiling oil versus egg yolks for the treatment of battlefield wounds (Packard 1921), an experiment brought on by necessity when the supply of the former ran out (fortunately for the patients). Lind (1757) described an experiment for the treatment of scurvy (conducted at sea), consisting of twelve patients, two each in treatment regimens as follows: cider, vinegar, vitriol, seawater, nutmeg, and oranges and lemons (the treatment that prevailed). These are but a few of many instances where those attempting to treat disease either consciously sought a method of prospective, direct observation in order to ascertain which option was more effective, or out of convenience or necessity were able to make a direct comparison that informed this decision. In the nineteenth century, empirical evaluation of medical treatments continued to gain ground. Claude Bernard's (1866) "Introduction to Experimental Medicine" laid out many principles of clinical experimentation, and placed great emphasis on removing personal bias on the part of the physician in evaluating treatment alternatives. Movement toward what we typically recognize as a prospective comparison that attempts to account for undue bias becomes clear in the case of Filiger, who advocated alternating treatment assignment of sequentially treated patients as a way to establish a concurrent, similar comparison group for the treatment in question (described in Doll 1998). Similar allocation schemes were used throughout the early twentieth century by the Medical Research Council in Great Britain (Doll 1998). However, not until the 1940s was treatment assignment by a random mechanism, the signifying element of RCTs, implemented in human trials. In 1946, the Medical Research Council began a randomized trial of immunization for whooping cough, followed shortly thereafter by a trial of streptomycin for tuberculosis. This latter trial, which became the first published RCT in 1948 (Medical Research Council 1948), was initiated by statistician Bradford Hill and physician D'arcy Hart, who both recognized that individual patient responses were highly variable and that treatments proposed and used for many years were yet to be validated. The streptomycin trial, which yielded unequivocal results within two years, set a new standard for the medical evaluation of treatments.

A landmark RCT conducted in the United States was the Salk vaccine trial begun in 1954 (described in Smith 1992) in an environment of competing medical views and resistance to a fully randomized study. The trial was carried out as a double-blind and independent of proponents of the vaccine, and is still recognized as an impeccably conducted study (Smith 1992). Randomized trials have been adopted across a spectrum of diseases since that time, with large organizations and networks being formed to specifically address diseases including diabetes, cancer, heart disease, and AIDS.

Hallmarks of the Randomized Controlled Trial

There are two essential design features of all RCTs:

Concurrent control group. The main purpose of concurrently evaluating individuals both receiving the standard treatment and the test treatment is to eliminate temporal trends in diagnosis, characterization of the condition, and ancillary care likely to be present in any comparison to a *historical control* group, by which we mean a cohort of individuals with an apparently similar condition treated differently at some other time and/or place. Concurrent evaluation also provides an implicit control over the commonly observed phenomenon of research participation itself having a positive effect on outcomes, regardless of the type of intervention.

Randomization. The fundamental means by which bias is removed from the measure of treatment effect is by disassociating treatment assignment from any and all extraneous factors on the part of the patient or the physician. This is accomplished by randomly assigning patients to one of a set of treatment regimes to then be prospectively compared. This process of randomization uniquely distinguishes RCTs from other approaches to clinical experimentation. Randomization will randomly (and usually equally) distribute factors associated with the outcome of interest between groups to be compared. While differences in characteristics between groups can be addressed to various degrees in other ways, typically by comparing "like with like" through matching, stratification into homogeneous groups, statistical modeling or adjustment, appropriately applied, only randomization will reliably assure this necessary condition for unbiased assessment. One reason is that it is often not the *known* potential confounding factors that we must concern ourselves with, but rather the *unknown* or uncollected factors, where other methods cannot address the potential bias. Also, randomization forms the theoretical basis for applying probability rules that we typically rely on for inference.

Additional Design Requirements for
RCTs to Provide Credible Information

Statistical power to detect realistic, clinically material treatment benefit. Suppose we have two treatments A and B to be compared. In the classical (e.g., frequentist) statistical hypothesis-testing paradigm, a quantity referred to as type II or β error equals the probability that a statistical test fails to produce a decision in favor of a difference between test treatment B and standard treatment A when in fact the two treatments differ. The complement of this quantity, or $1 - \beta$, is referred to as statistical power, and equals the probability of correctly deciding in favor of a treatment difference, that is, of detecting a difference when in fact it exists. This quantity depends on other parameters considered when planning the trial, specifically, the probability of incorrectly finding in favor of a difference when none exists (type I error, or alpha, is discussed below), the number of subjects evaluated (sample size), and an a priori specification of a difference between treatments that is both realistic and clinically material. It is imperative that RCTs be carefully designed with respect to statistical power, so as not to obtain equivocal findings that fail to answer the fundamental question concerning the worth of a new treatment under consideration. Underpowered studies can cause delay or even abandonment of promising avenues of treatment, and even a "negative" study that is adequately powered is an important finding in that energy and resources can be directed into other more promising alternatives. Recent commentaries lamenting the large number of underpowered trials that continue to be conducted even raise a concern as to whether such trials are ethical in the sense that it is probably not disclosed to the participant that the study has little chance of resulting in a medically important finding (Halpern, Karlawish, and Berlin 2002).

Control of multiplicity in hypothesis testing. The other key parameter in statistical hypothesis testing is the probability of incorrectly deciding in favor of a treatment difference when none exists, an inevitable consequence of using a probabilistic mechanism and frequentist hypothesis testing to make decisions. Typically this probability is set at some small value, such as 0.05 or 0.01. A complication that arises with RCTs is the practice of conducting periodic interim evaluations of the data; each evaluation consists of an evaluation of the primary hypothesis. These interim analyses are conducted to ensure that if definitive evidence of benefit (or harm) emerges prior to the anticipated end of the study, then actions can be taken to benefit the welfare of trial participants. It might also be determined partway through a trial that a treatment benefit is very unlikely, and stopping the trial early may be considered. In any case, appropriate statistical methodology for dealing with multiple examinations of the data and early trial stopping have been developed (Jennison and Turnbull 2000), and a methodological plan describing the approach should be devised at trial initiation and adhered to throughout trial conduct. Failure to account for a multiplicity of analyses can result in spurious "positive" findings, and can also diminish the influence of trials even when results are favorable, if there is a perception that a study had been terminated prematurely due to apparently favorable results (George et al. 1994).

Unbiased, accurate assessment of response or outcome. Randomization alone cannot ensure that an unbiased treatment comparison will result from an RCT, because subjectivity can readily enter the comparison after randomization has taken place in the form of biased assessment of outcomes. Both the participant and the assessor can influence outcomes whenever there is a degree of subjectivity in the response variable. For example, studies of pain relief, memory or cognitive improvement, physical mobility, and similar endpoints may be perceived by participants differently according to whether or not they are receiving active treatment, and those assessing the participants may introduce similar biases. For outcomes representing definitive disease states or events, or of course, deaths, problems with subjectivity of assessment are reduced, but still depend on equal ascertainment in each treatment group, that is, following participants with equal rigor to obtain all outcome events. Finally, when diagnostic films or other materials are assessed, it is desirable to have assessments made without knowledge of the patient's treatment group assignment. In all of these cases, partial or complete "blinding" of the treatment assigned is an essential tool for assuring minimal bias in treatment effect estimates.

A related concept is that of treatment compliance. Blinding is considered essential in studies with self-administered agents in order to keep participants from losing enthusiasm for adherence to the assigned regimen or continued participation. Such was the case with the Physician's Health Study, which relied on careful design of this element of the study in order to maintain compliance to either a placebo or an aspirin regimen over an extended period among over 22,000 men (Steering Committee of the Physician's Health Study Research Group 1989). In studies where treatments are administered within health-care facilities, compliance by those administering treatments must also be monitored. In either case, poor compliance can erode the ability to accurately estimate treatment benefit, and may cause the dismissal of effective treatments.

ALTERNATIVES TO RANDOMIZED CONTROLLED TRIALS

Randomized controlled trials were controversial since their introduction into medicine and remain so, primarily because of randomization. Despite the fact that any ethically designed trial uses as a control group the current standard treatment, which may indeed be no treatment or an inactive treatment (e.g., placebo), there nonetheless is the perception that participants are "guinea pigs" and may receive substandard care if assigned to the control group. This is not an altogether unreasonable view, since the impetus for the trial is usually the belief by some that the new treatment will result in a superior outcome. Alternatively, patients do incur risks when receiving either treatment and in particular the new treatment, about which less is known typically, and although they would incur these same risks were the treatment to be used independent of the trial, there may be a perception that such risks may be misrepresented or ignored in order to further the trial goals. Finally, the relinquishment of treatment assignment to a randomization mechanism is distasteful to many physicians and awkward to explain to patients. Indeed, there remain situations where RCTs are infeasible, and other study designs must be considered (Black 1996). A large body of literature exists regarding ethics of randomized trials, with some of the more interesting views put forth by statisticians (see Royall 1991).

The most obvious alternative to randomization is that mentioned earlier—a carefully controlled nonrandomized concurrent trial, but for reasons described above this design is generally insufficient to rule out bias in treatment evaluation. Even this design is unpalatable to some, as it still requires denial of a potentially better treatment to some individuals (Hellman and Hellman 1991). Thus, some advocate relying on observational studies with historical controls and analyses of data gathered over time from medical practice, coupled with the use of statistical methods to account for potential confounding of treatment effects and other factors. Numerous problems with observational studies have been identified, including temporal changes in disease definition (DuPont 1985), inexplicable large variations in effect when the same treatment is evaluated in sequential studies (Pocock 1977), nonstandardization of data and data quality issues

(Byar 1980), and use of out-of-date historical data that tends to inflate effects for new therapies (Moertel 1984).

Randomized Trial and Observational Study Findings Can Differ Greatly

Perhaps the clearest evidence of the superiority of RCTs over observational studies for unequivocally establishing treatment benefit comes from the unexpected findings that have frequently arisen when RCTs are conducted following observational studies. In fact, so many examples exist where the value of what has become a widely used or even standard practice in medicine based on uncontrolled observational studies is later overturned by an RCT that we need but cite only a few highly visible cases. In some instances, not only was the treatment not beneficial, but it actually caused serious harm. In other cases, treatments may have much more limited application and value than previously thought, dramatically changing the risk-to-benefit considerations that are part of clinical decision making as to its use. In the Cardiac Arrhythmia Suppression Trial (CAST), two antiarrhythmia drugs that were already in wide use were compared to placebo. The trial was terminated early when evidence of no benefit emerged, and later there were definitive findings of *increased* mortality among those receiving the drugs (Echt et al. 1991). In a second example, hormone replacement therapy (HRT) has become firmly established as beneficial in ameliorating menopausal and postmenopausal symptoms, as well as in providing long-term cardiac and other benefits for women. The basis for this intervention was scientifically rational and bolstered by numerous observational studies. In the Heart and Estrogen/progestin Replacement Study (HERS) trial, women with a history of heart disease were randomized to receive HRT or placebo. Early trends indicated no benefit in reduction in heart disease for women on HRT, and in longer-term follow-up, these findings persisted (Hulley et al. 1998). Because the trial was conducted among women with disease history, it was still considered plausible (and perhaps more likely) that healthy women would incur the heart-protective benefit previously seen in the observational trials. In 2002, results of the Women's Health Initiative (WHI) trial, a blinded, placebo-controlled trial of over 16,000 women, were released after the investigators and an independent data and safety monitoring committee concluded that a heart disease benefit would not be realized (Writing Group for the Women's Health Initiative Investigators 2002). Other anticipated risks, such as increased breast cancer incidence, were also documented, leaving women and physicians to ponder whether these risks were worth the benefit of HRT, which may be limited to the control of menopausal symptoms without the attendant long-term benefits that had been all but assumed to exist. In a final example, again where a therapy gained wide use while still under evaluation in randomized trials, high-dose chemotherapy with bone marrow transplant to replenish immune function, which is seriously compromised by the treatment, was used throughout the 1990s with intent to cure breast cancer. When results of RCTs finally became available, no material benefit in survival was evident, and with the many significant risks and costs that this regimen entails, oncologists have retreated from it as a standard therapy.

In addition to these instances where possible or definite harm was revealed for interventions considered to be beneficial, there have been numerous trials showing the relative worthlessness of therapies or procedures that are in common use. Recent examples include arthroscopic knee surgery for arthritis (versus a nontherapeutic intervention) (Moseley et al. 2002) and pulmonary artery catheters (versus standard care) in elderly high-risk surgical patients (Sandham et al. 2003). Both of these therapies showed no difference in outcomes for the alternative interventions. These issues will be revisited later.

While the primacy of the randomized clinical trial has been regularly questioned since its advent in medical research, it has repeatedly been shown to be the most reliable means by which treatment progress can be documented, and in many cases has overturned medical practice standards that were ineffective or harmful.

RCTS AS EVIDENCE-GENERATING MECHANISMS

Hierarchy of Evidence

Rating schemes establishing a hierarchy of evidence have been developed in order to aid in interpreting existing and new findings for use in clinical medicine. For example, the National Cancer Institute uses the definition of Levels of Evidence shown in table 6.1. Randomized controlled trials are given the highest weight, followed by nonrandomized concurrently controlled trials, then observational studies without control groups.

Role of RCTs in Evidence-Based Medicine

The medical community has increasingly embraced *evidence-based medicine* as both a pedagogical and clinical decision-making tool. Evidence-based medicine can be described in general as a system of weighing available information from different settings and synthesizing this information in a way that reflects the strength and credibility of the evidence, providing a framework for clinical decision making that reflects a greater degree of reliance on objective information sources (Evidence-Based Medicine Working Group 1992). Coupled with this objective view, there necessarily remains

Table 6.1.   Typical "'Levels of Evidence'" Scheme Used by the National Institutes of Health to Rank Types of Clinical Studies

Level	Type of Evidence
I	Randomized trials with low false-positive and low false-negative errors (high power). Evidence obtained from meta-analysis of multiple well-designed, controlled studies may also be considered.
II	Evidence obtained form at least one well-designed experimental study. Randomized trials with high false-positive and /or negative errors (low power).
III	Evidence obtained from well-designed, quasi-experimental studies such as non-randomized, controlled single-group, pre-post, cohort, time, or matched case-control series.
IV	Evidence from well-designed, non-experimental studies such as comparative and correlative descriptive and case studies.
V	Evidence from case reports and clinical examples.

the autonomous decision-making process of the individual caregiver, and thus the approach is not intended to be wholly algorithmic. Indeed, while RCTs rank highest in terms of evidence in this approach, the applicability of trial findings to individual patients who may differ from the trial participants in important ways must be considered for each case at hand (Dans et al. 1998; Guyatt et al. 1999).

RCTs and the Regulatory Environment

In contrast, the perspective and practices of regulatory concerns such as the U.S. Food and Drug Administration (FDA) might be viewed as essentially objective, since their principal concern is safety and efficacy of agents in well-defined populations, and aside from allowance for contraindicating conditions, results regarding the use of the agents in question are intended to be applicable to all similar clinical settings. In most instances (and nearly exclusively in the case of the FDA), information for this evidence-based approach to treatment for diseases arises from RCTs.

STRENGTHENING AND COMBINING EVIDENCE FROM RCTS

Confirmatory Trials

The planning, infrastructure, time, and cost required to conduct definitive efficacy trials necessitate that the studies be carefully designed to avoid equivocal findings, or in other words, to provide definitive evidence for whether the therapy in question is worthwhile. Nonetheless, even clear positive findings will invariably leave questions unanswered and may prompt little change in treatment practice. If we are to view the randomized trial as an exercise of the scientific method, as many have, then there is an important role for replication of trial findings. This is particularly important for clinical decision making, where trial results reflecting the benefit realized among participants must be translated to an individual patient's utility for one treatment option versus another. When benefits are moderate, as, for example, is the case in most cancer treatment advances (Berry 1996; Parmar, Ungerleider, and Simon 1996), these confirmatory trials may be necessary in order to effect change. Trials of similar design considered together have particular appeal to those interested in obtaining a more general quantitative measure of benefit (and risk). However, even when the trials are not formally combined, there is substantial qualitative value over and above any quantitative summary when findings are replicated in independent trials. It is also not uncommon that replicated trials fail to obtain the same results, providing an opportunity for closer scrutiny of the study populations and determination of how broadly applicable trial findings may be (DeMets and Califf 2002a).

Meta-Analysis

A more rigorously quantitative means of combining evidence from trials is by meta-analysis, a widely used analytic tool in many areas of social and medical science. Meta-analysis refers to a process whereby data from independent studies are gathered and combined to form a quantitative summary estimate of a given effect. Randomized trials may in fact be more suited to meta-analysis than nearly all other types of research designs, as within a given disease setting, there is likely to be greater uniformity in definition of the disease state, study design features, classes of therapeutic agents or procedures, and endpoints, and these features are increasingly likely to be well documented in studies of high quality (Moher et al. 2001). Meta-analyses were initially carried out primarily by extracting effect estimates from published literature to be combined into a single estimate using statistical techniques, but it is generally accepted now that in medical meta-analysis studies, it is imperative to obtain patient-level data from each study included, a laborious process that may involve seeking data from unpublished trials. Once these data are acquired and standardized for a common endpoint, the individual effect measures per study may be combined using an appropriate statistical model into a summary effect estimate (with an accompanying variability estimate). Results of each trial are also presented, and in cases where there is evidence of significant heterogeneity among trials, a summary measure may be inappropriate and thus omitted. Usually, some quality weights based on design considerations are assigned to the trials, providing a natural opportunity to evaluate trial quality.

Some positive aspects of meta-analyses are the ability to evaluate consistency among trial findings and possibly uncover small treatment effects that were not statistically significant in any one trial (although the meta-analysis is generally not considered the equivalent of an adequately powered RCT), and standardization of trial conduct. One disadvantage is that when combining heterogeneous trials and treatments into summary estimates, one may illustrate only a "proof of principle" that is of little use for clinical decision making. Furthermore, findings may be incorrect, as meta-analyses are essentially observational studies and are subject to attendant limitations. In particular, temporal trends in treatment and ancillary care render comparisons of newer versus older treatment uninterpretable or misleading.

Example: Early Breast Cancer Trialists' Collaborative Group Worldwide Meta-Analysis of Treatment for Breast Cancer

Since the mid-1980s, the Early Breast Cancer Trialists' Collaborative Group (EBCTCG) has undertaken a worldwide effort to collect and synthesize randomized trial data on the treatment of early breast cancer, that is, breast cancer that can be removed surgically but may require additional radiotherapy, hormonal, or chemotherapy treatment. For early breast cancer, these interventions entered trial testing during the 1970s, and while each showed promise and has continued to be developed, disease alleviation and survival gains are generally modest and incremental, and thus a meta-analysis of trials might strengthen evidence and foster wider use and further research efforts for this common cancer. At five-year intervals, data from trials around the world are gathered and synthesized by EBCTCG coordinators in Oxford, United Kingdom, and a meeting of trialists is then held to review data, discuss findings, and begin to prepare manuscripts describing findings.

The effort has been successful in obtaining a large proportion of the relevant information. For example, in the meeting in 1995, coordinators considered data from 37,000 women in 55 trials examining the hormonal treatment tamoxifen; this figure represented 87 percent of all known trial data for this agent. A publication of findings appeared in 1998 (Early Breast Cancer Trialists' Collaborative Group 1998). The EBCTCG has advanced findings from individual trials in several important ways, strengthening evidence for (a) the benefit of tamoxifen in reducing disease recurrence and lowering breast cancer mortality in women of all ages, (b) the value of chemotherapy in reducing recurrence and lowering mortality, (c) the safety and efficacy of less extensive surgery for primary tumor removal, and (d) the benefits and risks associated with radiotherapy after surgery.

CONSENSUS DEVELOPMENT

To fully transition from individual and aggregated findings from RCTs to a standard treatment policy, it is necessary to achieve consensus on the totality of evidence. This section describes a prototypical consensus-building exercise used in medical research in the U.S. Structure and Function of the National Institutes of Health Consensus Development Program.

The National Institutes of Health (NIH) Consensus Development (CD) Conference Program provides an example of how RCTs and other evidence are synthesized in a semiquantitative manner in order to provide health-care practitioners and researchers with information on the given state of knowledge and outstanding issues for a specific health issue (National Institutes of Health Consensus Development Panel 2001). The conference program began in the 1970s in response to concerns about the transfer of innovative medical technology into medical care practice. The Office of Medical Applications of Research (OMAR) was formed in the late 1970s and began the CD program. The conferences are jointly sponsored by OMAR, one or more of the NIH specialized institutes or centers (e.g., National Cancer Institute, National Heart, Lung, and Blood Institute), and the Office of the Director of the NIH. In addition, the Agency for Healthcare Research and Quality (AHRQ) participates by conducting a systematic literature review and assembling a bibliography of information relevant to the topic.

The stated purpose of the CD program is to evaluate information pertinent to a biomedical technology and develop a consensus statement. An "independent, broad-based, non-Federal, non-advocacy panel with appropriate expertise" listens to invited experts and formulates the statement based on the evidence presented. Since RCTs remain the most definitive evidence for treatment efficacy, they play a central role in CD deliberations and statements whenever evaluation of medical interventions is concerned. The CD statement is not intended to be a practice guideline and in particular, is specifically distanced from appearing as a mandate on health care by the NIH through the exclusion of federal employees from the panel. However, the statement is widely disseminated to the media, is typically submitted for publication in appropriate high-profile medical journals, and is disseminated to American Hospital Association directors of continuing medical education programs, to health maintenance organizations and preferred provider organizations, and federal health agencies (all prior statements are published on the CDP website).

Example: The NIH Consensus Development Program and Breast Cancer

A specific example of the activities and recommendations of the NIH Consensus Development Conference Program concerns therapy for breast cancer, for which conferences were held in 1979, 1980, 1985, 1990, and 2000. Through this process we can trace an evolution of therapy guidelines and examine how RCTs have influenced treatment standards.

In 1979, the first RCTs comparing total mastectomy (simple removal of the breast) to the standard radical mastectomy (a considerably more extensive and disfiguring procedure) had been completed, and the panel advocated the former as an acceptable alternative that should be more widely used. They also encouraged ongoing research into even less extensive procedures than total mastectomy. In 1980, the weight of evidence for chemotherapy was considered, with the recommendation that it be considered in cases where tumor cells had spread to the lymph nodes (node-positive). For node-negative patients, chemotherapy was not recommended, and for both types of patients, evidence for the benefit of hormonal therapy was insufficient for its recommendation. By 1985, sufficient evidence (from RCTs) had amassed so that chemotherapy was definitely recommended for younger node-positive patients and to be considered for postmenopausal women, where hormonal therapy was also supported. Node-negative patients were still considered generally not candidates for these interventions, due to a favorable prognosis without such treatments, but for some women these treatments should be considered, and further research was advocated. By 1990, several large RCTs had revealed significant disease reduction benefits for node-negative patients receiving chemotherapy or hormonal therapy, and so a cautious recommendation was made pending further follow-up to determine if mortality gains would be realized. Another major change in 1990 was the support of breast conservation surgery for removal of the primary tumor. In 2000, additional refinements to these recommendations were made, and a notable decision of the panel was to defer support of high-dose chemotherapy and the addition of a new class of drugs (taxanes) to standard chemotherapy until more definitive evidence of benefit was apparent (National Institutes of Health Consensus Development Panel 2001).

SHORTCOMINGS OF RCTS AS EVIDENCE FOR TREATMENT STANDARDS

In addition to flaws in essential RCT design features described earlier, there are some other ways in which RCTs may be limited with respect to providing evidence on which to base therapy standards.

Problems with Publication of Trial Findings

Underrepresentation of trials with negative findings, whether due to so-called publication bias or other reasons, can erode the credibility of RCTs as the basis for broader treatment policies. The term *publication bias* refers to the increased propensity for trials showing favorable effects for the new treatment to be published in high-profile journals, or in some cases to be published at all (Dickersin et al. 1987; Easterbrook and Berlin 1991). This phenomenon will have the effect of skewing evidence in favor of the new treatment. Publication bias is usually attributed to the medical review process, but can effectively be self-imposed when those conducting the trial lose enthusiasm and defer or avoid publication of results that they deem clinically uninteresting. However, negative trials with adequate statistical power are equally important in establishing treatment standards by ruling out avenues that have not been successful. Some high-profile trials with findings that are either negative or favor the control group (CAST, WHI, described earlier) are readily published because of the implications for patient care when the agents or procedures in question may already be in wide use outside of clinical trials.

A more serious form of publication bias and its consequent "filtering" of the body of RCT literature occurs when sponsors delay or impede the publication of findings, often by simply dropping resource commitments necessary to complete the trial. In one example discussed by DeMets (DeMets and Califf 2002), the Flovan International Randomized Survival Trial (FIRST) results showed significantly increased (rather than decreased as intended) mortality risk, but lack of support from the trial sponsor resulted in the trial steering committee's being left to publish an incomplete report of findings (DeMets and Califf 2002; Califf et al. 1997). Incidents of outright blockage of dissemination of trial findings (and legal action following publication) of a negative trial have also been documented (DeMets and Califf 2002b).

In most cases, responsibility for publication bias resides simply with investigators and journals. Analysis of recent time-to-publication of oncology trials after presentation at major oncology professional meetings found a correlation between negative findings and delay in publication (Krzyzanowska, Pintilie, and Tannock 2003). These authors note that failure to publish findings can be seen as an ethical breach of the agreement between investigators and participants at study initiation.

Generalizing Results to the Population at Large

Randomized controlled trials are often viewed as studies conducted exclusively in medical research settings that may have little resemblance to wider medical practice. Trials are often intentionally conducted in carefully defined patient cohorts, with the employment of numerous inclusion and exclusion criteria in order to reduce extraneous factors that may attenuate the treatment effect. While this practice is perfectly valid with respect to generating an unbiased assessment of the relative benefit of the treatment in the study cohort, the ability to generalize results to patients at large may be compromised. Even in trials of common diseases that enroll patients from different care settings, studies have demonstrated (a) underrepresentation of women and the elderly in large-scale heart disease trials (Lee et al. 2001); (b) underrepresentation of the elderly in oncology trials (Hutchins et al. 1999), a particularly ironic situation, since the majority of cancer patients are elderly in the typical sense of being over sixty-five years of age at diagnosis (Yancik and Ries 2000); and (c) underrepresentation of racial and ethnic minorities in RCTs for many diseases. Socioeconomic factors and care access, elitism on the part of the medical community, and cultural factors, some of which are promoted by historical cases of mistreatment, have contributed to this last deficiency (Gamble 1997).

Advocates of trials as a means to guide clinical practice argue that evidence from large trials still offers more sound information for reliable prediction of benefit for future treatment situations than do personal anecdotes (Califf and DeMets 2002). Studies of systemwide adoption of recommended practice changes brought about by clinical trials seem to bear this out (Allison et al. 2000; Chen et al. 1999), but they do not directly address whether certain patient subsets may be nonresponsive or experience unexpected negative consequences of new treatments discovered in RCTs with dissimilar patients.

DETERMINING THE IMPACT OF RCTS ON CLINICAL PRACTICE

Measuring Effectiveness: Outcomes Research

Outcomes research is a growing area in health-care evaluation. The National Library of Medicine describes outcome assessment (the listed term closest to *outcomes research*) as "research aimed at assessing the quality and effectiveness of health care as measured by the attainment of a specified end result or outcome. Measures include parameters such as improved health, lowered morbidity or mortality, and improvement of abnormal states (such as elevated blood pressure)" (National Library of Medicine, under "Medical subject headings"). With respect to disease treatment, this definition implies that outcomes research addresses questions beyond the demonstration of efficacy, which is narrowly defined as disease-specific response in a given evaluative setting (e.g., an RCT), and may encompass the study of: (a) dissemination and use of medical knowledge about treatments; (b) access to and delivery of those treatments and ancillary care in diverse health-care settings; (c) benefits and consequences of treatments using metrics that are alternative to the usual efficacy measures; and (d) the sum impact of these treatments on morbidity and mortality burden in the total patient community.

Adoption of Treatment Guidelines Arising from
NIH Consensus Conferences

The impact of CD conferences on medical practice has been the subject of a number of studies. Study types and the outcomes evaluated generally fall into two categories, the first measuring physician knowledge of CD statements and likelihood of adopting treatment strategies that are congruent with these guidelines (Ferguson 1993), and the second measuring changes in medical practice directly in temporal relation to the CD statements (Kosecoff et al. 1987; Lazovich et al. 1991; Sherman et al. 1992; Lomas et al. 1989). There have also been detailed studies and critiques of the CD program and its processes, as well as commentaries reflecting how the program is perceived by some in the medical community (Byar 1980). In general, results have been mixed, with several studies seeming to indicate that, while specific recommendations from the CD statement appear to be heeded, a trend of increased uptake after the conference is difficult to document. This situation suggests that the issue in question was already gaining wider acceptance (Sherman et al. 1992). Other studies do suggest a shift toward adoption of new treatment strategies that were advocated in CD statements. One concern that remains is limited awareness by physicians of the CD statements or other practice guidelines (Cabana et al. 1999; Ferguson 1993).

In 1988, a detailed study and critique of the process based on interviews and observation of the process identified several problematic elements of the program, including: (a) the lack of a well-defined process for choosing topics, questions, panelists, and speakers, potentially raising concerns about the relevance of topics and a well-rounded, unbiased consensus process; (b) reliance on expert testimony only, without concurrent independent literature review; (c) limited preparation time for nonexpert panelists from disciplines other than medicine and science; and (d) lack of broad coverage of societal, ethical, legal, and economic dimensions of the questions under study (Wortman, Vinokur, and Sechrest 1988). It should be noted that progress on at least some of these points has been made since the appearance of this study.

A Case Study of RCTs and Clinical Practice: Pediatric Oncology

One striking example of how clinical trials have changed medical practice (and in effect have become one and the same with it) is the case of pediatric oncology. Through networks of researchers and institutions supported by the National Cancer Institute's Cancer Cooperative Group program, RCTs have become the de facto standard of care, with patients readily being enrolled into clinical trials that have steadily built on prior incremental gains in earlier findings; and despite a lack of any one dramatic therapeutic advance, this incremental progress has resulted in a marked improvement in survival (see figure 6.1) (Lukens 1994; SEER Program (National Cancer Institute (U.S.), National Institutes of Health (U.S.), National Cancer Institute (U.S.), and Surveillance Program 2003). Over 70 percent of pediatric oncology patients are treated in clinical trials, and studies have shown that many pediatric oncologists largely see the trials as representing the best available treatment option for their patients (Joffe and Weeks 2002). An

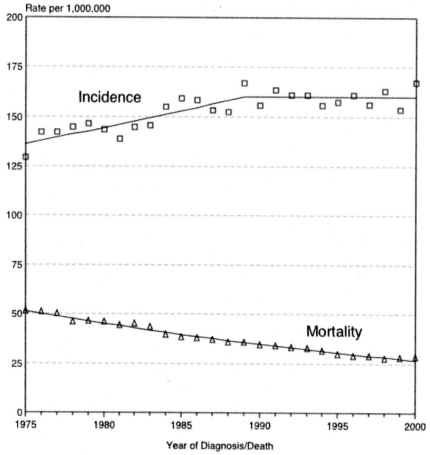

Figure 6.1.   Trends in U.S. Childhood Cancer Incidence and Mortality, 1975–2000

interesting contrast is the case of pediatric cardiology, where fewer than thirty trials have been conducted over the same period with a consequent lack of care standards (Califf and DeMets 2002).

CAN TRIALS BE DESIGNED TO BETTER INFLUENCE CARE POLICY?

Since the goal of RCTs is to discover new, more efficacious therapies that have applicability outside the specific clinical research setting, or to establish the relative worth of equally efficacious alternatives in terms of adverse effects, convenience, cost, or other considerations and thus similarly cause a shift to a new treatment regimen, we might consider how trials could be designed to be maximally influential on the target audience of practitioners. In this section, a number of ways in which this goal may be accomplished are discussed.

Decision Science and Trial Design

A trial design that naturally reflects the ways in which physicians and patients weight risk and benefit trade-offs would seem more likely to prompt adoption of the trial findings as valid and applicable. With this in mind, Parmar and colleagues (Stenning and Parmar 2002) have described a process by which physicians are queried as to their range of expectation in terms of the new versus standard treatment, and how large a difference between treatments would represent sufficient evidence for a change in practice. Similar approaches to elicitation of prior beliefs have been proposed in the context of Bayesian statistics applications to clinical trials (Spiegelhalter, Freedman, and Parmar 1994).

A particularly illustrative approach is the case of so-called equivalence trials, which seek to establish that two treatment approaches have equal efficacy. In reality (and statistically), *equivalence* means that there is an acceptably small difference between the treatments, so that treatment preference may then be based on other considerations such as toxicity, convenience, or cost. For example, in the United Kingdom, the standard treatment for localized testicular cancer is 30 gigavolts (g) of radiotherapy administered over a period of three weeks. An alternative being considered is a 20 g treatment course over a shorter time period; this would have less deleterious side effects but could lead to a small increase in relapse rate relative to the more extensive course. Physicians were surveyed to determine a range in the amount of increase in recurrence rates that would still lead them to consider the 20 g regimen as a reasonable risk given its benefits. They also indicated boundaries at which they would definitely choose 30 g or 20 g. This information was compiled and it was determined that the trial would need to be of sufficient size to rule out a difference of 3–4 percent between groups (e.g., for the study to show "equivalence," the observed difference must be smaller than this range). Without this information, one might conduct a trial in which the acceptable difference is too large for physicians to accept the alternative as reasonable, and thus the alternative would not be likely to be adopted. Alternatively, a trial to rule out a very small difference that physicians would consider inconsequential would be larger and more costly than necessary.

Incorporation of Secondary Measures and Endpoints

Prospective studies of secondary endpoints relevant to disease management and patient care may be embedded in the clinical trial protocol in order to answer a broader array of clinical questions. The rigorous collection of clinical and pathologic characteristics, demographic information, and treatment course history in clinical trials provides a high-quality environment for the study of quality of life, psychological effects, physical function, and other aspects of disease and its treatment. For example, quality of life (QOL) studies have become an integral component of most clinical trials in cancer. The scope of such studies is wide, including well-planned, hypothesis-driven assessments of how cancer treatment affects physical function, psychological well-being, sexuality, cognition, daily life activities and lifestyle, and other factors. These considerations are particularly relevant when the difference between treatments is minimal or absent, and thus treatment choice may depend essentially on these secondary endpoints.

Diversity in Enrollment

In 1993, the NIH Revitalization Act was signed into law; the law addressed a number of perceived problems with the federally funded research process. The new law included a mandate that clinical research include sufficient numbers of women and persons from traditionally underrepresented minority groups so that it could be assured that findings apply to these groups (National Institutes of Health 1994). This mandate initially raised considerable concern over its feasibility because, for example, a trial adequately powered to definitively determine efficacy in each minority group would be prohibitively large. However, researchers adapted to the spirit of the law and have since sought to improve the representativeness of RCT cohorts (Freedman et al. 1995). An increased racial/ethnic diversity of participants is desirable in clinical trials. More diverse participation will enhance justification for extrapolating from trial results to the population as a whole, ensure dissemination of quality care in accordance with current treatment guidelines, and provide the necessary data for continued investigations of the role of ethnic, social, and cultural factors in cancer prognosis and optimal treatment (Sung et al. 2003).

With respect to some diseases such as cancer, the demographic composition (with respect to whites, blacks, and Hispanics) of NCI-sponsored treatment clinical trials has in fact been found to be generally representative of the incident cancer burden in the population of adults and children (Tejeda et al. 1996; Bleyer et al. 1997; Ross et al. 1996). It has been argued by some that the clinical trial framework provides high-quality care that might otherwise not be obtained (Gelber and Goldhirsch 1988), and that participation by physicians in this research will itself standardize and improve treatment uniformity and quality, particularly with regard to surgical and staging procedures (Lukens 1994).

Trials Designed Specifically to Fill Gaps in Knowledge: Pragmatic Trials

One criticism of the present clinical research agenda is that practical questions of great interest to medical practitioners, payers, health policy planners, and patients often go unanswered (Tunis, Stryer, and Clancy 2003). The primary reason for this is that these stakeholders are not the driving force in the clinical trial enterprise, but rather those efforts and resources arise from the need to evaluate new interventions (drugs, devices, etc.) in the interest of obtaining approval for marketing. Consequently, technology assessments and overviews frequently identify gaps in knowledge, in the form of a lack of comparative studies of new versus older (and usually less costly) interventions, new interventions evaluated in diverse practice settings, or even any evidence of effectiveness of medical procedures or devices already in use.

Since these types of questions are of immediate interest to many stakeholders in health care, it would seem that RCTs focused on these problems would have great impact. Trials to address these questions have sometimes been called *practical trials* or *pragmatic trials*, having in common characteristics of relative simplicity of design, relevant endpoints that may include measures other than clinical efficacy, diverse enrollment with respect to both patients and types of participating centers, and comparison of agents or procedures that may already be in wide use. This last attribute often necessitates that the trial be funded by means other than pharmaceutical or medical device industry manufacturers, who may have little to gain or stand to incur loss from such trials. The NIH and the AHRQ have funded trials of this type, and the Veterans Administration (VA) Cooperative Groups Studies network has supported a number of landmark trials to answer practical care questions. However, more funding for infrastructure and operational costs of such trials is needed, as current resources are too limited to support this activity (Sung et al. 2003; Tunis, Stryer, and Clancy 2003). For example, the AHRQ and FDA jointly oversee the Center for Education and Research in Therapeutics (CERTS), which is charged with conducting studies for drugs and other therapies not being addressed by industry or NIH, but CERTS is not adequately funded to do more than identify questions in need of trials.

Some striking findings have arisen from trials conducted to address "practical" medical care questions. For example, a recent VA trial found that a nontherapeutic intervention was equally as effective as the standard surgical procedure for osteoarthritis of the knee (Moseley et al. 2002). This discovery prompted the Medicare program and the VA to reconsider support for this costly procedure. Trials in many other common conditions, including low-back pain, benign prostatic hypertrophy, hypertension, and depression have revealed important information about the relative worth of various intervention alternatives (Tunis, Stryer, and Clancy 2003).

SUMMARY AND CONCLUSIONS

Randomized controlled trials are among the most significant advances in medical research in recent times, and in a span of less than sixty years have revolutionized care for a large number of diseases. As biomedical technology and knowledge continue to advance at a record pace, this effort must grow and diversify to meet the need for objective, high-quality evidence regarding the merits of new interventions.

7

Linking Program Implementation and Effectiveness: Lessons from a Pooled Sample of Welfare-to-Work Experiments[1]

Howard S. Bloom, Carolyn J. Hill, and James A. Riccio

Over the past few decades, in large part due to the increased use of random assignment experiments, important advances have been made in building a convincing body of evidence about the effectiveness of social programs. Furthermore, researchers have greatly expanded the knowledge about program implementation—how social policies and program models operate in the real world. Meanwhile, much less has been learned about the relationship between implementation and effectiveness.

This disconnect is explained partly by the fact that implementation studies often do not include impact analyses. Thus, although these studies provide a wealth of information about leadership strategies, operating practices, and patterns of client involvement, they cannot determine how these factors affect client impacts.[2] The prevailing disconnect is also due to the fact that, although most random assignment impact studies include implementation analyses, they seldom have enough sites for a meaningful statistical analysis of how implementation and impacts are related. Thus, researchers can only speculate about which of the many implementation differences they observed caused the variation in impacts they documented.

The present chapter presents preliminary findings from a research synthesis study to help bridge this gap. The study pools data from a series of large-sample, multisite experiments of mandatory welfare-to-work programs conducted by MDRC during the past fifteen years. These experiments, which reflect the experiences of 69,399 sample members from fifty-nine locations in seven states, have the unusual (if not unique) virtue of including consistently measured indicators of program implementation for all sites.[3] Multisite experiments that measure program implementation and effects in a consistent manner offer a powerful way to "get inside the black box" of social programs to explore why programs perform as well—or as poorly—as they do (Greenberg, Meyer, and Wiseman 1994; Raudenbush and Liu 2000). And pooling data across such experiments is a promising way to obtain enough sites for a meaningful research synthesis.[4] However, in order to create opportunities for such a synthesis, researchers must build up an adequate supply of appropriate studies over time. Thus, in this chapter we try to illustrate why researchers and funders from different policy domains and program areas should consider developing long-term research agendas that use random assignment experiments with strong implementation studies and comparable measures and methods to accumulate knowledge about "what works best for whom."

In the following sections we discuss the theoretical and policy background for our research, and describe the programs, samples, data, and analytic framework upon which it is based.[5] Our findings illustrate the profound influence that implementation can have on the effectiveness of social programs.

DIMENSIONS OF IMPLEMENTATION

Policy makers, program administrators, program staff members, and researchers have debated for decades the influence of four sets of implementation-related factors on the effectiveness of welfare-to-work programs: (1) how programs are managed and what frontline practices they emphasize, (2) the kinds of activities that clients participate in, (3) the economic environment in which programs operate, and (4) the characteristics of clients whom they serve. Our analysis tests the following hypotheses that grow out of these debates.

Management Choices and Frontline Practice

Many experts contend that how frontline workers interact with clients and the social climate or institutional culture within which they interact can be powerful determinants of a program's success (Bane 1989; Behn 1991; and Mead 1983, 1986).[6] Yet, when it comes to which frontline practices work best, expert opinion often differs because of limited evidence. We examine the influence of several such debated practices.

Quick Employment

Emphasis on quick employment reflects how forcefully a program urges its clients to move quickly into jobs—even low-paying ones. Advocates of this approach believe that almost any job is a positive first step that can promote future advancement through the acquisition of work experience, job-related skills, and a track record of employment. Opponents believe that welfare recipients would do better by increasing their human capital through education and training so that they can qualify for better jobs before looking for work.

Programs can manifest these contrasting philosophies in many ways. For example, the prevailing philosophy can be evident in the initial activity that is encouraged or mandated: job search versus education or training. In addition, it can be reflected by how strongly job search activities stress rapid employment instead of holding out for a better job. Furthermore, it can be reflected by how long participants who are assigned to education or training are allowed to wait before looking for work. Therefore, efforts (or lack of efforts) to promote rapid employment can pervade staff interactions with clients regardless of the program activities to which the clients are assigned.[7] In examining this issue, several past random assignment experiments have found that counties with the largest employment impacts were places where, among other things, staff strongly encouraged quick client employment (Hamilton et al. 2001; Riccio, Friedlander, and Freedman 1994). Hence, there is some prior evidence on this issue.

Personalized Client Attention

A second practice that we examine is the extent to which frontline staff get to know their clients' personal situations, needs, and goals; arrange services that support these needs and goals; continue to work with clients over time to assure their success; and adjust client service plans to meet the clients' changing situations. Many managers believe that such a personalized approach is more effective than one in which clients are handled in a narrowly prescribed way (where "one size fits all"). These managers emphasize that "getting close to the customer" is key to properly addressing clients' aspirations and situations. Others see scarce program resources and less payoff from this investment of time. Although this issue has not been widely studied, one past random assignment experiment casts doubt on the benefits of increased personalized attention (Riccio and Orenstein 1996).

Closeness of Client Monitoring

Monitoring clients' participation in mandatory welfare-to-work programs is believed by many to be important for enforcing participation requirements and for helping clients to get the most from a program. Careful monitoring can help staff learn whether clients are showing up for their assigned activities and whether they are progressing in them. Based on what staff learn, they may start formal enforcement proceedings if participation obligations are being ignored; initiate assistance with personal problems or circumstances that might be interfering with clients' progress; or consider alternative client services and activities.[8] Thus, monitoring may contribute in various ways to a program's performance. However, close monitoring can be difficult for programs where employment-related activities occur at many different institutions or locations, and this can be especially problematic when tracking systems are deficient (Freedman et al. 2002; Riccio, Friedlander, and Freedman 1994; Wiseman 1987).

Consistency of Staff Views

Program performance may suffer when staff members are divided— whether due to confusion or disagreement—over what a program should be doing or how something should be done. Thus, it is frequently hypothesized that managers can improve program performance by focusing staff efforts on a common purpose and instilling in them a strong organizational culture (Behn 1991; Miller 1992; Nathan 1993).

Size of Staff Caseload

It is often argued that large caseloads prevent program staff members from spending enough time with their clients to be effective (Gueron and Pauly 1991). The only direct evidence on this issue is from one small-scale experiment (Riccio, Friedlander, and Freedman 1994). It compared client outcomes for a standard caseload, averaging ninety-seven clients per worker, and a reduced caseload, averaging fifty-three clients per worker. No differences were found.

Program Activities

The three main types of job-related program activities tested here are job search assistance, basic education, and vocational training. The relative effectiveness of these activities has been debated for many years as part of a broader philosophical controversy over how best to promote economic self-sufficiency for welfare recipients.

Job search assistance has been a staple of welfare-to-work programs since their inception. However, during the past two decades, federal and state governments have begun to invest more heavily in basic reading and math classes, preparation for the General Educational Development (GED) degree, and courses in English as a Second Language (ESL). To a lesser extent, they also have begun to invest more in vocational training.

Other activities provided by some welfare-to-work programs include unpaid work experience positions through which clients work at public or not-for-profit jobs in exchange for their welfare grants ("workfare"), and enrollment in four-year colleges or associate's degree programs at community colleges. Neither of these activities is highly prevalent, however.

Findings from an early welfare-to-work experiment in California cast doubt on the efficacy of immediately assigning welfare recipients with especially weak educational backgrounds to basic education classes (Freedman et al. 1996; Riccio, Friedlander, and Freedman 1994).[9] Partly in response to this finding, a later six-state welfare-to-work experiment directly compared (in three of its sites) a labor force attachment approach (which emphasized job search first) to a human capital development approach (which emphasized education and training first) (Hamilton 2002; Hamilton et al. 2001). This study did not find the anticipated advantage of human capital development over five years of follow-up.[10] However, both prior studies found that programs with the largest earnings impacts were ones that took a mixed approach, allowing clients to choose education and training or job search as their initial activity.

Local Economic Conditions

That local economic conditions can affect the performance of welfare-to-work programs seems almost self-evident. Nevertheless, there are two competing views about the likely direction of this effect. One view is that program performance will be better when unemployment rates are lower because low unemployment rates imply more jobs for clients. Thus, if a program can motivate and prepare clients for these jobs, it can increase their employment appreciably.

An opposing view is that programs perform less well when unemployment rates are lower because it is easier for welfare recipients to find jobs without extra help. Thus, even though a program may have a high placement rate, it might be producing little success beyond what would have been achieved in its absence. Furthermore, welfare recipients who are not working when unemployment rates are low may be especially hard to employ, thus making it particularly difficult for programs to increase employment for them.

The empirical evidence on this issue is limited because few past studies have been able to compare site-level impact estimates from random assignment experiments to measures of local economic conditions. An exception is Heinrich (2002), who found a negative but statistically insignificant relationship between the local unemployment rate and program impacts in JTPA. Other attempts to measure the relationship between local economic environment and site impacts (for example, Riccio and Orenstein 1996) are based on small numbers of sites; this limits the studies' ability to control for other local differences.

Client Characteristics

Programs that serve different types of clients may have more or less success not because of what they do, but, rather, because of whom they are trying to serve. Thus, understanding variation in program effectiveness requires taking into account cross-program variation in client characteristics that reflect the clients' employment potential and employment barriers.[11] The most widely used indicators of this client characteristic are formal education, prior employment experience, and past welfare receipt. Formal education and prior employment experience represent individual human capital; past welfare receipt predicts future reliance on welfare. Other indicators include race and ethnicity (to reflect potential labor market discrimination), number and age of children (to reflect alternative demands on clients' time), and physical and mental health status (to reflect clients' abilities to participate in the labor market).

The limited research that exists on this issue suggests that there is no simple relationship between program impacts and client characteristics. Some evidence indicates that many welfare-to-work programs of the mid-1980s and 1990s were effective with a broad range of clients (Michalopoulos, Schwartz, and Adams-Ciardullo 2001). At the same time, some subgroups fared much better than others in certain programs. These findings suggest that it is important to incorporate client characteristics into any analysis of program effectiveness.

PROGRAMS, SAMPLES, AND DATA

Our analysis is based on three MDRC random assignment evaluations of mandatory welfare-to-work programs: the Greater Avenues for Independence (GAIN) program conducted in twenty-two local offices in six California counties (Riccio and Friedlander 1992), Project Independence (PI) conducted in ten local offices in nine Florida counties (Kemple and Haimson 1994), and the National Evaluation of Welfare-to-Work Strategies (NEWWS) conducted in twenty-seven local offices in ten counties in California, Georgia, Michigan, Ohio, Oklahoma, and Oregon (Hamilton 2002; Hamilton et al. 2001). These initiatives were operated as each state's version of the federal Job Opportunities and Basic Skills Training (JOBS) program funded by the Family Support Act of 1988.

The programs studied through GAIN, PI, and NEWWS included varying mixes of work-promoting activities such as job search assistance, basic education, and vocational training. They also provided clients with support services such as child care and transportation. Clients were assigned to local staff members who arranged for them to attend program activities, helped them gain access to support services, and monitored their participation and progress. Participation in the programs was mandatory, and failure to attend assigned activities without "good cause" could result in reduction of a family's welfare grant. The original reports from these evaluations document in detail how programs were implemented and evaluated.

Each evaluation measured program impacts on client employment, earnings, and welfare receipt by comparing post-random-assignment outcomes for individuals randomly assigned to the program with those for individuals randomly assigned to a control group. Program group members were required to enroll in the program. Control group members were exempted from these requirements and excluded from program activities and services. However, they could seek assistance from other sources.

By randomly determining which sample members were assigned to the program and which were assigned to control status, each evaluation created two groups that in large samples are comparable in all ways.[12] Hence future outcomes for the control group provide valid indicators of what these outcomes would have been for the program group without the program. In other words, they identify the program group counterfactual. The difference between the actual experience of program group members and their counterfactual is a valid measure of the impact of the program (that is, how the program changed the outcome).

For the present study we pooled comparable data from these three evaluations, yielding a sample of 69,399 program and control group members from 59 local welfare-to-work offices. Although some of the original sample members were men, we focus only on female single parents in order to create a homogeneous sample. This sample includes 46,977 women from 27 local NEWWS offices, 18,126 women from 22 local GAIN offices, and 4,296 women from 10 local PI offices. Sample members per local office range from 177 to 4,418 and average 1,176.

Intake forms provided information on all program and control group members' socioeconomic backgrounds, which we used to measure client characteristics.

Administrative records from state unemployment insurance (UI) agencies provided data on all program and control group members' quarterly earnings during the first two years after random assignment, which we used to measure client outcomes.

Staff surveys of 1,225 caseworkers and 194 supervisors from local program offices provided data on how programs were run, which we used to measure their implementation. The number of respondents per office ranged from 1 to 83 caseworkers and from 0 to 14 supervisors, and averaged 21 and 3 per office, respectively. Completion rates exceeded 90 percent for most offices.

Follow-up surveys of a random subsample of 15,235 program and control group members provided data that we used to measure participation in employment-related activities sponsored by the program or other local organizations. Subsamples ranged from 27 to 2,159 individuals per office and averaged 258. Response rates ranged from 70 to 93 percent across counties in the studies.

County-level statistics on unemployment rates from the U.S. Bureau of Labor Statistics and California Employment Development Department were used to measure the local economic environment.

VARIATION IN PROGRAM EFFECTS

The dependent variable—the measure of local program effectiveness—is the estimated impact on sample members' mean total earnings (measured in constant 1996 dollars) for the first two years after random assignment.[13] The average program increased clients' earnings by $879 during their two-year follow-up period, or by 18 percent of what these earnings would have been otherwise. This is a sizable impact relative to those documented for other welfare-to-work programs (Gueron and Pauly 1991).

More importantly for the present analysis, the variation across offices in unconditional[14] impact estimates is large (see figure 7.1), ranging from −$1,412 to $4,217. Of the office-level impact estimates, 13 are negative, although not statistically significant at conventional levels. In contrast, 24 of the positive impact estimates are statistically significant, and many are quite large. Hence, the variation in impact estimates across local offices is highly statistically significant (beyond the 0.001 level).

Overall, these results show that there is plenty of impact variation to model, and that this variation reflects true differences in program impacts, not just estimation error.[15] The magnitude of the variation also underscores the importance from a policy perspective of trying to account for why some offices performed so much better than others.

MULTILEVEL MODELS USED TO EXPLAIN VARIATION IN EXPERIMENTAL IMPACT FINDINGS

To explore what created this variation in effects, we attempt to isolate the independent influences on it of the implementation factors described above. This requires accounting for the multilevel structure of the data in which sample members (level 1) are grouped by local program office (level 2). To do so we estimate a two-level hierarchical model (Raudenbush and Bryk 2002).[16] Level 1 of the model comprises a linear regression for individual sample members; this serves two purposes. It indicates how client characteristics influence program impacts; this indication is of direct substantive interest. And it produces estimates of conditional impacts for each program office (holding client characteristics constant), which is the main dependent variable for level 2.

Three linear regressions for local program offices comprise level 2 of the model. The first regression represents how conditional program effects depend on program implementation, activities, and environment. The parameters of this regression are our core findings. The second regression represents how the conditional mean control group outcome for each office (holding client characteristics constant) varies with the local economic environment. This provides an estimate of the counterfactual for each office. The third regression (which is an artifact of how the original experiments were conducted) accounts for the fact that several sites changed the ratio of their program and control groups over time.[17]

By estimating these relationships as a two-level model, we simultaneously determine all parameters at both levels, and each parameter represents the influence of a single factor holding constant the others.[18] For example, estimates of the influence of clients' prior education on program effectiveness hold constant all other client characteristics in level 1 plus all factors in level 2. Likewise, estimates of the influence of a particular feature

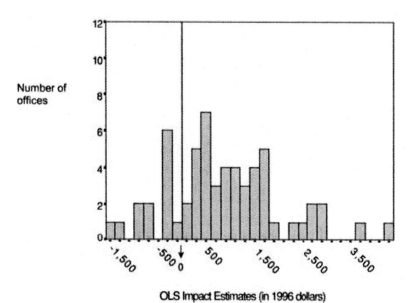

OLS Impact Estimates (in 1996 dollars)

Figure 7.1.   The Distribution of Unconditional Office-Level Impact Estimates

of program implementation hold constant all other factors in level 2 plus all client characteristics in level 1. Our model was specified as follows.
Level 1, for sample members:

$$Y_{ji} = \alpha_j + \beta_j P_{ji} + \sum_k \delta_k CC_{kji} + \sum_k \gamma_k CC_{kji} P_{ji} + \kappa_j RA_{ji} + \varepsilon_{ji}$$

$$(Eq.\ 1)$$

where:

Y_{ji} = the outcome measure for each sample member,

P_{ji} = a zero/one program group indicator for each sample member,

CC_{kji} = client characteristic k for each sample member (grand mean centered),[19]

RA_{ji} = a zero/one random assignment cohort indicator for each sample member,

α_j = the conditional control group mean outcome (counterfactual) for each local office,

β_j = the conditional program impact for each local office,

δ_k = the effect of client characteristic k on the control group mean outcome,

γ_k = the effect of client characteristic k on the program impact,

κ_j = a random assignment cohort coefficient (which has no substantive meaning) for each office,

ε_{ji} = a random component of the outcome for each sample member.

Level 2, for local offices:

$$\beta_j = \beta_0 + \sum_m \pi_m PI_{mj} + \sum_n \phi_n PA_{nj} + \psi EE_j + \mu_j$$

$$(Eq.\ 2)$$

$$\alpha_j = \alpha_0 + \lambda EE_j + \nu_j$$

$$(Eq.\ 3)$$

$$\kappa_j = \kappa_0 + \eta_j$$

$$(Eq.\ 4)$$

where:

PI_{mj} = program implementation feature m for each office (grand mean centered),

PA_{nj} = program activity n for each office (grand mean centered),

EE_j = economic environment for each office (grand mean centered),

β_0 = the grand mean impact,

π_m = the effect of program implementation feature m on program impacts,

ϕ_n = the effect of program activity n on program impacts,

ψ = the effect of economic environment on program impacts,

μ_j = a random component of program impacts for each office, and

α_0 = the grand mean control group earnings,

λ = the effect of economic environment on control group earnings,

v_j = a random component of control group mean earnings for each office, and

κ_0 = the grand mean random assignment cohort coefficient, and

η_j = a random component of the cohort coefficient for each office.

CONSTRUCTION AND ASSESSMENT OF THE IMPLEMENTATION MEASURES

The primary independent variables for each local office are measures of program implementation constructed from average staff survey responses.[20] Hence these measures reflect the perceptions of frontline workers. Survey questions were based on hypotheses about what works, drawn from the research literature and experience in the field. The first staff survey (for GAIN) was developed by MDRC and used by Riccio and Hasenfeld (1996) and Riccio and Orenstein (1996) to explore operational correlates of program impacts. This analysis was complemented by in-depth fieldwork to document local practices in order to better understand what was happening on the ground. Later surveys (for PI and NEWWS) evolved to reflect changing views about best practices. However, a common core of questions on issues that remain in the forefront of programmatic discussions was maintained. It is from these questions that we constructed our six measures of program implementation. Table 7.1 lists the questions used to do so.

Types of Measures

Program Practices

Three measures of program practices are multiquestion scales that were standardized to have mean values of zero and standard deviations of one across offices. A first measure—emphasis on quick job entry for clients—reflects the employment message conveyed to clients at each office—how much they were encouraged to take a job quickly, or to be more selective and wait for a better job or pursue education and training to improve their future prospects. A second measure—emphasis on personalized client attention—reflects the emphasis placed by each office on gaining in-depth understanding of clients' personal histories and circumstances to better accommodate their individual needs and preferences when making program

Table 7.1.   Staff Survey Questions for Scales of Program Implementation

Scale and Questions[a]

Emphasis on quick job entry for clients
- Does your unit emphasize helping clients build basic skills, or moving them quickly into jobs?
- Should your unit emphasize helping clients build basic skills, or moving them quickly into jobs?
- What would be your personal advice to a client who can either take a low-skill, low-paying job OR stay on welfare and wait for a better opportunity?
- What advice would your supervisor want you to give to such a client?

Emphasis on personalized client attention
- Does your program emphasize the quality of its services more than the number of clients it serves?
- During intake, does your unit spend enough time with clients?
- During intake, do staff make an effort to learn about clients' family problems?
- During intake, do staff make an effort to learn about clients' goals and motivation to work?
- How well is your program tailoring services to clients' needs?

Closeness of client monitoring
- How closely are staff monitoring clients?
- If a client has been assigned to adult basic education but has not attended, how soon would staff find out?
- If a client has been assigned to vocational education but has not attended, how soon would staff find out?
- How closely is your agency monitoring whether clients quit or lose part-time jobs?
- Once your agency learns a client lost a part-time job, how soon would she be assigned to another activity?

Staff caseload size
- How many clients are on your caseload today?

[a] The questions in this table paraphrase each staff survey question. Response categories generally took the form of a 5-point or 7-point Likert scale.

assignments. A third measure—closeness of client monitoring—reflects how closely staff at each office tracked client participation in assigned activities to keep abreast of their progress, their changing needs, and their involvement in the program.

A fourth measure of program practices—staff caseload size—reflects the average number of clients for whom each frontline staff member was responsible. This measure ranged across offices from 70 to 367 clients per staff member and averaged 136.

A fifth measure of program practice—staff disagreement—indicates the variability within each office of frontline staff responses to the first three sets of questions, while a sixth measure—frontline staff and supervisor disagreement—indicates the difference between average frontline staff and supervisor answers to these questions. Hence, these final two measures (which also were standardized to have means of zero and standard deviations of one) reflect the degree to which each office had a common vision of its program.

Participation in Activities

The next set of office-level independent variables concerns participation in employment-related activities. In constructing these measures, we take into account the fact that control group members often can obtain similar services in their communities without any help from the welfare-to-work program that is being evaluated (Gueron and Pauly 1991). Differences in program and control group participation rates are estimated for the most common activities: job search assistance, basic education, and vocational training.[21] Job search assistance includes self-directed individual job search and participation in group-focused job clubs. Basic education includes adult education classes, GED preparation, and ESL courses. Vocational training includes classroom training in basic occupational skills along with several less commonly used activities: on-the-job training, unpaid work experience, and postsecondary education or training. Differences in client participation rates, expressed in percentage points, represent the degree to which local programs increased exposure to each type of activity. These measures were constructed from follow-up survey data obtained roughly two years after random assignment for a random subsample of clients from each office. Appendix table 7.1a shows descriptive statistics for these estimated differences.

Economic Environment

The final office-level independent variable, representing the economic environment for each local office, was the average county unemployment rate during the client follow-up period for the office. Because sample enrollment often took several years at an office, the office's unemployment rate is an average of different periods for different sample members.

Client Characteristics

Independent variables for sample members include their education, number of children, age, race/ethnicity, recent past welfare receipt, and recent past earnings. These measures were constructed from data recorded on sample intake forms. Appendix table 7.2a shows descriptive statistics for these characteristics for the full sample, as well as across the fifty-nine offices.

Variability, Reliability, and Validity

Before using the preceding independent variables, we assessed them in terms of three requirements for a good measure: variability, reliability, and validity. Variability in a measure is required in order to determine its relationship with program impacts. For example, only if implementation varies across offices can one determine how impacts vary with implementation. Fortunately, the variation in eight of our ten office-level measures is statistically significant at beyond the 0.001 level (Bloom, Hill, and Riccio 2001, 109). The significance of variation for our staff disagreement measure could not be determined, and that for our staff/supervisor disagreement measure is low.[22] Nevertheless, both measures were maintained because of their conceptual importance.

A reliable measure has a high signal-to-noise ratio. Thus variation in its values reflects systematic differences in the subjects being observed, not just random error. This is necessary in order for an independent variable to obtain precise and unbiased estimates of its relationship to a dependent variable.[23] An unreliable measure of program implementation would produce an imprecise and distorted view of the true relationship between implementation and impacts.

Our multiquestion implementation measures—emphasis on quick job entry, emphasis on personalized attention, and closeness of monitoring—have two separate dimensions of reliability. One dimension, interquestion reliability (often called interitem reliability), reflects the consistency of answers to different questions used to construct each scale. High interquestion reliability refers to a scale whose component questions are highly correlated. The second dimension, interrespondent reliability, reflects the consistency of responses from different staff members at each office. High interrespondent reliability refers to a scale whose values for different staff members at the same office are highly correlated. Fortunately, our measures are reliable in both regards, with interquestion reliability coefficients between 0.76 and 0.84 and interrespondent reliability coefficients between 0.76 and 0.83.[24]

A valid measure is one that represents what it is intended to represent. Thus systematic variation in its values reflects true variation in its intended construct. This is necessary for an independent variable to obtain unbiased estimates of its relationship to a dependent variable. Thus an invalid measure of program implementation would produce a misleading view of the relationship between implementation and impacts.

Two types of validity were considered when assessing office-level independent variables: face validity and construct validity. Face validity is the degree to which the survey questions used for each independent variable appear, on their face, to convey the meaning that the variable is intended to convey. In other words, the components of the variable must accord with common sense. We believe that our variables meet this standard. Moreover, findings from the field research conducted across program offices for the original evaluations also support the face validity of the staff survey measures (Bloom, Hill, and Riccio 2001).

Construct validity asks whether the measures correlate with one another in ways that would be expected for the office-level constructs they are supposed to represent. We find this to be the case.[25] For example, program emphasis on quick job entry is positively correlated with increased participation in job search assistance and negatively correlated with increased participation in basic education or vocational training. In addition, program emphasis on personalized client attention and closeness of client monitoring are positively correlated with each other and negatively correlated with average staff caseload size. Furthermore, local unemployment rates are negatively correlated with average control group earnings.

Thus it was possible to estimate our model with an office-level dependent variable that had substantial variation and a series of office-level independent variables that were variable, reliable, and valid.

FINDINGS

Table 7.2 presents estimates of how program implementation, activities, and environment affect program impacts. The regression coefficients in column 1 indicate the change in program impacts per unit change in each variable listed, holding constant all others in the model. The partially standardized regression coefficients in column 2 indicate the change in program impacts per standard deviation change in each variable, holding constant all of the others.[26] Note that the unstandardized and standardized regression coefficients are the same for some of our program implementation scales because these scales were defined to have a standard deviation equal to one. The p-values in column 3 of the table indicate the statistical significance of each coefficient estimate and the standard errors in column 4 indicate their precision. These findings indicate the following important points.

A Strong Employment Message Is a Powerful Medium

The emphasis placed by programs on quick client employment has by far the largest, most statistically significant, and most robust effect on program impacts of all that we observed. Both the unstandardized and standardized coefficients for this multiquestion survey scale indicate that when the coefficient

Table 7.2.   The Effects of Program Implementation, Activities, and Environment on Program Impacts

Program Characteristic	Regression Coefficient	Partially Standardized Regression Coefficient	Statistical Significance (p-value)	Standard Error
Program Implementation				
Emphasis on quick job entry	$720***	$720***	2×10^{-6}	$134
Emphasis on personalized service	428***	428***	0.0002	107
Closeness of monitoring	−197	−197	0.110	121
Staff caseload size	−4***	−268***	0.003	1
Staff disagreement	124	124	0.141	83
Staff/supervisor disagreement	−159 *	−159*	0.102	96
Program Activities				
Basic education	−16**	− 208**	0.017	6
Job search assistance	1	12	0.899	9
Vocational training	7	71	0.503	11
Economic Environment				
Unemployment rate	−94***	−291***	0.004	30

Regression coefficients are reported in 1996 dollars per unit change in each independent variable. Partially standardized regression coefficients are reported in 1996 dollars per standard deviation change in each independent variable. These coefficients are estimated simultaneously with those reported in table 7.3. The grand mean impact is $879 or 18 percent of the counterfactual. Statistical significance is indicated by * for the 0.10 level, ** for the 0.05 level, and *** for the 0.01 level.

increases by one unit (which by definition equals one standard deviation of its distribution across local offices), program impacts increase by $720, other things being equal. To place this in perspective, recall that the grand mean program impact is $879. This is the estimated impact when all variables in the model are at their mean values. If the quick employment scale increases by one unit and all other variables remain constant, the estimated program impact increases to $1,599. In percentage terms this represents an increase from 18 percent of the average counterfactual to 33 percent.[27] The third column in the table indicates that the *p*-value for the quick client employment coefficient estimate equals 2×10^{-6}, which is well beyond conventional levels of statistical significance.

In addition, sensitivity tests demonstrate that this finding is highly robust to a wide range of variation regarding which program offices are included in the analysis.[28] For example, the finding did not change materially when as many as ten local offices with the most extreme program impacts (the dependent variable) or the most extreme emphases on quick employment (the independent variable) were eliminated from the analysis. Hence the finding does not appear to be confined to a small group of sites.

Further sensitivity tests were conducted to assess the extent to which the finding reflects only differences in the overarching programs examined (GAIN, PI, and NEWWS), or the state programs in the sample instead of variation across local offices within these larger aggregates.[29] However, even when these sources of variation are removed, the basic finding stays the same.

Getting Close to the Client Counts

Findings for personalized client attention are also striking, statistically significant, and robust. The unstandardized and standardized regression coefficients for this variable indicate that increasing it by one unit (one standard deviation of its distribution across offices) increases program impacts by $428, other things being equal. Thus if all variables in the model are at their mean value and the personalized attention scale is increased by one unit, the estimated program impact will increase from $879 to $1,307, or from 18 percent to 27 percent of the average counterfactual. The p-value for the coefficients is 0.0002, which indicates that they are highly statistically significant. In addition, sensitivity tests demonstrate that this finding is robust to variations in sample composition and whether or not cross-program or cross-state variation is included in the analysis. Hence the finding strongly suggests that personalized attention can make a big difference for clients above and beyond whatever services they receive and above and beyond other features of a program and its environment.

Monitoring Alone Is Not Enough

As noted earlier, knowing in a timely fashion how clients are progressing in their assigned program activities is presumably essential if frontline staff are to provide helpful case management or enforce participation mandates. It is therefore surprising that we find that offices that more closely monitor clients have smaller effects, other things being equal. Specifically, the unstandardized and standardized regression coefficients for this variable in table 7.2 indicate that increasing monitoring by one unit (a standard deviation) reduces program impacts by $197. However, these coefficients are not quite statistically significant ($p = 0.110$) and are not robust to sensitivity tests.

When interpreting this finding, note that the monitoring measure we use focuses on the timeliness of staff knowledge about client participation and progress. It does not focus on efforts to enforce compliance or provide assistance. Thus local offices that took a very tough stance or a very lenient stance toward enforcement could have rated high on this scale. Perhaps then what really matters is not just staff awareness of client behavior, but what staff members do with this information.

Large Caseloads Can Produce Small Impacts

Staff members' client caseload has a large and statistically significant negative effect on program impacts. The regression coefficient for this variable indicates that office impacts decline by $4 per additional client per caseworker, other things being equal. And its *p*-value of 0.003 is highly statistically significant. It is more helpful, however, to view this finding through the lens of a partially standardized regression coefficient. This parameter implies that increasing caseload size by one standard deviation of its distribution across offices (67 clients) reduces program impacts by $268, which is substantial.

Sensitivity tests indicate that this finding is robust to variations in the mix of local offices included. Thus it is pervasive and not just confined to a few unusual sites. However, the finding is sensitive to controlling for the evaluation in which sample members were originally involved. Close inspection of this result does not suggest a clear interpretation for it, however.[30]

Although consistent with conventional wisdom, our finding that increased caseload reduces program impacts conflicts with prior results from the Riverside GAIN caseload experiment (Riccio, Friedlander, and Freedman 1994), which found no difference in earnings impacts between sample members randomly assigned to staff with a standard caseload (averaging 97 clients per caseworker) versus those assigned to staff with a reduced caseload (averaging 53 clients per caseworker). However, our analysis examines caseloads that typically are much larger and vary much more than those for Riverside GAIN. The mean caseload size for a program office in the present study is 136 and its standard deviation across offices is 67. Thus, plus-or-minus one standard deviation from the mean spans a range from 69 clients per caseworker to 203 clients per caseworker. It therefore stands to reason that program impacts will erode substantially when caseloads begin to approach the higher end of this range, where staff may have very little time to devote to each client.

The Importance of Consistency in Staff Views Is Ambiguous

Findings are mixed for our two final measures of implementation—staff-versus-staff and staff-versus-supervisor disagreement about how to provide client services. The regression coefficient for staff-versus-supervisor disagreement is statistically significant (*p* = 0.102) and indicates that program impacts decline by $159 as this form of disagreement increases by one standard deviation, other things being equal. This is what we hypothesized.

However, the regression coefficient for staff-versus-staff disagreement is not statistically significant and thus cannot be distinguished from random error. Therefore, on balance it is not clear whether these findings support or challenge the widely held organizational imperative that managers should instill a common sense of mission and method among their staff.

Increasing Basic Education Reduces Short-Run Effects

Findings in table 7.2 indicate that programs that increase client use of basic education produce smaller-than-average effects on short-run earnings gains. The regression coefficient for this variable is negative and statistically significant ($p = 0.017$). It implies that program impacts decline by $16 for each one-point increase in the program-induced percentage of clients who receive basic education, other things being equal. The partially standardized regression coefficient indicates that program impacts decline by $208 when the program-induced percentage of clients who receive basic education increases by one standard deviation (13 percentage points).

Although this short-run effect for basic education is consistent with the original findings from the GAIN and NEWWS evaluations (Hamilton 2002; Riccio, Friedlander, and Freedman 1994), it is not clear why vocational training does not also depress short-run impacts, because it too imposes an opportunity cost of time required in the classroom that might have been spent producing earnings in the workplace. However, basic education often does not have a clear employment focus or a direct connection to the world of work, whereas vocational training usually has both of these features. In addition, program clients are often required to attend basic education as an initial activity. For such persons basic education might be less effective than for others who choose this option for themselves.[31]

At the same time, it is important to recall that the local programs found most effective by the original GAIN and NEWWS studies included basic education in their mix of client activities. Thus it may be that a more extreme emphasis on mandatory immediate basic education may be particularly detrimental but that in moderation and on a voluntary basis this activity might be effective.[32]

Job Search Activities Alone Do Not Assure Success, and the Effect of Vocational Training Is Unclear

Given the central role that job search has had in many past successful programs, it is noteworthy that its coefficient in our model is nearly zero and is not statistically significant. However, this finding does not necessarily mean that job search is unimportant for program success, nor that some programs could operate just as effectively without it. Instead it might be the case that the particular kinds of messages and assistance that get conveyed to clients within job search activities may determine whether those activities are effective. For example, job search assistance may be an important vehicle for operationalizing a quick employment message for clients; but holding constant this message, job search assistance may have little or no impact.

It should also be noted that vocational training did not have a statistically significant influence on program effectiveness, and although its regression coefficient was positive, it was much smaller than that for basic education. Thus, more or less use of this activity did not seem to influence program effectiveness appreciably. Like the finding for job search, it is possible that the finding for vocational training reflects that the specific employment-related activity used by a program matters less than the way it is used. And perhaps what most distinguishes job search and vocational training from basic education is that the first two are directly related to employment, whereas the third is not.

It's Hard to Raise Earnings When Jobs Are Scarce

The regression coefficient for the unemployment rate in table 7.2 is highly statistically significant ($p = 0.004$) and implies that a 1 percentage point increase in the unemployment rate reduces program impacts by $94, other things being equal. The partially standardized regression coefficient indicates that an increase of one standard deviation in the unemployment rate (3.1 percentage points) will reduce program impacts by $291. This sizable estimated decline was robust to sensitivity tests.

Thus it appears that other things being equal, the performance of welfare-to-work programs declines when unemployment rates rise and jobs for clients become harder to find. This result has particular relevance for setting performance standards in the current depressed economic climate.

Constellations of Program Characteristics Can Really Count

Perhaps the most useful way to apply the findings in table 7.2 is to use them to project the likely effectiveness (impacts) of welfare-to-work programs with different constellations of approaches to serving clients. Consider the following examples:

Approach #1: Employment focus with close direction of program staff and clients

- Staff encourage clients to get jobs quickly.
- Staff support this strategy through personal client attention.
- Staff monitor client progress closely.
- Staff share this vision with each other.
- Staff share this vision with their supervisors.

Approach #2: Laissez-faire management of staff and clients

- Client-to-staff ratios are very high.
- Clients do not receive personal attention.
- Client progress is not monitored closely.
- Staff do not share a common vision with each other.
- Staff do not share a common vision with their supervisors.

The preceding examples involve program features that managers can influence. Hence, projecting the likely impacts of each example can help illustrate how managers might improve program performance.

For example, if each factor listed for approach 1 were one standard deviation from its mean value and all other factors in the model were at their mean value, the findings in table 7.2 suggest that approach 1 would increase client earnings by $986 more than would the average program in the present sample. Hence, approach 1 would increase client earnings by $1,865 or 38 percent of the mean counterfactual. (Note that this finding does not account for potential nonlinearities such as interaction effects or threshold effects, which we plan to explore in future work.)

If each factor listed for approach 2 were one standard deviation from its mean value and all other factors in the model were at their mean value, the findings in table 7.2 suggest that approach 2 would reduce impacts by $534 compared to the average program in the present sample. Hence, approach 2 would increase client earnings by only $345 or 7 percent.

Now compare the projected effectiveness of the two examples. Approach 1 would increase client earnings by $1,865 or 38 percent whereas approach 2 would increase client earnings by only $345 or 7 percent. These projections suggest that differences in program implementation can produce important differences in program effectiveness even with the same types of clients, the same mix of program activities, and the same economic conditions.

The Types of People Served Have Some—but Limited—Consequences for Program Performance

Table 7.3 indicates how program impacts vary with each client characteristic in our model, holding constant all other client and program characteristics. These findings are estimates of regression coefficients for equation 1.

Because client characteristics are defined as distinct categories and represented in the model by zero or one indicator variables, it is necessary to report only the regression coefficient for each category plus its p-value and standard error. (Partially standardized regression coefficients do not add useful information.) These coefficients represent the regression-adjusted difference in mean program impacts for a sample member with the specified characteristic and a sample member in the omitted category for that characteristic, other things being equal.

For example, the regression coefficient of $653 for clients with a high school diploma or GED at random assignment (in the first row of the table) implies that the impact for sample members with this credential is $653 greater than the impact for clients without it, other things being equal. This finding is highly statistically significant ($p = 0.001$). It implies that, on average, if programs differed only in terms of the proportion of their clients having a high school credential, those serving a higher proportion of such people would have larger impacts than those serving a smaller proportion.

Table 7.3.   The Relationships between Client Characteristics and Program Impacts

	Regression Coefficient	Statistical Significance (p-value)	Standard Error
Was a high school graduate or had a GED	$653***	0.001	$187
Was a recent welfare applicant	−145	0.532	232
Had received welfare for past 12 months	444*	0.085	258
Had a child under 6 years old	34	0.841	171
Had one or no children (omitted category)			
Had two children	301	0.160	214
Had three or more children	591***	0.003	199
Was less than 25 years old	206	0.557	351
Was 25 to 34 years old	105	0.707	281
Was 35 to 44 years old	305	0.376	345
Was 45 or older (omitted category)			
Was white, non-Hispanic (omitted category)			
Was black, non-Hispanic	−178	0.369	199
Was Hispanic	−213	0.527	337
Was Native American	−696	0.115	442
Was Asian	353	0.560	606
Was some other race/ethnicity	726	0.487	1,044
Had zero earnings in the past year (omitted category)			
Had earned $1 to $2,499	−186	0.222	152
Had earned $2,500 to $7,499	72	0.787	267
Had earned $7,500 or more	22	0.965	501

Regression coefficients represent the conditional difference in mean impacts on follow-up earnings (in 1996 dollars) for the category specified and the omitted category listed or implied. These coefficients are estimated simultaneously with those reported in table 7.2. The grand mean impact is $879 or 18 percent of the counterfactual. Statistical significance is indicated by * for the 0.10 level, ** for the 0.05 level, and *** for the 0.01 level.

It is straightforward to extend this type of interpretation to characteristics with more than two categories. Consider the number of children that clients had at the time of random assignment. The regression coefficient for "had three or more children" (which is highly statistically significant) indicates that program impacts for clients in this category are $591 greater than for those who are similar in all other ways except that they "had one or no children" (the omitted category for this characteristic).

The only other statistically significant coefficient in the table is for women who received welfare during all twelve months before random assignment and thus were more welfare dependent than average. This coefficient indicates that program impacts for women with this characteristic were $444 larger than for those who were less welfare dependent, other things being equal.

Taken together, the findings in table 7.3 reflect a mixed picture of how client characteristics affect program impacts. Impacts are not consistently larger or smaller for clients who are likely to be easier or harder to employ. Thus, while some characteristics matter to program effectiveness, others do not.

Another way to understand the relative importance of the types of people served is to consider how much of the cross-office variance in the unconditional impacts is explained by the cross-office variation in the characteristics of clients. (This is determined, in essence, by measuring how much lower the variation in conditional impacts is relative to the variation in unconditional effects.) Client characteristics explain about 16 percent of the variation in program impacts across offices. By contrast, much more variance is explained by the set of implementation-related factors (that is, program strategies and economic context). When these are added to the model, the variance explained jumps to 80 percent. In sum, a program's effectiveness is only modestly determined by the nature of its clientele; what is done for and with them matters much more.

CONCLUSIONS

This chapter illustrates what can be achieved by a quantitative synthesis of original data from random assignment experiments that provide valid and reliable estimates of program impacts for many sites, plus valid and reliable measures of how these sites implemented their programs. Thus, this chapter is an example of research that uses multiple levels of information, with high-quality data from a number of sites. Lynn, Heinrich, and Hill (2001) argue that such research can provide the most useful insights for public sector governance.

Our findings, which were substantial in magnitude, statistically significant, and robust to variations in sample composition and structure, demonstrate that, holding other factors in the model constant:

- Management choices for how welfare-to-work programs are implemented matter a great deal to the programs' success. In particular: a strong employment message is a powerful medium for stimulating clients to find jobs, a clear staff focus on personal client attention can markedly increase their success, and large client caseloads can undercut program effectiveness.
- Increased reliance on mandatory basic education reduces short-run program effectiveness. Thus, programs that directly emphasize employment are more successful in the short run.
- The local economic environment is a major determinant of program success; programs are much less effective when jobs are scarce.
- Welfare-to-work programs can be effective for many different types of clients, although some client characteristics may make a difference. However, it is not clear that targeting clients who are especially job ready (or not) influences program effectiveness.
- Overall, the way that a program is implemented has much more influence on its effectiveness (impacts) than do the types of clients it serves.

These findings are based on a solid foundation of valid and reliable impact estimates from random assignment experiments for fifty-nine local program offices. Nevertheless, they also rely on a nonexperimental model of the natural variation in these impacts. Therefore, these findings are only as valid as the model upon which they are based. To maximize their validity, we have carefully specified our model to ensure that it represents all four general categories of factors likely to influence program effectiveness—implementation, activities, environment, and client characteristics. And within each category we have attempted to include specific factors that are judged by researchers and practitioners to be most relevant for program success. Furthermore, we have subjected our findings to a series of stringent sensitivity tests. Thus, we have confidence in the results presented but acknowledge that certainty about them is not possible.

In closing, we emphasize that our research was possible only because of the careful, comprehensive, and consistent data collection efforts of the experiments that we pooled and the broad range of circumstances that they represent. Thus, as social scientists and policy researchers develop their research agendas and as government agencies and foundations make their future research funding plans, we urge them to emphasize a long-run strategy for accumulating program knowledge based on:

1. random assignment experiments that make it possible to obtain valid and reliable estimates of program effectiveness
2. multisite experiments that reflect the existing range of natural variation in program effectiveness
3. careful specification of the likely determinants of program effectiveness based on social science theory, past empirical research, and experiential knowledge of practitioners
4. equally careful and consistent measurement of these hypothesized determinants across studies and sites
5. adequate support for and attention to quantitative syntheses of this information

In this way we believe that the most progress possible can be made toward unpacking the "black box" of social programs and thereby acquiring the information needed to improve them.

APPENDIX

Table 7.1a.   Client Participation in Employment-Related Activities

	Basic Education	Job Search Assistance	Vocational Training
Mean percentage of program group members who participated in the activity	19	22	27
Mean percentage of control group members who participated in the activity	8	5	22
Mean difference in participation rates between program and control group members	11	17	5
Standard deviation across the 59 offices of the difference in participation rates	13	12	10
Range across the 59 offices of the difference in participation rates	−11 to 50	−13 to 47	−21 to 35

Source: MDRC surveys of randomly sampled program and control group members from each local office.

Table 7.2a.   Client Characteristics[a]

At Random Assignment the Sample Member:	Percentage of Full Sample of Individuals	Cross-Office Range (%)
Was a high school graduate or had a GED	56	17 to 74
Was a welfare applicant	17	0 to 99
Had received welfare for past 12 months	44	0 to 96
Had a child under 6 years old	46	7 to 73

(*continued*)

Table 7.2a.   (*continued*)

At Random Assignment the Sample Member:	Percentage of Full Sample of Individuals	Cross-Office Range (%)
Had one or no children	42	30 to 56
Had two children	33	28 to 50
Had three or more children	25	11 to 39
Was younger than 25 years old	19	1 to 42
Was 25 to 34	49	23 to 57
Was 35 to 44	26	14 to 45
Was 45 or older	6	2 to 34
Was white, non-Hispanic	41	1 to 87
Was black, non-Hispanic	41	0 to 98
Was Hispanic	14	0 to 92
Was Native American	2	0 to 21
Was Asian	2	0 to 23
Was some other race/ethnicity	< 1	0 to 5
Had zero earnings in the past year	56	29 to 81
Had earned $1 to $2,499	21	10 to 30
Had earned $2,500 to $7,499	14	6 to 26
Had earned $7,500 or more	9	2 to 27

Sample size = 69,399

[a] The sample in this analysis is restricted to females only.

NOTES

1. This chapter is reprinted with permission of the *Journal of Policy Analysis and Management*, which awarded it the Vernon prize for best article of 2003. The authors thank Larry Lynn for his collaboration on the conception and initiation of the project that forms the basis for this chapter; Judy Gueron for her feedback and support throughout the project; colleagues at MDRC for helping us to understand the programs studied and data used; and The Pew Charitable Trusts for funding the project.

2. We are not implying that all implementation studies should analyze the connections to program effects. Examples of informative implementation studies that are not explicitly designed to look at impacts include Behn (1991); Brodkin (1997); Hagen and Lurie (1994); Mead (1986); and Meyers, Glaser, and MacDonald (1998).

3. Earlier efforts to explore the statistical relationships between implementation and impacts using a smaller set of welfare-to-work sites were conducted by Riccio and Hasenfeld (1996) and Riccio and Orenstein (1996).

4. For a similar analysis using a smaller sample of Job Training Partnership Act (JTPA) sites, see Heinrich (2002).

5. For further background on this study, see Bloom, Hill, and Riccio (2001) and Riccio, Bloom, and Hill (2000).

6. For example, based on her review of existing research and firsthand experience as a state welfare administrator, Bane (1989, 287) argues that the central challenge in building effective programs is " how to shape an organizational culture that . . . delivers a clear message that the goal is jobs, sets a clear expectation that clients can get jobs and that workers are obligated to make that happen, monitors performance, and provides necessary resources."

7. For example, Riccio, Friedlander, and Freedman (1994, xxv) described efforts in California's Riverside County GAIN program, which epitomized the quick-employment philosophy, "to communicate a strong 'message' to all registrants . . . , at all stages of the program, that employment was central, that it should be sought expeditiously, and that opportunities to obtain low-paying jobs should not be turned down."

8. Unfortunately, we do not have a consistent measure of the degree of enforcement across all the offices in this study.

9. Counties in that evaluation that most strongly emphasized basic education did not produce the consistently larger earnings impacts for that subgroup of clients, and some had no statistically significant effect on their earnings at all over a five-year follow-up period.

10. This study found that among clients who did *not* have a high school diploma or GED at the time of random assignment, the labor force attachment strategy had larger impacts on earnings over the five-year follow-up period than did the human capital development strategy, which emphasized basic education activities. In contrast, for sample members who entered the study with a high school credential the human capital development strategy, which emphasized vocational training or post-secondary education for this subgroup, was about as effective as the labor force attachment approach—albeit substantially more expensive (and, therefore, less cost-effective).

11. Understanding how program performance varies with client characteristics is also important for wisely targeting program resources and setting performance standards. Program resource targeting decisions are usually based on two criteria—equity and efficiency. Equity concerns lead to targeting in accord with clients' need for assistance. Efficiency concerns lead to targeting in accord with clients' ability to benefit. Evidence that client characteristics actually do influence program impacts would encourage giving higher priority to serving individuals who are most likely to benefit from the program and establishing performance standards that take the composition of the program's caseload into account.

12. Strictly speaking, randomization produces groups whose expected values are equal for all variables. The larger the sample randomized, the more closely it approximates this ideal. Given the especially large samples for the present analysis, the program and control groups were quite similar.

13. Earnings were expressed in constant 1996 dollars using the CPI-U (Economic Report of the President 2000).

14. Unconditional impacts refer to impacts estimated without controlling for cross-office variation in measured client characteristics. They are distinguished from conditional impacts, discussed later, which do control for these characteristics.

15. Raudenbush and Bryk (2002, 63–64) describe the two tests that we used to assess the statistical significance of the variation in program impacts across local offices.

16. Hierarchical models—also called *random effects models, mixed models,* or *variance component models*—are a major advance in the analysis of data where observations are grouped within aggregate units such as students in schools, employees in firms, residents in neighborhoods, and clients in programs.

17. See Bloom, Hill, and Riccio (2001, 23) for further details.

18. This is accomplished through a combination of maximum likelihood and weighted least squares procedures (Raudenbush and Bryk 2002).

19. Raudenbush and Bryk (2002, 31–35) describe how different ways of centering variables affect the interpretation of their coefficients in a hierarchical model.

20. Bloom, Hill, and Riccio (2001, 88) describe how these averages were regression adjusted to control for office differences in staff characteristics. Although these adjustments were minimal they help to hold constant differences that may exist in the perceptions of different types of staff members.

21. Bloom, Hill, and Riccio (2001, 91) describe how these participation differences were regression adjusted to control for minor differences in the background characteristics of program and control group members at each office. This was done to increase the precision of program activity measures and to estimate them in a way that is consistent with the estimation of program impacts.

22. This probably is because there were only one or two supervisors per office.

23. See Greene (1993, 435–40) for a discussion of this problem.

24. See Bloom, Hill, and Riccio (2001, 88–89) for further details.

25. See Bloom, Hill, and Riccio (2001, 94, 95, and 108) for further details.

26. The partially standardized regression coefficient equals the original coefficient multiplied by the standard deviation of the independent variable that it represents.

27. The counterfactual (control group conditional mean earnings) was $4,871.

28. See Bloom, Hill, and Riccio (2001, app. D).

29. Cross-program variation was removed from the analysis by adding dummy variables for GAIN and PI (with NEWWS the omitted category) to equations 2, 3, and 4. Doing so eliminated the fixed effects of these overarching programs. Cross-state variation was removed by adding dummy variables for six of the seven states to equations 2, 3, and 4. This eliminated state fixed effects. The only major finding to change in either case was that discussed later for caseload size.

30. When a dummy variable for GAIN was added to equations 2, 3, and 4, the coefficient for caseload size in equation 2 dropped almost to zero. However, the pattern of correlations for this dummy variable with program impacts, caseload size, and other local office features did not produce a clear explanation of why its presence in the model affected the caseload size coefficient.

31. See Hamilton and Brock 1994.

32. Our findings apply only to short-run effects. Effectiveness of job search, basic education, and vocational training during a period up to five years after random assignment are examined by Hamilton et al. (2001) for NEWWS; and by Freedman et al. (1996) for GAIN. Hotz, Imbens, and Klerman (2000) examine an additional four years of effects for GAIN (when the restriction that prevented controls from being served by the program was no longer in effect).

8

Forecasting the Effects of Scaling Up Social Programs: An Economics Perspective

Robert A. Moffitt

The problem of scale-up, or forecasting the effects of interventions at a larger scale than that for which their estimated effects were originally obtained, occurs across many different applications, programs, and disciplines. Economic models of scale-up, which are the concern of this chapter, have focused on particular types of scale-up effects that occur frequently in interventions where economic outcomes are the major interest and where program beneficiaries—in this case, students, rather than teachers or schools—are usually the actors making the decision of whether to take up the intervention. However, because they have the ambition to provide a general model of individual choice behavior, economic models have a much wider applicability than to economic outcomes alone and to the decisions of students alone. Economists have indeed begun in recent years to apply their models to broader sets of outcomes and issues, such as the effect of educational interventions on noncognitive outcomes, the importance of peer effects within schools, and the effects of special education programs. However, this work is still relatively immature as a subfield and in addition, economists have done almost no work, and have developed almost no models, for certain types of scale-up effects, particularly those concerning the change in the nature of the intervention itself, the effect on which program operators most often focus.

It is argued here that economics has nevertheless much to contribute to the problem of scale-up. First, the economic model of production processes provides a natural framework within which to discuss the problem of scale-up in general, and to develop a taxonomy of different types of scale-up effects. As an example of its usefulness, I argue below that it allows one to provide alternative explanations for one of the most common findings in the scale-up literature, namely, that effects at larger scales always seem to be weaker than at smaller scales. Second, the economic model provides particularly good insights into some, but not all, of the types of effects listed in such a taxonomy, particularly those having to do with scale-up effects in inputs and outputs. Third, the economic model has led to a general framework for empirical evaluation research and causal inference that can be usefully employed in the measurement of scale-up effects, particularly by nonexperimental means using natural variation. While none of the fundamental problems of measuring scale-up effects are "solved" by the econometric models, these models do provide suggestions for an approach and a framework within which evidence can be accumulated and progress can be made.

This chapter is not concerned with the question of how a researcher can get a successful small-scale program to be adopted by a larger set of schools, how it can be managed at a larger scale, why some interventions appear to "spread" and others do not, or what characteristics of a successful small-scale intervention are most likely to result in its being taken to scale. As important as these questions are, they require an analysis of how schools and institutions actually adopt innovations, and this is beyond the scope of this chapter and indeed, they are not questions (perhaps unfortunately) that economists in the evaluation literature have generally considered.[1] This chapter is instead concerned with the scientific question of how to forecast the actual effects of an intervention prior to its being adopted at a larger scale.

The chapter first lays out a conceptual, economic model within which scale-up effects can be discussed, and then provides some discussion of those effects on which the economic model has something to say. Then issues of measuring and estimating scale-up effects (i.e., the forecasting problem) are discussed.

SCALE-UP CONCEPTS

As stressed by Hedges in his chapter, conceptual models are necessary to make progress on the problem of scale-up. Purely statistical models alone are unlikely to be satisfactory because there are too many causal effects involved in the scale-up problem, and purely statistical models will most likely not adequately separate the different confounding factors and individual effects that are at work. Like all difficult problems where the complexity of the real world is much greater than the data and the methods at our disposal, having a theoretical framework to guide thinking and to interpret the data concerning the scale-up problem is essential.

Production Function Model

The production function model is very familiar to education researchers and needs no elaboration, for it has been used repeatedly as a framework within which the effects of educational inputs on student outcomes can be understood (Levin 2001; Lazear 1999). It has its critics as a useful model to understand the nature of the educational process (Hanushek 1986; Mayston 1996), but here it will be used in a more general way to describe the nature of the mechanism by which individuals are drawn into treatments and later enter a posttreatment state, with selection mechanisms at work at both ends. Figure 8.1 illustrates the simplest such model. A population of individuals exists, from whom a subset are drawn into the program and receive the intervention. It is probably sufficient to define the population as the "eligible" population although this can be deceptive if the criteria for eligibility are endogenous, for in that case the size and nature of the eligible population can change as the program is scaled up. There is a process, defined as a specific set of treatments applied to a set of individuals (possibly differentially by individual characteristics), which constitutes the intervention. Individuals emerge at the other end and outcomes are observed for them individually, and the distribution of outcomes for the entire exiting group is observed as well. Those who drop out of the intervention prior to its completion are included in the exiting group, and their outcomes are regarded as part of the outputs of the intervention, even though their effects may be zero or close to it. Outcomes are subdivided into short-run and long-run outcomes; this by itself is an innocuous distinction but is useful because scale-up effects differ along those dimensions, as discussed below.

The paradigmatic case is that in which estimates have been obtained on a small program, but interest centers on its effects when the program is put in place in a larger area, such as city- or statewide, or even nationally. For example, a curricular innovation has been tested and found favorable in the schools in one area but now is being considered for adoption statewide. Typically one obtains from the small-scale evaluation (whether experimental or

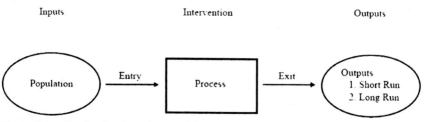

| Inputs | Intervention | Outputs |

Figure 8.1. Production Function Model

nonexperimental) estimates of the effect of an intervention on some outcome variable Y of some population P. The effects may differ for those with different values of a set of individual characteristics, or contextual factors, X. The population P represents characteristics of the sample in the evaluation in addition to X, and often is measured by some indicators of the nature of the process by which individuals enrolled in the program and how they were selected to be in it. Often participants join the program on their own accord, but they may also be referred or required to participate. Statistically, we can say that the small-scale evaluation provides estimates of the function $E(Y|T,X,P)$ for different values of T and X, but generally for only a single value of P (though this may vary as well, as described below).

Economists distinguish the concept of scale-up from the larger problem of generalizability, or external validity, but educational researchers in this area often do not do so. For example, moving from a small scale to a larger scale may result in an enrolled population with a different set of individual characteristics or in areas with different contextual factors (X) from that of the individuals and areas used for small-scale estimation. Perhaps the educational innovation was tested on children in a middle-income school but it is being considered for adoption in a low-income school. Or the innovation was tested on students of largely one ethnic or racial group and is being considered for adoption in schools where a different ethnic or racial group constitutes the majority. Economists term this a problem of generalizability because the effects of the innovation may differ for students of different income levels, or different racial and ethnic groups, and therefore an extrapolation problem must be solved when forecasting the effects of the innovation to the different group or different context (assuming no direct estimates are available for the different group). Economists do not consider this to be a problem of scale because it exists even in cases where scale is not an issue—that is, where the innovation's effects were measured in a small area (e.g., one school) and the innovation is being considered for adoption in a different small area (e.g., a different school with different students and context) and one is trying to forecast the effect in the different school. Economists instead reserve the term *scale-up* for problems of generalization that have a change in scale as an intrinsic element, and that would occur even if the types of individuals or schools involved in the initial evaluation were the same as those in the areas where adoption is being considered. This chapter concentrates on problems where scale-up is an intrinsic issue, and does not use as examples problems that involve attempts to forecast the effects of innovations on different areas or types of individuals per se. However, in practice both problems tend to occur together, for large scale-up almost always involves bringing under the intervention some types of areas or individuals who were not in the tested areas, as well as changes of scale itself. The empirical problem of forecasting is, however, the same problem, and this will be discussed below when that problem is addressed.

Scale-Up Effects in Inputs

Table 8.1 lists a taxonomy of scale-up effects that will be discussed here. The table divides the effects into those pertaining to inputs, those pertaining to the intervention, and those pertaining to outputs, and distinguishes between short-run and long-run effects.

In the category of inputs, a short-run scale-up effect occurs if there is some voluntary element to participation in the program and if knowledge of the program diffuses through the population rather than occurring instantly. Such effects can occur whether the program in question is completely new, and its impact was estimated initially on only a small set of individuals drawn into the program by some special process, or it is an existing program where a reform has been made and it is the effect of the reform on entry that is the issue at hand. Some reforms can conceivably be viewed unfavorably by many in the population, in which case diffusion of information about it may reduce entry rather than increase it.

Thinking about how individuals in the population will view the new program or the reform raises immediately the important question of how individuals, or schools in some cases, would come to be enrolled or involved in the program after scale-up. The long-run effect in table 8.1 of change in entry mix reflects the fact that the individuals or schools involved in the large-scale program may differ in some way from those in the estimation sample in ways that could not be measured in the latter. One example that often comes up in purely voluntary programs, where individuals or schools make their own participation decisions, is that the estimation sample is often conducted on individuals or schools that are particularly advantaged or

Table 8.1. Taxonomy of Scale-Up Effects

Stage of Production	Effects	
	Short Run	*Long Run*
Inputs	Knowledge of diffusion	Change in entry mix Migration Other endogenous responses
Intervention	Knowledge build-up on best technology for intervention	Change in nature of the treatment Change in resources per recipient
Outputs	Lags in effects of output scale-ups	Market responses Social interactions Policy-institutional reactions

disadvantaged relative to the population as a whole. For example, interventions are often initially conducted on a particularly disadvantaged sample. An intervention that is aimed at very disadvantaged individuals but which, after scale-up, brings into the program less-disadvantaged individuals who benefit less from the program, will result in a dilution of the program effects when measured as an average. This is one effect that is consistent with the commonly observed reduction in intervention effects when going to scale (mentioned in the introduction), and can occur even if the intervention, or treatment itself, is unchanged after scale-up; merely the composition of the enrolled population may change.

If the selection mechanism involves some voluntary elements, then another possibility that arises is that the individuals or schools considering participation may be able to obtain information on the effectiveness of the program, and make their decisions on that basis. If they do, and if they perceive, rightly or wrongly, that the effectiveness of the program is different after scale-up from before, that too can affect entry and the composition of the enrolled population after scale-up. This will be mentioned again below in the discussion of output effects.

The nature of these effects will differ depending on selection. If those administering the program do not allow purely voluntary participation, then the question is how the selection mechanism will change after scale-up. That question has to be answered on a case-by-case basis, depending on the application in question.

Economists have been relatively successful in constructing plausible, and empirically verified, models of the voluntary participation decisions of individuals in social programs. The standard model for such effects is some kind of benefit-cost calculation, either expected utility maximization or some related concept. Economists have made less progress in modeling the decisions of program operators in deciding whom to admit to a program in those cases where enrollment is not entirely voluntary. Modeling the decision process of organizations is much more difficult than modeling that for individuals.

The relevance of entry and diffusion effects to classroom innovations of various kinds is still present but is likely to operate in a different fashion because individual students cannot select themselves in and out of a classroom where an intervention has been implemented. An exception occurs when parents, guardians, and/or teachers lobby effectively on behalf of individual students to include or remove them from classrooms selected for implementation of the intervention during scale-up. Nevertheless, there could be effects of classroom innovations on the nature of the students entering that classroom if those innovations affect curriculum or student or teacher behavior at earlier grades, or if schools likewise make alterations. A small-scale intervention in only one classroom may not affect school or teacher policy in earlier or later grades, but a large-scale intervention may. It is one of the paradoxes of entry effects that entry mix effects are likely to be small if the intervention itself is small and incremental, and does not have a large impact on outcomes; but the more successful the intervention, and the larger the effects on outcomes, the more entry mix is likely to be a problem.

It is also difficult to separate measurement from theory in this case because whether these types of spillover effects into earlier classrooms are a problem depends on whether the "small-scale" intervention took as its unit of observation the student in the classroom where the intervention was taking place, or the school. To the extent that the school was the unit of observation, and the innovation was implemented "schoolwide," the effects mentioned above may very well be captured.

Table 8.1 also lists migration and other endogenous responses as long-run input effects. If migration occurs as individuals move into (or out of) the areas where the intervention is offered, or across areas because the intervention differs across those areas, this can also generate a scale-up effect that is not captured by the small-scale estimates. Individuals moving into a school district where a particularly successful intervention has been brought up to scale—or out of a district where the intervention is of a type that some parents dislike—may, likewise, change the input mix and therefore the average effectiveness of the program in question. This is really a subcategory of the entry mix problem. Other endogenous responses of this kind are possible, such as changes in personal or family characteristics to make oneself eligible for a program (income, family structure, etc.).

Scale-Up Effects in Intervention

Many practitioners think of scale-up effects as occurring primarily in the nature of the intervention itself. This effect is most often described as the problem of "implementation," meaning getting the program operators (in this case, teachers and schools) to actually implement the program in the same way it was implemented in the small-scale test. In some of the discussions in the educational scale-up literature, where this problem is considered to be overwhelmingly the most important one, a "successful" educational innovation is defined not only as one that has a positive effect on outcomes of students in the small-scale test, but also as one that is easily implementable by schools and teachers in the larger educational system.

The economics literature on program evaluation discusses several reasons for the presumed importance of implementation. One is the general notion that it is more difficult organizationally to administer a program to a large group of individuals than to a small group; this is another explanation for a diminution of effects when going to scale. However, this notion needs to be parsed and some important distinctions, though perhaps only conceptual ones, need to be made. Administering a program to a large number of individuals does not technically require any different treatment process than administering a program to a small set of individuals provided the technology of the treatment is kept the same; for example, if the intervention is administered to groups of the same size as in the small-scale program (meaning necessarily more groups). There may be administrative difficulties higher up in the organization that may yield inefficiencies, but this is a very different type of effect. In many cases, instead, the notion that the program is harder to administer to a large set of individuals than to a small set arises because the technology is not held fixed and the treatment given at the individual level in the small-scale program is not replicated at the larger level. Sometimes this can be thought of purely as a resource issue because a smaller amount of resources per enrollee may be devoted at the larger scale than at the smaller scale. That individuals might be treated more uniformly, and with less personal attention, in a large-scale rather than a small-scale program is an example of the treatment's actually changing when going to scale.

These effects are listed as long-run effects in table 8.1, and it is fair to say that economists have not studied these issues much, partly because they are so difficult. To do so properly requires a model of how treatments are administered at different scales, and how the nature of an intervention changes with scale, and this is an inherently difficult problem. Many small-scale evaluations do conduct "process" evaluations or studies of how services are actually delivered in a particular small-scale intervention (the Bloom, Hill, and Riccio chapter in this volume is one of the better illustrations of this type of work), but one of the weaknesses of most analyses of that kind is that they are not fed into any type of structured model that could be used for extrapolation and generalization to other, and larger-scale, types of programs.

A rather different, short-run effect of scale-up in the intervention occurs when those running the program change the nature of the treatment (in a positive direction, presumably) as more effective ways of serving the population are continually discovered. Programs are rarely static and unchanging, and new programs in particular almost always evolve over time. Nevertheless, this is listed as a short-run problem in table 8.1 on the presumption that the program will eventually stabilize if left in place long enough, and it is this long-run effect that is of most interest to the evaluator.

Scale-Up Effects in Outputs

Economists have conducted the majority of their work on scale-up effects in outputs, which are sometimes lumped together as "general equilibrium" effects. The textbook example is that of a market response that occurs when an intervention becomes large enough in scale to affect supply and demand in a market and hence changes the equilibrium price. In many examples, the price response to a large-scale intervention acts to reduce the average effect of that intervention—for example, increases in the supply of more skilled labor reduces its equilibrium wage—making the estimate from the small-scale intervention too large. This provides a third possible explanation for the commonly observed diminution in program effectiveness after going to scale (in addition to the dilution of the nature of the entry pool, and reduction in the effectiveness of the treatment itself for a constant entry pool). Economists are well equipped to study clearing of markets and to consider the multiple feedback effects that can occur when an intervention is large enough to affect markets.

The relevance of these effects to classroom interventions below the adolescent years is questionable, because the main type of effect studied by economists is the effect of the productivity of the school-leaving pool on the youth labor market. Interventions that were large-scale and close to the school-leaving point, and which had a large enough effect to (for example) increase the skill level of graduates could conceivably have an effect of this kind. However, the more important "general equilibrium" effect of this kind for classroom innovations is its effect downstream, that is, on classrooms at later grades. A truly successful intervention that improves the cognitive skills of students in a particular dimension will undoubtedly have effects on how material is taught in later grades, and this will not be captured by a tested intervention that is so small in magnitude as to not affect the average skill level of students in the upper grades.

But there are two other scale-up effects in outputs, aside from the classic market example, which are potentially important as well. One is the presence of social interactions, as they may be called, which arise only when a program is scaled up. An example is the development and establishment of social norms and expectations that arise when large numbers of individuals undertake a treatment and become aware that others have done so. The feedback effects so generated make the small-scale impact estimates invalid. If the feedback effects are positive in sign, this is one case where the small-scale intervention may underestimate the large-scale effect because the latter reinforces and extends the former by propagation through the larger student population. Another example is where the individuals affected by an intervention affect the outcomes of individuals not in the program. For example, students whose performance improves may have positive effects on the performance of students who have never been in the program if they are in the same classrooms or have some other type of social contact. Peer effects are one specific example of such effects. Economists have recently begun to model these kinds of effects but have made only modest progress to date (Kremer and Levy 2003; Nechyba 1996; Epple, Figlio, and Romano 2004).

Another even larger-scale output scale-up effect occurs if the institutional or policy environment changes in response to the scale-up of the program. Typically this is of concern only when the intervention in question is a very large-scale, structural change in an entire program or system. Examples include welfare reform in the United States in the mid-1990s, and possibly the No Child Left Behind legislation. The effects in question here arise if programs other than those that have been affected change their service offerings in response to the reform of the initial program. In the case of welfare reform, if new child-care programs spring up, if the nature of job training programs changes to serve a different clientele, if new tutoring or remedial programs are created after the intervention, or other changes in the local policy environment occur, these truly "macro" effects can also affect individual outcomes and therefore cause the small-scale estimates to be invalidated.

All output effects can have effects on inputs if the effectiveness of, or payoff to, the program affects program entry decisions. Programs that have some voluntary element, for example, can be expected to bring in more enrollees if the program is perceived as successful as it is unsuccessful. Likewise, changes in the treatment discussed earlier can affect entry decisions if the nature of the treatment is correctly perceived by the population and there are voluntary elements to enrollment.

MEASURING SCALE-UP EFFECTS

Measuring scale-up effects is a difficult task and requires departing from the standard experimental or nonexperimental model, both of which consider the impact of a treatment on a set of individuals or organizations holding constant the scale of the program, the entry pool, the nature and implementation of the intervention, and the scale of the output effects. Therefore measurement must go in other directions.

Because evaluation methodology becomes important in the discussion of measuring scale-up, the following discussion separately considers experimental, natural variation, and simulation methods. In all cases, it is assumed that valid small-scale estimates of the effect of an intervention on outcomes for a particular population are available.

Experimental Methods

The typical small-scale randomized field trial (RFT) does not capture scale-up effects. Generally, the typical modification in experimental methodology to capture scale-up effects is to conduct experiments at the community level and to make them saturation experiments. Thus, randomizing a set of areas or school districts into treatment and control groups would almost by definition capture most entry scale-up effects (except for immigration from other areas), and at least some output scale-up effects (although not those market responses that occur in other areas), and will include some intervention-related scale-up effects. In short, by testing a program by implementing it on the entire population of an area, it is possible to obtain a direct estimate of the total effect of a program, thus capturing scale-up. If a large number of areas is tested, this approach essentially is a partial implementation of the actual program on a large scale, and consequently it is not surprising that it should capture many scale-up effects.

Unfortunately, there are many difficulties with implementing this idea and, as a result, it is rarely a viable option. One problem is that enrolling a sufficient number of areas to gain a reasonable level of statistical significance is extraordinarily costly and beyond virtually all research budgets. The common practice of pairing single comparison areas with single treatment areas is subject to too much variability to be reliable, and there are many examples in areas of social welfare intervention where comparison-site designs have proved faulty because of random events in one of the two areas. A second difficulty that often arises is simply a political one, for it is often difficult to obtain the cooperation of large numbers of political entities in a randomized trial, at least in our decentralized government where mandates from the top are rarely possible. A third difficulty is that controlling the treatment to make it homogeneous across the areas is always quite problematic. For all these reasons, a statistically reliable saturation-side experiment to capture scale-up effects is a nonstarter.

Natural Variation

Some types of input and output effects can be captured by statistical analysis using natural variation in scale across areas. Using this variation, however, does require the construction of some type of statistical model that can relate the scale-up effects to the effects available from the small-scale estimation. The small-scale estimation will provide, for example, "first stage" estimates of the effect of the intervention on outcomes of the individuals enrolled. A statistical model is then required to relate the effects of such a change in outcomes, generalized to a larger population, that work through feedback, either through market responses or social interactions. Estimating those feedback effects is possible with nonexperimental data, using natural variation across areas in other dimensions. Market output responses, for example, require estimates of the price responsiveness to a shift in a supply or demand curve, and there is an extensive econometric literature on how to estimate such types of relationships with natural variation using observational data. Social interaction effects, while much more difficult to measure, can in principle be measured with the right kind of exogenous, cross-area or cross-group variation in the mix of individuals with different outcomes, allowing estimation of peer effects and social norm effects.

Entry effects are more difficult to measure because small-scale estimation typically provides no information at all on how individuals would come to be enrolled in a scaled-up program. Exceptions sometimes occur when small-scale estimates are available for different areas, or for different sets of individuals; these exceptions at least provide some estimates on how the outcomes will differ for a different input mix (the population P referred to previously). A model of entry is required, and one must develop a model of how individuals or organizations make choices to participate in similar programs which can be extrapolated or mapped into the entry effects of the program in question. The "similar" natural variation may be difficult to locate in existing programs or past evaluations, but this is required to capture input mix effects.

There are definite limits to these types of exercises, however, for they work only in some circumstances and with the availability of natural variation in the first place. They are typically not possible for scale-up effects that occur in the intervention, where there is rarely direct natural variation or relevant natural variation in a related treatment which can be used instead, but only in output and input effects. Imprecision in many nonexperimental estimators of this kind, and the threats to internal validity which arise so frequently, further weaken this approach.

Simulation

In many cases the only, or most promising, approach, is to construct a theory-based simulation model that can be used to forecast the magnitude of the scale-up effects of various kinds. Entry mix, market and social interaction responses, and even how the nature of treatments varies with scale can in principle be formally modeled. Calibrating such simulation models is the difficult part, and must rely on previous estimates obtained from natural variation to inform the values of the parameters assumed. In some cases, there may be no reliable estimates of parameters in the simulation model, in which case the best that can be done is to simulate with a plausible range of parameters and to leave the final estimates uncertain and only falling into a range. Theory-based simulation is also only as good as the theory used to construct the models, and some theories have been validated more than others from past research. Nevertheless, there are many ways to quasi validate simulation models from outside data to ensure that they are correctly representing at least existing, or historical, behavior, and this allows such models to be grounded more firmly than they would be otherwise.

Different Populations and Contexts

Finally, as noted previously, the problem of generalizing the estimates of a small-scale intervention to areas or schools with different types of students or different contextual factors is not a scale-up problem per se but can nevertheless be likewise discussed under experimental, natural variation, and simulation methods. Experimental methods would seem to be very appropriate here—and feasible, provided that sufficient numbers of schools can be persuaded to test an innovation. The recommendation for multisite designs made by Hedges in his chapter in this volume is exactly aimed at obtaining information on how the effects of an innovation that was successful in one particular school in one particular area would differ for different schools, students, and areas. Multisite designs would have the additional advantage of providing information on the much-discussed problem of what educational innovations are "adaptable," meaning that they can be implemented successfully in different schools and in different populations than those in the initial study. Natural variation is the nonexperimental counterpart to randomization, where natural variation in some type of school innovation is necessary for estimation. Simulation is the ultimate solution if nothing else is available; in this case, a model of how treatment effects differ by student, school, and area would have to be developed, using as a research base the knowledge gleaned from past studies of other educational interventions on how impacts vary along those dimensions. Once again, the uncertainty inherent in this type of forecasting would require sensitivity testing and the production of a range of estimates rather than a single one.

SUMMARY

Analyzing scale-up effects is difficult and requires different models and methods than those used for the typical small-scale evaluation. In light of the difficulties involved, it is important to begin by conceptualizing the problem correctly, forming a taxonomy of different scale-up effects, and relating them coherently to one another. Indeed, constructing a theoretical model of scale-up is important simply to organize any empirical approach to the problem. None of the empirical means of measuring scale-up effects is particularly attractive, but the approach most likely to yield insights—though not "solutions"—is a simulation model based on theory, which is informed by the collection of empirical estimates available or which can be reliably obtained from nonexperimental analysis, possibly from using natural variation across areas.

NOTE

1. The area of economic research where a somewhat related set of issues has been discussed is the literature on incentives in organizations and, to some extent, game theory. Very little of this literature has specifically focused on organizational determinants of the adoption of innovations, however.

III

BREAKING BOUNDARIES: SUCCESSFUL SCALE-UP IN TRANSFORMING ORGANIZATIONS

9

Breaking Boundaries: Scaling Collaboration in Time and Space

Ian Foster and Carl Kesselman

In many domains of human endeavor, work is performed increasingly within distributed teams that link participants from different locations and perhaps even from distinct organizations. This trend has received much attention from organizational theorists, who have coined terms such as *networked organization* (Sproull and Kiesler 1992), *virtual team, distributed collaborative group,* and *virtual organization* (Palmer and Speier 1997) to refer to the different organizational and collaborative structures enabled by information technology (Yager 1997).

This trend is particularly marked within the physical and biological sciences, wherein distributed communities can function as "knowledge societies" (Knorr Cetina 1999) within which participants engage in the collaborative construction of knowledge artifacts (Nentwich 2003). Participants advance their individual and common goals by exchanging information and/or by sharing physical resources (storage, computers, scientific instruments). The term *collaboratory* (Bair 1999; National Research Council 1993) has been coined to refer to such "laboratories without walls."

The emergence of these virtual locales for collaboration is motivated by many factors, with technology playing an important role as both enabler and driver. The development of the Internet, web, and high-speed networks makes it possible for distributed groups to collaborate in new ways. Within the hard sciences, rapid increases in the volume of available data and/or in the complexity and fidelity of computer models are demanding increasingly close cooperation within and across disciplines (National Science Foundation 2003). For example, in the life sciences, which were traditionally data poor, new genomes are being acquired on a daily basis; thus, research advances depend increasingly on the ability to integrate across many data sets

189

(Goble, Pettifer, and Stevens 2004; Stein 2002). In climate research, advances in both scientific understanding and supercomputer performance mean that researchers now work not with numerical models of the atmosphere, ocean, or biosphere in isolation, but with coupled climate system models (Blackmon et al. 2001). The construction of these models is a team effort, and the data sets that the models produce are themselves knowledge artifacts of interest to large communities of scientists and policy makers.

Our purpose in this chapter is to introduce some of the concepts and approaches that are being used to enable effective collaboration beyond traditional institutional boundaries. We explain the need to scale participation, capability, and efficiency, and illustrate with examples of how various scientific communities are applying so-called Grid technologies (Foster and Kesselman 2004) to achieve this scaling. We focus on the hard sciences in which these concepts and technologies have found early adoption, and with which we have the most experience.

SCALING ISSUES IN COLLABORATION

There are few tasks that cannot benefit from the contributions of more than a single person, whether those contributions amount to human expertise or other resources. Historically, collaboration has required collocation, which is why human development is to a significant extent a history of physical institutions such as the town, factory, and university.

While physical institutions have many advantages, they are necessarily limited in terms of the human expertise and physical resources that they can accumulate and bring to bear on any particular problem. Thus, it is not surprising that with the advent of modern telecommunications we see a flowering of new forms of collaboration that expand beyond traditional geographic and organizational boundaries. In so-called virtual organizations (VOs) (Foster, Kesselman, and Tuecke 2001), participants are connected by common interests rather than institutional affiliations, and they share resources and work together to achieve a common goal (see figure 9.1). With the emergence of virtual organizations, collaborations are no longer limited in scale to the individual's institution, but can be dynamically expanded to include any participant who can bring value, regardless of location or affiliation.

While the creation and ubiquitous deployment of the Internet and web have enabled considerable progress toward effective distributed collaboration, significant obstacles remain to scaling along the axes of participation, capability, and efficiency, as we now explain.

All collaboration is built on a foundation of trust. Trust is not an absolute quality, but rather quantifies the extent to which a participant is expected to

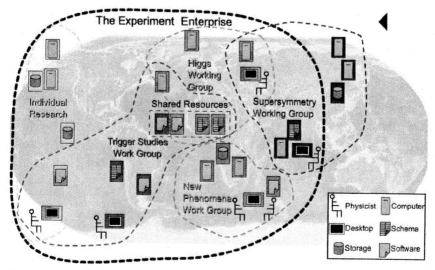

Figure 9.1.   Schematic View of the Various Overlapping Virtual Organization Structures That Apply within a Particular Scientific Community

conform to the explicit and implicit rules and mores of a collaboration. Establishment of some form of trust relationship with other participants is therefore a necessary precondition for an individual's *participation* in a collaborative venture. Trust is an input that is used to create the rules or *policies* that apply to any participant. These rules constrain the terms of participation, the role(s) that an individual may assume, and ultimately, the activities that the participant is allowed—or wishes—to undertake. Technology can facilitate collaboration by automating policy enforcement and enabling the implementation of more flexible and/or open policies. Whether or not a particular individual or community finds more open policies desirable is a separate issue that we do not address here, except to note that in the physical sciences at least, enhanced collaboration has often been found to yield competitive advantage (Knorr Cetina 1999).

The value of a virtual organization to its participants can depend on its collective *capability*: the various resources to which it provides access. The Internet and web allow access to people and websites, but more sophisticated collaboration modalities can require access to large and diverse databases, simulation systems, software services, scientific instruments, and sensors of various kinds. The effective integration of these capabilities into collaborative systems can require new technologies, policies, and social structures.

Finally, the *efficiency* with which a collaboration functions depends not only on the ease with which it can establish and maintain participation and capability, but also on the ease with which its members can engage in their various tasks. Thus, a vital part of scaling collaboration is good tools for such things as discovering the resources available to the collaboration, managing workflows that use those resources, federating distributed databases, and responding to changes in the structure and work of the collaboration.

Scaling Participation

A collaboration is defined above all by its participants; specifically, their identities, contributions, and roles. Participants need not be people: computational components such as services, databases, simulation programs, and intelligent agents are becoming increasingly important elements in many collaborative systems and must be considered as participants in many respects (e.g., from the perspectives of trust and discovery).

Approaches to allowing, inviting, or encouraging participation in collaborations have historically been rooted in existing social structures and thus often build on personal relationships and organizational structures. For example, a researcher might provide a password to a colleague wishing to access a database. However, while such approaches have the advantage of familiarity, they can limit the ability of a collaboration to scale in terms of numbers—and, equally importantly, to respond to changing demands by evolving the composition, functions, or roles of its participants.

Scaling collaboration requires that participation extend beyond personal trust relationships. It is here that technology can help, not by requiring the adoption of any particular policy, but by assisting with the implementation and enforcement of more flexible policies (decision rules) that may allow access based on other criteria. For example, rather than providing passwords to immediate colleagues, we might want to allow access to a resource by any accredited employee of an institution, or by any individual recommended by a colleague. To implement such policies, we require means by which trust, identities, and roles can be established and maintained automatically and without direct reference to personal relationships. Of course, such policies also imply a desire to share information or other resources more widely.

The emergence of e-commerce has spurred the wide deployment of protocols for secure authentication. However, these protocols are used primarily for validating existing client-server trust relationships (e.g., for accessing bank account information) rather than for supporting the development of communities based on more symmetric trust relationships. One consequence of this asymmetry is that these systems are not typically used to pool resources but rather simply to provide access to the single web server that supports the e-commerce service.

Grid security technologies provide basic mechanisms that are widely used to enable cross-organizational trust relationships within collaborations that depend on resource sharing for their operation. These mechanisms allow participants (both human and computational) to acquire identities that are independent of the participants' institutional affiliation(s). They also provide single-sign-on capabilities so that an individual can authenticate once and then access many resources. Related mechanisms allow for participants to delegate roles and privileges to computational agents that may perform tasks on their behalf, and allow resource owners to manage who is allowed to access their resources. These mechanisms underlie, for example, the Grid2003 (The Grid2003 Project 2004) and TeraGrid (Cartlett 2002) systems that have been created to support the U.S. scientific community, and the Network for Earthquake Engineering Simulation (NEESgrid) that is being created to enable remote access to experimental facilities and data archives by the U.S. earthquake engineering community (Pearlman et al. 2004).

Despite these successes, such Grid deployments still depend on largely manual methods for declaring and maintaining bilateral trust relationships between institutions and between individuals and designated authorities within the virtual organization in which they participate, combined with mechanisms for restricted delegation of authority. For example, NEESgrid and Grid2003 both require that authorized individuals (so-called registration authorities) vouch for the credentials of local participants. More dynamic and scalable mechanisms for creating and maintaining trust relationships are required if we wish to scale to larger and more diverse communities of participants. For example, we might want to allow any enrolled student of an approved university or any chartered engineer to participate in a NEESgrid experiment as an observer. A key to implementing such policies is the ability for users to assert attribute information ("I am a student" or "I am an engineer") reliably and securely. Recent work in policy federation is providing infrastructure for such purposes. For example, the Security Association Markup Language (SAML) standard and such implementations of this standard as Shibboleth (Erdos and Cantor 2002) provide an interoperable protocol for discovering and exchanging policy information.

Online communities (which have long been innovators in collaboration technology) are another source of increasingly sophisticated approaches to managing trust, including mechanisms for structuring communication (e.g., chat rooms), establishing reputation (e.g., eBay), and extending communities via personal recommendations (e.g., Friendster). However, these systems are not concerned (primarily) with sharing resources but with communication. The Access Grid (Stevens 2004) system is an example of how collaboration tools can enable not only communication but also the sharing of such resources as programs and data.

The use of Grid security mechanisms to support collaboration in the climate modeling community provides a good illustration of how a set of participants can use technology to implement policies that meet goals of both data protection and openness. The Earth System Grid, which can be seen at

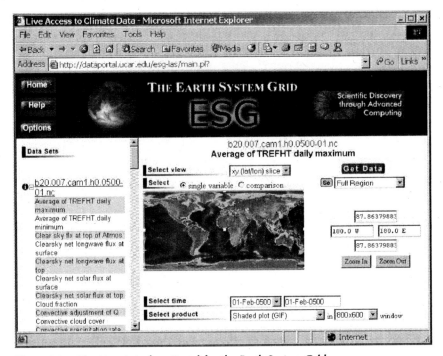

Figure 9.2.   The User Interface Portal for the Earth System Grid

www.earthsystemgrid.org (Allcock et al. 2001), is concerned with enabling community access to large amounts of numerical simulation data by a large community of researchers and policy makers (see figure 9.2). The following set of access patterns arises:

- A small set of expert climate modelers is responsible for generating the simulation data.
- Once prepared, this data is accessed by a set of scientists affiliated with the modelers, for purposes of quality control and early research.
- Finally, the data are made available to the wider community for general use.

Thus we have three forms of participation, or roles: the data producers, an initial trusted user community, and the broad climate community. Participation in the first two roles is both well defined and important to control carefully, for reasons of both scientific integrity and professional reputation. Membership in the second is far less well defined and indeed need not be controlled—but does need to be monitored in order to demonstrate that value is being delivered to the community.

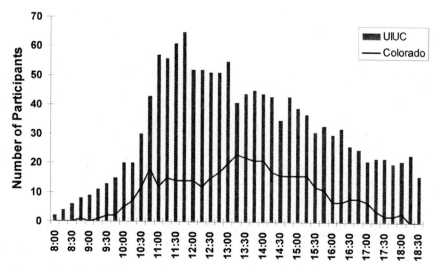

Figure 9.3. Plot Showing the Number of Participants as a Function of Time That Observed a Distributed Earthquake Engineering Experiment Run over NEESgrid

The Earth System Grid addresses these diverse concerns as follows. All accesses are authenticated by using the same standard public key infrastructure (PKI) credentials and mechanisms, as supported by the Grid Security Infrastructure, supported by an open source software system called the Globus Toolkit. However, quite different mechanisms are used to generate credentials for different purposes. Members of the first and second sets of users obtain their credentials via a carefully controlled registration process based on personal vetting by designated staff at participating institutions who act as registration authorities. Members of the second group request their credentials via a web form, which serves simply to validate the e-mail address provided. The Earth System Grid portal then performs authorization according to both the identity of an individual and the quality of the credential supplied.

A similar scheme has been applied successfully within the NEESgrid system referred to above, which shows the broad participation that can be achieved for online experiments when this sort of infrastructure is in place.

Scaling Capability

One immediate benefit of scaling participation in a collaboration may be a corresponding increase in aggregate capability. From the perspective of human capital, scaling the number of participants can bring in new talent, enhancing the ability of a collaboration to achieve its goals. Of particular importance is the ability to respond to changing requirements by bringing in domain experts with a scope outside the original focus of the collaboration. Note that almost by definition, these new domain experts will be drawn from "outside" organizations that specialize in the new problem area. This observation reinforces our assertion that scaling up collaboration requires the ability to span organizational structures dynamically.

Recall, however, that our definition of *participant* includes not only people but also computational elements such as computers, databases, applications, sensors, and other instruments. The pooling of these resources within a collaborative structure can provide researchers with access not only to greater total capability (e.g., greater computational capacity) but also to entirely new capabilities constructed from synergistic combinations of services and resources contributed by different participants.

The NEESgrid environment provides a good illustration of this point. As noted above, NEESgrid is a distributed collaboration environment designed to support earthquake engineering. A common activity within earthquake engineering is conducting the physical test of a structure by placing a model on an experimental apparatus so that it may be subjected to forces and accelerations such as one would find during an earthquake. For example, the response of a steel or concrete column may be determined by fixing the column to an extremely rigid structure (called a *reaction wall*) and subjecting the column to loading via large hydraulic actuators. On the other hand, the dynamic response of the interface between the soil and a structure sitting on it, such as a bridge piling, is typically determined by building a scale model of the soil substructure and piling and measuring the dynamic response when the box containing the soil is shaken. To compensate for the effects of scaling, the soil model and associated structural model are subjected to scaled gravitational forces by being placed in a centrifuge.

Shared remote access to either of these two capabilities when considered in isolation represents a significant enhancement to the capabilities of the NEESgrid collaboration. However, if these two capabilities are combined with numerical simulation models, we can couple the detailed simulation of the large structure with the complex dynamics of the solid mechanics. The result is an entirely new type of earthquake engineering experimental capability, as depicted in figure 9.4. Thus, NEESgrid provides the technological underpinnings that allow innovative researchers to explore new problem-solving approaches.

Grid technologies support the scaling of capability by defining standard and interoperable protocols and interfaces for interacting with and managing remote resources, thus facilitating the integration of those resources into the aggregate capability of a collaboration. They also define mechanisms for organizing resources into collections, for discovering available capabilities and their characteristics, and for composing different capabilities to provide new functionality. These basic mechanisms allow new *virtualized*

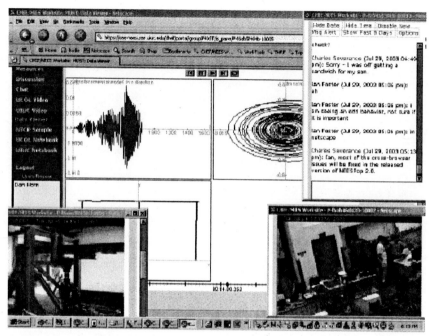

Figure 9.4.   The NEESgrid Portal Allows Collaborators to Interact with an Ongoing Earthquake Engineering Experiment

services, such as the NEESgrid experimental capability, to be created by combining and abstracting underlying, more basic capabilities.

Scaling Efficiency

Efficiency is the final aspect of collaboration scaling that we consider. While a formal definition of efficiency could be attempted, we use the term here somewhat loosely to describe a decrease in the time and/or the cost required for a collaboration to perform a task.

Efficiency issues are not totally independent of the scaling of capability. For example, expanding a collaboration's capabilities to embrace larger computers or faster software may reduce the time it takes to complete various tasks. Outsourcing tasks to external resource providers or to other human experts can further increase efficiency by decreasing the cost of performing an operation.

Other mechanisms can have a more direct impact on efficiency. For example, the integrated trust and policy mechanisms described above (see "Scaling Participation") make it possible for collaboration participants to assign tasks to remote computational services without regard to issues of ownership. When combined with appropriate discovery and brokering functions, such mechanisms can allow the collaboration to achieve far more efficient distribution of tasks to participants and thus better response times for individual tasks as well as better throughput for the collaboration as a whole. The right balance between individual response times and aggregate throughput may be a question of collaboration policy, and may be enforced by distributed policy-management techniques.

Efficiency of collaboration can be further scaled by creating tools that reduce the time to specify and perform the steps required for task completion. We illustrate this point with an example from astronomy: creating a *mosaic*, that is, an image of a specified region of the sky from a catalog of smaller images (Williams et al. 2003). As in the climate modeling example above, the original data in the catalog are created by a small number of producers and made available to the community, in this case for use in astronomical research. Producing a mosaic for a given region of the sky turns out to be a nontrivial task. First, the files that store the required data must be identified. Since the data may come from different surveys, the data must then be projected into a common coordinate space so that different components align. Images must then be flattened so that they can be coregistered, and then the individual images must be composed to generate the desired result.

The process of creating the final integrated image can involve many steps over thousands of images. Performing this task by hand would be tedious and error prone. Instead, we can create tools that start with a high-level description of the desired result and automatically construct from this description a *workflow* that defines the sequence of steps required to generate the desired result. A Grid-based execution tool can then process this workflow, mapping individual tasks to available execution capabilities while taking into account availability, performance, and possible failure conditions.

The development and broad deployment of tools such as this mosaic generation system depend, first of all, on the scaling of a collaboration's participation and capabilities, so that required data sources and processing power can be aggregated. At the same time, that scaling of participation and capability would serve little purpose if tools such as the mosaic generation system were not available to make efficient use of collaboration resources.

A final example illustrates the impact that Grid technologies can have on participation, capability, and efficiency. Figure 9.5 shows the number of computational resources delivered to various virtual organizations participating in a major U.S. Grid deployment, Grid2003, during a three-month period in late 2003 and early 2004. The Grid2003 system exploits all of the mechanisms described above to achieve broad participation in its activities (twenty-eight institutions and more than one hundred physicists, at the time of writing), to integrate considerable capability into its collaborative

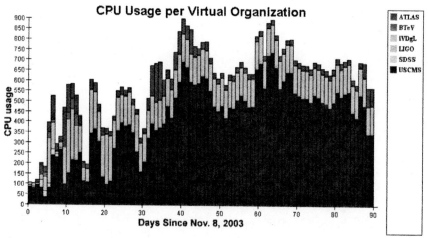

Figure 9.5. Computational Resources Delivered to the Various Virtual Organizations That Participated in the Creation of Grid2003

system (close to 3,000 CPUs), and to enable efficient use of the aggregate resources by its various participants.

FUTURE TECHNOLOGY DIRECTIONS

We review here two emerging technology trends that we expect to have a significant impact on our ability to scale participation, capability, and efficiency within collaborative teams.

The first trend is the increased deployment of *service-oriented architectures* based on Web-services technologies. The distinguishing characteristic of a service-oriented architecture is that we can interact with any system element or *service* in a standard and well-defined manner, by sending messages to that service with a format specified by an interface definition associated with the service. For example, the interface definition for a database service might define message exchanges for requesting the schema of the database and for retrieving elements from the database. Service-oriented architectures simplify the integration of disparate organizations into an integrated collaboration, as participants do not need to know anything about how a capability is implemented in order to access it—they simply need to know its interface. Initial Web-service approaches assumed a static service set. However, recent developments are enabling a more dynamic environment (Foster et al. 2002).

The second trend is concerned with the augmentation of service-oriented environments with rich semantic descriptions of service function (Goble et al. 2004). Such service descriptions can provide a basis for inference and discovery, concerns that are becoming increasingly important in many disciplines. Traditional approaches to service description are to annotate the service with a predefined set of attributes. For example, a database of genome sequence data might annotate each putative gene with information about source, presumed function, size, and so forth. Information about the computational steps used to derive new data from old can also be useful (Foster et al. 2002). Semantic approaches create *ontologies* to represent fundamental concepts and use such knowledge-representation languages as OWL (van Harmelen et al. 2003) to represent and reason about complex relationships between concepts. These technologies might be used, for example, to encode that a gene is a type of genetic sequence, thus supporting inference and discovery concerning the sorts of programs that can be applied to genes. Application of semantic representation within both standard web-based environments (e.g., the Semantic Web [Berners-Lee, Hendler, and Lassila 2001]) and service-oriented environments enhance the users' ability to discover, configure, and use the services that are most relevant to them. Early experiences suggest that the impact of semantics on the construction of virtual organizations can be dramatic, significantly decreasing the amount of overhead required to integrate a new participant or capability into a collaboration.

SUMMARY

The vision of computer networks enabling a new type of human-machine and human-human interaction was first enunciated in the late 1960s by pioneers such as Licklider, Engelbart, and Kleinrock (Engelbart and English 1968; Licklider and Taylor 1968). These scientists advanced the idea of networks' being used to create a new type of collaborative space within which remote computers, data, storage devices, and other devices would be shared to advance the work of distributed communities. With the broad deployment of the Internet and the advent of Grid technology, this vision is now being realized on an ever-increasing scale.

We have used examples from several scientific communities, to discuss various approaches to increasing participation, capability, and efficiency within distributed virtual organizations. We have described, in particular, how Grid technologies are being used to enable the formation of effective collaborative teams that span institutions and countries. Our examples illustrate how collaborative groups that extend beyond the confines of a single physical institution can allow significant increases in the aggregate human expertise and other capabilities that can be applied to challenging problems.

We have emphasized what can be done today, but significant obstacles remain to be overcome before collaborations are no longer defined by slow-moving, organizationally centralized mechanisms, but can instead form spontaneously; be managed in a user-empowered and distributed manner; and be protected and monitored by an infrastructure that maintains and enforces trust relationships. These obstacles motivate our current and future research.

10

Sociodigital Formations: Constructing an Object of Study

Saskia Sassen

One of the distinctive capabilities of computer-centered technologies is the rescaling of social relations and domains. What has tended to operate or be nested at local scales can now move to global scales, and global relations and domains can now, in turn, become directly articulated with local settings. As a result of the growing presence and use of these technologies, an increasing range of social relations and domains have become, de facto, transboundary. Understanding the place of these new computer-centered technologies and the ways in which they are transforming social relationships is the focus of an initiative launched by the Social Science Research Council (SSRC) in 2000 to contribute to the development of a social science of information technology (IT). The SSRC initiative aims at a specific component of this broad agenda for research on and conceptualization of IT, one that focuses on the work of constructing the object of research that speaks to social scientists as opposed to, for instance, computer engineers.[1]

This task presents several challenges for social scientists. We—SSRC's Committee on Information Technology and International Cooperation—decided to address two of these. One involves avoiding technological determinism or limiting research to the "impacts" of information technology on existing social arrangements. In a nutshell our concern with respect to this issue was to recognize that these technologies have contributed to construct whole new domains of interaction. To gain some closure on the effort, we confined our focus to computer-centered interactive technology and to interactive electronic information and communication structures. A second challenge is to go beyond what is one of the most evident and powerful capabilities that these technologies bring to interactive domains: decentralized access. In practical terms this has meant the possibility of reaching far more people—as consumers, as students, as activists—and firms and institutions. But these technologies evince at least two other basic capabilities that we need to factor into social science research. One is interconnectivity (i.e., each point of access can interact directly with all other such points); the other is simultaneity (same-time transacting). In combination with the first, these two capabilities have the capacity to produce significant qualitative transformations in communication and information structures.

QUALITATIVE TRANSFORMATIONS: TWO EXAMPLES

In my own research, I find electronic financial markets to be a good illustration of such a qualitative transformation that comes about when all three capabilities—decentralized access, interconnectivity, and simultaneity—are in play. One of the key and most significant outcomes of digital technology in finance has been the jump in orders of magnitude and the extent of worldwide interconnectedness. There are basically three ways in which digitization has contributed to this outcome. One is the use of sophisticated software, a key feature of the global financial markets today and a condition that in turn has made possible an enormous amount of innovation. Second, the distinctive features of digital networks can maximize the implications of global market integration by producing the possibility of simultaneous interconnected flows and transactions, as well as decentralized access for investors and for exchanges in a growing number of countries. The key background factor here is that since the late 1980s, the trend has been for more and more countries to de- and reregulate their economies according to a particular set of criteria that has ensured cross-border convergence, the linking of different markets, and the global integration of their financial centers. Third, because finance is particularly about transactions rather than simple flows of money, the technical properties of digital networks assume added meaning. Interconnectivity, simultaneity, decentralized access, and software instruments all contribute to multiply the number of transactions, the length of transaction chains (i.e., distance between instrument and underlying asset), and thereby the number of participants. The overall outcome is a complex architecture of transactions. These three features of today's global market for capital are inextricably related to the new technologies.

This example makes clear that new technologies are partly embedded in institutional environments that have the power to inscribe such technology. As a result, the outcome does not reflect exclusively the features of the particular technology at work. One focus of the SSRC's efforts to contribute to a social science of information technology has been to capture the interactions between the technical and social logics at work in producing distinctive outcomes across different social contexts in which information technologies are used. These new technologies have had a deeply transformative effect but they do not dislodge the fact that a substantive agenda organizes market actors. Today's global capital market is a complex formation markedly different from earlier global financial markets partly because of its extensive digitization. But digitization does not replace the financial—as different from digitization—logic driving actors even as it changes the composition of their options. Finance remains embedded in a larger set of economic institutions. The global capital market is a particularly helpful case for examining these dynamics of transformation and embeddedness.

Electronic activist networks provide a contrasting example of the transformative potential of information technologies, illustrating how the local can become embedded in the nonlocal, specifically global networks and global agendas. Through their practices, these local but globally connected activists are developing a particular type of global politics, one that runs through localities and is not predicated on the existence of global institutions. Simultaneous decentralized access can help local actors have a sense of participation in struggles that are not necessarily global, but are globally distributed in that they occur in locality after locality. Computer-centered interactive technologies facilitate multiscalar transactions and simultaneous interconnectivity among those confined largely to a locality.[2]

Both of these instances are examples of scaling that incorporate all three capabilities of computer interactive technologies. They suggest that the scale-up of such technologies is not simply a matter of reaching larger numbers of people, but has the potential to transform social structures and relationships. The SSRC's effort to construct a different type of object for research from those that are typical in the social sciences might also be of interest to researchers in other fields pursuing innovative ways of using these technologies. For example, "Grid technology" that makes possible scientific collaboration discussed by Foster and Kesselman (in this volume) would seem to factor in all three capabilities of IT.

THE SSRC PROJECT: SPECIFYING THE PROBLEM

SSRC's project on information technology is designed to capture the distinctiveness and variable weight of computer-centered interactive technologies in a broad range of electronic communication and information structures.[3] A key objective is the development of analytic categories that would allow the researcher to factor in this variability.[4] Models centered on technology as the explanatory variable—a common choice—can capture intensity of impact (weak, strong) but cannot adequately capture other features of this variability (e.g., the formation of new interactive domains). Understanding the place of these new computer-centered technologies and their capabilities from a social science perspective requires avoiding a purely technological interpretation and recognizing the embeddedness and the variable outcomes of these technologies for different economic, political, and social orders. They can indeed be constitutive of new social dynamics, but they can also be derivative or merely reproduce older conditions. Further, while some of their capabilities are distinct and exclusive to these technologies, others simply amplify the effects of older technologies.

Methodologically, this concern required us to go beyond the notion that understanding these technologies can be reduced to the question of impacts. There is a growing literature that examines the impacts of these technologies on familiar domains long constructed as objects of study by the various social sciences.[5] But impacts are only one of several forms of the intersection of society and technology. Others have to do with the constitution of whole new sociotechnical interactive domains—what we call digital formations—which in turn need to be constructed as objects of study. This means examining the specific ways in which these technologies are embedded in (often very specialized) distinct contexts. And it requires examining the mediating cultures that organize the relation between these technologies and users—among which we might include matters as diverse as gendering or the utility logics that organize use. These mediating cultures can be quite diverse and particular; for example, when the objective is control and surveillance, the practices and dispositions involved are likely to be different from those involved in using electronic markets or engaging in large-scale computer-based conversations.

If these technologies can transform existing, and even constitute whole new interactive domains, we cannot confine the analytic development of this field of inquiry to framing analyses in terms of independent and dependent variables, by far the most common approach in the social sciences. We also need to develop analytic categories able to capture formations that incorporate into one entity what would be conceived of as mutually exclusive conditions or attributes in the independent-dependent variable framing, a subject I return to later.

HOW WE WENT ABOUT SPECIFYING
COMPUTER-CENTERED INTERACTIVE SETTINGS

We established what we might call disciplining conditions for executing the second step of our project: specifying the properties of actual interactive settings. First, we confined our project to electronically structured interactive domains.[6] Second, we selected actually operating domains, rather than simulated environments, since we were not interested in game-theoretic models but wanted to understand the properties of actual interactive settings, including their possibly erratic character. Finally, we narrowed the choice of researchers and foci for analysis to a specific substantive field: interactive domains that are or are becoming part of the world of transnational and international relations.

Proceeding inductively seemed the most effective option given our aim of understanding key features of actual working domains in order to develop an analytic category or model that could then be used for examining other such electronic interactive domains. Since one of our key concerns is to get at the properties of new interactive domains made possible by these technologies, we decided to focus on multiple and very diverse empirical instances of such interactive domains. To that end we selected researchers (both social scientists and computer scientists) working on, among other topics, large-scale Internet-based conversations; global communication systems of major multinational corporations; early conflict-warning systems; electronic financial markets; electronic activist networks; knowledge spaces; and open source software development communities. These are all interactive domains structured electronically, and they are all actual empirical cases.

One way of addressing our concerns in the project was to emphasize the variable interaction between the diverse capabilities (technical and social) involved. First, we defined as technical capabilities those endogenous to electronic information and communication structures. Insofar as these interactive electronic structures involve people (there are those that do not), we defined them as containing endogenized social logics directly affecting the transactions—for example, rationales and utility functions of users, whether traders, open source software developers, or the other actors the project focuses on. Each of the domains we selected contains a specific type of interaction between endogenous technical capabilities and endogenized social logics. Second, we recognized that the weight of either the technical or the social will vary according to the domain and according to the cumulative causation or path dependence (i.e., closing out the full range of possibilities that may have existed at one time) set in motion with each of these combinations.[7] The particular techniques and methods to be deployed to capture this variability will depend partly on the particular digital formation under study. The key is that they should accommodate variability of interaction between technical and social factors (as defined in our project), and tendencies toward path dependence in the development of these interactions.

Let me elaborate briefly on the above. An important issue for us was, as I indicated earlier, to avoid technological determinism yet at the same time to recognize the specific capabilities of computer-centered interactive technologies. One reason for this was, again, that these technologies can constitute whole new domains for social interaction and cannot be confined to the status of an independent variable as is so often the case. In their digitized form, these domains exhibit properties of their own that derive from technical capabilities enabling specific patterns of interaction. These properties are then endogenous to these digitized structures rather than the product of an exogenous context—that is, financial system, educational system, the interstate system—even though the technologies themselves tend to result from nontechnical rationales (e.g., much of the development in electronic interactive domains has been driven by finance and its objectives). Among these endogenous properties are the simultaneity of information exchange, distributive outcomes, and capacity for electronic storage and memory, in combination with the new possibilities for access and dissemination that characterize the Internet and other computer-centered information systems.

But insofar as these are interactive social domains they are also characterized by an endogenizing of social logics. By social logics we intend to refer to a broad range of conditions, actors, and projects, including specific utility logics of users as well as the substantive rationalities of institutional and ideational orders. These endogenized social logics will (a) vary from one domain to another (e.g., electronic financial markets and electronic activist networks both use the three technical capabilities described earlier, but they do so for very different purposes), and (b) will variously alter the straightforward technical effect—that is, they may reduce, enhance, or distort the technical capabilities.[8] Further, social logics can produce whole new possibilities and push technical advances, as has clearly been the case in electronic financial markets, for example. In brief, from a social science perspective, as compared to a purely engineering one, such digitized information and communication structures and dynamics are mixed domains in that they filter, and are given meaning by, social logics.

This way of approaching our problem allows us to conceive of these electronic information and communication structures as resulting from various mixes of computer-centered technical capabilities and the broad range of social contexts that provide the utility logics, substantive rationalities, and cultural meanings for the particular types of digital interaction involved. In this regard then the digital spaces that concern us in this project are sociodigital.

Digital formation is the construct we settled on in the project to designate these specific types of information and communication structures. Digital formations are then to be distinguished from digital technology tout court. Further, not all digital networks are digital formations. The latter are mixed outcomes in that they result from endogenous technical properties and endogenized social logics. They are digitized structures but are partly shaped and given meaning by social, political, economic, ideational, and often visual conditions that exist typically outside of or, at the minimum, transcend the technology as such.

Digital formations can assume a variety of forms. Among those familiar to the social sciences are networks, markets, and communities. But there are other ways of typifying these formations both within and outside the conceptual framing of the social sciences. We can also expect new types of forms to emerge as the use of these technologies widens. The multiplication of digital formations over the last decade means that these can in turn begin to function as social, albeit digitized, conditionings for new technical developments.

The presence of social logics in the structuring of these formations means, from a social science perspective, that the technical capabilities of these new technologies are characterized by both variability and specificity. Technical capabilities are deployed or used in ways that are uneven and contradictory within diverse digital formations. They unfold in particular contexts—that is, they do not exist as purely technological events. This in turn makes it difficult to generalize their transformative effects. Variability and specificity are crucial dimensions emerging from the diverse foci of analysis in our project. The choice of researchers in the project sought to address this as each focuses in great detail on a different subject. While variability and specificity make generalization difficult, detailed study can illuminate patterns and structures helpful in hypothesizing future trends and in developing agendas for research as IT continues to evolve.[9]

BEGINNING THE WORK OF
LOCATING DIGITAL FORMATIONS

A key issue in the project is the construction of digital formations as an object of study. There are several analytic vocabularies that can be used to do this. Identifying and also developing such vocabularies is part of the conceptual mapping of this field of inquiry and the effort to generate research agendas on the subject. Each of the researchers in the project worked in a specialized discipline and hence used a distinct analytic vocabulary and focused on a distinct puzzle or theme.[10] Here I will simply discuss some strategies for beginning the work of locating a digital formation in a conceptual field that allows us to capture both endogenous technical properties and "external" social logics. Which of these external social logics become endogenized will depend on the particular domain under study.

We identify analytic operations that allow us to factor in the intersection of technologies and social logics. These analytic operations should hold whether these technologies are derivative, transformative, or constitutive. And they should hold for a broad range of specific types of digital formations. Such analytic operations can assume multiple forms. We have opted for three such operations, sufficiently complex as to accommodate a broad range of outcomes. We specify these as a first approximation for locating digital formations by understanding the broader field within which they emerge and eventually get constituted as electronic information and communication structures.

At the most general level we want to emphasize the importance of analytic categories and frames that allow us to capture the complex imbrications between the computer capabilities that concern us here and the contexts within which they are deployed or used. A second set of analytic operations concerns the mediating practices and cultures that organize the relation between these technologies and users in order to understand more precisely the social logics at work. (This would seem to be a crucial issue for the implementation of computer-centered interactive initiatives in the educational system.) Until quite recently there was no critical elaboration of these mediations because it was assumed that questions of access, competence, and interface design fully captured mediating experience. A third set of analytic operations is aimed at recognizing questions of scaling, an area where these particular technologies have evinced enormous transformative and constitutive capabilities. In the social sciences, scale (not to be confused with scale-up) has largely been conceived of as a given or as context and has, in that regard, not been a critical category. The new technologies have brought scale to the fore precisely through their destabilizing of existing hierarchies of scale and notions of nested hierarchies. Thereby they have contributed to launch a whole new heuristic, which, interestingly, also resonates with developments in the natural sciences where questions of scaling have surfaced in novel ways. The next three sections develop these issues very briefly.

Digital/Social Imbrications

Using the term *imbrication* is a way of specifying an interaction that is not characterized by hybridity or blurring: the technical and the social can shape and condition each other but each is and remains specific and distinct.[11] And such interactions can occur in often short or long chains, where one outcome (social) contributes to a new technical element that can contribute to a new social condition that in turn behaves like a conditioning for the technical. Throughout these interactions the specificity is maintained even as each is transformed, and in that sense this process can be described as one of imbrications.

As a first approximation we can identify three features of this process of imbrication. To illustrate, we can use one of the key capabilities of these technologies, that of raising the mobility of capital and thereby changing the relationship between mobile firms and territorial nation-states. This is further accentuated by the "dematerialization" brought about by the digitization of much economic activity. Digitization raises the mobility of what we have customarily thought of as not mobile, or barely mobile. Once digitized, an economic activity or good gains hypermobility—instantaneous circulation through digital networks with global span. Both mobility and digitization are usually seen as mere effects or at best functions of the new technologies. Such conceptions erase the fact that achieving this outcome requires multiple conditions, including such diverse ones as infrastructure and legal changes.

The first feature, then, is that "producing" capital mobility and dematerialization takes capital fixity—state-of-the-art-built environments, a talented professional workforce on the ground at least some of the time, legal systems, and conventional infrastructure from highways to airports and railways. These are all partly place-bound conditions. Once we recognize that the hypermobility of the instrument had to be *produced*, we introduce nondigital variables in our analysis of the digital. Such an interpretation carries implications for theory and practice. For instance, simply having access to these technologies does not necessarily alter the position of resource-poor countries or organizations in an international system with enormous inequality in the power to shape larger regulatory frames for the use of these technologies.[12]

A second feature that needs to be recovered here is that the capital fixity needed for hypermobility and dematerialization is itself transformed in this process. The real estate industry illustrates some of these issues. Financial-services firms have invented instruments that liquefy real estate, thereby facilitating investment and circulation of these instruments in global markets. Yet, part of what constitutes real estate remains very physical. At the same time, however, that which remains physical has been transformed by the fact that it is represented by highly liquid instruments that can circulate in global markets. One way of capturing the difference would be to call it a form of extreme landlord absenteeism. It may look the same, it may involve the same bricks and mortar, it may be new or old, but it is a transformed entity.

The nature of place-boundedness here differs from what it may have been one hundred years ago when it was far more likely to be a form of immobility. Today it is a place-boundednesss that is in turn inflected or inscribed by the hypermobility of some of its components, products, and outcomes. Both capital fixity and mobility are located in a temporal frame where speed is ascendant and consequential. This type of capital fixity cannot be fully captured through a description confined to its material and locational features.

A third feature in this process of imbrication can be captured through the notion of the social logics organizing the process. Many of the digital components of financial markets are inflected by the agendas that drive global finance, and these are not technological per se. The same technical properties can produce outcomes that differ from those of electronic financial markets. Much of our interacting in digital space would lack any meaning or referents if we were to exclude the nondigital world. It is deeply inflected by the cultures, the material practices, the legal systems, the imaginaries that take place outside digital space. It is necessary then to distinguish between the technologies and the digital formations they contribute to make possible. The types of digital spaces of concern to our project are not exclusively technical conditions that stand outside the social. They are embedded in the larger societal, cultural, subjective, economic, imaginary structurations of lived experience and the systems within which we exist and operate.

In this regard then digitization is multivalent. It brings with it an amplification of both mobile and fixed capacities. It inscribes the nondigital but is itself also inscribed by the nondigital. The specific content, implications, and consequences of each of these variants are empirical questions—objects for study. So what is conditioning the outcome when digital technologies are at work and what is conditioned by the outcome? We have difficulty capturing this multivalence through our conventional categories that tend to dualize and posit mutual exclusivity: if it is immobile, it *is* immobile, and if it is mobile, it *is* mobile (a type of endogeneity problem). Using the example of real estate signals that the partial representation of real estate through liquid financial instruments produces a complex imbrication of the material and the dematerialized moments of that which we continue to call real estate. And so does the partial endogeneity of physical infrastructure in electronic financial markets.

Mediating Practices and Cultures

One consequence of the above is that the articulations between digital space and users—whether social, political, or economic actors—are constituted in terms of mediating cultures and/or practices. They result partly from the values, cultures, power systems, and institutional orders within which users are embedded. Use is not simply a question of access and understanding how to use the hardware and the software.

There is a strong tendency in the literature to assume use to be an unmediated event and hence to make it unproblematic (once access and competence are given). There is in fact much more of a critical literature when it comes to questions of access. At best, recognition of a mediating culture has been confined to that of the "techie," one that has become naturalized rather than recognized as one particular type of mediating culture. Beyond this thick computer-centered-use culture, there is a tendency to flatten the practices of users to questions of competence and utility.

From the perspective of the social sciences, use of the technology should be problematized rather than simply seen as shaped by technical requirements and the necessary knowledge, even though this might be the perspective of the computer scientist and engineer who designed it. For instance, in his research on use of the Internet by different types of Arab groups, Jon Anderson (2003) found that the young "westernized" Arabs in his study made the same use as many youths in our societies: cruising, chat clubs, shopping. In contrast, scholars of the Koran, the most traditional group in his study, made a far more sophisticated use of the technology as they hyperlinked their way through the text and prior text annotations. Being scholars of the text, they had a complex mediating culture that allowed them to use the technology (no matter how "traditional" the activity) far more intensely and to derive a far greater utility. These mediating cultures also can produce a subject and a subjectivity that become part of the mediation. For instance, in open source networks much meaning is derived from the fact that these practitioners contest a dominant economic-legal system centered in private-property protections; participants become active subjects in a process that extends beyond their individual work and produces a culture. There are multiple ways of examining the mediating cultures organizing use. Among others, these can conceivably range from small-scale ethnographies to macrolevel surveys, from descriptive to highly theorized accounts, from a focus on ideational forms to one on structural conditions.

Scaling: The Transformative and Constitutive Capabilities of New Digital Technologies

Narrowing the discussion of scaling to the formation of transboundary domains (e.g., transnational civil society, transnational corporate networks, regional integration)—the overall focus in our project—we can identify four types of scaling dynamics in the constitution of global digital formations. These four dynamics are not mutually exclusive, as becomes clear when we use the example of what is probably one of the most globalized and advanced instances of a digital formation: electronic financial markets. A first type of scaling dynamic is the formation of global domains that function at the self-evident global scale, for example, some types of very large-scale conversations (see, e.g., the chapter by Sack in Latham and Sassen 2005).

A second type of scaling can be identified in the local practices and conditions that become directly articulated with global dynamics, not having to move through the traditional hierarchy of jurisdictions. Electronic financial markets also can be used as an illustration here. The starting point is floor- or screen-based trading in exchanges and firms that are part of a worldwide network of financial centers. These localized transactions link up directly to a global electronic market. What begins as local gets rescaled at the global level.

A third type of scaling dynamic results from the fact that interconnectivity and decentralized simultaneous access multiplies the cross-border connections among various localities. This produces a very particular type of global formation, one that is a kind of distributed outcome: it resides in the multiplication of lateral and horizontal transactions, or in the recurrence of a process in a network of local sites, without the aggregation that leads to an actual globally scaled digital formation as is the case with electronic markets. Instances are open source software development, certain types of early conflict-warning systems, and worldwide activist networks (see, e.g., chapters by Weber, Alker, Bach and Stark, and Sassen in Latham and Sassen 2005).

A fourth type of scaling dynamic results from the fact that global formations can actually be partly embedded in subnational sites and move between these differently scaled practices and organizational forms in a continuous two-way flow. For instance, the global electronic financial market is constituted both through electronic markets with global span, and through locally embedded conditions—that is, financial centers and all they entail, from infrastructure to systems of trust. So are the global communication flagships of multinational corporations (see chapter by Ernst in Latham and Sassen 2005).

The new digital technologies have not caused these developments, but they have in variable yet specific ways facilitated them and shaped them. The overall effect is to reposition the meaning of local and global (when internetworked) in that each of these will tend to be multiscalar. For example, much of what we might still experience as the "local" (an office building or a house or an institution right there in our neighborhood or downtown) actually is a microenvironment with global span insofar as it is internetworked. Such a microenvironment is in many senses a localized entity, but it is also part of global digital networks that give it immediate far-flung span. To continue to think of this as simply local is not very useful. It is a multiscalar condition. Part of the work of constructing electronic information and communication structures as an object for socioscientific study entails locating these structures against the scalar complexity that the new technologies have made possible rather than taking scales as givens and self-contained.

NOTES

1. The results of this initiative can be found in Latham and Sassen (eds.), *Digital Formations: Information Technologies and New Architectures in the Global Realm* (Prince-

ton, NJ: Princeton University Press, 2005). Details about the various components of the initiative can be found on the Committee on Information Technology and International Cooperation's website at ssrc.org. See also *Items* (the official publication of the SSRC), Spring 2004. We thank the Ford Foundation for its generous support.

2. Both of these examples are developed in detail in my chapter "Electronic Markets and Activist Networks: The Weight of Social Logics in Digital Formations," in Latham and Sassen (eds.), *Digital Formations: Information Technologies and New Architectures in the Global Realm* (Princeton, NJ: Princeton University Press, 2005).

3. We do not assume that technology and society are actually separate entities, and accept many of the propositions in the critical social science literature that posit that technology is one particular instantiation of society—society frozen; that is to say, one moment in a trajectory that once might have been experienced as simply social. Without losing this critical stance we want, nonetheless, to isolate the variable we will refer to as *technology*.

4. We are, to some extent, working against a profuse scholarship centered on the technical properties of the new interactive computer technologies and their capacities for producing change. These technologies increasingly dominate explanations of contemporary change and development, with technology seen as the impetus for the most fundamental social trends and transformations. Such explanations also tend to understand these technologies exclusively in terms of their technical properties and to construct the relation to the social world as one of applications and impacts.

5. For critical examinations that reveal particular shortcomings of technology-driven explanations, see, for example., Wajcman 2002; Loader 1998; Nettime 1997; Hargittai 1998; and more generally Latour 1991; Munker and Roesler 1997; MacKenzie 1999; MacKenzie and Wajcman 1999; World Information Order 2002; Howard and Jones 2004; and Avgerou et al. 2004.

6. There are important types of capabilities inherent to these technologies that fall outside the focus of this project, notably robotics, routine automated data processing, and the design of virtual environments. Further, a number of novel formations resulting from these technologies are not explored here. In Sassen (2006, part 3), I identify several highly specialized, novel, cross-border assemblages that result from a dislodging of bits of territory, authority, and rights once lodged in the nation state. Among the more familiar instances is the new International Criminal Court and the new types of global jurisdictions it enables..

7. Just to recapitulate, by the *technical* we mean here the digital technologies in play, and by the *social*, the logics or utility functions that drive users—whether individuals or organizations.

8. Factoring in endogenized social logics and capturing their effect on technical properties is a crucial methodological element in the project. I have examined some of these issues in "Electronic Markets and Activist Networks: The Weight of Social Logics," referred to in note 2. This type of understanding also would contest the still-common assumption that a new technology will ipso facto replace all older technologies that are less efficient, or slower at executing the tasks the new technology is best at.

9. The uneven and often contradictory character of these technologies and their associated information and communication structures also leads us to posit that

these technologies should not be viewed simply as factor endowments. This type of view is present in much of the literature, often implicitly, and represents these technologies as a function of the attributes of a region or an actor—ranging from regions and actors fully endowed, or with full access, to those without access.

10. It is clearly impossible to summarize this material here, and summaries would be of little use. We can only refer the interested reader to the published collection (see note 1). Each chapter in the volume that resulted from the project is concerned with a distinct digital formation and illustrates a particular research strategy and theoreticoempirical specification.

11. Please refer to the qualifications in note 4.

12. Much of my work on global cities has been an effort to conceptualize and document the fact that the global digital economy requires massive concentrations of material and social resources in order to be what it is (see, e.g., Sassen 2001). Finance is an important intermediary in this regard: it represents a capability for liquefying various forms of nonliquid wealth and for raising the mobility (i.e., hypermobility) of that which is already liquid. But to do so, even finance needs significant concentrations of material resources.

11

Measuring and Managing Successful Organizational Scale-Up

Eric G. Flamholtz and Yvonne Randle

This chapter provides a framework for understanding, measuring, and managing the process of organizational scale-up in business enterprises. In this context, scale-up is viewed in terms of the movement from one stage of organizational growth to another over an enterprise's life cycle after the stage of "birth" has been successfully completed. Specifically, *scale-up* refers to the process of developing the set of "organizational capabilities" or "form" required by an enterprise as it increases in size and complexity.

In this chapter we present a specific organizational life cycle model that can be used to identify the point at which specific scale-ups to the business enterprise should occur. We use this model in conjunction with an organizational effectiveness or success model (Flamholtz 1986, 1995) that has been and is being empirically tested (Flamholtz 2003) to indicate what needs to be done for successful scale-up as well as what can go wrong. In addition, we describe two different instruments—the Organizational Effectiveness Survey and the Growing Pains Questionnaire—which can be used to assess the extent to which an organization scales successfully as it develops over time.

We first provide an explanation and definition of scale-up in economic organizations. Next, we present a review of life cycle models of organizational growth, which enable us to identify the critical points of organizational scale-up. Third, we present a model of organizational scale-up that specifies what must be done to build a successful organization at different stages of growth that is based on our own and others' research. Next, we present and describe two instruments that can be used to assess the extent to which an organization has been successful to date in "scaling up" and the extent to which it is positioned for future scale-ups.

217

THE CONCEPT AND CONTEXT OF SCALE-UP

Scale-up in economic organizations cannot be explained simply in terms of growth in size (e.g., in revenues, people, etc.). In fact, organizations can literally "choke" on their own growth when they have not developed the internal capabilities to support it (Flamholtz and Randle 1987). Research by many organizational life cycle theorists (Greiner 1972; Adizes 1979; Quinn and Cameron 1983; Churchill and Lewis 1983; Flamholtz and Randle 2000) provides a framework to understand the problem of scale-up in economic enterprises that takes other factors into consideration. Life cycle models suggest that there are definable states in the growth of enterprises from birth to expansion to maturity and ultimate decline. Each stage of growth after successful "birth" occurs at a specific point in an organization's life and brings with it a predictable set of organizational development issues that must be successfully dealt with if the organization is to move on to the next stage (that is, to scale up) effectively.

Accordingly, we define scale-up in economic enterprises as "the extent to which an organization's design (systems, processes, and structures) fits with its stage of growth/development." An organization whose internal capabilities effectively support the challenges it faces at a given stage of growth/development has scaled up effectively. If an organization fails to develop and implement the systems, structures, and processes needed to support its growth/development, it has not scaled up effectively. As a result, it will experience difficulties—and may even be in jeopardy of failing.

ORGANIZATIONAL LIFE CYCLE MODELS AND THE POINT OF SCALE-UP

Life cycle theorists suggest that organizations evolve through a predictable series of stages. Based on a review of the life cycle literature, this section briefly describes the theoretical foundation of these models as well as the dimensions of the models themselves. We conclude with a summary of the strengths and limitations of this approach for explaining organizational growth and in turn, organizational scale-up.

Background

The organizational life cycle models are based on the structural contingency approach to the study of organizations; in this case that approach focuses on the relationship between organizational size and structure. Research on this relationship suggests that increasing size—operationalized as physical capacity, personnel, organizational inputs/outputs, and/or resources (Kimberly 1976)—is related to increasing differentiation (Blau and Schoenherr 1971; Meyer 1972), increasing specialization (Pugh, Hickson, and Hinnings 1969; Blau and Schoenherr 1971), and increasing decentralization of decision-making authority and formalization of role activities (Child 1973). The theory underlying all of these findings is that, as organizations increase in size, they become more bureaucratic (Weber 1947) or mechanistic (Burns and Stalker 1961) in form. In other words, as organizations grow, functions or skills needed to perform certain tasks become specialized, rules and procedures come to govern performance of the organization's members, roles and responsibilities become more clearly defined, a hierarchy develops to coordinate the efforts of members, and rewards become increasingly based on performance.

Organizational life cycle theorists build on this idea that as organizations grow, they change from what Mintzberg (1984, 207) calls a "simple entrepreneurial structure" to a "more elaborated, bureaucratic structure" by dividing the various changes in structure that occur over a company's life into predictable stages.

Stage Models of Growth and Development

From a biological perspective, the concept of a life cycle suggests that there is a relationship between an organism's age and its development (both physical and psychological). In life cycle models, development is viewed as a series of stages that proceed in an orderly and invariant fashion (Worchel and Cooper 1983). Stages are characterized by a particular physical or psychological "form." Human physical development, for example, may be broken down into the stages of childhood, adolescence, adulthood, and old age. Examples of life cycle models of human psychological development include those proposed by Freud (1933) and Piaget (1932).

Like their biological counterparts, organizational life cycle theorists divide development into a series of stages, each characterized by a different organizational structure or form. These stages are assumed to be sequential and not easily reversed (Lavoie and Culbert 1978). Some organizational life cycle models use the relationship between age and form to define stages (Thain 1969; Scott 1971; Adizes 1979; Quinn and Cameron 1983). In other models, stages are defined in terms of the relationship between size and form (Cowen, Middaugh III, and McCarthy 1984; Flamholtz 1986, 1995), while still others define stages in terms of the relationship between form and both age and size (Greiner 1972; Churchill and Lewis 1983).

Whatever definition of "stage" is used, the applicability of most life cycle models is limited because they do not adequately operationalize age and size. This leads to a situation in which the actual occurrence of a particular stage of organizational development remains vague. In most models, both age and size are defined in relative terms, with age ranging from "young to mature" and size ranging from "small to large."

In addition to inadequate definitions of age and size dimensions, there is a problem with models like Greiner's (1972) in which both age and size are used to define organization stages: they usually assume a direct relationship between the two dimensions such that as an organization ages, it also increases in size. This does not seem to mirror reality since, depending on the industry, a company could be a ten-year-old entrepreneurship (defined here as a small organization) or a ten-year-old $1 billion bureaucracy. A local coffee roaster, established in 1971, the year Starbucks was founded, may gross less than $100,000 a year today, while Starbucks has grown in size during the same time period to annual revenues in excess of $3 billion.

It appears then that the relationship between age, size, and form may not be as direct as some life cycle theorists assume it is. Further, the use of age by organizational life cycle theorists may not be as valid as size in determining the timing of stages. According to Child and Keiser:

> Although a definition [of development] in terms of age has the advantage of incorporating the temporal dimension unambiguously, it does not direct attention to the fundamental question of why, how, and through which progressions organizations change along with the passage of time. These questions are recognized more explicitly when organizational development is defined as a change in an organization's condition [of which size is one dimension]. (1981, 28)

The inability of most theorists to clearly define the specific relationship between age and/or size and form greatly restricts the usefulness and testability of most life cycle models. There are, however, two models (Miller and Friesen 1984; Flamholtz 1986, 1995) that use specific criteria to define when stages should occur. Miller and Friesen (1984) use age (less than ten years) and structure information (e.g., "informal structure") to define the first stage of their model, thereafter relying on sales growth percentages and structure to differentiate stages (e.g., the growth phase is defined by sales growth greater than 15 percent and a functional structure). Their framework may be difficult to apply to some firms. For example, if a firm is less than ten years old, growing at more than 15 percent per year, with an informal structure, it could be classified in their framework as operating either in the birth or growth phase.

Flamholtz uses specific revenue ranges based on "data obtained from actual companies" (1986, xiv; 1995) to define the stages of organizational growth in his model. At least one empirical test supports the validity of these revenue ranges for tracking organizational growth (see Randle 1990). Such a classification scheme improves on that provided by Miller and Friesen, as it precludes simultaneous classification into multiple categories.

The Five Generic Stages of Organizational Growth

Randle (1990) suggests that there are five basic "stages" of growth. These are: birth, growth, maturity, diversification, and decline. While some models (Lippett and Schmidt 1967; Scott 1971; Quinn and Cameron 1983) ignore the growth stage, only a few (Adizes 1979; Miller and Friesen 1984; Flamholtz 1986, 1995) include a decline stage, and some contain more than five stages (Greiner 1972; Adizes 1979; Churchill and Lewis 1983; Flamholtz 1986, 1995), there does appear to be at least some consensus with respect to the existence of these five stages as shown in the appendix to this chapter.

Life cycle theorists suggest that at each stage of development, organizations assume a new and different form. This form can be defined in terms of two dimensions: (1) formalization of organizational structure (e.g., roles, responsibilities, career hierarchy) and organizational systems (e.g., accounting, inventory, personnel); and (2) management focus or strategy.

Consistent with the structural contingency perspective, life cycle theorists suggest that as an organization grows, its structure (e.g., roles, responsibilities, career hierarchy) and systems become (or should become) increasingly more formalized in order to meet the challenges created by this growth. Coupled with the formalization of structure, however, is the idea that there are certain problems that managers must resolve at each stage of growth that can affect long-term success (Miller and Friesen 1984; Cameron and Whetten 1983). This suggests that there is also a "strategy" component that helps define organizational form at each stage of development. As defined by Chandler, strategy is "the determination of the basic long-term goals and objectives of the enterprise, and the adoption of courses of action and the allocation of resources necessary for carrying out these goals" (Chandler 1962, 13). In the life cycle models, "long-term goals" focus on growth and the "courses of action" are the steps taken to overcome the problems confronted at each stage of development.

Based on a review of the literature and drawing on the information presented in the appendix, the remainder of this section presents a description of organizational form at each of the five defined stages of development.

The Birth Stage

New organizations are created when an individual or group of individuals recognizes a market opportunity that is not currently being met and begins to build a business to serve this need (Freeman 1982; Flamholtz 1986, 1995). Life cycle theorists suggest that at this stage, the emphasis is on identifying a market need and creating products or services to meet this need. The organization is small and roles and responsibilities have yet to be defined.

While there are accounting, planning, and control systems, they are not formalized. For example, the owner/entrepreneur tends to do much of the planning in his or her head at this stage of development rather than relying on more formalized strategic or operational planning systems. The atmosphere that exists at the organization is characterized as creative and innovative (Lyden 1975; Quinn and Cameron 1983).

Miller and Friesen (1984) suggest that organizations remain in the birth stage until they are ten years old. Flamholtz argues that manufacturing firms transition from this stage when they achieve approximately $1 million in annual revenues. Service organizations encounter the challenges of each stage earlier in their growth, and thus should multiply their revenues by three to track their development using the revenue ranges Flamholtz (1986, 1995) provides.[1] Whatever the length of the birth stage, its primary function might be termed *proof of concept*; it lasts until there is evidence of the economic viability of the business concept.

The signal that the birth stage is ending and that the organization is entering a new stage (the growth stage in these models) is a rapid increase in sales. Thus the growth stage is the first point of scale-up for organizations, as discussed below.

The Growth Stage

This stage is characterized by a rapid increase in sales and the size of the organization as measured by the number of personnel. According to Miller and Friesen (1984), sales growth is greater than 15 percent annually, and Flamholtz (1986, 1995) suggests that sales can double or even triple over the course of a year for firms in this stage. In Flamholtz's model, this stage usually occurs when organizations reach annual sales revenues over $1 million and lasts until they reach annual revenues of $100 million.

Rapid growth has two major effects on economic organizations. First, the organizations begin to feel that their resources (e.g., plant and equipment, human) are being stretched to their limits (Flamholtz 1986, 1995) as the demand for products or services offered by the company increases. In response to this increasing demand for its products or services, the organization must scale up. This means that the organization in the growth stage must focus on acquiring more resources to support the demand (Lyden 1975; Miller and Friesen 1984). This is the stage during which many companies seek outside financing from investors. Second, organizational members will begin to feel as if the business is "out of control." This results, in part, from underdeveloped operating systems (e.g., accounting, billing, inventory, etc.) that cannot support the larger entity the organization has become (Flamholtz 1986, 1995).

According to Flamholtz (1986, 1995), once the company has acquired adequate resources to support its continued growth and its operating systems are in place, it should begin focusing on its management systems. This includes developing formalized planning and control systems, defining the organization's structure by formalizing roles and responsibilities and communicating them to the organization's members, and creating a formalized management development program that will ensure the organization has "professional" managers who will help it reach the next stage of development. While the development of these systems represents a separate stage in Flamholtz's (1986, 1995) model, the *professionalization stage*, it is treated here as a part of the growth stage of development. This is consistent with the description of this stage provided by others (Lyden 1975; Miller and Friesen 1984).

As a result of the development of both operating and management systems, the organization that attains the growth stage of development is becoming increasingly more formalized. It must, in essence, become more formalized if it is going to survive to the next stage because its informal systems and structure can no longer support its operations. Blau and Schoenherr (1971) suggest, for example, that increasing size results in increased communication and coordination problems that are resolved through changes in organizational structure (such as divisionalization and changes in the size of the administrative component).

The fundamental characteristic of the growth stage is expansion in revenues, in people, and in complexity. All of the life cycle models suggest that the organization must develop the internal capabilities to match its increased size and complexity. In brief, the central problem of the growth stage is for the organization to scale up its form or capabilities to match its current or anticipated size.

The Maturity Stage

An organization reaches this stage, according to Miller and Friesen (1984), when, after a period of rapid growth, sales growth declines to less than 15 percent a year. According to Flamholtz (1986, 1995), this stage should be attained by the time a firm reaches approximately $100 million in annual revenues. The organization, at this stage, has become "professionalized" in the sense that it now has formal operating, control, and planning systems, and its structure (roles, responsibilities, and relationships between roles) is clearly defined.

The focus at this stage is on increasing the efficiency of the systems developed during the growth stage through helping personnel adapt to and accept the changes that these systems represent. The emphasis at this stage then is on what Lippett and Schmidt (1967) call "developing stability." According to Flamholtz and Randle (2000), this stage is a critical part of making the successful transition from a "pure entrepreneurship" to an "entrepreneurially-oriented professionally managed firm."

According to Flamholtz (1986, 1995), this transition is best accomplished by focusing on explicitly defining and managing the organization's culture. To be consistent with the structures and systems now employed by the company, the culture must begin to emphasize planning, efficiency in procedures, and professionalism rather than promoting the informality inherent in the culture of entrepreneurial firms. To change the organization's culture, managers need to first identify what the existing culture is through diagnosing the meaning attached to company symbols, rites and rituals, and heroes (Deal and Kennedy 1982). Next, managers need to develop strategies for changing aspects of the culture. Deal and Kennedy (1982) suggest that training can be useful in facilitating such change and Schein (1985) suggests that corporate leadership plays a critical role in this process.

This stage is a subtle but critical part of successful scale-up. As a company has grown rapidly, and developed the advanced systems and processes necessary to support its increased size and complexity, many people, especially those who were part of the founding of the enterprise, have typically begun to mourn the passing of "the way things were" when it was a much smaller enterprise. They may, in fact, actively or passively resist the change in organizational form and procedures.

A critical part of successful scale-up is then to manage the cultural change to make the transition from a "pure entrepreneurship" to an "entrepreneurially-oriented professionally managed firm." Empirical research has indicated that successful culture management can have a direct impact upon financial performance (Flamholtz 2000).

The Diversification Stage

The fourth stage in the life cycle models has been referred to as the "revival" phase by Miller and Friesen (1984) while Flamholtz (1986, 1995) calls it the "diversification" stage. Miller and Friesen (1984) suggest that this stage is reached when, after the maturity stage, the organization again experiences a rapid increase in sales as a result of entering new market niches. Flamholtz (1986, 1995) suggests that it occurs when a company reaches the growth limit for a single product or service and decides to diversify. In their model, this normally occurs when the annual sales exceed $500 million.

According to Flamholtz (1986, 1995), if a company wants to grow further once it has reached the limit for one product, it must re-create the entire growth process from birth to maturity. This occurs, most typically, in the context of new product divisions managed by a parent firm (Thain 1969;

Scott 1971). The focus of management at this stage is on identifying new markets, creating new products or services to meet the needs of that market, and acquiring the resources to support the production process (Cowen, Middaugh III, and McCarthy 1984). In the absence of declining markets, some organizations may not diversify through product or market expansion but may remain in the maturity stage indefinitely. However, if a company fails to diversify in the face of a declining market, it may eventually fail.

Diversifying companies face the problem of integrating new product divisions into existing structures (Miller and Friesen 1984).[2] Provided that new product divisions have been successful at identifying new markets, and demand for products begins to increase, these divisions will face the same problems the entire organization faced as it grew. At the same time, however, the organization as a whole will be faced with the problem of integrating the various product divisions into a cohesive unit. Management should focus then on operating and management systems, as well as on managing the corporate culture in order to achieve integration and reduce inefficiencies.

This stage represents a different kind of scale-up. During the first three stages the enterprise was growing and scaling up a single business. Once an organization has reached this stage it will have more than one business, and the problem is to create the organizational form that is appropriate for managing a set of business enterprises, not just different product lines. Examples of successful enterprises that have achieved this stage are General Electric, Johnson & Johnson, and Nestle.

The Decline Stage

According to Miller and Friesen (1984), the decline phase is reached when demand for products levels off, product innovation is minimal, and profitability starts to drop. In Flamholtz's (1986, 1995) model, this can occur at any point in the organization's life as a result of decreasing demand for products or services offered. It can also result from management's failure to make the required changes in organizational structure, systems, and strategy to meet the challenges presented by growth.

If an organization enters this stage, it becomes critical that management focus on defining new markets or creating new markets for the existing products or services. Management should also focus on evaluating existing systems and their ability to take the organization into new markets. These steps can prevent organizational death, the final stage in the model proposed by Adizes (1979).

The decline stage can be characterized by scale-down or scale-up. Mergers and acquisitions lead to scale-up. If the problem is one of declining growth in a particular industry, then organizations might try to employ a "consolidation" strategy and acquire competitors. For example, Compaq acquired DEC and was later acquired by Hewlett-Packard, creating a behemoth organization. This form of increased size and growth creates a special problem of scale-up. It requires that a totally new organization be designed from the combined "parts" (individual businesses), and that the organization successfully transform itself to the new design.

The Nature of Organizational Transitions and Scale-Up

Most life cycle models do not directly deal with the question of how organizations move from one stage to the next at a specific age or size. Instead, most models focus on identifying what Quinn and Cameron refer to as "the consistent pattern of development [that] seems to occur in organizations over time, and [how] the organization's activities and structure in a stage are not the same as the activities and structures present in another stage" (1983, 40). These models assume that there is what Haire (1959) has termed a "lawfulness" to organizational growth and internal development and that progression from one stage to the next is a given: once an organization reaches a certain size or age it will reach the corresponding stage of development. This is captured best by Churchill and Lewis (1983, 34): "Those companies that remain in business become Stage II [or whatever stage is next in the model] enterprises."

As is true of the structural contingency perspective, in general (Dalton et al. 1980), few life cycle models offer explanations for why some organizations continue to succeed, while others fail. The answer to this question appears to lie in the change process. Research suggests that since organizations tend toward inertia (Hannan and Freeman 1984; Tushman and Romanelli 1985), changes (like the movement from one stage to the next) can be highly disruptive and sometimes "fatal" (Miller 1982). Therefore, the process through which an organization changes from one form to another (in these models, moves from one stage to the next) can be a critical determinant of success.

While the transition process appears critical, only a few life cycle theorists (Greiner 1972; Miller and Friesen 1984; Flamholtz 1986, 1995) explicitly include descriptions of this process in their models. In Greiner's (1972) model, a management "crisis" serves as the signal that the organization needs to change its form. If, and when, the crisis is overcome, the organization moves to the next stage of development. Implicit in this model is the notion that if the crisis is not overcome, the organization will fail.

In Miller and Friesen's (1984) model, the organization experiences crises of a different kind during transition periods. In this model, the crisis is usually related to performance, either in terms of profits or in terms of inefficiencies of internal operations. As performance declines, decision makers must act to fundamentally transform the organization if it is to survive. This involves simultaneously changing a number of structural factors (Miller 1982) and often includes replacement of executive leadership. Such changes occur during turbulent transition periods that are followed by periods in which the organization is relatively stable.

As is true of the other two models, in Flamholtz's (1986, 1995) model of organizational growth, transition periods in most cases are particularly traumatic for the organization. The need for a transition results from a "mismatch" between the organization's "form" and the requirements of the stage at which it should be operating, given its size. In this growth model, organizational "form" or structure consists of six key components, or "building blocks": markets selected, products (including services), resources to support growth, operational systems, management systems, and culture. The first two of these components relate to the particular business the organization is in, while the last four comprise what might be termed "organizational infrastructure."

Under this growth model, the challenge in building an organization is to combine these six key components appropriately at given stages of organizational growth. If the organization is able to achieve the necessary design and it changes its structure, systems, and management focus before it reaches a particular stage (as indicated by size), it will either not experience problems or they will be minimized.

The lack of "fit" between size and organizational design leads to problems, which Flamholtz (1986, 1995) refers to as "organizational growing pains." These growing pains indicate that change is needed if the organization is to continue operating effectively and thus reduce the likelihood of failure. They also indicate a lack of successful scale-up. If, for example, a company does not focus on developing the systems needed to support its operations at $10 million to $100 million in annual revenues, it will essentially operate as a birth stage organization even though its size (and growth) is consistent with the growth stage. This will place it at risk of failure (Flamholtz 1986; Flamholtz and Randle 1987). Life cycle theorists then suggest that success depends on the ability of managers to recognize and make the necessary changes in organizational form at the appropriate time. As Flamholtz and Randle (2000, 360) state: "The key to making this change [in form] is for the entrepreneur to recognize that the company's former mode of operation will no longer be effective." Operationally, the problem is to create the appropriate design for the organization, given its stage of growth. In other words, successful scale-up depends, to a great extent, on the organization's ability to create internal systems, structure, processes, and design commensurate with its size.

Summary of Life Cycle Models

In a sense, all life cycle models attempt to provide "blueprints" for successful organizations at each stage of development. Assuming these blueprints are valid, they can be used by decision makers to assess their own organization's development and by researchers in examining organizational success and failure.

While all models appear to offer prescriptions for successful growth, only Flamholtz's (1986, 1995) model is explicit enough to be used by both organizational decision makers and researchers. This is the only model in which the relationship between size and "organizational form" is made explicit by clearly defining both dimensions. This model identifies, in terms of revenues, when the stages should occur; suggests what managers should focus on at each stage; and describes what the "structure" of the organization should be, given its stage of development. Such descriptions increase both the applicability and testability of this life cycle model.

While Flamholtz's (1986, 1995) model is testable, it still suffers from a major limitation of most life cycle models: it does not explicitly recognize the impact that the environment can have on an organization's success or failure. Further, these models tend to treat organizations as if they operate in a vacuum, that is, theorists tend to focus on a single organization as the unit of analysis. Specifically, these models ignore an important driving force for organizational change: competition. According to Porter (1985, 1), "Competition is at the core of the success or failure of firms. Competition determines the appropriateness of a firm's activities that can contribute to its performance, such as innovation, a cohesive culture or good implementation."

It may be that the management crises (Greiner 1972), declining performance (Miller and Friesen 1984), and growing pains (Flamholtz 1986, 1995) that organizations experience as they grow result from increasing competition, not just increasing size. In fact, it may be that these problems would not arise if organizations had little or no competition. Assuming there is a market for a company's product, in a competition-free environment, an organization could adopt any form and continue to be successful since customers would have no alternative source for its products and/or services. As long as demand for its products and/or services continued to exist, there would be little incentive for the organization to adopt a different form, especially given the disruptive nature of the change process.

Competition then may have a direct impact on the need for organizations to change from one form to another over the course of their lives. It may in fact determine when these changes should occur. In the face of severe competition, for example, an organization may need to make the transition to the maturity stage of development earlier than $100 million (as proposed by Flamholtz and Randle 1998, 2000), if it is to continue being competitive. In the face of little or no competition and with adequate demand, the organization could remain indefinitely in the growth stage.

A further limitation of these models is that, with the exception of the work of Flamholtz and Kurland (2005), there has been relatively little empirical research devoted to examining the success and failure rates of organizations adopting various forms at various sizes. Some of the initial empirical research that has been performed focuses upon testing whether or not the stages occur in a sequential fashion (Miller and Friesen 1984) and whether managers' definition of effectiveness varies by stage (Cameron and Whetten 1981, 1983). While these are important questions in light of claims by some theorists that predictable stages do not occur (Tushman and Romanelli 1985), this line of research does not address the underlying causes of success and failure. More recently, Flamholtz and Kurland have conducted empirical research to address the causes of organizational success and failure (Flamholtz and Kurland 2005).

USING A LIFE CYCLE APPROACH TO EXPLAIN ORGANIZATIONAL SCALE-UP

All life cycle models implicitly describe scale-up in terms of the successful movement (defined in terms of developing the internal capabilities to support the new stage of growth/development) from one stage of growth to the next. One major problem with most models, however, is that they provide little guidance to managers with respect to when specific scale-ups are likely to occur and what managers might do to prepare for them.

While Flamholtz's (1986, 1995) model suffers from some of the same limitations as other life cycle models, its usefulness in this context is that it identifies the point at which scale-ups should occur, based on the size of the organization as measured in terms of annual sales. The model is also useful because it prescribes the organizational components, or "form," that must be developed in order to be successful at each stage of growth.

Flamholtz's model describes seven stages of organizational growth and development, with each stage defined in terms of annual revenues and one or more critical tasks that *should* receive attention at each stage of development. These critical tasks comprise what Flamholtz (1995) calls the "six building blocks of organizational" success. These tasks, all of which have been supported by previous research, are:

- Identification and definition of a viable market (Adizes 1979; Brittain and Freeman 1980; Freeman and Hannan 1983)

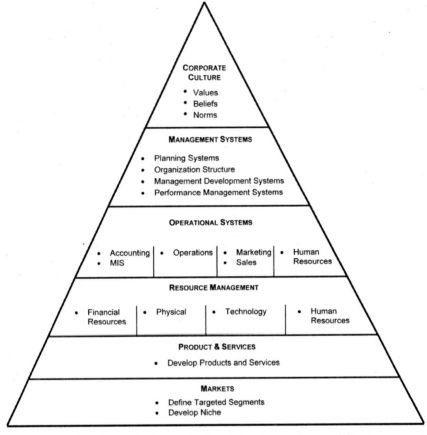

Figure 11.1. The Pyramid of Organizational Development, copyright Management Systems Consulting Corp., 2004

- Development of products and/or services for the chosen market (Burns and Stalker 1961; Midgley 1981)
- Acquisition, development, and management of resources required to operate the organization (Pfeffer and Salancik 1978; Brittain and Freeman 1980; Carroll and Yangchung 1986)
- Development of day-to-day operational systems (Starbuck 1965)
- Development of the management systems (i.e., planning, structure, management development, and performance management systems) needed to support the long-term functioning of the organization (Child and Keiser 1981; Tushman, Virany, and Romanelli 1985)

Growth Stage	Critical Development Areas	Approximate Organizational Size ($ in Millions of Sales)
I. New Venture	Markets and Products	Less than $1 million
II. Expansion	Resources and Operational Systems	$1 to $10 million
III. Professionalization	Management Systems	$10 to $100 million
IV. Consolidation	Corporate Culture	$100 to $500 million
V. Diversification	Markets and Products	$500 million to $1 billion
VI. Integration	Resources. Operational Systems. Management Systems. Culture	$1 billion +
VII. Decline	All Six Tasks	Any size organization

Figure 11.2.   The Stages of Organizational Growth

- Managing the corporate culture so that its supports the enterprise's current and long-term goals (Peters and Waterman 1982; Walton 1986)

Flamholtz (1986, 1995) embeds these six critical tasks in what he calls a "pyramid of organizational development" (shown in figure 11.1), suggesting that the tasks must be performed in a stepwise fashion. In fact, Flamholtz argues that if the organization is to function effectively and increase its chance of long-term success, the six key tasks making up the pyramid must be developed individually and as a system.

The emphasis that should be given to each task differs depending upon the size of the organization—that is, the stage of growth. Figure 11.2 identifies critical development areas associated with each stage of growth, as well as the approximate size (measured in millions of dollars of sales revenue) at which an organization can be expected to or should scale up to the next stage.

Successful scale-up—and long-term success—depends on the extent to which the organization's design "fits" with its size. When an organization has not effectively developed the systems, structures, and processes needed to support its size, it will begin to experience what Flamholtz (1986, 1995) calls "growing pains"—symptoms that the organization has not yet made the successful transition (matched its organizational design) to its current stage of development (defined in terms of revenue). In brief, growing pains indicate that the organization has not successfully scaled up and that it needs to do so.

Nature and Causes of Organizational Growing Pains

Growth, though essential to organizations over the long term, creates its own set of problems—the growing pains described above. Growing pains indicate that the "infrastructure" of an enterprise (i.e., the resources, internal operational and management systems, and culture it needs at a given stage of growth) has not kept up with its size, as measured by its revenues. Stated differently, it means that scale-up has not been successful. For example, a business with $200 million in revenue may only have an infrastructure to support the operations of a firm with $50 million in revenue, or one-fourth its size. This type of situation typically occurs after a period of growth, sometimes quite rapid growth, where the infrastructure has not been changed to adjust to the new size and complexity of the organization. The result is an "organizational development gap" (that is, a gap between the organization's actual infrastructure and that required at its current size or stage of development), which produces the growing pains.

The severity with which an organization experiences growing pains indicates the extent to which it is experiencing problems scaling up (to the next stage of development). When these growing pains are extreme, the organization is in jeopardy of failing if it does not take the steps needed to develop the systems, processes, and design needed to take it fully into the next stage of growth (i.e., have a design that "fits" with its size).

Empirical research (Flamholtz and Hua 2002b) has indicated that there is a statistically significant relationship between organizational growing pains and financial performance. Flamholtz has developed two instruments that assess:

1. The extent to which an organization is experiencing problems in scaling up—that is, the extent to which the organization is experiencing "growing pains"
2. The extent to which an organization has developed the systems and structures needed to operate effectively at its stage of growth (i.e., the extent to which an organization has "scaled up")

Growing Pains Questionnaire

Figure 11.3 presents a questionnaire Flamholtz (1986, 1995) developed to measure the extent to which an enterprise is facing problems in making the transition from one stage of development to the next. Respondents are asked to indicate the extent to which they believe their organization is suffering from each "growing pain" on a five-point Likert scale (Likert 1932) that ranges from "to a very great extent" to "to a very slight extent." Scores on the questionnaire can range from a low of 10, which suggests that successful scale (i.e., organizational transition) has occurred, to a high score of 50, which means that the company is facing severe problems with respect to scale-up that may ultimately lead to its failure.

We have used this survey for more than twenty-five years and collected a database of "organizational growing pains scores" from companies of all

Name: _____   Date:_____

Position/Title:_____   Firm: _____

To what extent do each of the following describe your organization? Place a check mark in the appropriate column.

Growing Pains	A To A Very Slight Extent	B To A Slight Extent	C To Some Extent	D To A Great Extent	E To A Very Great Extent
1. *People feel that there are not enough hours in the day.*	☐	☐	☐	☐	☐
2. *People are spending too much time "putting out fires."*	☐	☐	☐	☐	☐
3. *Many people are not aware of what others are doing.*	☐	☐	☐	☐	☐
4. *People lack understanding of where the firm is heading.*	☐	☐	☐	☐	☐
5. *There are too few good managers.*	☐	☐	☐	☐	☐
6. *Everybody feels "I have to do it myself if I want to get it done correctly."*	☐	☐	☐	☐	☐
7. *Most people feel our meetings are a waste of time.*	☐	☐	☐	☐	☐
8. *When plans are made, there is very little follow-up and things just don't get done.*	☐	☐	☐	☐	☐
9. *Some people feel insecure about their place in the firm.*	☐	☐	☐	☐	☐
10. *The firm has continued to grow in sales but not in profits.*	☐	☐	☐	☐	☐

Figure 11.3.   Organizational Growth Pains Questionnaire

sizes in all industries (see Flamholtz and Randle 2000, chapter 3). Data from this source indicate that growing pains increase at each stage of growth from stages I to V and decline in stage VI of the Flamholtz life cycle model. This suggests that the "survivors" have sufficiently developed their infrastructure so that it is appropriate for their stage of growth. Stated differently, organizations that survive to stage VI have achieved successful scale-up, and, as a result, have reduced growing pains.

Organizational Effectiveness	A To A Very Slight Extent	B To A Slight Extent	C To Some Extent	D To A Great Extent	E To A Very Great Extent
1. Overall, we have enough of the right technology/information systems to be an effective organization.	☐	☐	☐	☐	☐
2. Overall, we are effective in making day-to-day operational decisions.	☐	☐	☐	☐	☐
3. Our company has a well-developed planning process that addresses operational (day to day) issues.	☐	☐	☐	☐	☐
4. We effectively gather and use information about our customers and competition.	☐	☐	☐	☐	☐
5. People's behavior is consistent with our organization's stated culture/values.	☐	☐	☐	☐	☐

Figure 11.4.   Organizational Effectiveness Survey

Organizational Effectiveness Survey

Flamholtz developed the Organizational Effectiveness Survey (1986, 2003) to assess the extent to which an organization has developed the systems and structures needed to support current and promote continued growth. The survey focuses on assessing the extent to which the organization has scaled up overall by assessing the extent to which it has developed appropriate systems, processes, and structures at each of the six levels in the pyramid of organizational success. The survey also includes a seventh dimension—financial results—defined as the extent to which the organization has the capacity and systems in place to effectively manage the financial aspects of its business. Respondents are asked to indicate the extent to which sixty-five items describe their organization on a five-point Likert scale (Likert 1932) that ranges from "to a very slight extent" to "to a very great extent." Figure 11.4 contains five sample survey items.

Two different measurements are calculated from these results: *extent developed* and *percent favorable* scores. "Extent developed" scores range from 1 to 5 and indicate the extent to which the organization has developed the processes, systems, structures, and so forth, overall and at each level in the pyramid of organizational success.

We have developed a set of proposed "norms" for strategic organizational development. As shown in figure 11.5, scores of successful organizations depend upon the organization's size. This figure indicates the minimum score thought to be required at each stage of growth. The hypothesis

Level of Pyramid	Stage I	Stage II	Stage III	Stage IV	Stage V
Markets	≥ 3.0	≥ 4.0	≥ 4.0	≥ 4.0	≥ 4
Products/Services	≥ 3.0	≥ 4.0	≥ 4.0	≥ 4.0	≥ 4
Resources	≥ 2.0	≥ 3.0	≥ 4.0	≥ 4.0	≥ 4
Operational Systems	≥ 2.0	≥ 3.0	≥ 4.0	≥ 4.0	≥ 4
Management Systems	≥ 2.0	≥ 2.0	≥ 3.0	≥ 4.0	≥ 4
Culture	≥ 2.0	≥ 2.0	≥ 2.0	≥ 3.0	≥ 4

Figure 11.5. Organizational Effectiveness Scoring Norms

(consistent with life cycle research) is that larger organizations require more well-developed/sophisticated systems. Therefore, as the organization advances from one stage of growth to the next, the scores need to successfully increase.

The second set of scores calculated from results is *percent favorable*. Percent favorable scores—ranging from 0 percent to 100 percent—indicate the extent to which an organization is experiencing problems overall with respect to one of the six tasks contained in the pyramid of organizational success, and/or with respect to financial results. In brief, an organization may have developed the structures and processes needed for its current stage of growth, but if "percent favorable" scores in any area or overall are less than 50 percent, the organization may not be well positioned to move to the next stage of growth. In other words, "extent developed" scores indicate the extent to which the organization has "scaled up," while "percent favorable" scores indicate the extent to which the organization is prepared for the next stage of development (i.e., is prepared to continue scaling up).

EMPIRICAL RESEARCH ON SUCCESS AND FAILURE OF ORGANIZATIONAL SCALE-UP

To assess the validity of the framework presented above as well as their related hypotheses, Flamholtz and others have been engaged in a program of empirical research. Summarized below is a selection of empirical research studies undertaken to test the model's predictive validity and related hypotheses regarding strategic organizational development and financial performance.

Strategic Organizational Development and Financial Performance

Flamholtz and Aksehirili (2000) performed an empirical test of the proposed link between the organizational development model and the financial success of organizations. They used a paired comparison of a natural experiment to test the hypothesis "the success of a company in managing the six key tasks of the organizational development pyramid framework positively affects the financial performance of the firm." Naturally occurring experiments are occurrences in the environment where only the variables of interest change and other conditions remain approximately the same. Sixteen companies from eight industries were selected as matched pairs. Firms within each pair have roughly similar products and/or services and operated at approximately the same time periods. Due to the necessity of measuring financial performance, the firms selected were chosen from publicly traded companies. In order to maximize the potential variance in the sample, each pair of companies included one company that was successful and another that was, a priori, believed to be less successful. The rationale was that if there was not sufficient variance between the pairs when there were differences in success, then the hypothesized relationship was unlikely to exist.

To test this hypothesized relationship, Flamholtz and Aksehirili analyzed financial and nonfinancial information relevant to the hypothesized model for eight pairs of companies in different industries. Each company was evaluated in terms of the six key strategic building blocks, and scores were assigned to indicate the degree of the organization's development. Average return on equity (ROE) was used as an indicator of financial performance.

The organizational development score and measures of financial performance were used in a Friedman two-way analysis of variance as well as in a regression analysis to test the predictive validity of the framework. Friedman two-way analysis of variance was appropriate since the data consisted of two matched samples (Siegel 1956). The Friedman test determines whether the pairs come from the same set of companies or differ significantly regarding their scores in the pyramid of organizational development. Regression analysis was used to evaluate the relationship between organizational development pyramid success and financial performance. To assess the ability of the organizational development pyramid framework to predict the financial performances of a firm, the total organizational development pyramid score and average ROE were used in a regression analysis as independent and dependent variables, respectively. Both analyses found a statistically significant relationship between the development of the six critical success factors and overall financial success of organizations.

Strategic Organizational Development and
Financial Performance: Additional Evidence

Flamholtz and Hua (2002a) provide another empirical test of the hypothesized link between the Flamholtz organizational development model and a firm's financial performance. Here the authors tested the hypothesis (that "the success of a company in managing the six key tasks of the organizational development pyramid framework positively affects the financial performance of the enterprise") within a single firm, using a set of fifteen relatively comparable divisions. The authors also report the results of related, exploratory research on the thresholds of strategic organizational development for profitability of individual companies or operating units.

The Flamholtz and Hua study was conducted as part of a program of action research on a medium-sized industrial enterprise operating in the United States, the Banner Corporation. Banner, a parts manufacturer for industrial, truck, and other automotive businesses (e.g., Ford Motor Company, Navistar, and Dana Corporation), represented the classic "old economy." The company was formed primarily through acquisitions in a classic "roll-up" strategy of industry consolidation through acquisition. Banner was comprised of fifteen divisions, each of which had been a stand-alone entrepreneurial company, with revenues between $25 million and $100 million (i.e., at stage III on the pyramid of organizational development).[3]

At the time of this study, the divisions totaled about $700 million in annual revenue. These divisions consisted of a set of reasonably related technologies, such as foundries and forges. The foundries ranged from processing capacity for grey iron to ductile iron to lost foam to other similar technologies. The nature of the business of such entities is job order manufacturing. The similarities between the divisions present a relatively unusual opportunity for research because of their comparability.

Each division was evaluated by senior management in terms of the six key strategic building blocks. Scores were assigned (using a five-point Likert scale) to indicate the degree of each division's strategic organizational development. This score and a measure of financial performance (earnings before interest and taxes, or EBIT[4]) were used in a regression analysis to test the predictive validity of the framework.

Flamholtz and Hua ran a regression between: (1) the degree to which each division was perceived as being developed in terms of the six key strategic building blocks as a whole (i.e., "the average pyramid development score") and (2) EBIT. Stated differently, the hypothesis is that the highest-performing divisions are those that are the most developed in terms of the pyramid, whereas the lowest-performing divisions (financially) are those that are least developed in terms of the six key strategic building blocks.

The regression equation describing the relationship among variables is:

$$y \, (\text{EBIT}) = -17.14 + 7.77 * \text{Pyramid Score}$$

Adjusted R^2 is 0.55, and is statistically significant at the 0.0003 level. This means that approximately 55 percent of EBIT is explained by the six variables comprising the pyramid of organizational development. This result provides support for the hypothesis of a relationship between the degree of strategic organizational development and the financial performance of organizations. The study by Flamholtz and Hua (2002a) has been replicated with similar results in an independent research site in a different industry (financial services) by Flamholtz and Kurland (2005).

CONCLUSIONS

This chapter provides a framework for understanding, measuring, and managing the process of organizational scale-up in commercial enterprises. Scale-up is viewed in terms of the movement from one stage of organizational growth to another over an enterprise's life cycle after the stage of "birth" has been successfully completed. Specifically, scale-up refers to the process of developing the set of "organizational capabilities," or "form," required by an enterprise as it increases in size and complexity.

We have presented a specific organizational life cycle model that can be used to identify (measure) the point at which specific scale-ups to the business enterprise should occur. The chapter uses this model in conjunction with an organizational effectiveness, or success, model that has been and is being empirically tested to indicate what needs to be done for successful scale-up as well as what happens when scale-up is unsuccessful (i.e., "growing pains"). In addition, we have described two different instruments—the Organizational Effectiveness Survey and the Growing Pains Questionnaire—which can be used to assess the extent to which an organization has accomplished successful scale-up (given its current stage of growth).

We have made the construct of "scale-up" more concrete, or operationally measurable, by indicating the organizational capabilities that need to be developed at each stage of growth. Although there are pitfalls, it is possible to manage the process of organizational scale-up successfully.

APPENDIX

Factors Defining the Stages of Organizational Growth: Birth Stage[5]

Birth: The small organization operates on an informal basis.
Operating systems and structure are ill defined.
Decision-making authority is centralized in the owner/founder.
Management is focused on identifying and beginning to exploit a market niche.
Lippett and Schmidt (1967), "birth stage": Management focus is on creating an operating system and becoming viable.
Thain (1969), "Stage 1": The organization is small and simple. Management is autocratic.

Scott (1971), "Stage 1": The organization has little or no formal structure, produces only one product, operates with a high level of personal control, and uses paternalistic rewards to control individual behavior.

Greiner (1972), "Creativity Stage": The organization is informal in structure. Management focuses on developing products and identifying markets. Communication is frequent and informal. Individuals work long hours for modest salaries.

Lyden (1975): The organization focuses on identifying or creating a market niche.

Adizes (1979), "Infant Organization": The organization's policies and procedures are ill defined. Management focus is on acquiring resources. Authority is centralized in the owner/founder.

Cameron and Whetten (1981), "Entrepreneurial and Creativity": Management focus is on marshalling resources, achieving a niche, and establishing priorities for the organization's future.

Churchill and Lewis (1983), "Stage I: Existence": Management focus is on obtaining customers, delivering products, and acquiring the financial resources to achieve these goals. Formal systems are nonexistent.

Quinn and Cameron (1983), "Entrepreneurial Stage": Management focus is on innovation, niche formation, and creativity.

Cowen, Middaugh III, and McCarthy (1984), "Birth Stage": The organization is managed by the entrepreneur. Management focus is on products and markets. No formal systems exist.

Miller and Friesen (1984), "Birth Stage": The firm is less than ten years old, has an informal structure, and is dominated by the owner/manager.

Astley (1985), "Stage I": The organization operates under the personal control of the owner/entrepreneur. Creativity is high and structure is informal.

Flamholtz (1986, 1995), "The New Venture": The organization is between $0 and approximately $1 million in annual sales. Management focus is on defining markets and developing products. Decision-making authority is concentrated in the owner/entrepreneur.

Factors Defining the Stages of Organizational Growth: Growth Stage

Growth: The organization is experiencing rapid growth as a result of its successful identification of a market niche and creation of products to meet customer needs. It has not yet become a "bureaucratic" organization, but is moving toward this end. Its structure and systems are becoming more formalized. Roles and responsibilities (organization structure) are beginning to be defined. Operating systems are becoming more formalized and decision-making authority is becoming decentralized. Management focus is on acquiring the resources needed to meet

increasing demand for products or services and on formalizing operating systems so as to make more efficient use of the resources acquired.
Lyden (1975): The organization focuses upon the acquisition of resources. It begins to focus upon increasing the efficiency of production.
Adizes (1979), "Go Go Stage": The organization begins to move faster to take advantage of opportunities and, as a result, begins to grow.
Churchill and Lewis (1983), "Stage IV: Take-Off": Management focus is on acquiring resources to support growth, delegating authority, creating formal operating systems, and maintaining effective leadership. Systems are becoming strained.
Miller and Friesen (1984), "Growth Stage": The firm experiences greater than 15 percent annual growth in sales. It has a functionally organized structure and has begun to formalize policies. Management focus is on achieving rapid sales and acquiring resources to support both internal development and growth.
Flamholtz (1986, 1995), "Expansion": The firm is expanding rapidly in terms of sales revenue, number of employees, etc. For most firms, this stage begins when they reach somewhere between $1 million and $10 million in annual sales. Organizational resources are stretched to the limit by increasing demand. Management focus is on acquiring more resources and formalizing operating systems so as to use resources more efficiently.
"Professionalization": The firm's management begins to focus more explicitly on formalizing organization structure, control and planning systems, and management development programs. Organizations reach this stage of development when annual sales reach between $10 million and $100 million.

Factors Defining the Stages of Organizational Growth: Maturity Stage

Maturity: The organization's growth has stabilized as a result of a maturing market. The majority of its operating systems are now formalized and it tends to function as a bureaucratic organization. Management focus is on refining the systems that were developed during the growth stage and helping the organization's employees accept these changes.
Lippett and Schmidt (1967), "Youth Stage": Management focus is on developing stability and earning a reputation.
Thain (1969), "Stage 2": The organization is large and is functionally specialized. Managers operate as a team.
Scott (1971), "Stage 2": The organization is characterized by functional specialization, institutionalized search, and impersonal rewards.
Greiner (1972), "Direction Stage": The organization installs a strong manager and embarks on a period of sustained growth. Management

focus is on efficiency and creating an organization with top-down communication. Formal control and accounting systems are being increasingly utilized.

Lyden (1975): The organization focuses on pattern maintenance (increasing stability) and institutionalization of structure.

Adizes (1979) "Adolescent Stage": Focus is on planning and coordination. Policies and procedures are formalized and formal training programs are in place. Stability, rather than growth, is sought.

"Prime Organization": Systems are in place to help achieve increased efficiency. Growth has stabilized.

Cameron and Whetten (1981), "Formalization and Control": Management focus is on formalizing goals and increasing production efficiency.

Churchill and Lewis (1983), "Resource Maturity": Management focus is on eliminating inefficiencies of growth through creating formal budgeting, strategic planning, and control systems. There is also concern over how to maintain the entrepreneurial spirit.

Quinn and Cameron (1983), "Collectivity Stage": Management focus is on creating high cohesion and commitment.

"Formalization and Control Stage": Management focus is on stability and institutionalization.

Cowen, Middaugh III, and McCarthy (1984), "Youth Stage": The organization is managed by specialists. Management focus is on bringing the product or service to market efficiently. Performance evaluation, control, and reward systems are formalized.

Miller and Friesen (1984), "Maturity Stage": After a period of high growth, the firm experiences sales growth of less than 15 percent. Sales growth stabilizes and innovation declines. The organization has become fairly bureaucratic and the emphasis is placed on increasing efficiency.

Astley (1985), "Stage II": The organization has become mechanistic. Emphasis is on increasing efficiency, standardizing tasks, and creating a functional structure.

Flamholtz (1986, 1995), "Consolidation": Management focus is on explicitly managing the corporate culture (the values, beliefs, and norms) so that it supports the changes that were instituted during the growth phase of development. This stage usually occurs when an organization reaches approximately $100 million in annual sales.

Factors Defining the Stages of Organizational Growth: Diversification

Diversification: As a result of declining sales or the desire to expand into other domains, an organization's management will begin to look for or develop new market niches. The firm's structure becomes division-alized and management must now deal with the problem of integrat-ing the new divisions into the existing organization. The birth-growth-maturity cycle of development begins again with respect to the new division(s). Management simultaneously focuses on identifying mar-kets, creating products, and acquiring resources. At the same time, em-phasis must also be placed on designing operating and management systems to support the new organization.

Thain (1969), "Stage 3": The organization has a divisionalized structure. Division managers manage as if they were directing independent com-panies.

Scott (1971), "Stage 3": The organization offers multiple product lines. Management focus is on research and development and growth.

Greiner (1972), "Delegation Stage": The organization's market is ex-panding. Management focus is on decentralizing authority.

"Coordination Stage": The organization has formal operating systems to allow for greater coordination among product groups. Growth begins again.

Quinn and Cameron (1983), "Structure Elaboration and Adaptation Stage": Management focus is on domain expansion and decentralization.

Cowen, Middaugh III, and McCarthy (1984), "Maturity": Management focus is on finding new products and markets. Structure shifts so as to promote better coordination of divisions.

Miller and Friesen (1984), "Revival": The organization diversifies and ex-pands. Management focus is on planning and control to achieve both diversification and integration. Sales growth again increases to greater than 15 percent per year.

Astley (1985), "Stage III": The organization is divisionalized and highly structured. Decision-making authority is decentralized.

Flamholtz (1986, 1995), "Diversification": If a firm decides to grow be-yond the revenue that can be generated by a single product line (usu-ally about $500 million), it will begin to look for new markets and products and generally create a new entity (division) to produce and market these products.

"Integration": Management focus is on integrating the operations of the new product division(s) created by diversification into the existing business. This involves redesigning the operating and management sys-tems and, perhaps, redefining the corporate culture.

Factors Defining the Stages of Organizational Growth: Decline

Decline: If the market for an organization's products or services declines at any point in the organization's life, or if it fails to make the required changes in its form at the appropriate size, it will experience a decline in sales, profit, and/or productivity. Organizations at this stage must focus on redefining their market niche and rebuilding their internal operations if they are to survive.

Adizes (1979), "Maturity Stage" to "Aristocratic Stage" to "Early Bureaucracy" to "Bureaucracy" to "Death": The focus in the maturity stage is no longer on productivity and growth. Less time is spent on research and development. This pattern of deemphasizing results becomes increasingly more intense as the organization progresses through the remaining three stages. If the pattern is not curtailed, the organization will "die."

Miller and Friesen (1984), "Decline": The organization experiences stagnation as its markets dry up. Product demand levels off and innovation is low. Profits start to decline.

Flamholtz (1986, 1995), "Decline": The organization has failed to recognize that its initial product or service success is no longer viable. The key challenge for these firms is to discover new market opportunities and begin rebuilding the entire set of organizational components (e.g., markets, products, resources, etc.).

NOTES

1. For example, a $333,333 service firm is equivalent to a $1 million manufacturing firm in Flamholtz's model.

2. While "integration" represents a separate stage in Flamholtz's (1986, 1995) model, others (Cowen, Middaugh III, and McCarthy, 1984; Miller and Friesen, 1984) suggest that it is part of the diversification stage and is treated in this fashion here.

3. Fourteen of the divisions had revenues between $25 million and $50 million.

4. EBIT is a classic measure of financial performance and was the one the Banner Corporation used to assess its own divisional performance.

5. Research by Flamholtz and others has provided empirical support for the proposed six-variable model (Flamholtz and Aksehirili 2000; Flamholtz and Hua 2002a; Flamholtz and Kurland 2003).

IV

SYNTHESIZING CONCEPTS OF SCALE-UP FOR EDUCATION

12

Toward a Program of Research on Scale-Up: Analytical Requirements and Theoretical Possibilities

Mark A. Constas and Kevin L. Brown

Terms such as "scale-up," "up-scaling," or "scaling up" are commonly used to describe efforts to implement an intervention or group of interventions across large numbers of varied settings. Understood as a problem of magnitude (how many individuals or sites will be involved?), breadth (what populations and settings will be involved?), and programmatic complexity (how will different configurations of program components be reliably implemented across settings?), the chapters in this volume show that scaling up is viewed as an ongoing challenge across many sectors, including medicine, business development, manufacturing, and engineering. While scaling up is a topic of widespread programmatic interest, little attention has been given to understanding how scaling up may be conceptualized and studied as a topic of substantive interest. Even less attention has been given to developing a theoretically informed knowledge base to guide scientific studies of scale-up. Addressing such knowledge deficits as they pertain to education research is the focus of the first section of this book.

Solving the problem of how to design studies that will yield generalizable findings about effective scale-up strategies requires a systematic approach to research—most probably a combination of approaches. Ideally, such approaches are built upon a set of disciplinary-based theoretical propositions and analytical models capable of guiding decisions about how best to collect, analyze, and interpret data. Currently, no well-codified set of propositions or empirically anchored analytical frameworks exist. The chapters in this book raise questions and offer solutions that may help us formulate the kinds of propositions and specify the types of models needed to advance our thinking about how to conceive of and conduct studies on scale-up. This chapter attempts to describe elements of a program of research based on the conceptual and analytic insights presented in part I. Offered as a heuristic device, our multidimensional model specifies the types of variables and modeling procedures that might be used to develop a research program focused on the contextual complexities of large-scale implementation.

A FEW OBSERVATIONS: WHERE'S THE THEORY?

Much attention has been given to the topic of school reform (e.g., Ravitch 2000; Tyack and Cuban 1995). Few studies, however, have sought to identify, through systematic empirical research, factors that influence the success of various reforms as they are scaled up in varied educational settings across different populations of students and teachers in different types of schools. One of the more comprehensive contemporary works on scale-up in the United States came out of the RAND project on New American Schools. The 1998 book by Susan Bodilly, *Lessons from New American Schools' Scale-up Phase*, identified school structural factors, selection process factors, jurisdictional and institutional factors, and design and team factors as important correlates of successful implementation (Bodilly 1998). This work was useful because it represents one of the most focused attempts to identify variables that influence the success of broad scale-up. Yet while this work was useful, and in some ways seminal, it did not propose a theoretical framework upon which future studies of scale-up might be based. Another shortcoming of this research was that it did not attempt to connect reform efforts to student outcome data.

A more recent publication by Berends, Kirby, Naftel, and McKelvey (2001) on the New American Schools program identified teachers' perceptions, school characteristics, design and design team assistance, and district support as being critical. Here, student-level data were included, but no robust effects were found—the absence of effect being attributed to what the authors describe as "wide variations in implementation and environments" (Berends et al. 2001, xxvi). As was the case in earlier work by Bodilly (1998), no theoretical framework was developed.

Work related to scale-up has been carried out in the United Kingdom under the banner of "school improvement research." While this work seeks to develop a theoretical orientation to the problem (see Hopkins 1996; Tymms 1996), little progress has been made in developing anything that resembles a comprehensive theory about how school improvement works and how such efforts might be scaled across schools, across programs, and across populations of students and teachers. Indeed, David Hopkins has lamented, "Despite increased practical work in this area, the level of discourse about how school improvement works remains disturbingly low" (Hopkins 1996, 31).

Highlighting a methodology deficiency in the literature, Tymms observes that "perhaps the greatest flaw in the school effectiveness research is the almost total lack of experimental data" (Tymms 1996, 123). With reference to building theoretical foundations for this area of research, Tymms also notes that "theoretical progress has been disappointing simply because a firm foundation does not exist on which to build" (1996, 123). To date, only two resources have attempted to lay such a foundation. One, an edited volume that resulted from a 2003 Harvard conference (Dede et al. 2005), discusses the role of technology in overcoming barriers to scale-up. The other, a digital library on *Scaling Up School Reform Initiatives* created for the North Central Regional Educational Laboratory (National Institute for Social Science Information 2001), provides a searchable database of scholarly research on the principles of, challenges to, and strategies for successful scale-up.

How the field of education needs to approach the topic of scale-up is perhaps best illustrated, in a negative sense, by an article that was published in the August 2003 issue of *Education Research*: "Rethinking Scale: Moving Beyond the Numbers to Deep and Lasting Change." Following Elmore (1996) and Gamson (1998), Coburn argues that "as the issue of 'scale' emerges as one of the key challenges for educational reform, it remains largely under theorized in the educational literature" (2003, 3). After preparing rhetorical ground for her work by citing the need for a more fully developed definition of scale-up, Coburn contends that conceptualization of scale-up should be made up of four concepts: depth, sustainability, spread, and shift in reform ownership. Her work illustrates one of the fundamental problems of how conventional forms of "theory" development proceed in many areas of educational research.

Here is the problem. The definition of scaling up offered, while useful in some conceptual sense, lacks a few elements, elements that are central to developing theoretical and analytical models needed to support a program of disciplined research. Coburn's discussion of scaling up did not: (1) provide explicit, readily discernible connections to a set of disciplinary-based constructs and explanations; (2) identify the need to develop measurement tools to support research on scaling up; (3) emphasize the importance of developing a program of research that has prediction as its ultimate goal; or (4) seek to develop a formal theoretical perspective.

In an article titled "What Theory Is Not," Robert Sutton and Barry Staw (1995) noted that references, data, variables, diagrams, and hypotheses do not qualify as theory. While Sutton and Staw were offering advice to investigators in organizational behavior and management, their observations apply equally well to the field of education. The type of theory that we should have in mind here as we try to develop a theoretical framework for scaling up research is more formal than what is typically found in the field of education. According to Nagel (1961), a theory should include the following: "(1) an abstract calculus that is the logical skeleton of the explanatory system, and that implicitly defines the basic notions of the system, (2) a set of rules that in effect assign empirical content to the abstract calculus by relating it to the concrete materials of observation and experiment, (3) an interpretation or model for the abstract calculus which supplies some flesh for the skeletal structure in terms of more or less familiar conceptual or visualizable materials" (90).

Nagel's description of theory provides a useful outline to guide how we might work to develop a program of research on scale-up. His *abstract calculus* points to the need for clear, well-developed constructs that can be arranged as a set of functionally interrelated propositions. His reference to rules highlights the need for measurement precision and research design. Finally, the reference to *interpretation or a model for the abstract calculus* suggests the need for conceptual clarity, concrete representation, and analytic specificity. Introducing his definition of theory here is important because we need to think about theory as something more technically sophisticated and analytically generative than a graphic representation of a few loosely connected ideas that have little or no connection to an accumulated body of empirical evidence.

CUTTING THROUGH THE CONCEPTUAL FOG

The four chapters in part I of this volume represent two different approaches to establishing a conceptual base for scale-up research in education. The chapters by Cohen and Baker take a "top-down" approach in the sense that they build a concept of scale-up by generalizing from previous efforts to take successful innovations to scale. On the other hand, Hedges and Reichardt take a "bottom-up" approach by conceptualizing scale-up as a methodological problem, that is, by asking what analytical techniques or research designs are most likely to provide evidence that a particular innovation might successfully be taken to scale. The question, then, is whether these two approaches to producing conceptual clarity overlap. In other words, is there a theory of scale-up that can provide the basis of, and is subject to, a rigorous analytical research program?

Predicting Scale-Up Success

Reichardt outlines seven commonly used or "prototypical" research designs, and details the "threats to validity" of each design. He acknowledges the practical constraints placed on education researchers and emphasizes designing studies in ways that minimize (rather than eliminate via randomized assignment) potential sources of bias in estimates of treatment effects. This often may mean "embellishing" or modifying the prototypical research design in a way that addresses the most plausible threats to validity. Reichardt's chapter is an important reminder that the validity of nonexperimental studies can be improved greatly with a modest investment of planning in the research design stage. However, anticipating possible threats to validity as a way of best estimating treatment effects, while an extremely useful thought experiment, presumes rather than produces a theory of scale-up.

This presumption is made clearer in Hedges's highly original contribution to this volume. Drawing an analogy with psychometric generalizability theory, which views interactions with context as measurement errors, Hedges creates both quantitative and qualitative measures of the generalizability of treatment effects to varying educational contexts. Hedges's "generalizability coefficient" provides a way of predicting scale-up success by calculating the fraction of variance in treatment effects that is explained by the main treatment effect. Treatment effects are said to be reproducible if they are largely independent of context. What that context is, however, remains to be specified.

Hedges himself makes the plausible assumption that context often will mean classrooms, schools, and districts, and he proceeds to show how design considerations affect the ability to estimate the variance components needed to calculate generalizability coefficients at these different levels. Like Reichardt, Hedges argues that researchers need to design studies of treatment effects in ways that increase our ability to predict scale-up success (via more accurate estimates of both direct and indirect effects). Taken together, these methodological considerations bring us substantially closer to what might count as evidence for a theory of scale-up; however, neither approach alone brings us closer to a specific theory of scale-up itself. Classrooms, schools, and districts may well be important dimensions of scale, but how and why they affect scale-up efforts remains to be explained.

Predictors of Scale-Up Success

Qualitative methods often are needed to look inside the "black box" of evaluation research to find evidence of why a treatment is effective or not. Baker, herself an early champion of experimental designs in education research, calls this a distinction between knowledge-producing and decision-related studies. For scale-up researchers, however, making good predictions of success means having some idea of the predictors or contextual factors involved. Drawing on her own work, Baker argues in her first of seven "principles for scale-up" that researchers must acknowledge that "affecting the course of education requires attention to a number of socially connected practices," including the instability of urban schools, a climate of distrust about researcher motives, local political constraints on sample populations, changes in state education policies, and teacher interactions. She says that literature reviews (what she calls "the history of stable scientific findings") and multiple trial studies are one way of identifying potential confounding factors. Modifications of treatment design and testing procedures along with measures for transfer, implementation, and user reaction then can be used to refine this list of what makes interventions scalable and sustainable.

Taking a broader historical view, Cohen observes that we have a handful of very general explanations for why interventions fail but almost no evidence about why they succeed. He argues that the success of innovations depends on both the innovation itself and the implementation environment. Innovations themselves can vary by their target adopter, strength of sponsorship, and amount of departure from conventional practice. Environmental predictors of scale-up success include incentives to innovate, standards for classroom practice, degree of local or state control, availability of resources, and political climate. Cohen predicts, for example, that an innovation is more likely to succeed with broad sponsorship, more incentives for change, and common standards of (quality) practice. He also argues that adapting innovations to increase adoption rates often means reducing the fidelity of implementation in the current environment of U.S. schooling. Finally, Cohen observes that the factors affecting scale-up may even vary by the type of innovation itself (e.g., instruction, assessment, licensing, hiring, professional development, etc.), making it even more difficult to elaborate a priori any theoretical basis upon which to build. So, in the end, any program of scale-up research must use theoretical possibilities and analytical rigor in tandem to develop a formal conceptual framework to guide future research.

TOWARD A FRAMEWORK FOR SCALE-UP RESEARCH

Taken together, the views expressed by the authors in part I provide some useful guidelines that can inform our thinking about how best to develop a framework for scale-up research. Referencing some of the foundational literature in the philosophy of science (Nagel 1961; Quine 1991), we find three elements that are central to building a scientific theory of scale-up:

1. Reference to disciplinary perspectives that can be used to frame the problem
2. Identification of an empirically justifiable set of variables and measures used to define and investigate scale-up
3. Specification of a clearly articulated prediction model to focus the study of scale-up

Using these three elements, the sections that follow describe components of a potential program of research on scale-up.

Framing the Problem

As noted earlier, the chapters in this part approach the concept of scale-up in education from different perspectives. Hedges and Reichardt are more focused on the research design issues for measuring and predicting treatment outcomes in varying contexts. Cohen and Baker are more focused on understanding the contextual complexity of scale-up and suggest that the research designs we employ must find ways to unravel and explain the effects of such complexity. In the end, each author defines scale-up as the process of testing the broad effectiveness of an already-proven educational intervention as it is implemented in large numbers of complex educational contexts.

The question that remains is whether this definition of scale-up can be operationalized in a way that is methodologically sound. *Implementation*, as the first definitional construct, is conceptualized as a set of economic variables that focus on variations in commodities or costs (e.g., financial resources, human resources) needed to scale an intervention, and on abstract qualities (e.g., perceived costs and benefits) attributed to the intervention. Within economics, implementation theory (e.g., Corchon 1996; Saijo, Tatamitani, and Yamoto 1996; Maskin and Moore 1998) provides the tools needed to identify the set of implementation variables and measures to be included in the proposed study. An economically oriented analysis of scaling up would, for example, focus on teachers' and administrators' perceptions of the value of the intervention and on the influence of financial resources as reported at the school and district level.

Educational context, or what Cohen calls the "environment" of implementation, is conceptualized as a set of psychological/developmental variables (e.g., teacher qualifications, demographic characteristics of the student body) and structural factors (e.g., school size, school achievement record) that can be used to describe how an intervention being scaled is influenced by critical factors in school settings. From this perspective, developmental systems theory (Ford and Lerner 1992; Lerner and Benson 2003), and its forerunner, developmental contextualism (Lerner and Kauffman 1985; Lerner and Fisher 1994), provide useful empirically based insights to guide how educational context can be defined and measured over time. The problem then is to integrate economic models, which help explain cost-benefit conditions (in both real and perceived terms), with developmental models, which describe the way in which environments and entities (e.g., individuals or interventions) interact and change over time. The identification of variables and the construction of a prediction model are derived from this integration.

Identifying Variables and Measures

Empirical findings used to identify predictors of scale-up success may be drawn from evaluations of large-scale school reforms (e.g., Berends, Kirby, Naftel 2001; Bodilly 1998), from studies of the effects of conflicting school reforms (Berends et al. 2002), from studies of implementation variation (e.g., Lipsey and Corday 2000), and from investigations of how schools and teachers respond to change and innovation (e.g., Altrichter and Elliot 1999; Finnan and Meza 2003; Hall and Hord 2001). Across these areas of work, three categories of variables are regularly cited as important predictors of implementation success: (1) teacher variables, (2) institutional variables, and (3) policy variables. The following proposed study of the large-scaled effectiveness of the CAP reading comprehension program provides an example of how to identify and measure each of these variables.

Teacher variables in the study ask questions about the influence of teachers' perceptions of the intervention, about the effect of teachers' backgrounds, and about the fidelity of implementation. The *perception of the intervention* variable asks, "How might teachers' views about the benefits and costs associated with the intervention affect the success of the scaling effort?" Data for this variable will be collected in two stages. Stage 1 involves constructing an intervention perception scale for teachers (ISP-T) based on analysis of responses from a sample of teachers across school districts. The survey will be administered in stage 2 to all teachers who participate in the study. The *teacher's background/capacity* variable asks, "To what extent will variations in general training (educational level) and specific training (reading specialist, training related to the intervention) affect the success of the scaling effort?" Data for this variable will come both from district and state records and from a posttest to assess teachers' understanding of the basic components and procedures associated with the intervention. The *fidelity of implementation* variable asks, "How well do teachers implement the intervention as prescribed and in what ways do variations in implementation affect student outcomes?" To capture variations in implementation (over time and between student populations), each class will be observed for three one-hour sessions, distributed over a three-month period. The resulting Likert scale, the implementation variability scale (IVS), will be administered a minimum of three times annually after the first year of the project.

Institutional variables ask questions about school leadership, district commitment, and school type. The *school leadership* variable asks, "To what extent might the perceptions and levels of commitments of school principals, school leaders (e.g., school reading lead) affect the success of the scaling effort?" Stage 1 of data collection for this variable involves interviewing a sample of principals and reading leads from schools participating in the study. Stage 2 involves the administration of an intervention perception scale for administrators (IPS-A) to all principals and reading leads that participate in the study. The *district commitment* variable asks, "To what extent do the perceptions and levels of commitment of district level officials and district offices affect the success of the scaling effort?" A sample of superintendents and district-level officials will be used to create an intervention perception scale for districts (IPS-D) that will be administered to all superintendents and district officials who participate in the study. The *school type* variable asks, "Which structural factors (e.g., location and demographics, size, resource base), achievement (school achievement histories) or combination of factors offer the best prediction of the success of the intervention being scaled?" Data associated with this variable will be collected from school and district databases.

Policy variables ask questions about the effect of mandated testing, and curricular competition. The *mandated testing* variable asks, "In what ways might the content and process of state requirements affect the success of the scaling effort?" Data for this variable will be derived from a content analysis that compares the reading-related cognitive demands of mandated tests with the cognitive characteristics of the intervention. The *curricular competition* variable asks, "To what extent might other curricular interventions affect the success of the scaling effort?" Data for this variable will be derived from a content analysis of other interventions and from interviews with a sample of teachers from each of the districts sampled. Data for both policy variables will be collected at the outset of the study and then at least annually over the course of the investigation. Because this is a single-state study, policy variables are not "variables" in the true sense of the term but can be treated as such since different aspects of the intervention (e.g., creative, analytical, practical) will be more or less consistent with the content of mandated tests and more or less consistent with the demands of competing curricular interventions.

The array of teacher, institutional, and policy-related dimensions of scale-up offers a potentially useful set of empirical indicators to focus a study of scale-up. Table 12.1 provides a tabular summary of the dimensions, variables, measures, and theoretical constructs upon which the empirical study of scale-up will be based.

Specifying a Prediction Model

The organization of scaling up dimensions and variables into a prediction model is based on the logic of multilevel regression (e.g., Raudenbush and Bryk 2002) where classroom/teacher effects are nested within school effects, which are ultimately nested within district effects. Figure 12.1 provides a

Table 12.1.   **Framework to Support Scale-Up Research**

Scale-Up Dimensions	Variable	Measure/Data Source	Construct
Teachers	Perceptions of the value of the intervention	Interviews and scales	Implementation
	Education and training	District records	Context
	Fidelity of implementation	Observational data and scales	Implementation
Institutions	School leadership	Interviews and scales	Implementation
	District-level commitment	Interviews and scales	Implementation
	School type	Review of school, district, and state files	Implementation and Context
Policies	Testing and accountability	Policy analysis and content analysis	Context
	Curriculum requirements	Policy analysis and content analysis	Context

graphic depiction of hypothesized predictive relations that describe how an analysis might be conceptualized. Specifically, the predictors of scale-up success include teacher, institution, and policy variables. Each of these predictors, in turn, will have different effects on intervention outcomes depending on the level of analysis.

The only task remaining, then, is to specify the research design in such a way that the sampling and analytical techniques employed address any unspecified "threats to validity" and allow for the estimation of enough variance components to make meaningful predictions about how successfully the intervention will scale up at different levels and under varying conditions.

SUMMARY

Consistent with the goals of the conference that generated this volume, and directly supportive of the ambition to develop theoretical and analytical models of scale-up, the chapters in part I provide useful insights to help forge a new program of research. Acknowledging both the conceptual complexities and the methodological challenges of such a program, the recommendations offered by the authors can help guide our thinking about the types of variables, measures, and analysis needed to establish a program of research that is scientifically valid and practically useful. The sample research project outlined above provides one illustration of how we might

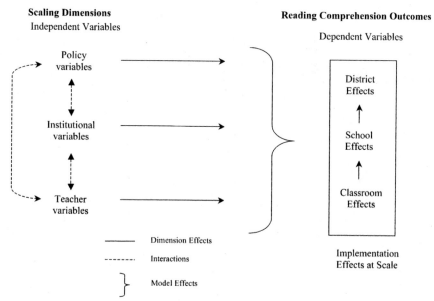

Figure 12.1. Prediction Model to Support Research on Scale-Up

proceed as we work to create an empirically based body of knowledge on scale-up. However, one oft-hidden environmental factor is the research team itself, and without mechanisms for ensuring that an innovation that is highly "generalizable" to classrooms, schools, and districts actually will be used elsewhere once the research is done often means, as Cohen puts it, that in America "one would expect plenty of innovative activity at every level of education, but typically sketchy implementation." Part II of this volume provides lessons for gauging the generalizability of educational interventions in the American sociopolitical context from other disciplines where innovations routinely are taken to scale.

13

Successful Scale-Up in Three Stages: Insights and Challenges for Educational Research and Practice

Paul Horwitz

To be successfully scalable, an educational innovation must go through three stages. First, it must be shown to be effective—that is, credible evidence must be adduced that the innovation actually has measurable (and desirable!) effects. Second, it must be shown that the initial favorable results can be replicated in multiple settings that are representative of the population of intended implementation sites. Finally, in order for the innovation to spread widely, there must be in place some institutional mechanism to accomplish that scale-up. In a free-market economy the most likely candidate for such an institution is a commercial or nonprofit enterprise.

SCALING UP IN THREE SUCCESSIVE STAGES

The chapters by Dignam; Bloom, Hill, and Riccio; and Flamholtz and Randle cover each of these successive stages. Dignam describes the design of individual experiments involving innovations in medicine, Bloom and his colleagues are concerned with measuring the effectiveness of an existing intervention in the area of public welfare, and Flamholtz and Randle deal with features that characterize successful scale-up of innovations in firms. Each of these areas of application has similarities with education, yet differs from education in important respects. Accordingly, each chapter offers a point of view quite different from that of the education community, but with sufficient overlap between their concerns and ours to make each of them insightful and relevant for the problems faced by our community as we attempt to scale up educational innovations.

"From Efficacy to Effectiveness: Translating Randomized
Controlled Trial Findings into Treatment Standards"

Randomized controlled trials (RCTs) have become the "gold standard" in medical research; increasingly, they are perceived as such in education as well (National Research Council 2002). What are the implications of this trend? How are RCTs likely to play out in education research? Is education research even capable of carrying out effective RCTs? As we attempt to carry out effective RCTs, what lessons can we learn from the experience of medical researchers? What, in short, are the similarities and differences between education and medicine with respect to RCTs?

Dignam points out that a successful RCT requires a "concurrent" control group—in other words, that the control and experimental groups must take part in the experiment simultaneously, or nearly so. Concurrency is more of a problem for medicine, where one is tempted to compare the treatment group to historical data, than for education research, where, given the scarcity of good data together with the fact that standards and assessments change rather rapidly, an education researcher would probably be hard pressed to find a historical control group! There are, however, obstacles to using control groups for education research that differ from those encountered by medical researchers.

One obvious difference is that education research need not be concerned with a "placebo" effect, whereby subjects who have not received the treatment get well anyway. To make the point, imagine the following experimental protocol: (1) take two high school math classes with students randomly selected from the same population; (2) teach one of the classes plane geometry, say, using the innovative technique under study; let the other class go out for recess during math class. Keep this up all year long, then (3) give both classes a test in order to measure their knowledge of geometry. This protocol is obviously unfair to the "placebo" class. There being no immune system for education, the control class in this fictional scenario is quite unlikely to learn geometry all on its own. The result of the proposed procedure is thus not in serious question, and in fact it would be considered highly unethical (not to mention ridiculous) to adopt it.

There is another, not quite so obvious, reason why education control groups tend to be more problematic than medical ones: it is not usually possible to hide who is in which group. RCTs depend on "double-blind" procedures—neither the participating clinicians nor the patients can know which patient is receiving the treatment and which the placebo. Educational interventions, by their very nature, are usually obvious to all interested parties, a fact that raises the oft-heard complaint, "Why do I (or my child) have to be in the control group?" Moreover, the novelty of the treatment and the increased attention inevitably paid to the treatment class are likely to affect the outcome of the experiment.

RCTs depend, as the name suggests, on *randomization*. It is imperative that treatment and control groups be randomly selected from the same population. Always a daunting requirement, this is arguably more difficult to achieve in education than in medicine. In fact, in many cases it is impossible to make the control group statistically identical to the experimental group along all the dimensions that might logically be expected to correlate to the outcomes of interest. Even if one can get the same teacher to teach two different classes, for instance, one using the innovation, the other the traditional method of instruction, the very fact that the classes necessarily occur at different times may have a significant effect on their makeup. For example, two college-prep physics classes may be quite different because one of them coincides with a calculus course (and therefore does not have any of the calculus students in it).

An additional requirement for RCTs is that they have adequate statistical power. The research design must ensure a reasonable likelihood that the experiment will detect a difference of the expected magnitude between the experimental intervention and the traditional treatment if such a difference in fact exists. This often translates into doing research on a rather large scale, perhaps involving thousands or tens of thousands of patients or students. While this has become common practice in medical research, it is still quite rare in education—presumably for lack of adequate funding. Moreover, since effects of treatments in both fields tend to be cumulative, there is a growing need for long-range research projects that extend over many years, yet these are also quite rare in education.

Treatment compliance is a problem common to both medicine and education research; in education it is generally referred to as the need to ensure "faithfulness of implementation." In medicine it is often difficult, particularly in long-term studies involving expensive or inconvenient treatments, to ensure that patients are actually following through with the treatment. The analogy in education is that once a study has progressed from the very early, single-classroom stage, subsequent implementations are rarely entirely faithful to the original research design. This obviously weakens the claims made either for or against a certain treatment.

A major problem with RCTs in education, not shared by medicine, is that there is often no widely accepted standard for what constitutes "success." The expected outcome of a medical intervention is usually well defined (e.g., the patient returns to health) although, to be sure, the *assessment* of that outcome is subject to variability and human judgment. But in education there is even controversy over the *expectations*. Educational standards and curricula vary, sometimes significantly, from state to state. Standardized test scores have the advantage of being easily measured but may fail to capture the multifaceted outcome of an intervention.

Dignam's chapter points to several interesting cases in medicine where RCTs have arrived at findings that were in conflict with expectations based on casual observation. Such cases are rare but not unheard of in education. For example, early investigations of the GenScope program (Horwitz et al. 1998) indicated that it was very successful in teaching genetics, based on informal observations of classrooms. However, later, when RCTs were used to investigate several different interventions, it was found that the GenScope groups rarely performed at a level superior to that of the control classes (Horwitz and Christie 2000; Hickey et al. 1999; Hickey et al. 2003).

Dignam describes a well-defined process for consensus development that the NIH has put in place through its Office of Medical Applications of Research. There is nothing equivalent to this in education. Indeed, one looks forward to the day when evidence-based research in education will attain a level of maturity that would justify the Department of Education's performing the same service.

Among the limitations of RCTs, Dignam mentions the problem in medical research of underrepresentation of trials with negative findings. This can occur due to publication bias or simply because researchers are reluctant to report such findings, either because they fear that such publication will reflect badly on them, or simply because they "burn out" on a project that they perceive to be unsuccessful and fail to complete the steps necessary to prepare a publication. I have seen no evidence bearing on the extent of this problem in education research, but it is reasonable to assume that it exists.

There are also problems associated with the generalization of results from RCTs to larger populations. In medicine, RCTs may be viewed by clinicians as irrelevant to their medical practice; in education, a common complaint by teachers or administrators is, "That study wouldn't apply to my kids (or my school)." This highlights the need to follow up RCTs with studies designed to ascertain whether or not the results are applicable on a broader scale. Particularly these days, with the No Child Left Behind Act mandating a flurry of additional reporting requirements, such follow-up studies might be able to take advantage of data being collected for other purposes in schools that have chosen to implement some form of the treatment under study—which leads neatly to the next chapter under consideration here.

"Linking Program Implementation and Effectiveness: Lessons from a Pooled Sample of Welfare-to-Work Experiments"

This chapter is an excellent example of a "metastudy"—an analysis of data taken from other research efforts. Such studies are very hard to pull off, and it is encouraging to have an existence proof that the necessary integration of disparate data generated for different purposes can actually be done successfully (Glass 1977b).

A major advantage of the study, and one that is all too often missing in education research, is that the authors started out with a ready-made, quantitative assessment rubric: namely, the employment status and earnings of the clients of different welfare-to-work programs, measured a fixed time period (two years) after the clients received services. The effects of improvements in education are harder to assess (necessitating, for example, a reliance on standardized tests), and furthermore, remarkably few education research projects even collect long-term (e.g., multiyear) data bearing on outcomes.

The data in this chapter were analyzed using a two-level model: level 1 measured sample members, and level 2 measured local program offices. Level 1 used a linear regression for individual sample members that (1) indicates how client characteristics influence program impacts, and (2) estimates the impact of each program office. Level 2 comprised three linear regressions. The first represents how conditional program effects depend on program implementation, activities, and environment; the second describes how the conditional mean control group outcome for each office varies with local economic environment; and the third is a technical correction that accounts for the fact that several sites changed the ratio of their program and control groups over time. In the analysis, all parameters at both levels are determined simultaneously, and each parameter represents the magnitude of a partial derivative—that is, the influence of a single factor, holding all the others constant.

The findings from this study are not particularly intuitive; they are useful and could not have been guessed at by "common sense." Would that we had a few more educational studies of this kind! To pick one example close to my heart: Wouldn't it be nice to have a really definitive study of the effect of technology on learning? How would one go about it? Which technologies would one study? Could one compare across different technologies? How? What outcomes would one look for? How would one collect the data? How would one analyze it? Studies of this kind have been done, of course (Mandinach and Linn 1986; Kulik and Kulik 1991), but none that I am aware of were performed with the rigor and care demonstrated here.

Why is this? What is so hard about obtaining this kind of information, which would be so useful to educational policy makers?

One problem, clearly, is the lack of reliable measures of educational outcomes at the appropriate level of granularity. It was straightforward for Bloom and his colleagues to use as an indicator of success the earnings of back-to-work clients two years after their participation in the different programs. The data were available, since the programs in question had followed up on their clients, and the data were a reliable measure of a desired outcome of the programs. In contrast, the expected results from education are harder to measure and often more long term. Scores on standardized tests, for instance, while convenient and available, do not measure how well prepared students are for leading productive, happy lives after they leave school. Other "quality of life" indicators such as annual income or criminal record five, ten, or twenty years after graduation from high school are not readily available.

To return to the example above, the problem is particularly acute with respect to assessing the use of information technology in education. There is little hard information bearing on this issue at present, in part because the technology changes rapidly, in part because results are inevitably confounded by many nontechnological factors. For example, the ability of schools to faithfully implement technology-rich interventions is closely tied to their ability to install and maintain the technology, which in turn is related to other factors closely correlated to the overall quality of the schools. This situation calls for wide-scale studies that collect fine-grained data and to the extent possible steer clear of "samples of convenience" consisting primarily of schools with above-average technological infrastructure. A promising approach to achieving this goal is described at the end of this chapter.

Measures of effectiveness and "scalability" aside, the mechanism for achieving widespread adoption of a promising educational innovation would seem to rest with the private sector, through the agency of firms. This fact points up the relevance of a third chapter, by Flamholtz and Randle.

"Measuring and Managing Successful Organizational Scale-Up"

Even assuming that a definitive research result could be obtained demonstrating the effectiveness of a given educational intervention, it is by no means clear that the innovation would find its way into a significant number of schools nor that, once introduced, it would be sustained for long enough to become a permanent feature of the operation of those schools that did adopt it. The issues of *scalability* and *sustainability* would still remain.

In a free-market economy, large-scale adoption of innovations does not usually happen primarily through government intervention alone. Except in those cases where the government itself is the main customer for the innovation, most innovations spread through the economy through the actions of commercial or not-for-profit firms. Government funding, whether for research or technology development, though useful and perhaps even essential at the early stages of the innovation cycle, is generally insufficient to ensure the widespread dissemination of an innovation (Horwitz 1979). To study the conditions necessary for such dissemination, therefore, one must turn to research on firms that operate essentially independently of such government-funded research programs.

The Flamholtz and Randle chapter describes a model for the life cycle of firms as they evolve through five stages, identified as birth, growth, maturity, diversification, and decline. Scalability of an innovation is thus closely correlated in this chapter to the growth of an individual enterprise, whereas the same term in education research generally refers to the dissemination and diffusion of an innovation.

The disparity between the two definitions can be appreciated simply by examining the stages delineated above: each is associated with the *growth* of the subject firm. But schools do not grow, or if they do they are reacting to demographic pressure rather than to any internal imperative. The factor that drives the evolution of a school is likely to be a reaction to failing test scores, community pressure, or other extrinsic measures of performance, rather than the desire for revenue growth that drives for-profit firms. Further differences between the two kinds of institutions abound: firms compete, but schools, for the most part, do not; firms enjoy considerable freedom to diversify their product in response to changing market pressures; schools do not; firms measure their relative success in terms of profitability, while schools have no comparable means to compare performance; and finally, firms compete for market share, whereas the vast majority of schools are guaranteed a fixed number of "customers" selected purely on the basis of geographical criteria.

The relevance of this chapter to the scalability of educational innovations derives from the fact—largely ignored by most of the research in the field— that ultimately the success or failure of an innovation is likely to depend on the fortunes of the commercial firms that attempt to carry it to market, and those firms are likely to traverse the life cycle described in the chapter regardless of the exact nature of the innovation under study.

Indeed, Flamholtz and Randle's chapter takes a theoretical stance that explicitly ignores the details of what it is that any individual firm actually *does*. Much of the power of their approach, in fact, derives from its applicability across domains, technologies, and markets. Nevertheless, I would draw attention to a few idiosyncrasies of the education market that may affect details of their model as it plays out in profit-seeking firms whose customers are schools.

One often-overlooked difference is that in education the customers for goods and services are not the ultimate beneficiaries. While educational innovations are intended to benefit children, purchasing decisions are made by adults. This gives rise to many of the peculiarities that distinguish education from other markets.

The educational market space is highly fractionated. In all but a few states (e.g., Texas, California, Florida), purchasing decisions are made independently by school districts—sometimes by individual schools. This increases the complexity, and thus the cost, of marketing products and services to the education sector, which in turn raises the barrier to new entries, where most innovation is traditionally to be found.

As mentioned above, public schools do not compete directly either for funds or for students. (In some states this is beginning to change, due to the rise in charter and independent schools. The growing home-school market may also pose a competitive threat in the next few years.) This means that the pressure to adopt an educational innovation typically comes from within a school district, and is driven by absolute goals and objectives, rather than by comparisons between school districts.

That said, we must note that the education marketplace is currently undergoing vast changes brought about by regulatory actions at the federal and state levels. New accountability standards (e.g., the No Child Left Behind Act of 2002) have had, and continue to have, an enormous effect on the way schools do business. Changes in the regulatory environment are a well-known factor in promoting innovation in for-profit firms (Ashford, George, and Heaton 1979)—their effect, in this instance, on the education sector of the economy has yet to play itself out.

MODELING ACROSS THE CURRICULUM: THE CONCORD CONSORTIUM IERI PROJECT

The Concord Consortium is currently running an Interagency Education Research Initiative (IERI) project called "Modeling Across the Curriculum," or "MAC" for short, that addresses some of the problems described by the three chapters discussed above. As the principal investigator of this project, I cannot resist the temptation to describe it here.

Information technology developed by the MAC project makes it possible to conduct education research that closely resembles the independent random trials that Dignam describes. In our project the treatment under review consists of having students interact with computer software designed to help them learn to use appropriate mental models in understanding scientific concepts. The Internet enables us to extend the reach of the project at very low cost to a large number of schools, teachers, and students.

We expose students to interactive, scaffolded models of scientific phenomena. As the students work with these materials, their actions are logged and uploaded to a central server where the data are accumulated and analyzed. The technology has been designed to be scalable in the sense that any teacher who wishes to participate can do so simply by going to our website[1] and registering for the project. We then make the software available to the teacher, and every time a student runs one of our activities we collect the data, parse them, and return to the teacher and student in the form of a report on the student's work.[2]

Our project is therefore open to a rather large number of participating schools, teachers, and students. We have, in fact, designated two types of schools: "member schools" and "contributing schools." The former are official participants in the project and are treated as such. Project staff have visited each member school at least once, and a second visit took place during the spring semester of 2004, for the purpose of holding teacher workshops. Each member school also receives a small grant from the project, which it can use for purchasing or updating technology. Teachers are compensated for attending the workshops and implementing the curriculum, and a designated "contact point" at each school also receives a stipend for helping with the project.

The "contributing" schools, in contrast, have not had any direct contact with the project. They are simply visitors to our website who have chosen to register with us and to download our software. Nevertheless, we collect the same data from them as we do from the member schools, we analyze them in the same way, and we send back the same reports. (The names of all the participating students are encrypted in our database to preserve their confidentiality, but the schools can decode the names so that they can use the reports for evaluation and grading.)

The project currently has enrolled fifteen member schools. This is the number we reference in our original IERI proposal, and we have no plans to recruit additional schools. As of this writing, however, (mid-March 2004), however, over fifty additional schools from twenty-five U.S. states and seven foreign countries have signed up as contributing schools. Fifteen percent of the roughly 5,500 students currently participating in the study are from contributing schools. Given that the website has been open for registration only since the beginning of January 2004, it is significant that the contributing schools have so quickly outpaced the member schools, and although the volume of data produced by the latter is still much less than half the total it is clear that the curves are about to cross there, too.

The technology we have developed on the MAC project also enables us to solve the problem, alluded to by Dignam, of randomly selecting a control group from the same population as the experimental group. We can simply produce multiple versions of the same software and randomly assign different treatments to different students within the same class. Thus, one version of an activity might confine itself to helping the students learn to perform well within that activity; a second, model-based version might frame its scaffolding in the form of repeated references to the model that underlies the activity. The expectation would be that students in the second group, though they might not succeed at the activity as well as those in the first group, would learn the science better, as evidenced by their ability to transfer their learning to other domains or assessment modalities. As long as the various versions of the activities are sufficiently similar, such random assignment of treatment can even be implemented as a "double-blind" procedure—that is, neither the teacher nor the students need know which treatment variation a given student was receiving.[3]

The MAC project, and the technology that underpins it, provides a good example of a way to collect useful, fine-grained data from a very large number of schools. By continuing this data collection over the lifetime of the project, we will be able to study the same students as they progress from one grade level to another. Such multiyear longitudinal studies are rare in education research, but useful though they are, they remain inadequate to inform policy. For instance, we have no way at present to continue to track these students beyond their high school years. As the Bloom, Hill, and Riccio chapter makes clear, such tracking is essential if we are ever to obtain valid estimates of the true life cycle value of an educational intervention.

Finally, as mentioned above, no educational intervention, however successful, will have a significant effect on society as a whole unless it is implemented on a very large scale. One model entity for doing that is the for-profit firm, hence the relevance of Flamholtz and Randle's chapter. With this in mind, and with respect to the MAC project in particular, the Concord Consortium has spun off a small company, Educational Network Services, Inc. (ENS), for the express purpose of commercializing and disseminating the technology and expertise that the MAC project, and other Concord projects, have generated. With support from a Phase 1 Small Business Innovative Research (SBIR) grant from the National Science Foundation, ENS is currently conducting a study to determine the feasibility of a plan to install and maintain interactive, educational software for math and science in grades six through twelve. Each of the programs ENS delivers will combine student-centered problem solving and investigative activities with the delivery and automated scoring of assessment instruments for use in grading and to meet reporting requirements. By analyzing and maintaining this assessment data for schools, ENS will help to reduce their costs while improving the scope and quality of information they need for planning and for complying with state and federal reporting requirements.

NOTES

1. The URL for this project is mac.concord.org.
2. As a central aspect of our ongoing research on this project, we are finding ways to analyze the data, which are extremely fine grained and contain a lot of information, and to improve the reporting of the data back to the schools.
3. We had originally planned to pursue this line of research, so our technology is capable of delivering the different versions and keeping track of which student is getting which version. But for the moment, at the request of NSF, we have restricted our protocol to delivering a single version of the treatment (the model-based one), using the number of activities completed as our independent variable.

14

Technology and Scale-Up: Implications for Research and Practice

Sarah-Kathryn McDonald and Michelle Llosa

The impact of technology on education in the past thirty years has been staggering. New technologies have enabled the development of new curricular materials, methods of delivering instruction, and ways of monitoring the use and impacts of interventions. Technology has been used to create new and more efficient ways of collecting, analyzing, and disseminating more information more quickly to inform instruction. In particular, technology has been praised for its promise both to enable the rapid diffusion of educational innovation across schools within the nation and globally to stimulate the development of new, potentially scalable interventions. This point was highlighted in the 1997 *Report to the President on the Use of Technology to Strengthen K–12 Education*, which led to the establishment of the Interagency Education Research Initiative (U.S. Office of Science and Technology Policy 1997), and in subsequent IERI program solicitations (see, e.g., National Science Foundation 1999, 2000, 2001, 2002, 2004).

The pervasiveness of computer-based technologies in society at large, the investments required to successfully scale "technology-reliant innovations . . . in educational environments," and technology's capacity to change what and how students learn in and out of classrooms are being widely discussed in a growing literature (see, e.g., Dede and Honan 2005, 238; Dede, Honan, and Peters 2005; Roschelle et al. 2000). Our purpose here is not to summarize or comment on these issues, but instead to consider when such technology-enabled changes to the educational system are likely to affect scale-up research and our ability to accumulate rigorous evidence of interventions' effects over time as a basis for educational policy making and practice.

TECHNOLOGY, TIME, AND CONTROL:
MANAGING THE PACE AND PERVASIVENESS OF CHANGE

Computer-centered information and communication technologies are ubiquitous. They enable the rapid adoption of select interventions in multiple contexts with the prospect that even more contexts will be reachable (via broadband or satellite) in the near future. Virtual communities of teachers in training and in service are being established and growing every year. Virtual student communities also are sprouting across the globe, but their relatively smaller penetration and typically more dynamic nature (with less cohesiveness among community members) raise questions regarding the likelihood they will become significant forces for scale-up in the near term. The Internet and related technologies facilitate distance learning, including the provision of a wide range of curricular and other learning materials to those who study and are schooled at home—but it is an open question whether the delivery system they provide will ever stimulate fundamental modifications to the organization of public education. How, then, do we gauge the likely impact of technology on scaling and scale-up research?

In chapter 8, "Forecasting the Effects of Scaling Up Social Programs: An Economics Perspective," Robert Moffitt is "concerned with the scientific question of how to forecast the actual effects of an intervention prior to its being adopted at a larger scale." His analysis suggests three critical points at which technology can, directly or indirectly, affect efforts not just to enact interventions at scale but also to evaluate their outcomes. Prior to scale-up, it may be possible to use technology to engineer fidelity of implementation (to core if not all aspects of an innovation). For example, it is increasingly possible to choose whether or not to build into an intervention features that prescribe identical delivery on each enactment, or allow for minor adaptations to be made within predefined limits. Used this way, technology has the potential to help control for key "scale-up effects in intervention" suggested by the application of a production function model, a positive impact for scale-up research. The logic of scientific inquiry requires fidelity of implementation. The investigator prescribes the treatment and must be able to control its administration to ensure that changes in outcomes are not attributable to changes in inputs. Treatments that vary from those prescribed cannot be warranted by the same evidence that demonstrates the efficacy of the intervention as designed. Technology is beneficial to scale-up when it services the researchers' need to minimize, if not eliminate, the possibility of discrepancies between the intervention as delivered and designed.

During scale-up, in education as in manufacturing (see Conley and Wolcott in this volume), technology increasingly enables and/or encourages developers and practitioners to continually refine, rapidly adjust, and itera-tively adapt interventions. While such refinements may be desirous as a means of ensuring interventions achieve the intended results in diverse con-texts, widespread adaptation is incompatible with efforts to demonstrate the effectiveness of "the intervention." When adaptation becomes the norm, a key element of experimental control—the integrity of the treatment (fidelity of implementation)—is missing. Scientifically, adaptation is prob-lematic not because it stops an intervention from working (necessarily), but because it prevents us from making claims regarding the intervention's effi-cacy. In Moffitt's terms, embedding fast-response product evaluation and re-design capabilities in innovations can introduce important short-run "ef-fects in intervention" that challenge the possibility of achieving meaningful longitudinal analysis of treatment effects, a negative consequence for scale-up research.

Before, during, and after implementation, technology may be intention-ally employed (by an intervention's designers) or exploited (e.g., by indi-viduals outside the intended treatment or control groups) to rapidly dis-seminate information about innovations and their outcomes. In such situations selection mechanisms ("scale-up effects in inputs") can be af-fected in significant ways, posing additional challenges to scale-up research (e.g., by reducing the sample of those who could serve as a potential con-trol group). This is particularly problematic when those mechanisms in-clude the opportunity to continue or exit from an ongoing intervention.

These examples underscore technology's capacity to affect both the re-search designs and methodologies required to assess interventions' impacts and the ability to accumulate this knowledge in meaningful ways. They also suggest that the nature and significance of these secondary effects are influ-enced only indirectly by the ubiquity of the underlying technology and the likely pace of additional change in the near term. What matters most for ed-ucational research is not the rapidity of technological innovation and the rate with which technological innovations are adopted; it is not even the ex-tent to which technology affects the speed and ease with which we can col-lect, analyze, and share assessment and other data used to evaluate inter-ventions' success. The crucial consideration is whether the ubiquity and rapidity of technological change are stabilizing or destabilizing our ability to control, statistically if not in reality, the interventions (treatments) that are administered, the composition and characteristics of experimental groups, and the context within which educational experiments take place. To illustrate we consider the implications of three technology-enabled phe-nomena for scale-up research: the rapid adoption of select interventions in multiple contexts and the establishment of virtual communities of teachers and students.

Technology and the Rapid Adoption of
Select Interventions in Multiple Contexts

There are at least two ways in which technology facilitates more rapid adoption of select educational interventions in multiple contexts than was likely—if even possible—until quite recently. Both are the result of developments in the information and communication facilities of high-speed networks, the Internet, and the worldwide web.

First is the ability to deliver a wide range of interlinked and cross-referenced multimedia materials quickly and (once infrastructure investments are factored out of the equation) inexpensively to geographically dispersed locations linked to the global computer (Internet) network. Here technology fundamentally provides a mechanism for delivering interventions to more users in more contexts—a capacity that also stimulates the development of innovations amenable to transmission this way. Second, the enhanced communication capacities associated with these technological developments make it possible to share not only innovations but also information about them quickly and easily within and across current and potential markets. Whether such information is targeted by innovators and providers to particular audiences (e.g., through e-mail marketing campaigns, the placement of online advertisements, the addition of new and linked content to carefully selected web pages) or shared by others more informally (e.g., via Listservs, chat rooms, and web logs), it has the potential to stimulate (or quell) demand for innovations, greatly facilitating (or complicating) the prospects of scale-up.

Many IERI projects take advantage of these information and computing technologies in the design and dissemination of innovations, including the Modeling Across the Curriculum project Horwitz describes in the preceding chapter, and Project LISTEN's automated Reading Tutor, described in the companion to this volume (see Mostow and Beck 2006).[1] In both cases technology enables innovations to be delivered easily to networked individuals, be they students in the classroom or, in the case of the Reading Tutor, teachers who wish, whether at home or at school, to access reports on students' use and progress with the intervention. Both projects' use of technology facilitates extensive data collection (e.g., at very fine-grained sizes from session logs), a capability with considerable implications for cognitive science, systems development and research, and education research.[2] These implications notwithstanding, such technology-enabled and -enhanced dissemination capabilities do not seem to challenge the adequacy of current research designs and methodologies in significant ways. To the contrary, it is frequently possible, as both the Horwitz and the Mostow and Beck chapters note, to use the technological features that facilitate delivery and data collection to embed experiments in the interventions far more easily than can often be achieved in other scale-up paradigms. Indeed, in these instances technology, far from posing challenges to our methodologies and study designs, can enable the intervention developers and scale-up researchers to tackle many of the obstacles to scaling noted elsewhere in these two volumes.

Technology and the Creation of Virtual Teacher Communities

Technology provides opportunities for teachers to share resources and experiences easily, quickly, and securely over large distances, around the clock. Internet-enabled tools make it possible for educators to access extensive libraries of lesson plans, curricular materials, assessment tools, online educational information, and archived records of information exchanges.[3] More recent advances have made it possible for educators not only to access but also to upload materials to websites where they can be stored and subsequently retrieved by individuals outside both the teachers' schools and social networks. Alternatively—or in addition—teachers can take advantage of a variety of opportunities for more interactive exchanges, again with individuals known and unknown to them (e.g., through Listservs, web logs— "blogs"—threaded discussions, and chat rooms).

Clearly these changes in information flows and social relations have implications for scaling and scale-up research. Instructors can quickly bring their adaptations of and reactions to interventions being scaled to audiences that may include members of control, treatment, and other groups of teachers—potentially both introducing confounds into current studies and reducing the pool eligible for inclusion in subsequent scientific examinations of an intervention's effects. More problematic for educational researchers, however, may be the emergence and promotion of virtual teacher communities.

Virtual teacher communities can be self-starting or (more or less actively) established and promoted by third parties. The former can easily arise from technology that "introduces" previously unfamiliar practitioners (e.g., in a chat room, via a Listserv), then provides mechanisms for those motivated to extend the contact (e.g., interacting via e-mail before, in odd breaks during, or at the end of a busy day in school). The latter may be artifacts—or objectives—of interventions that employ online technologies (e.g., web-delivered courses, web-based multimedia resources, access to hypermedia-based video cases) to provide teacher professional development and enhance preservice teacher education.[4] Virtual communities also may be facilitated by vehicles such as Tapped In®, a web-based environment in which networks of educators can form, develop, be sustained, and intersect. Within three years of its launch in 1997, Tapped In® was supporting fifteen organizations and 6,000-plus members (Fusco, Gehlbach, and Schlager

2000); at the time of writing Tapped In® reported that twelve organizations (providers of preservice and postgraduate education and professional development services, and state and local education agencies) and "scores of small local groups from around the globe" were availing themselves of its services, including the opportunity to participate in more than 700 special interest groups (Tapped In® 2006).

We may have some time before the full potential—and implications—of virtual teacher communities are realized. Bull, Bull, and Kajder (2004) note that "teachers do not yet appear to have formed widespread virtual communities of practice" (35), particularly when compared with their student counterparts (see below). Importantly, as developers of Tapped In® highlight, online communities of practice rarely map onto the communities of practice that we expect to find in education (i.e., within school buildings or, perhaps less strongly defined, within districts). This is perhaps not surprising, given the difficulties of building, sustaining, and integrating such communities ("groups of people informally bound together by shared expertise and passion for a joint enterprise") within traditional organizations (Wenger and Snyder 2000, 139, 140) and the relatively poor understanding of the nature of such communities within education (Schlager and Fusco 2003, 207; see also Brown and Duguid 1991; Cochran-Smith and Lytle 1999; Lortie 1975; McLaughlin and Talbert 2001). As Foster and Kesselman and Sassen note in this volume, it is an open question whether the sociological impediments to their development will be challenged in meaningful ways by technologies (or more instrumental motivations, such as the advantages associated with collaboration observed in the physical sciences, see Knorr Cetina 1999), perhaps making the virtual community more attractive than the one bounded by bricks and mortar. Given the emphasis that theories in the sociology of education place on the significance of school- and district-based professional community for student learning, it will be very important to monitor developments in this area and think creatively about the implications for educational research design and data analysis.

Technology and the Creation of Virtual Student Communities

While the anticipated benefits of new learning technologies have sometimes lagged expectations (e.g., as resource and other constraints have slowed the pace of classroom penetration), the creation of new, transboundary, technology-enabled virtual communities has continued unabated. This last category of technological transformation is perhaps most troubling, both because its ability to redraw social boundaries is difficult to forecast and because it is its impacts which hold the greatest potential to undermine traditional research designs—a powerful argument for proactively revisiting the logic and methods employed in educational scale-up research.

The ubiquity of information and communication technologies (ICTs) creates enormous (until recently, unimaginable) opportunities for school-aged children to "meet" and interact with individuals whose only similarity to them may be the access they have to compatible ICTs. Internet-based resources (e.g., blogs and student websites) are increasingly being used to establish virtual student communities, with the promise to grow and change rapidly. An example is Facebook (www.thefacebook.com), the "online directory that connects people through social networks at schools" (Facebook 2006). Developed by Mark Zuckerberg while he was a student at Harvard University, Facebook was publicly launched in February 2004. Nearly two years later Facebook supports local networking at "more than 2500 schools in many countries" (Facebook 2006) and is "consistently in the Top 10 of the most visited sites in the U.S.," with 93 percent of the site's 8.5 million registered users logging on to the site monthly and 65 percent daily (Sedarevic 2006).

Facebook is only one example of the rapidly diffusing mechanisms expanding the number and size of virtual student communities. Adding to the online facilities allowing students to connect virtually to a vast network of peers, education researchers and individual instructors develop and promulgate web interfaces that enable students to work collaboratively on tasks across classes, grades, schools, and districts. An example from the IERI project portfolio is the *One Sky, Many Voices* BioKIDS project that Songer describes in the companion to this volume (Songer 2006). *One Sky, Many Voices* utilizes technology to facilitate interactive study, allowing "students, teachers, parents and scientists . . . [to] participate from classrooms, homes, after-school programs or other educational settings" in "inquiry-based K–12 science curricula" (One Sky, Many Voices 2001). BioKIDS (one of three *One Sky, Many Voices* projects) utilizes technology to "allow students to compare and share their findings with students and researchers around the world" (One Sky, Many Voices n.d.). Perhaps stimulated by such deliberate attempts to encourage students to engage in connected online learning, the Pew Internet and American Life Project in 2002 had identified "the Internet as virtual study group" as one of five metaphors for how students "think about and use the Internet for school" (Levin and Arafeh 2002, 6).

The development of virtual student communities poses two distinct challenges to scale-up research. First, it clearly increases the prospects that students outside the schools in which interventions are being implemented will learn about and potentially be exposed to key features of them. This raises the specter of the contamination of efforts to assess intervention outcomes scientifically. Similarly, the potential for uncontrolled diffusion of information about interventions may severely restrict the population eligible to participate in future randomized controlled trials. This is particularly important with respect to knowledge accumulation. Single studies are less likely to influence policy makers' and practitioners' understandings of complex education phenomena and subsequent courses of action (see Stevenson 2000; McDonald et al. forthcoming). This is both reasonable and desirable; our intuitions (like the logic of scientific inquiry) tell us that valid findings in support of an intervention are necessary but insufficient to warrant the intervention's adoption in high-stakes situations. Evidence-based decision making implies a preponderance of rigorous, reinforcing findings. It assumes multiple trials—replications with and without differences—will converge to demonstrate the merits of an innovation. Reliability may be logically impossible to achieve, however, when subjects and the contexts in which they receive interventions are constantly in flux.

The second fundamental challenge virtual student communities pose to scale-up research is one that Sassen encourages us to ponder: what happens when technologies contribute to the construction of "whole new domains of interaction" that do not neatly align with preexisting conceptualizations or maps of the spaces within which social relations occur? Empirical evidence demonstrates the critically important role classroom-based instruction plays in student achievement. Classrooms also assume important roles in the social lives of students and teachers, and provide a locus and the rationale for parent-teacher interactions. For students, the classroom is their community of learning; the teacher, the community leader. Individual classrooms are understood to reside, metaphorically as well as literally, in buildings within whose boundaries learning climates are more or less student centered, academic pressure is more or less keenly felt, and teachers are more or less encouraged to take active roles in leading the school and creating the atmosphere in which instruction and learning occur. Classrooms and schools are acknowledged to be dynamic systems, yet student behavior (in particular learning in response to classroom-based instruction) is understood in the context of a well-described hierarchical system of contextual influences. Education researchers use this conceptualization of the social organization of schools to create innovations to modify and instruments to assess social interplay within and across classrooms. It is critical to consider how scale-up research will be affected when new technological advances redraw the boundaries of the instructional and/or the learning environment.

TECHNOLOGY AND THE ORGANIZATIONAL STRUCTURE OF THE PUBLIC EDUCATION SYSTEM

The preceding examples illustrate the power of technology to facilitate, even drive, the development of new networks of students, teachers, and, potentially, other individuals and organizations with a stake in instruction, learning, and educational improvement. Technology also makes it possible to service the demand for education in new ways. Distance learning is of course not a new phenomenon, and while "correspondence courses" may once have been colloquially understood to be somehow inferior to teaching enabled by face-to-face interaction with qualified instructors, the many enhancements and quality controls that can be engineered into communication via the Internet and grid-based interactions have encouraged the entrance of new, premium brands into that marketplace. This is particularly the case with respect to postsecondary education, although opportunities for using distance learning at the pre-K–12 level—as a supplement to or replacement for classroom-based instruction—are being explored as well.[5] Such online tools are valuable resources to instructors who teach online full-time (1,600 K–12 nationwide in the 2002–2003 school year, expected to increase to over 2,000 by 2004–2005; see Blair 2002). Flamholtz and Randle in this volume suggest that these are trends education administrators should follow—decreasing demands for "traditional" educational services and experiences and/or failures to "make the required changes in organizational structure" lead to organizational decline, ultimately demise. Our theories were developed from intuitions and evidence regarding the factors that influence one predominant mode of K–12 learning: that which takes place in the classroom. Although these theories acknowledge that classroom-based learning is heavily contextualized, and we routinely consider a wide range of level-2 or level-3 forces that are understood to account for variation in student achievement,[6] technology has the potential to transform the fabric of those relationships. The implications for scientific social science research on scale-up are tremendous. Whether or not individual schools, districts, or the public education system at large will perceive (and respond to) these trends as threats to their continued viability remains to be seen. Either way it seems prudent for education researchers to monitor and think proactively about the potential effects of new computer-based technologies on the adequacy of our theories and research designs.

NOTES

1. For additional information on the Concord Consortium's Modeling Across the Curriculum project see mac.concord.org/; for information on the Reading Tutor see Project LISTEN at www.cs.cmu.edu/~listen/.

2. The issues raised by educational research projects that generate extensive student log files were addressed by IERI and other researchers in the symposium "Logging Students' Learning in Complex Domains: Empirical Considerations and Technological Solutions" at the 2005 Annual Meeting of the American Educational Research Association, in Montreal, Canada.

3. See, for example, the Educator's Reference Desk4 (www.eduref.org), the Gateway to Educational Materials (www.thegateway.org).

4. Examples from the IERI project portfolio include Brandon's study of the "effects of professional development and long-term support on curriculum implementation and scaling-up"; Palincsar's investigation of the "feasibility of scaling up effective reading comprehension instruction using innovative video-case-based hypermedia"; Osborn's project to assess "how distance learning for teachers can enable inquiry sciences in rural classrooms"; and Labbo's exploration of "best practices—teacher preparation—technology: connections that enhance children's literacy acquisition and reading achievement." Information on these and other IERI projects is available from the NSF-funded Data Research and Development Center's website, at drdc.uchicago.edu.

5. Examples from the IERI project portfolio include an exploration of "cognitively-based multimedia support for a balanced approach to the development of early reading in school and home contexts" that "explores how technology-supported tools may benefit children's (grades K, 1, 2) word recognition skills in meaningful contexts and provide new avenues for school-home connections" (see drdc.uchicago.edu/community/projects/sharp_goldman.shtml); the development of tools to support the Math Forum (www.mathforum.org), an "online community [that] includes teachers, students, researchers, parents, educators, and citizens at all levels who have an interest in math and math education" (www.mathforum.org/about.forum.html); and an exploration of how the Math Forum catalyzes and nurtures "online workgroups to power virtual learning communities" (see www.nsf.gov/awardsearch/showAward.do?AwardNumber=0325447 and www.nsf.gov/awardsearch/showAward.do?AwardNumber=0325872).

6. For example, "educational and occupational aspirations (influenced by family characteristics and individual abilities and interests), social contexts, community influences, norms, values, cultural capital, the social organization of schooling, social relationships in school communities, curriculum differentiation and the allocation of social and material resources, and the roles and beliefs of members of the teaching profession (McDonald et al. forthcoming; see also Bidwell and Friedkin 1988; Dreeben 1994; Hallinan 2000; Levinson, Cookson, and Sadovnik 2001; and Schneider 2003).

References

Acumen. 2003. Case Study: Immunex. *Acumen Journal of Life Sciences* 1(4): 28–29.

Adizes, I. 1979. Organizational passages: Diagnosing and treating life cycle problems in organizations. *Organizational Dynamics* (Summer): 3–24.

Alkers, H. 2005. Designing information resources for transboundary conflict early warning networks. In *Digital formations: Information technologies and new architectures in the global realm*, ed. R. Latham and S. Sassen. Princeton, NJ: Princeton University Press.

Alkin, M. C. 1985. *A guide for evaluation decision makers*. Beverly Hills, CA: Sage.

Allcock, W., I. Foster, V. Nefedova, A. Chervenak, E. Deelman, C. Kesselman, J. Lee, A. Sim, A. Shoshani, B. Drach, and D. Williams. 2001. High-performance remote access to climate simulation data: A challenge problem for data grid technologies. In *SC 2001 Proceedings of the ACM/IEEE SC 2001 Conference, November 10–16, 2001, Denver, Colorado, USA*, ed. SC (Conference), 20. New York: ACM Press.

Allison, J. J., C. I. Kiefe, N. W. Weissman, S. D. Person, M. Rousculp, J. G. Canto, S. Bae, et al. 2000. Relationship of hospital teaching status with quality of care and mortality for Medicare patients with acute MI. *Journal of the American Medical Association* 284 (10): 1256–62.

Altieri, M. A. 2005. An agroecological basis for natural resource management among poor farmers in fragile lands. In *Participatory research and development for sustainable agriculture and natural resource management: A sourcebook*. Vol. 1, *Understanding participatory research and development*, ed. J. Gonsalves, T. Becker, A. Braun, D. Campilan, H. de Chavez, E. Fajber, M. Kapiriri, J. Rivaca-Caminade, and R. Vernooy. Ottawa: International Development Research Centre, www.idrc.ca/en/ev-85047-201-1-DO_TOPIC.html (accessed January 9, 2006).

Altieri, M. A., D. Buckles, R. Bunch, S. Carter, A. Casanova, P. Engel, R. Figueroa, and C. Venegas. n.d. Scaling up successful agroecological initiatives in Latin America and the Caribbean. nature.berkeley.edu/~agroeco3/sane/ (accessed January 9, 2006).

Altrichter, H., and J. Elliot. 1999. *Images of educational change*. Milton Keynes, UK: Open University Press.

Anderson, J. W. 2003. New media, new publics: Reconfiguring the public sphere of Islam. *Social Research* 70 (3): 887–906.

Ashford, N. A., J. George, and R. Heaton. 1979. Environment, health, and safety regulation and technological Innovation. In *Technological innovation for a dynamic economy*, ed. C. T. Hill and J. M. Utterback. New York: Pergamon Press.

Astley, W. G. 1985. The two ecologies: Population and community perspectives on organizational evolution. *Administrative Science Quarterly* 30: 224–41.

Avgerou, C., C. Ciborra, and F. Land. 2004. *The social study of information and communication technology innovation, actors, and contexts*. Oxford, UK: Oxford University Press.

Bach, J., and D. Stark. 2005. Recombinant technology and new geographies of association. In *Digital formations: IT and new architectures in the global realm*, eds. R. Latham and S. Sassen, 37–53. Princeton, NJ: Princeton University Press.

Bair, R. 1999. Collaboratories: Building electronic scientific communities. In *Impact of advances in computing and communications technologies on chemical science and technology*, ed. National Research Council, 125–140. Washington, DC: National Academy Press.

Baker, E. L. 1973. The technology of instructional development. In *Second handbook of research on teaching*, ed. R. M. W. Travers, 245–85. Chicago: Rand McNally.

Baker, E. L. 1994. Learning-based assessments of history understanding. Special issue. *Educational Psychologist* 29 (2): 97–106.

Baker, E. L., M. Freeman, and S. Clayton. 1991. Cognitive assessment of history for large-scale testing. In *Testing and cognition*, ed. M. C. Wittrock and E. L. Baker, 131–53. Englewood Cliffs, NJ: Prentice Hall.

Baker, E. L., J. L. Herman, and M. Gearhart. 1996. Does technology work in schools? Why evaluation cannot tell the full story. In *Education and technology: Reflections on computing in classrooms*, ed. C. Fisher, D. C. Dwyer, and K. Yocam, 185–202. San Francisco: Jossey-Bass.

Baker, E. L., and R. E. Mayer. 1999. Computer-based assessment of problem solving. *Computers in Human Behavior* 15 (3/4): 69–282.

Baker, E. L., D. Niemi, H. Herl, A. Aguirre-Muñoz, L. Staley, and R. L. Linn. 1996. *Report on the content area performance assessments (CAPA): A collaboration among the Hawaii Department of Education, the Center for Research on Evaluation, Standards, and Student Testing (CRESST) and the teachers and children of Hawaii* (Final Deliverable). Los Angeles: University of California, National Center for Research on Evaluation, Standards, and Student Testing.

Baldwin, C. Y., and K. B. Clark. 2000. *Design rules*. Vol. 1, *The power of modularity*. Cambridge, MA: MIT Press.

Bane, M. J. 1989. Welfare reform and mandatory versus voluntary work: Policy issue or management problem? *Journal of Policy Analysis and Management* 8 (2): 285–89.

Bardach, E. 1977. *The implementation game: What happens after a bill becomes a law*. Cambridge, MA: MIT Press.

Behn, R. 1991. *Leadership counts: Lessons for public managers from the Massachusetts welfare, training and employment program*. Cambridge, MA: Harvard University Press.

Berends, M., J. Chun, G. Schuyler, S. Stockly, and R. J. Briggs. 2002. *Challenges of conflicting school reforms: Effects of New American Schools in a high-poverty district.* Santa Monica, CA: Rand.

Berends, M., S. Kirby, S. Naftel, and C. McKelvey. 2001. *Implementation and performance in New American Schools: Three years into scale-up.* Santa Monica, CA: RAND.

Berman, P., and M. W. McLaughlin. 1979. *Federal programs supporting educational change.* Vol. 8, *Implementing and sustaining innovations.* Santa Monica, CA: Rand.

Bernard, C. L. 1866. *Introduction à l'étude de la médecine expérimentale.* Rev. ed. Paris: Garnier-Flammarion.

Berners-Lee, T., J. Hendler, and O. Lassila. 2001. The semantic web. *Scientific American* 284 (5): 34–43.

Berry, D. A. 1996. When is a confirmatory randomized clinical trial needed? *Journal of the National Cancer Institute* 88 (22): 1606–7.

Bidwell, C. E., and N. E. Friedkin. 1988. Sociology of education. In *Handbook of sociology,* ed. N. J. Smelser, 449–71. Newbury Park, CA: Sage.

Black, N. 1996. Why we need observational studies to evaluate the effectiveness of health care. *British Medical Journal* 312 (7040): 1215–18.

Blackmon, M. B., B. Boville, F. Bryan, R. Dickinson, P. Gent, J. Kiehl, et al. 2001. The community climate system model. *Bulletin of the American Meteorological Society* 82 (11): 2357–76.

Blair, J. 2002. The virtual teaching life. *Education Week on the Web.* counts.edweek .org/sreports/tc02/article.cfm?slug=35virtual.h21 (accessed January 26, 2006).

Blau, P., and R. Schoenherr. 1971. *The structure of organizations.* New York: Basic Books.

Bleyer, W. A., H. A. Tejeda, S. B. Murphy, O. W. Brawley, M. A. Smith, and R. S. Ungerleider. 1997. Equal participation of minority patients in U.S. national pediatric cancer clinical trials. *Journal of Pediatric Hematology and Oncology* 19 (5): 423–27.

Bloom, B. S., G. F. Madaus, and J. T. Hastings. 1981. *Evaluation to improve learning.* New York: McGraw-Hill.

Bloom, H. S., C. J. Hill, and J. Riccio. 2001. Modeling the performance of welfare-to-work programs: The effects of program management and services, economic environment, and client characteristics. New York: MDRC.

Bodilly, S. 1998. *Lessons from New American Schools' scale-up phase.* Santa Monica, CA: Rand.

Boothroyd, P., and G. Dewhurst. 1983. Design for assembly: Selection of the right method. *Machine Design* 10: 94–98.

Boruch, R. F. 1976. On common contentions about randomized field experiments. In *Evaluation studies review annual,* ed. G. V. Glass, 1: 158–94. Beverly Hills, CA: Sage.

Boruch, R. F. 1997. *Randomized experiments for planning and evaluation: A practical guide.* Thousand Oaks, CA: Sage.

Boruch, R. F., and H. Gomez. 1977. Sensitivity, bias, and theory in impact evaluations. *Professional Psychology* 8: 411–34.

Bracht, G. H., and G. V. Glass. 1968. The external validity of experiments. *American Educational Research Journal* 5: 437–74.

Bransford, J. D., and M. K. Johnson. 1972. Contextual prerequisites for understanding: Some investigations of comprehension and recall. *Journal of Verbal Learning and Verbal Behavior* 11: 717–26.

Brittain, J. W., and J. Freeman. 1980. Organizational proliferation and density-dependent selection. In *The organizational life cycle issues in the creation, transformation, and decline of organizations*, ed. J. R. Kimberly and R. H. Miles, 291–338. San Francisco: Jossey-Bass.

Brodkin, E. Z. 1997. Inside the welfare contract: Discretion and accountability in state welfare administration. *Social Service Review* 71 (1): 1–33.

Brooks, F. P. 1995. The *mythical man month: Essays on software engineering*, 20th anniversary ed. Reading, MA: Addison-Wesley.

Brown, J. S., and P. Duguid. 1991. Organizational learning and communities-of-practice: Toward a unified view of working, learning and innovation. *Organization Science* 2: 40–57.

Brown, S. F. 2002. Growing drugs is a tricky business. *Fortune*, November 25.

Buchenau, B., and J. Fulton-Surrey. 2000. *Experience prototyping*. San Francisco: IDEO Publishing.

Bull, G., G. Bull, and S. Kajder. 2004. Tapped in. *Learning & Leading with Technology* 31 (5): 34–37.

Burns, T., and G. M. Stalker. 1961. *The management of innovation*. London: Tavistock.

Byar, D. P. 1980. Why databases should not replace randomized clinical trials. *Biometrics* 36 (2): 337–42.

Cabana, M. D., C. S. Rand, N. R. Powe, A. W. Wu, M. H. Wilson, P. A. Abboud, et al. 1999. Why don't physicians follow clinical practice guidelines? A framework for improvement. *Journal of the American Medical Association* 282 (15): 1458–65.

Califf, R. M., K. F. Adams, W. J. McKenna, M. Gheorghiade, B. F. Uretsky, S. E. McNulty, et al. 1997. A randomized controlled trial of epoprostenol therapy for severe congestive heart failure: The Flolan International Randomized Survival Trial (FIRST). *American Heart Journal* 134 (1): 44–54.

Califf, R. M., and D. L. DeMets. 2002. Principles from clinical trials relevant to clinical practice: Part I. *Circulation* 106 (8): 1015–21.

Cameron, K. S., and D. A. Whetten. 1981. Perception of organizational effectiveness over organizational life cycles. *Administrative Science Quarterly* 26: 525–44.

Cameron, K. S., and D. A. Whetten. 1983. Models of the organizational life cycle: Applications to higher education. *Review of Higher Education* 55: 212–41.

Campbell, D. T., and J. C. Stanley. 1963. Experimental and quasi-experimental designs for research. In *Handbook of research on teaching*, ed. N. L. Gage, 171–246. Chicago: Rand McNally.

Cappelleri, J. C., R. B. Darlington, and W. M. K. Trochim. 1994. Power analysis of cutoff-based randomized clinical trials. *Evaluation Review* 18: 141–52.

Carroll, G. R., and P. H. Yangchung. 1986. Organizational task and institutional environments in ecological perspective: Findings from a local newspaper industry. *American Journal of Sociology* 91: 838–73.

Cartlett, C. 2002. The TeraGrid: A primer. Available at www.teragrid.org/about/TeraGrid-Primer-Sept-02.pdf.

Chalmers, T. C., P. Celano, H. Sacks, and H. Smith. 1983. Bias in treatment assignment in controlled clinical trials. *New England Journal of Medicine* 309: 1358–61.

Chandler, A. D. 1962. *Strategy and structure*. Cambridge, MA: MIT Press.

Chen, J., M. J. Radford, Y. Wang, T. A. Marciniak, and H. M. Krumholz. 1999. Do "America's Best Hospitals" perform better for acute myocardial infarction? *New England Journal of Medicine* 340 (4): 286–92.

Chi, M. T. H., R. Glaser, and M. Farr, eds. 1988. *The nature of expertise.* Hillsdale, NJ: Lawrence Erlbaum Associates.

Child, J. 1973. Predicting and understanding organization structure. *Administrative Science Quarterly* 18: 168–85.

Child, J., and A. Keiser. 1981. Development of organizations over time. In *Handbook of organizations: Adapting organizations to their environments,* ed. P. C. Nystrom and W. H. Starbuck, 28–64. New York: Oxford University Press.

Churchill, N. C., and V. L. Lewis. 1983. The five stages of small business growth. *Harvard Business Review* (May–June): 30–50.

Clark, D. L. 1985. Emerging paradigms in organizational theory and research. In *Organizational theory and inquiry: The paradigm revolution,* ed. Y. S. Lincoln, 43–78. Newbury Park, CA: Sage.

Coburn, C. E. 2003. Rethinking scale: Moving beyond the numbers to deep and lasting change. *Educational Researcher* 32: 3–12.

Cochrane, A. L. 1989. Archie Cochrane in his own words: Selections arranged from his 1972 introduction to "Effectiveness and efficiency: Random reflections on the health services." *Controlled Clinical Trials* 10 (4): 428–33.

Cochran, W. G., and D. B. Rubin. 1973. Controlling bias in observational studies: A review. Sankhya (Series A), 35, 417–46.

Cochran-Smith, M., and S. L. Lytle. 1999. Relationships of knowledge and practice: Teacher learning in communities. *Review of Research in Education* 24: 249–305.

Cohen, D. K. 1987. Educational technology, policy, and practice. *Educational Evaluation and Policy Analysis* 9 (Summer): 153–70.

Cohen and Hill. 2001.

Cohen, D. K., and D. L. Ball. 2003. Instruction, innovation, and the problem of scale. Unpublished draft, Ann Arbor.

Cohen, D. K., and J. Spillane. 1993. Policy and practice: The relations between governance and instruction. In *Review of research in education,* ed. G. Grant, 18: 3–49. Washington, DC: American Educational Research Association.

Cohen, W. A., and D. A. Levinthal. 1990. Absorptive capacity: A new perspective on learning and innovation. *Administrative Science Quarterly* 35 (1): 128–52.

Conley, J. G. 1996. *Ryobi outdoor products: A case study in rapid production innovation.* Teaching Case Study written for McCormick-Kellogg MMM program.

Conley, J. G. 2002. *Hewlett-Packard blades.* Teaching Case Study, Kellogg School of Management Case Series.

Conley, J. G., K. Craw, J. Glaspie, M. Hernandez, and C. Janes. 2002. *New product development at the Harley Davidson Motor Company.* Teaching Case Study, Kellogg School of Management Case Series.

Conley, J. G., B. Moran, and J. Gray. 1998. A new paradigm for the design of safety critical castings. *Journal of Materials and Manufacturing, SAE Transactions* 107.

Conley, J. G., and R. C. Wolcott. 2004. Design for securability. Working Paper, Center for Research on Technology and Innovation, Kellogg School of Management, Northwestern University.

Cook, T. D., and D. T. Campbell. 1979. *Quasi-experimentation: Design and analysis issues for field settings.* Boston: Houghton Mifflin.

Cooper, H., and Hedges, L. V. 1994. The Handbook of research synthesis. New York: Russell Sage Foundation.

Corbett, D. H., and B. L. Wilson. 1998. Scaling within rather than scaling up: Implications from students' experiences in reforming urban middle schools. *The Urban Review* 30 (4): 261–93.

Corchon, L. 1996. *The theory of implementation of socially optimal decisions in economics.* New York: St. Martin's Press.

Corchon, L., and I. Ortuono-Ortin. 1995. Robust implementation under alternative information structures. *Economic Design* 1: 159–71.

Cowen, S. S., J. K. Middaugh III, and K. Mccarthy. 1984. Corporate life cycles and the evolution of management (part I). *Management Decision* 22: 3–11.

Cronbach, L. J. 1957. The two disciplines of scientific psychology. *American Psychologist* 12: 671–84.

Cronbach, L. J. 1975. Beyond the two disciplines of scientific psychology. *American Psychologist* 12: 116–27.

Cronbach, L. J. 1982. *Designing evaluations of educational and social programs.* San Francisco: Jossey-Bass.

Cronbach, L. J., S. R. Ambron, S. M. Dornbusch, R. D. Hess, R. C. Hornik, D. C. Phillips, et al. 1981. *Toward reform of program evaluation.* San Francisco: Jossey-Bass.

Cronbach, L. J., H. Nanda, N. Rajaratnam, and G. C. Gleser. 1972. *The dependability of behavioral measurements.* New York: Wiley.

Cronbach, L. J., and P. Suppes. 1969. *Research for tomorrow's schools: Disciplined inquiry for education.* Stanford, CA: National Academy of Education, Committee on Educational Research. New York: Macmillan.

CSFB. 2002. *Patents and pipelines: A guide for pan-European investors.* CSFB Equity Research, New York, February 12.

Cuban, L. 1993. *How teachers taught: Constancy and change in American classrooms, 1890–1990.* 2nd ed. New York: Teachers College Press.

Dalton, D. R., W. D. Todor, M. J. Spendoli, G. J. Fielding, and L. W. Porter. 1980. Organization structure and performance: A critical review. *Academy of Management Review* 5: 49–64.

Dans, A. L., L. F. Dans, G. H. Guyatt, and S. Richardson. 1998. Users' guides to the medical literature: XIV. How to decide on the applicability of clinical trial results to your patient. *Journal of the American Medical Association* 279 (7): 545–49.

Deal, T. E., and A. A. Kennedy. 1982. *Corporate cultures: The rite and rituals of corporate life.* Reading, MA: Addison-Wesley.

Dede, C., and J. P. Honan. 2005. Scaling up success: A synthesis of themes and insights. In *Scaling up success: Lessons from technology-based educational improvement,* ed. C. Dede, J. P. Honan, and L. C. Peters. San Francisco: Jossey-Bass.

Dede, C., J. P. Honan, and L. C. Peters, eds. 2005. *Scaling up success: Lessons from technology-based educational improvement.* San Francisco: Jossey-Bass.

Dell, M., and J. Magretta. 1998. The power of virtual integration: An interview with Dell Computer's Michael Dell. *Harvard Business Review* 76 (2): 72–84.

DeMets, D. L., and R. M. Califf. 2002a. Lessons learned from recent cardiovascular clinical trials: Part I. *Circulation* 106 (6): 746–51.

DeMets, D. L., R. M. Califf. 2002b. Lessons learned from recent cardiovascular clinical trials: Part II. *Circulation* 106 (7): 880–86.

Dickersin, K., S. Chan, T. C. Chalmers, H. S. Sacks, and H. Smith Jr. 1987. Publication bias and clinical trials. *Controlled Clinical Trials* 8 (4): 343–53.

Doll, R. 1998. Controlled trials: The 1948 watershed. *British Medical Journal* 317 (7167): 1217–20.

Dreeben, R. 1994. The sociology of education: Its development in the United States. In *Research in sociology of education and socialization,* ed. A. M. Pallas, 10: 7–52. Greenwich, CT: JAI Press.

DuPont, W. D. 1985. Randomized vs. historical clinical trials: Are the benefits worth the costs? *American Journal of Epidemiology* 122 (6): 940–46.

Early Breast Cancer Trialists' Collaborative Group. 1998. Tamoxifen for early breast cancer: An overview of the randomized trials. *Lancet* 351 (9114): 1451–67.

Easterbrook, P. J., and J. A. Berlin. 1991. Publication bias in clinical research. *Lancet* 337 (8746): 867–72.

Echt, D. S., P. R. Liebson, L. B. Mitchell, et al. 1991. Mortality and morbidity in patients receiving encainide, flecainide, or placebo. The Cardiac Arrhythmia Suppression Trial. *New England Journal of Medicine* 324 (12): 781–88.

Eckert, W. A. 2000. Situational enhancement of design validity: The case of training evaluation at the World Bank Institute. *American Journal of Evaluation* 21: 185–93.

Economic Report of the President. 2000. Washington, DC: U.S. Government Printing Office.

Elmore, R. 1996. Getting to scale with successful educational practice. *Harvard Educational Review* 66: 1–26.

Engelbart, D. C., and W. K. English. 1968. A research center for augmenting human intellect. In *Proceedings of AFIPS 1968 fall joint computer conference,* ed. Fall Joint Computer Conference, 33: 395–410. Washington, DC: Thompson Book.

Epple, D., D. Figlio, and R. Romano. 2004. Competition between private and public schools: Testing stratification and pricing predictions. *Journal of Public Economics* 88: 1215–45.

Erdos, M., and S. Cantor. 2002. *Shibboleth architecture.* Abstract. shibboleth.internet 2.edu/docs/draft-internet2-shibboleth-arch-v05.pdf (accessed January 14, 2006).

Evidence-Based Medicine Working Group. 1992. Evidence-based medicine. A new approach to teaching the practice of medicine. *Journal of the American Medical Association* 268 (17): 2420–25.

Facebook. 2006. Customer service: The most frequently asked questions. www.facebook.com/help.php (accessed January 24, 2006).

Ferguson, J. H. 1993. NIH consensus conferences: Dissemination and impact. *Annals of the New York Academy of Sciences* 703 (1): 180–98.

Fetterman, D. M. 1982. Ibsen's baths: Reactivity and insensitivity. *Educational Evaluation and Policy Analysis* 4: 261–79.

Finnan, C., and J. Meza. 2003. The accelerated schools project: Can a leader change the culture and embed reform? In *Leadership lessons from comprehensive school reform,* ed. J. Murphy and A. Datnow, 83–108. Thousand Oaks, CA: Corwin Press.

Fisher, R. A., Sir. 1951. *The design of experiments.* 6th ed. Edinburgh, UK: Oliver and Boyd.

Flamholtz, E. G. 1986. *How to make the transition from an entrepreneurship to a professionally managed firm.* San Francisco: Jossey-Bass.

Flamholtz, E. G. 1995. Managing organizational transitions: Implications for corporate and human resource management. *European Management Journal* 13 (1): 39–51.

Flamholtz, E. G. 2000. Corporate culture and the bottom line. *European Management Journal* 9 (3): 268–75.

Flamholtz, E. G. 2003. Toward an integrative theory of organizational success and failure: Previous research and future issues. *International Journal of Entrepreneurship Education* 1 (3): 297–319.

Flamholtz, E. G., and Z. Aksehirili. 2000. Organizational success and failure, an empirical test of a holistic model. *European Management Journal* 18 (5): 488–98.

Flamholtz, E. G., and W. Hua. 2002a. Strategic organizational development and the bottom line: Further empirical evidence. *European Management Journal* 20 (1): 72–81.

Flamholtz, E. G., and W. Hua. 2002b. Strategic organizational development, growing pains, and corporate financial performance: An empirical test. *European Management Journal* 20 (5): 527–36.

Flamholtz, E. G., and W. Hua, with Z. Aksehirili. 2002c. Searching for competitive advantage in the black box. Unpublished Working Paper, Anderson School of Management, University of California, Los Angeles.

Flamholtz, E. G., and S. Kurland. 2005. Strategic organizational development infrastructure and financial performance. *International Journal of Entrepreneurial Education* 3: 117–42.

Flamholtz, E. G., and Y. Randle. 1987. How to avoid choking on growth. *Management Review* (May): 25–29.

Flamholtz, E. G., and Y. Randle. 1998. *Changing the game: Organizational transformations of the first, second and third kind.* New York: Oxford University Press.

Flamholtz, E. G., and Y. Randle. 2000. *Growing pains.* 3rd ed. San Francisco: Jossey-Bass.

Ford, D., and R. Lerner. 1992. *Developmental systems theory: An integrative approach.* Newbury Park, CA: Sage Publications.

Foster, I., and C. Kesselman, eds. 2004. *The grid: Blueprint for a new computing infrastructure.* 2nd ed. Amsterdam: Morgan Kaufmann.

Foster, I., C. Kesselman, J. M. Nick, and S. Tuecke. 2002. Grid services for distributed systems integration. *IEEE Computer* 35 (6): 37–46.

Foster, I., C. Kesselman, and S. Tuecke. 2001. The anatomy of the grid: Enabling scalable virtual organizations. *International Journal of Supercomputer Applications* 15 (3): 200–22.

Foster, I., J. Voeckler, M. Wilde, and Y. Zhao. 2004. Chimera: A virtual data system for representing, querying, and automating data derivation. In *Proceedings of the 14th International Conference on scientific and statistical database management,* ed. J. Kennedy, 37–46. Los Alamitos, CA: IEEE Computer Society.

Freedman, D., R. Pisani, and R. Purves. 1983. *Statistics.* New York: Norton.

Freedman, D., R. Pisani, R. Purves, and A. Adhikari. 1991. *Statistics.* 2nd ed. New York: Norton.

Freedman, S., D. Friedlander, G. Hamilton, J. Rock, M. Mitchell, J. Nudelman, A. Schweder, and L. Storto. 2002. *Two-year impacts for eleven programs.* Washington, DC: U.S. Department of Health and Human Services, Administration for Children and Families, Office of the Assistant Secretary for Planning and Evaluation and U.S. Department of Education, Office of the Under Secretary, Office of Vocational and Adult Education.

Freedman, S., D. Friedlander, W. Lin, and A. Schweder. 1996. The GAIN evaluation: Five-year impacts on employment, earnings, and AFDC receipt. New York: MDRC.

Freedman, L. S., R. Simon, M. A. Foulkes, L. Friedman, N. L. Geller, D. J. Gordon, et al. 1995. Inclusion of women and minorities in clinical trials and the NIH Revitalization Act of 1993—The perspective of NIH clinical trialists. *Controlled Clinical Trials* 16 (5): 277–85.

Freeman, H. E., and C. C. Sherwood. 1970. *Social research and social policy.* Englewood Cliffs, NJ: Prentice Hall.

Freeman, J. 1982. Organizational life cycles and natural selection processes. In *Research in organizational behavior,* ed. B. Staw and L. L. Cummings, 4: 1–32. Greenwich, CT: JAI Press.

Freeman, J., and M. J. Hannan. 1983. Niche width and the dynamics of organizational populations. *American Journal of Sociology* 88: 1116–45.

Freud, S. 1933. *New introductory lectures on psychoanalysis.* New York: W. W. Norton.

Friedman, M., and R. D. Friedman. 1962. *Capitalism and freedom.* Chicago: University of Chicago Press.

Fullan, M. 1982. *The meaning of educational change.* New York: Teachers College Press.

Fusco, J., H. Gehlbach, and M. Schlager. 2000. Assessing the impact of a large-scale online teacher professional development community. tappedin.org/tappedin/web/papers/2000/AssessingComm.pdf (accessed January 20, 2006).

Gage, N. L., ed. 1963. *Handbook of research on teaching.* Chicago: Rand McNally.

Gamble, V. N. 1997. Under the shadow of Tuskegee: African Americans and health care. *American Journal of Public Health* 87 (11): 1773–78.

Gamson, A. 1998. The challenge of going to scale: A review of the literature. Paper presented at the Pew Forum, Pittsburgh.

Gawer, A., and M. Cusumano. 2002. *Platform leadership: How Intel, Microsoft, and Cisco drive industry innovation.* Boston: Harvard Business School Press.

Gehan, E. A. 1984. The evaluation of therapies: Historical control studies. *Statistics in Medicine* 3 (4): 315–24.

Gelber, R. D., and Goldhirsch. 1988. Can a clinical trial be the treatment of choice for patients with cancer? *Journal of the National Cancer Institute* 80 (12): 886–87.

George, S. L., C. Li, D. Berry, and M. R. Green. 1994. Stopping a clinical trial early: Frequentist and Bayesian approaches applied to a CALGB trial in non-small-cell lung cancer. *Stat Med* 13 (13–14): 1313–27.

Gilmore, J. H., and B. J. Pine. 2000. *Markets of one: Creating customer-unique value through mass customization.* Boston: Harvard Business School Press.

Glass, G. V. 1977a. Downtime. *Outlook* 25: 3–6.

Glass, G. V. 1977b. Integrating findings: The meta-analysis of research. *Review of Educational Research* 5:351–79.

Goble, C., S. Pettifer, and R. Stevens. 2004. Knowledge integration: In silico experiments in bioinformatics. In *The grid: Blueprint for a new computing infrastructure,* ed. I. Foster and C. Kesselman. San Francisco: Morgan Kaufmann.

Goble, C. A., D. De Roure, N. R. Shadbolt, and A. Fernandes. 2004. Enhancing services and applications with knowledge and semantics. In *The grid: Blueprint for a new computing infrastructure,* ed. I. Foster and C. Kesselman. San Francisco: Morgan Kaufmann.

Greenberg, D., R. Meyer, and M. Wiseman. 1994. Multi-site employment and training evaluations: A tale of three studies. *Industrial and Labor Relations Review* 47 (4): 679–91.

Greene, W. H. 1993. *Econometric analysis*. Upper Saddle River, NJ: Prentice Hall.

Greiner, L. E. 1972. Evolution and revolution as organizations grow. *Harvard Business Review* (July–August): 37–46.

Grissmer, D. W., A. Flanagan, J. H. Kawata, and S. Williamson. 2000. *Improving student achievement: What state NAEP test scores tell us*. Santa Monica, CA: Rand.

Gueron, J., and E. Pauly. 1991. *From welfare to work*. New York: Russell Sage Foundation.

Guyatt, G. H., J. Sinclair, D. J. Cook, and P. Glasziou. 1999. Users' guides to the medical literature: XVI. How to use a treatment recommendation. Evidence-Based Medicine Working Group and the Cochrane Applicability Methods Working Group. *Journal of the American Medical Association* 281 (19): 1836–43.

Hagen, J. L., and I. Lurie. 1994. *Implementing JOBS: Progress and promise*. Albany, NY: Nelson A. Rockefeller Institute of Government.

Haire, M. 1959. Biological models and empirical histories of the growth of organizations. In *Modern Organizational Theory*, ed. M. Haire, 10: 272–306. New York: Wiley.

Hall, G. E., and S. M. Hord. 2001. *Implementing change: Patterns, principles and potholes*. Boston: Allyn and Bacon.

Hallinan, M. T., ed. 2000. *Handbook of the sociology of education*. New York: Kluwer Academic/Plenum.

Halpern, S. D., J. H. T. Karlawish, and J. A. Berlin. 2002. The continuing unethical conduct of underpowered clinical trials. *Journal of the American Medical Association* 288 (3): 358–62.

Hamilton, G. 2002. *Moving people from welfare to work: Lessons from the National Evaluation of Welfare-to-Work Strategies*. Washington DC: U.S. Department of Health and Human Services, Administration for Children and Families, Office of the Assistant Secretary for Planning and Evaluation and U.S. Department of Education, Office of the Under Secretary, Office of Vocational and Adult Education.

Hamilton, G., and T. Brock. 1994. *The JOBS evaluation: Early lessons from seven sites*. Washington, DC: U.S. Department of Health and Human Services, Administration for Children and Families, Office of the Assistant Secretary for Planning and Evaluation and U.S. Department of Education, Office of the Under Secretary, Office of Vocational and Adult Education.

Hamilton, G., S. Freedman, L. Gennetian, C. Michalopoulos, J. Walter, D. Adams-Ciardullo, A. Gassman-Pines, S. McGroder, M. Zaslow, J. Brooks, and S. Ahluwalia. 2001. *National evaluation of welfare-to-work strategies: How effective are different welfare-to-work approaches? Five-year adult and child impacts for eleven programs*. Washington, DC: U.S. Department of Health and Human Services, Administration for Children and Families, Office of the Assistant Secretary for Planning and Evaluation and U.S. Department of Education, Office of the Under Secretary, Office of Vocational and Adult Education.

Hannan, M. T., and J. Freeman. 1984. Structural inertia and organizational change. *American Sociological Review* 49: 149–64.

Hanushek, E. 1986. The economics of schooling: Production and efficiency in public schools. *Journal of Economic Literature* 24:1141–77.

Hanushek, E. A. 1989. The impact of differential expenditures on school performance. *Educational Researcher* (May): 45–62.

Hargittai, E. 1998. Holes in the net: The Internet and the international stratification. INET '98 Conferences: The Internet Summit, Geneva, Switzerland, July.

Hedges, L. V. 1997. Construct validity and causal inference: The concept of total causal inference error. In *Causality in Crisis?* ed. V. McKim and S. Turner, 325–41. Notre Dame, IN: Notre Dame University Press.

Hedges, L. V. 2004. Designing studies for evidence-based generalization in education. Presentation in the Presidential Invited Session Symposium, "Changing the Way We Think about Improving Student Learning Outcomes: Conceptualizing and Contextualizing Scale-Up in Educational Research," Annual Meeting of the American Educational Research Association, San Diego, California.

Heinrich, C. J. 2002. Outcomes-based performance management in the public sector: Implications for government accountability and effectiveness. *Public Administration Review* 62 (6): 712–25.

Hellman, S., and D. S. Hellman. 1991. Of mice but not men: Problems of the randomized clinical trial. *New England Journal of Medicine* 324: 1585–89.

Hickey, D. T., A. C. H. Kindfield, P. Horwitz, and M. A. Christie. 1999. Advancing educational theory by enhancing practice in a technology-supported genetics learning environment. *Journal of Education* 181: 25–55.

Hickey, D. T., A. C. H. Kindfield, P. Horwitz, and M. A. Christie. 2003. Integrating curriculum, instruction, assessment, and evaluation in a technology-supported genetics learning environment. *American Educational Research Journal* 40: 495–538.

Hively, W., H. L. Patterson, and S. H. Page. 1968. A "universe-defined" system of arithmetic achievement tests. *Journal of Educational Measurement* 5: 275–90.

Hopkins, D. 1996. Toward a theory for school improvement. In *Merging traditions: The future of research on school effectiveness and school improvement*, ed. J. Gray, D. Reynolds, C. Fitz-Gibbon, and D. Jesson, 30–50. London: Cassell.

Hopp, W. P., and M. Spearman. 2001. *Factory physics: The foundations of manufacturing management*. Burr-Ridge, IL: Irwin-McGraw-Hill.

Horwitz, P. 1979. Direct government funding of research and development: Intended and unintended effects on industrial innovation. In *Technological innovation for a dynamic economy*, ed. C. T. Hill and J. M. Utterback, 255–91. New York: Pergamon Press.

Horwitz, P., and M. Christie. 2000. Computer-based manipulatives for teaching scientific reasoning: An example. In *Innovations in science and mathematics education: Advanced designs for technologies of learning*, ed. M. J. Jacobson and R. B. Kozma, 163–91. Hillsdale, NJ: Lawrence Erlbaum Associates.

Horwitz, P., J. Schwartz, A. C. H. Kindfield, L. M. Yessis, D. T. Hickey, A. J. Heidenberg, and E. W. Wolfe. 1998. Implementation and evaluation of GenScope™ learning environment: Issues, solutions, and results. In *Proceedings of the Third International Conference of the learning sciences*, ed. by M. Guzdial, J. Kolodner, and A. Bruckman. Charlottesville, VA: Association for the Advancement of Computers in Education.

Hotz, V. J., G. W. Imbens, and J. A. Klerman. 2000. *The long-term gains from GAIN: A re-analysis of the impacts of the California GAIN program*. Cambridge, MA: National Bureau of Economic Research.

House, E. R. 1974. *The politics of educational innovation*. Berkeley: McCutchan.

Hovland, C. I., A. A. Lumsdaine, and F. D. Sheffield. 1949. *Experiments on mass communication*. Princeton, NJ: Princeton University Press.

Howard, P. N., and S. Jones, eds. 2004. *Society online: The Internet in context*. London: Sage.

Howard-Grabman, L., and G. Snetro. 2003. *How to mobilize communities for health and social change*. Baltimore, MD: Health Communication Partnership.

Hulley, S., D. Grady, T. Bush, C. Furberg, D. Herrington, B. Riggs, et al. 1998. Randomized trial of estrogen plus progestin for secondary prevention of coronary heart disease in postmenopausal women. Heart and Estrogen/Progestin Replacement Study (HERS) Research Group. *Journal of the American Medical Association* 280 (7): 605–13.

Hutchins, L. F., J. M. Unger, J. J. Crowley, C. A. Coltman Jr, and K. S. Albain. 1999. Under-representation of patients 65 years of age or older in cancer-treatment trials. *New England Journal of Medicine* 341 (27): 2061–67.

Iansiti, M., and A. MacCormack. 1997. Developing products on internet time. *Harvard Business Review* 75 (5): 108–18.

Improving America's Schools Act of 1994. Pub. L. No. 103–382, 108 Stat. 3518 (1994).

Integrated Development Enterprise software product available at www.ide.com/.

Ishii, K. 1995. Life-cycle engineering design. *ASME Journal of Mechanical Design* 117: 42–47.

Jennison, C., and B. Turnbull. 2000. *Group sequential methods with applications to clinical trials*. London: Chapman & Hall/CRC.

Joffe, S., and J. C. Weeks. 2002. Views of American oncologists about the purposes of clinical trials. *Journal of the National Cancer Institute* 94 (24): 1847–53.

Kaplan, A. 1964. *The conduct of inquiry: Methodology for behavioral science*. San Francisco: Chandler.

Keil, M., and R. Montealegre. 2000. Cutting your losses: Extricating your organization when a big project goes awry. *MIT Sloan Management Review* 41 (3): 55–68.

Kemple, J., and J. Haimson. 1994. Florida's Project Independence: Program implementation, participation patterns, and first-year impacts. New York: MDRC.

Kimberly, J. R. 1976. Organization size and the structuralist perspective: A review, critique, and proposal. *Administrative Science Quarterly* 21: 571–97.

Kirk, R. 1995. *Experimental design*. Belmont, CA: Brooks Cole.

Kish, L. 1965. *Survey sampling*. New York: John Wiley.

Knorr Cetina, K. 1999. *Epistemic cultures: How the sciences make knowledge*. Cambridge, MA: Harvard University Press.

Kosecoff, J., D. E. Kanouse, W. H. Rogers, L. McCloskey, C. M. Winslow, and R. H. Brook. 1987. Effects of the National Institutes of Health Consensus Development Program on physician practice. *Journal of the American Medical Association* 258 (19): 2708–13.

Kremer, M., and D. Levy. 2003. *Peer effects and alcohol use among college students*. Cambridge, MA: National Bureau of Economic Research.

Krzyzanowska, M. K., M. Pintilie, and I. F. Tannock. 2003. Factors associated with failure to publish large randomized trials presented at an oncology meeting. *Journal of the American Medical Association* 290: 495–501.

Kulik, C.-L. C., and J. Kulik. 1991. Effectiveness of computer-based instruction: An updated analysis. *Computers in Human Behavior* 7: 75–94.

Lam, J. A., S. W. Hartwell, and J. F. Jekel. 1994. "I prayed real hard, so I know I'll get in": Living with randomization. In *Critically evaluating the role of experiments*, ed. K. J. Conrad, 55–66. New Directions for Program Evaluation, no. 63. San Francisco: Jossey-Bass.

Landauer, T. K. 1995. *The trouble with computers: Usefulness, usability, and productivity.* Cambridge, MA: MIT Press.

Larkin, J. H., J. McDermott, D. P. Simon, and H. A. Simon. 1980. Expert and novice performance in solving physics problems. *Science* 208: 1335–42.

Latham, R. and S. Sassen, eds. 2005. *Digital formations: Information technologies and new architectures in the global realm.* Princeton, NJ: Princeton University Press.

Latour, B. 1991. Technology is society made durable. In *A sociology of monsters*, ed. J. Law, 103–31. London: Routledge.

Lavoie, D., and S. A. Culbert. 1978. Stages of organization and development. *Human Relations* 51: 417–38.

Lazear, E. 1999. *Educational production.* Cambridge, MA: National Bureau of Economic Research.

Lazovich, D. A., E. White, D. B. Thomas, and R. E. Moe. 1991. Underutilization of breast-conserving surgery and radiation therapy among women with stage I or II breast cancer. *Journal of the American Medical Association* 266: 3433–38.

Lee, P. Y., K. P. Alexander, B. G. Hammill, S. K. Pasquali, and E. D. Peterson. 2001. Representation of elderly persons and women in published randomized trials of acute coronary syndromes. *Journal of the American Medical Association* 286: 708–13.

Lerner, R. M., and C. B. Fisher. 1994. From applied developmental psychology to applied developmental science: community coalitions and collaborative careers. In *Applied Developmental Psychology*, eds. C. B. Fisher and R. M. Merner, 505–22. New York: McGraw-Hill.

Lerner, R. M., and M. B. Kauffman. 1985. The concept of development in contextualism. *Developmental Review* 5: 309–33.

Lerner, R., and P. Benson, eds. 2003. *Developmental assets and asset-building communities: Implications for research and policy.* Norwell, MA: Kluwer.

Levels of Evidence for Cancer Treatment Studies: Definition and Use (PDQ). www.nci.nih.gov/cancer_information/doc (accessed September 5, 2002).

Levin, D., and S. Arafeh. 2002. *The digital disconnect: The widening gap between Internet-savvy students and their schools.* Washington, DC: The Pew Internet & American Life Project. www.pewinternet.org/pdfs/PIP_Schools_Internet_Report.pdf (accessed January 20, 2006).

Levin, J. 2001. For whom the reductions count: A quantile regression analysis of class size and peer effects on scholastic achievement. *Empirical Economics* 26: 221–46.

Levin, M., ed. 2001. *Pharmaceutical process scale-up.* New York: Marcel Dekker.

Levinson, D., P. W. Cookson Jr., and A. R. Sadovnik, eds. 2001. *Education and sociology: An encyclopedia.* New York: Routledge Falmer Press.

Licklider, J. C. R., and R. W. Taylor. 1968. The computer as a communication device. *Science and Technology* (April): 21–31.

Likert, R. A. 1932. A technique for the measurement of attitudes. *Archives of Psychology* 140: 1–55.

Lind, J. A. 1757. *A treatise on the scurvy.* London: A. Miller.

Lindblom, C. E., and D. K. Cohen. 1979. *Usable knowledge: Social science and social problem solving.* New Haven, CT: Yale University Press.

Lippett, G. L., and W. H. Schmidt. 1967. Crisis in a developing organization. *Harvard Business Review* 45: 102–12.

Lipsey, M., and D. Corday. 2000. Evaluation methods for social intervention. *Annual Review of Psychology* 51: 345–75.

Loader, B., ed. 1998. *Cyberspace divide: Equality, agency and policy in the information age.* London: Routledge.

Lochner, R. H., and J. E. Matar. 1990. *Designing for quality.* Milwaukee: American Association for Quality Control Publishing.

Lomas, J., G. M. Anderson, K. Domnick-Pierre, E. Vayda, M. W. Enkin, and W. J. Hannah. 1989. Do practice guidelines guide practice? The effect of a consensus statement on the practice of physicians. *New England Journal of Medicine* 321 (19): 1306–11.

Lord, F. M. 1967. A paradox in the interpretation of group comparisons. *Psychological Bulletin* 68: 304–5.

Lord, F. M., and M. R. Novick. 1968. *Statistical theories of mental test scores.* Reading, MA: Addison-Wesley.

Lortie, D. C. 1975. *Schoolteacher: A sociological study.* Chicago: University of Chicago Press.

Lukens, J. N. 1994. Progress resulting from clinical trials: Solid tumors in childhood cancer. *Cancer* 74 (9): 2710–18.

Lumsdaine, A. A. 1965. Assessing the effectiveness of instructional programs. In *Teaching machines and programmed learning.* Vol. 2, *Data and directions,* ed. R. Glaser, 267–320. Washington, DC: National Education Association of the United States.

Lyden, F. J. 1975. Using Parsons' functional analysis in the study of public organizations. *Administrative Science Quarterly* 20: 59–70.

Lynn, L. E., Jr., C. J. Heinrich, and C. J. Hill. 2001. Improving governance: A new logic for empirical research. Washington, DC: Georgetown University Press.

MacKenzie, D. 1999. Technological determinism. In *Society on the line: Information politics in a digital age,* ed. W. H. Dutton, 41–46. Oxford: Oxford University Press.

MacKenzie, D., and J. Wajcman. 1999. *The social shaping of technology.* Buckingham: Open University Press.

Maiese, M. 2005. The scale-up problem. In *Beyond intractability,* ed. G. Burgess and H. Burgess. Boulder: Conflict Research Consortium, University of Colorado. www.beyondintractability.org/essay.jsa?id=38757&nid=5051 (accessed January 9, 2006).

Mandinach, E. B., and M. C. Linn. 1986. The cognitive effects of computer learning environments. *Journal of Educational Computing Research* 2 (4): 411–27.

Mann, C. C. 2003. The year the music dies. *Wired* 11 (2): 91–138.

Mark, M. M., C. S. Reichardt, and L. J. Sanna. 2000. Time series designs and analyses. In *Handbook of applied multivariate statistics and mathematical modeling,* eds. H. E. A. Tinsley and S. R. Brown, 353–89. New York: Academic Press.

Maskin, E. 1999. Nash equilbrium and welfare optimality. *Review of Economic Studies* 66: 23–38.

Maskin, E., and J. Moore. 1999. Incomplete contracts and renegotiation. *Review of Economic Studies* 66: 39–56.

Mayston, D. 1996. Educational attainment and resource use: Mystery or econometric misspecification? *Education Economics* 4: 127–42.

McDonald, S., V. Keesler, N. Kaufmann, and B. Schneider. 2006. Scaling up exemplary interventions. *Educational Researcher.*

McGrath, M. E., ed. 1996. *Setting the PACE in product development.* Boston: Butterworth Heinemann Books.

McLaughlin, M. W., and J. E. Talbert. 2001. *Professional communities and the work of high school teaching.* Chicago: University of Chicago Press.

Mead, L. M. 1983. Expectations and welfare work: WIN in New York City. *Policy Studies Review* 2 (4): 648–61.

Mead, L. M. 1986. *Beyond entitlement: The social obligations of citizenship.* New York: The Free Press.

Medical Research Council. 1948. Streptomycin treatment of pulmonary tuberculosis: A Medical Research Council investigation. *British Medical Journal* 2: 769–782.

Meier, P. 1972. The biggest public health experiment ever: The 1954 field trial of the Salk poliomyelitis vaccine. In *Statistics, a Guide to the Unknown*, eds. J. M. Tanur et al. San Francisco: Holden-Day.

Meyer, J., and B. Rowan. 1977. Institutionalized organizations: Formal structure as myth and ceremony. *American Journal of Sociology* 83: 340–63.

Meyer, M. H., and A. P. Lehnerd. 1997. *The power of product platforms.* New York: The Free Press.

Meyer, M. W. 1972. Size and the structure of organizations: A causal model. *American Sociological Review* 37: 434–41.

Meyers, M. K., B. Glaser, and K. MacDonald. 1998. On the front lines of welfare delivery: Are workers implementing policy reforms? *Journal of Policy Analysis and Management* 17 (1): 1–22.

Michalopoulos, C., C. Schwartz, and D. Adams-Ciardullo. 2001. *National evaluation of welfare-to-work strategies: What works best for whom? Impacts of twenty welfare-to-work programs by subgroup.* Washington, DC: U.S. Department of Health and Human Services, Administration for Children and Families, Office of the Assistant Secretary for Planning and Evaluation and U.S. Department of Education, Office of the Under Secretary, Office of Vocational and Adult Education.

Midgley, D. F. 1981. Toward a theory of the product life cycle: Explaining diversity. *Journal of Marketing* 45: 109–15.

Miller, D. 1982. Evolution and revolution: A quantum view of structural change in organizations. *Journal of Management Studies* 19: 131–51.

Miller, D., and P. Friesen. 1984. A longitudinal study of the corporate life cycle. *Management Science* 30: 1161–83.

Miller, G. 1992. *Managerial dilemmas: The political economy of hierarchy.* New York: Cambridge University Press.

Mintzberg, H. 1984. Power and organization life cycles. *Academy of Management Review* 9: 207–24.

Moertel, C. 1984. Improving the efficiency of clinical trials: A medical perspective. *Statistics in Medicine* 3 (4): 455–65.

Moher, D., K. F. Schulz, D. Altman, and CONSORT Group (Consolidated Standards of Reporting Trials). 2001. The CONSORT statement: Revised recommendations for improving the quality of reports of parallel-group randomized trials. *Journal of the American Medical Association* 285 (15): 1987–91.

Moore, G. A. 1995. *Crossing the chasm.* New York: Harper Business Books.

Moseley, J. B., K. O'Malley, N. J. Petersen, T. J. Menke, B. A. Brody, D. H. Kuykendall, et al. 2002. A controlled trial of arthroscopic surgery for osteoarthritis of the knee. *New England Journal of Medicine* 347 (2): 81–88.

Mostow, J., and J. Beck. 2006. When the rubber meets the road: Lessons from the in-school adventures of an automated reading tutor that listens. In *Scale-up in practice,* ed. B. Schneider and S. McDonald. Lanham, MD: Rowman & Littlefield.

Mukerjee, N. 1998. The rush to scale: Lessons being learnt in Indonesia. In *Who changes? Institutionalizing participation in development,* ed. J. Blackburn and J. Holland. London: Intermediate Technology Publications.

Munker, S., and A. Roesler, eds. 1997. *Mythos Internet.* Frankfurt: Suhrkamp.

Myers, D., and A. Schirm. 1999. *The impacts of upward bound: Final report for phase I of the national evaluation.* Washington, DC: Mathematica Policy Research.

Nagel, E. 1961. *The structure of science: Problems in the logic of scientific explanation.* London: Routledge & Kegan Paul.

Nathan, R. 1993. *Turning promises into performance: The management challenge of implementing workfare.* New York: Columbia University Press.

National Institute for Social Science Information (NISSI). 2001. *Smart library on scaling up school reform initiatives.* scalingup.smartlibrary.info/newinterface/main.cfm (accessed January 1, 2006).

National Institutes of Health. 1980. Pros and cons of NIH Consensus Conferences. *Journal of the American Medical Association* 244(13): 1413–1414.

National Institutes of Health. March 28, 1994. *NIH Guidelines on the Inclusion of Women and Minorities as Subjects in Clinical Research.* Federal Register, part VIII (59 FR 14508–13).

National Institutes of Health Consensus Development Panel. 2001. National Institutes of Health Consensus Development Conference Statement: Adjuvant therapy for breast cancer, November 1–3, 2000. *Journal of the National Cancer Institute* 93 (13): 979–89.

National Institutes of Health, Office of the Director, Office of Medical Applications of Research. 2001. *Guidelines for the planning and management of NIH Consensus Development Conferences Online.* Bethesda, MD: National Institutes of Health.

National Library of Medicine. *Medical subject headings.* www.nlm.nih.gov/mesh/ (accessed March 28, 2002). http://grants.nih.gov/grants/guide/notice-files/not94-100 .html.

National Research Council. 1993. *National collaboratories: Applying information technology for scientific research.* Washington, DC: National Academy Press.

National Research Council. 2002. *Scientific research in education.* Committee on Scientific Principles for Education Research, ed. R. J. Shavelson and L. Towne. Center for Education, Division of Behavioral and Social Sciences and Education. Washington, DC: The National Academies Press.

National Science Foundation. 1999. *Interagency Education Research Initiative (IERI), program announcement, NSF 99-84.* www.nsf.gov/pubsys/ods/getpub.cfm?nsf9984 (accessed December 31, 2004).

National Science Foundation. 2000. *Interagency Education Research Initiative (IERI), program solicitation, NSF 00-74.* www.nsf.gov/pubsys/ods/getpub.cfm?nsf0074 (accessed December 31, 2004).

National Science Foundation. 2001. *Interagency Education Research Initiative— revised version (IERI), program solicitation, NSF 01-92.* www.nsf.gov/pubs/2001/nsf0192/ nsf0192.htm (accessed December 31, 2004).

National Science Foundation, Directorate for Education and Human Resources, Division of Research, Evaluation and Communication. 2002. *Interagency Education Research Initiative (FY2002) (IERI) program solicitation, NSF-02-062.* www.nsf.gov/ pubsys/ods/getpub.cfm?nsf02062 (accessed December 31, 2004).

National Science Foundation, Directorate for Education and Human Resources, Division of Research, Evaluation and Communication. 2004. *Interagency Education Research Initiative (IERI) program solicitation, NSF 04-553.* www.nsf.gov/pubs/ 2004/nsf04553/nsf04553.htm (accessed December 29, 2004).

National Science Foundation. 2005. Interagency Education Research Initiative (IERI). www.nsf.gov/funding/pgm_summ.jsp?pims_id=5486 (accessed January 3, 2006).

National Science Foundation Blue-Ribbon Advisory Panel on Cyberinfrastructure. 2003. *Revolutionizing science and engineering through cyberinfrastructure.* www .communitytechnology.org/nsf_ci_report (accessed January 21, 2005).

Nechyba, T. 1996. *Public school finance in a general equilibrium tiebout world: Equalization programs, peer effects, and private school vouchers.* Cambridge, MA: National Bureau of Economic Research.

NEESgrid. 2004. *Distributed hybrid earthquake engineering experiments: Experiences with a ground-shaking grid application.* it.nees.org (accessed January 21, 2005).

Nentwich, M. 2003. *Cyberscience: Research in the age of the internet.* Vienna: Austrian Academy of Sciences Press.

Nettime. 1997. *Net critique,* comp. Geert Lovink and Pit Schultz. Berlin: Edition ID-ARchiv.

Nichols, E. G., and J. G. Conley. 2000. An airframe design perspective on casting process simulation. In *Proceedings of Simulation 2000, Ninth Conference on the modeling of casting, welding and solidification processes,* ed. P. Sahm, P. Hansen, and J. G. Conley. Aachen, Germany: TMS Publications.

Niemi, D., E. L. Baker, D. Steinberg, J. Wang, and E. Chen. Forthcoming. Strategies for validating large-scale assessments. In *Educational Assessment.*

NIH Guidelines on the Inclusion of Women and Minorities as Subjects in Clinical Research, 59 Fed. Reg. 14,508–14,513 (March 28, 1994).

Nye, B., L. V. Hedges, and S. Konstantopoulos. 2000. The effects of small classes on achievement: The results of the Tennessee class-size experiment. *American Educational Research Journal* 37: 123–51.

O'Day, J., and M. S. Smith. 1993. Systemic school reform and educational opportunity. In *Designing coherent education policy: Improving the system,* ed. S. H. Fuhrman, 250–312. San Francisco: Jossey-Bass.

One Sky, Many Voices. 2001. groundhog.sprl.umich.edu/ (accessed January 24, 2006).

One Sky, Many Voices. n.d. BioKIDS: Overview. groundhog.sprl.umich.edu/site/ biokids.html (accessed January 24, 2006).

Oxman, A. D., D. J. Cook, and G. H. Guyatt. 1994. Users' guides to the medical literature. VI. How to use an overview. Evidence-Based Medicine Working Group. *Journal of the American Medical Association* 272 (17): 1367–71.

Packard, F. R. 1921. *The life and times of Ambroise Paré, 1510–1590.* New York: Paul B. Hoeber.

Palakodaty, S., S. Walker, G. Townsend, P. York, and G. Humphreys. 2000. Scale-up and GMP plant design—pharmaceutical particle engineering by the SEDS process. Electronic version. *Pharmaceutical Contractor* (August): 60–63.

Palmer, J. W., and C. Speier. 1997. A typology of virtual organizations: An empirical study. In *Association for Information Systems 1997 Americas Conference,* ed. Association for Information Systems. Pittsburgh: The Association for Information Systems.

Parmar, M. K., R. S. Ungerleider, and R. Simon. 1996. Assessing whether to perform a confirmatory randomized clinical trial. *Journal of the National Cancer Institute* 88(22): 1645–51.

Patton, M. Q. 1978. *Utilization-focused evaluation.* Beverly Hills, CA: Sage.

Pearlman, L., C. Kesselman, S. Gullapalli, B. F. Spencer Jr., J. Futrelle, K. Ricker, I. Foster, P. Hubbard, and C. Severance. 2004. Distributed hybrid earthquake engineering experiments: Experiences with a ground-shaking grid application. In *Proceeding of the 13th IEEE International Symposium on High-Performance Distributed Computing,* 14–23. Los Alamitos, CA: IEEE Computer Society.

Peters, T. J., and R. H. Waterman. 1982. *In search of excellence.* New York: Harper and Row.

Petroski, H. 1998. *Invention by design: How engineers get from thought to thing.* Cambridge, MA: Harvard University Press.

Pfeffer, J., and G. R. Salancik. 1978. *The external control of organizations: A resource dependence perspective.* New York: Harper and Row.

Piaget, J. 1932. *The moral judgement of the child.* New York: Harcourt Brace Jovanovich.

Pine, B. J. 1999. *Mass customization: The new frontier in business competition.* Boston: Harvard Business School Press.

Pocock, S. J. 1977. Randomized clinical trials: Letter to the editor. *British Medical Journal* 1: 1661.

Porter, M. 1996. What is strategy? *Harvard Business Review* 74 (6): 61–78.

Porter, M. E. 1985. *Competitive advantage: Creating and sustaining superior performance.* New York: The Free Press.

Powell, A. G., E. Farrar, and D. K. Cohen. 1985. *The shopping-mall-high-school: Winners and losers in the educational marketplace.* Boston: Houghton Mifflin.

Pringle, D., J. Drucker, and E. Ramstad. 2003. A global journal report: World circuit: Cellphone makers pay a heavy toll for missing fads. *The Wall Street Journal* (Eastern Edition) October 30: A1.

Pugh, D., D. Hickson, and R. Hinnings. 1969. The context of organizational structures. *Administrative Science Quarterly* 14: 91–114.

Quine, W. 1991. *Pursuit of truth.* Cambridge, MA: Harvard University Press.

Quinn, R. E., and K. Cameron. 1983. Organizational life cycles and shifting criteria of effectiveness: Some preliminary evidence. *Management Science* 29: 33–51.

Randle, Y. 1990. Toward an ecological life cycle model of organizational success and failure. PhD diss., University of California, Los Angeles.

Raudenbush, S., and A. Bryk. 2002. *Hierarchical linear models: Applications and data analysis methods*, 2nd ed. Thousand Oaks, CA: Sage.

Raudenbush, S. W., and X. Liu. 2000. Statistical power and optimal design for multisite randomized trials. *Psychological Methods* 5 (2): 199–213.

Ravitch, D. 2000. *Left back: A century of failed school reforms*. New York: Simon & Schuster.

Reichardt, C. S. 1979. The statistical analysis of data from nonequivalent group designs. In *Quasi-experimentation: Design and analysis issues for field settings*, ed. T. D. Cook and D. T. Campbell, 147–205. Chicago: Rand McNally.

Reichardt, C. S., W. M. K. Trochim, and J. C. Cappelleri. 1995. Reports of the death of regression-discontinuity analysis are greatly exaggerated. *Evaluation Review* 19: 39–63.

Repenning, N. 2001. Understanding fire fighting in new product development. *Journal of Product Innovation Management* 18 (5): 285–300.

Repenning, N. 2002. A simulation-based approach to understanding the dynamics of innovation implementation. *Organization Science* 13 (2): 109–27.

Riccio, J., H. S. Bloom, and C. J. Hill. 2000. Management, organizational characteristics, and performance: The case of welfare-to-work programs. In *Governance and performance: new perspectives*, ed. Heinrich and Lynn, 166–98. Washington, DC: Georgetown University Press.

Riccio, J., and D. Friedlander. 1992. GAIN: Program strategies, participation patterns, and first-year impacts in six counties. New York: MDRC.

Riccio, J., D. Friedlander, and S. Freedman. 1994. GAIN: Benefits, costs, and three-year impact of a welfare-to-work program. New York: MDRC.

Riccio, J., and Y. Hasenfeld. 1996. Enforcing a participation mandate in a welfare-to-work program. *Social Service Review* 70 (4): 516–42.

Riccio, J., and A. Orenstein. 1996. Understanding best practices for operating welfare-to-work programs. *Evaluation Review* 20 (1): 3–28.

Ridgeway, J. E., J. S. Zawgewski, M. N. Hoover, and D. V. Lambdin. 2002. Student attainment in connected mathematics curriculum. In *Standards-based school mathematics curricula: What are they? What do students learn?* ed. S. L. Senk and D. R. Thompson, 193–224. Mahwah, NJ: Lawrence Erlbaum Associates.

Rogers, E. M. 2003. *Diffusion of innovations*. 5th ed. New York: The Free Press.

Roschelle, J. M., R. D. Pea, C. M. Hoadley, D. N. Gordin, and B. M. Means. 2000. Changing how and what children learn in school with computer-based technology. *Children and Computer Technology* 10(2): 76–101.

Ross, J. A., R. K. Severson, B. H. Pollock, and L. L. Robison. 1996. Childhood cancer in the United States: A geographical analysis of cases from the Pediatric Cooperative Clinical Trials groups. *Cancer* 77 (1): 201–7.

Rowan, B. 2002. The ecology of school improvement: Notes on the school improvement industry in the United States. *Journal of Educational Change* 3: 283–314.

Royal Society of Chemistry, Environment, Health and Safety Committee. 1999. Safety issues in the scale up of chemical reactions, version 1/3/99. London: The Royal Society of Chemistry. www.rsc.org/pdf/ehsc/scaleup.pdf (accessed January 3, 2006).

Royall, R. 1991. Ethics and statistics in randomized clinical trials (with discussion). *Statistical Science* 6 (1): 52–88.

Rubin, D. B. 1974. Estimation of causal effects in randomized and non-randomized studies. *Journal of Educational Psychology* 66: 688–701.

Sack, W. 2005. Discourse architecture in very large-scale conversations. In *Digital formations: Information technologies and new architectures in the global realm*, ed. R. Latham and S. Sassen. Princeton, NJ: Princeton University Press.

Saijo, T., Y. Tatamitani, and T. Yamoto. 1996. Toward natural implementation. *International Economic Review* 37: 949–80.

Sandham, J. D., R. D. Hull, R. F. Brant, L. Knox, G. F. Pineo, C. J. Doig, et al. 2003. A randomized, controlled trial of the use of pulmonary-artery catheters in high-risk surgical patients. *New England Journal of Medicine* 348 (1): 5–14.

Sarason, S. B. 1971. *The culture of the school and the problem of change.* Boston: Allyn and Bacon.

Sassen, S. 2001. *The global city: New York, London, Tokyo.* Princeton, NJ: Princeton University Press.

Sassen, S. 2005. Electronic markets and activist networks: The weight of social logics in digital formations. In *Digital formations: Information technologies and new architectures in the global realm*, ed. R. Latham and S. Sassen. Princeton, NJ: Princeton University Press.

Sassen, S. 2006. *Territory, authority, rights: From medieval to global assemblages.* Princeton, NJ: Princeton University Press.

Sawhney, M., and E. Prandelli. 2001. Communities of creation: Managing distributed innovation. *California Management Review* 42 (4): 24–55.

Schein, E. H. 1985. *Organizational culture and leadership.* San Francisco: Jossey-Bass.

Scherpereel, C. M. 2001. *Decision order theory: The semantic dimensions of decision making.* PhD diss., Northwestern University.

Schlager, M. S., and J. Fusco. 2003. Teacher professional development, technology, and communities of practice: Are we putting the cart before the horse? *The Information Society* 19 (3): 203–20.

Schneider, B. 2003. Sociology of education: An overview of the field at the turn of the twenty-first century. In *Stability and change in American education: Structure, process, and outcomes*, ed. M. T. Hallinan, A. Gamoran, W. Kubitschek, and T. Loveless, 193–226. Clinton Corners, NY: Eliot Werner Publications.

Scott, B. R. 1971. Stages of corporate development (Part I). Case No. 9-371-294. Intercollegiate Clearing House, Harvard University Business School.

Scriven, M. 1967. The methodology of evaluation. In *Perspectives of curriculum evaluation* (American Educational Research Association Monograph Series on Curriculum Evaluation), ed. R. W. Tyler, R. M. Gagne, and M. Scriven, 39–83. Chicago: Rand McNally.

Sedarevic, M. 2006. Where is my mind: The Facebook phenomenon. *Cherwell24.* www.cherwell.org/where_is_my_mind_the_facebook_phenomenon (accessed January 19, 2006).

SEER Program (National Cancer Institute (U.S.), National Institutes of Health (U.S.), National Cancer Institute (U.S.), and Surveillance Program. 2003. *SEER Cancer Statistics Review, 1975–2000.* Bethesda, MD: National Cancer Institute.

Shadish, W. R., and T. D. Cook. 1999. Comment—Design rules: More steps toward a complete theory of quasi-experimentation. *Statistical Science* 14: 294–300.

Shadish, W. R., T. D. Cook, and D. T. Campbell. 2002. *Experimental and quasi-experimental designs for generalized causal inference.* New York: Houghton Mifflin.

Shavelson, R., and L. Towne, eds. 2002. *Scientific research in education.* Committee on Scientific Principles for Education Research, Center for Education, Division of Behavioral and Social Sciences, National Research Council. Washington, DC: National Academy Press.

Shavers, V. L., C. F. Lynch, and L. F. Burmeister. 2002. Racial differences in factors that influence the willingness to participate in medical research studies. *Annals of Epidemiology* 12 (4): 248–56.

Sherman, C. R., A. L. Potosky, K. A. Weis, and J. H. Ferguson. 1992. The Consensus Development Program: Detecting changes in medical practice following a consensus conference on the treatment of prostate cancer. *International Journal of Technology Assessment in Health Care* 8 (4): 683–93.

Siegel, S. 1956. *Nonparametric statistics for the behavioral sciences.* New York: McGraw-Hill.

Smith, J. S. 1992. Remembering the role of Thomas Francis, Jr. in the design of the 1954 Salk vaccine trial. *Controlled Clinical Trials* 13 (3): 181–84.

Smith, M. S., R. Gabriel, J. Schoot, and W. L. Padia. 1976. Evaluation of the effects of Outward Bound. In *Evaluation Studies Review Annual: Volume 1*, ed. G. V. Glass, 400–21. Newbury Park, CA: Sage.

Songer, N. B. 2006. Rethinking sustainability of curricular innovations: Notes from urban Detroit. In *Scale-up in practice*, ed. B. Schneider and S. McDonald. Lanham, MD: Rowman & Littlefield.

Spiegelhalter, D. J., L. S. Freedman, and M. K. B. Parmar. 1994. Bayesian approaches to randomized clinical trials. *Journal of the Royal Statistical Society. Series A (Statistics in Society)* 157 (3): 357–416.

Sproull, L., and S. Kiesler. 1992. *Connections: New ways of working in the networked organization.* Cambridge, MA: MIT Press.

Stake, R. E. 1967. Toward a technology for the evaluation of educational programs. In *Perspectives of curriculum evaluation.* American Educational Research Association Monograph Series on Curriculum Evaluation, ed. R. W. Tyler, R. M. Gagne, and M. Scriven, 1–12. Chicago: Rand McNally.

Stake, R. E. and J. A. Easley Jr. 1987. Case studies in science education. Washington, D.C.: U.S. Government Printing Office.

Starbuck, W. 1965. Organizational growth and development. In *Handbook of Organizations*, ed. J. G. March, 451–533. Chicago: Rand McNally.

Steering Committee of the Physician's Health Study Research Group. 1989. Final report on the aspirin component of the ongoing Physician's Health Study. *New England Journal of Medicine* 321 (3): 129–35.

Stein, L. A. 2003. OWL, web ontology language reference. www.w3.org/TR/owl-ref (accessed January 21, 2004).

Stein, L. 2002. Creating a bioinformatics nation. *Nature* 317: 119–20.

Stenning, S. P., and M. K. B. Parmar. 2002. Designing randomized trials: Both large and small trials are needed. *Annals of Oncology* 13 (4): 131–38.

Stevens, R. 2004. Group-oriented collaboration: The Access Grid collaboration system. In *The grid: Blueprint for a new computing infrastructure*, eds. I. Foster and C. Kesselman, 191–99. San Francisco: Morgan Kaufmann.

Stevenson, D. L. 2000. The fit and misfit of sociological research and education policy. In *Handbook of the sociology of education*, ed. M. T. Hallinan. New York: Kluwer Academic/Plenum.

Stoll, H. 1999. *Product design methods and practices*. New York: Marcel Dekker.

Suh, N. P. 2001. *Axiomatic design: Advances and applications*. London: Oxford University Press.

Sung, N. S., W. F. Crowley Jr., M. Genel, P. Salber, L. Sandy, L. M. Sherwood, et al. 2003. Central challenges facing the national clinical research enterprise. *Journal of the American Medical Association* 289 (10): 1278–87.

Sutton, R., and B. Staw. 1995. What theory is not. *Administrative Science Quarterly* 40:371–84.

Tapped In®. 2006. Tenant partners. tappedin.org/tappedin/web/tenants.jsp (accessed January 20, 2006).

Tejeda, H. A., S. B. Green, E. L. Trimble, L. Ford, J. L. High, S. R. Ungerleider, et al. 1996. Representation of African-Americans, Hispanics, and Whites in National Cancer Institute cancer treatment trials. *Journal of the National Cancer Institute* 88 (12): 812–16.

TeraGrid. 2002. *The TeraGrid: A primer*. www.teragrid.org/about/TeraGrid-Primer-Sept-02.pdf (accessed January 14, 2005).

Thain, D. H. 1969. Stages of corporate development. *The Business Quarterly* (Winter): 33–45.

The Achievement Council. n.d. Independent evaluation of CRESST performance assignments (presented to the Los Angeles Unified School District). Los Angeles.

The Grid2003 Project. 2004. *The Grid2003 production grid: Principles and practice*. www.ivdgl.org/grid2003 (accessed January 21, 2005).

Trochim, W. M. K. 1984. *Research design for program evaluation: The regression-discontinuity approach*. Newberry Park, CA: Sage.

Tunis, S. R., D. B. Stryer, and C. M. Clancy. 2003. Practical clinical trials: Increasing the value of clinical research for decision making in clinical and health policy. *Journal of the American Medical Association* 290 (13): 1624–32.

Tushman, M. L., and E. Romanelli. 1985. Organizational evolution: A metamorphosis model of convergence and reorientation. In *Research in organizational behavior*, ed. B. Staw and L. L. Cummings, 171–222. Greenwich, CT: JAI Press.

Tushman, M. L., B. Virany, and E. Romanelli. 1985. Executive succession, strategic reorientation, and organizational evolution: The minicomputer industry as a case in point. *Technology in Society* 7: 297–313.

Tyack, D., and L. Cuban. 1995. *Tinkering toward utopia*. Cambridge, MA: Harvard University Press.

Tymms, P. 1996. Theories, models and simulations: School effectiveness at an impasse. In *Merging traditions: The future of research on school effectiveness and school improvement*, ed. J. Gray, C. Reynolds, C. Fitz-Gibbon, and D. Jesson. London: Cassell.

Ulrich, K. T., and S. D. Eppinger. 2004. *Product design and development*. 3rd ed. New York: McGraw-Hill/Irwin.

U.S. Office of Science and Technology Policy. President's Committee of Advisors on Science and Technology (PCAST). Panel on Educational Technology. 1997. *Report to the president on the use of technology to strengthen K–12 education in the United States.* Washington, D.C.: U.S. Government Printing Office. www.ostp.gov/PCAST/k-12ed.html (accessed January 19, 2006).

Uvin, P., and D. Miller. 1996. Paths to scaling up: Alternative strategies for local nongovernmental organizations. *Human Organization* 55 (3): 344–53.

van Harmelen, F., J. Hendler, I. Horrocks, D. L. McGuinness, P. F. Patel-Schneider, and E. von Hippel. 2003. *The sources of innovation.* New York: Oxford University Press.

von Hippel, E. 1988. The sources of innovation. New York: Oxford University Press.

Wajcman, J., ed. 2002. Addressing technological change: The challenge to social theory. Special issue, *Current Sociology* 50 (2): 347–63.

Walton, R. E. 1986. A vision-led approach to management restructuring. *Organizational Dynamics* (Spring): 9–16.

Weber, M. 1947. *The theory of social and economic organization.* New York: The Free Press.

Weber, S. 2005. The political economy of open source software and why it matters. In *Digital formations: Information technologies and new architectures in the global realm,* ed. R. Latham and S. Sassen. Princeton, NJ: Princeton University Press.

Weiss, C. H. 1977. Research for policy's sake: The enlightenment function of social research. *Policy Analysis* 3: 531–45.

Welch, W. W. 1979. Twenty years of science curriculum development: A look back. *Review of Research in Education* 7: 282–306.

Wenger, E. C., and W. M. Snyder. 2000. Communities of practice: The organizational frontier. *Harvard Business Review* (January–February): 139–45.

Wildavsky, A. 1993. *Speaking truth to power: The art and craft of policy analysis.* New Brunswick, NJ: Transaction Publishers.

Williams, R., B. Berriman, E. Deelman, J. Good, J. Jacob, C. Kesselman, C. Lonsdale, S. Oliver, and T. Prince. 2003. Multi-wavelength image space: Another grid-enabled science. *Concurrency and Computation: Practice and Experience* 15(6): 539–549.

Winship, C., and S. L. Morgan. 1999. The estimation of causal effects from observational data. *Annual Review of Sociology* 25: 659–707.

Wiseman, M. 1987. How workfare really works. *Public Interest* 89: 36–47.

Wittrock, M. C. 1974. Learning as a generative process. *Educational Psychologist* 11: 87–95.

Wittrock, M. C., and E. L. Baker, eds. 1991. *Testing and cognition.* Englewood Cliffs, NJ: Prentice Hall.

Wolcott, R. C., P. Tibrewal, and A. Saxena. 2004. Platforms and eco-systems: Value creation, capture, propagation and control. Working Paper, Center for Research in Technology and Innovation, Kellogg School of Management, Northwestern University.

Worchel, S., and J. Cooper. 1983. *Understanding social psychology.* 3rd ed. Homewood, IL: Dorsey Press.

World Health Organization. 2004. *An approach to rapid scale-up: Using HIV/AIDS treatment and care as an example.* Geneva: World Health Organization. www.who.int/hiv/pub/prev_care/en/rapidscale_up.pdf (accessed January 9, 2005).

World Health Organization. 2005. Nigeria: Summary country profile for HIV/AIDS treatment scale-up. Geneva: World Health Organization. www.who.int/3by5/ support/june2005_nam.pdf (accessed January 9, 2006).

World Information Order. 2002. *World information files.* Vienna: Institute for New Culture Technologies/Berlin: Center for Civic Education.

Wortman, P. M., A. Vinokur, and L. Sechrest. 1988. Do consensus conferences work? A process evaluation of the NIH consensus development program. *Journal of Health Politics, Policy, and Law* 13 (3): 469–98.

Writing Group for the Women's Health Initiative Investigators. 2002. Risks and benefits of estrogen plus progestin in healthy postmenopausal women: Principal results from the Women's Health Initiative randomized controlled trial. *Journal of the American Medical Association* 288 (3): 321–33.

Yager, S. E. 1997. Everything's coming up virtual. *ACM Crossroads* 4 (1).

Yancik, R., and L. A. Ries. 2000. Aging and cancer in America: Demographic and epidemiologic perspectives. *Hematology Oncology Clinics of North America* 14 (1): 17–23.

Zlokarnik, M. 2002. *Scale-up in chemical engineering.* Weinheim: Wiley-VCH Verlag GmbH & Co.

Index

About the Editors and Contributors

Eva L. Baker is a distinguished professor at UCLA. She is codirector of the National Center for Research on Evaluation, Standards, and Student Testing (CRESST) and director of the Center for the Study of Evaluation (CSE). She was chair of the Board on Testing and Assessment at the National Research Council and cochair of the Joint Committee on the Revision of the *Standards for Educational and Psychological Testing* (published in 1999). She is the current president of the American Educational Research Association (AERA) and former president of the Educational Psychology Division, American Psychological Association. She is currently involved in accountability and assessment research in the United States, England, Australia, and Korea, with a special interest in transfer. She has published over seven hundred chapters, reports, and articles.

Deborah Loewenberg Ball is dean of the School of Education and William H. Payne Collegiate Professor at the University of Michigan. Ball's work draws on her many years of experience as an elementary classroom teacher. Her research focuses on mathematics instruction and on interventions designed to improve its quality and effectiveness. Her research groups study the nature of the mathematical knowledge needed for teaching and develop survey measures that make possible analyses of the relations among teachers' mathematical knowledge; the quality of their teaching; and their students' performance. Of particular interest in this research is instruction that works to redress significant achievement disparities for students of color and students living in poverty. Ball is a principal investigator on the Study of Instructional Improvement, a large longitudinal study of efforts to improve instruction in reading and mathematics in high-poverty urban elementary schools. Ball is also codirector of the Center for Proficiency in Teaching Mathematics, a research and development center aimed at strengthening professional education of mathematics teachers. Ball has authored or coauthored over one hundred publications and has lectured and made numerous major presentations around the world. Her research has been recognized with several awards and honors, and she has served on several national and international commissions and panels focused on policy initiatives and the improvement of education.

Howard S. Bloom, chief social scientist for MDRC, has designed and implemented numerous large-scale experimental and quasi-experimental studies of employment and education programs, has taught applied statistics and research methods at Harvard University and New York University for many years, and has written several books and numerous articles on evaluation research. His most recent book, *Learning More from Social Experiments: Evolving Analytic Approaches*, explores how to effectively combine experimental and nonexperimental methods to measure causal effects.

Kevin L. Brown is a research scientist at the Data Research and Development Center (DRDC) at NORC, at the University of Chicago. Prior to joining DRDC, he worked as senior research analyst for the National Institute for Social Science Information (NISSI), managing the production of digital libraries on poverty and educational research. His research and professional interests are in social theory and the dissemination of research on social problems to policymakers, practitioners, and the public at large. He received an M.A. in Economics and Ph.D. in Sociology from the University of Chicago.

David K. Cohen is John Dewey Collegiate Professor in the School of Education and Walter Annenberg Professor of Public Policy in the Ford School of Public Policy at the University of Michigan. His research interests include education policy, the relations between policy and practice, and school improvement. With Brian Rowan and Deborah Loewenberg Ball, he has directed the Study of Instructional Improvement at the University of Michigan.

James G. Conley is a clinical professor in the Kellogg School of Management and the McCormick School of Engineering at Northwestern University. He also serves as a faculty fellow in the Institute for Design Engineering and Application. His academic interests are at the nexus of innovation and creativity, management strategy, and intellectual property law. This research is informed by professional practice in his role as a principal of the Chicago Partners consulting firm.

Mark A. Constas is associate professor of research methodology and program evaluation in the Department of Education at Cornell University. His research focuses on the development and examination of designs that make use of qualitative and quantitative data. He is also interested in strategies used to build connections between research and practice and has recently published a book with Robert Sternberg, *Translating Theory and Research into Educational Practice: Developments in Content Domains, Large-Scale Reform, and Intellectual Capacities.*

James J. Dignam is an assistant professor in the Department of Health Studies at the University of Chicago and an investigator at the University of Chicago Cancer Research Center. He received a Ph.D. in biostatistics from the University of Pittsburgh in 1994. His research interests include cancer clinical trial design and interim monitoring, racial/ethnic background and cancer prognosis, and competing risks and multiple endpoints in survival analysis.

Eric G. Flamholtz is president of Management Systems Consulting Corporation and professor of management at UCLA's Anderson School of Management. He is a member of the Board of Directors of 99 Cents Only Stores, a NYSE company. He received a Ph.D. from the University of Michigan. His dissertation, which helped pioneer the area of human resource accounting, was cowinner of the McKinsey Foundation Doctoral Dissertation Award. His research deals with organizational scale-up in entrepreneurial enterprises.

Ian Foster is director of the Computation Institute at Argonne National Laboratory and the University of Chicago, where he is also the Arthur Holly Compton Distinguished Service Professor of Computer Science. His research deals with distributed and parallel computing and computational science.

Larry V. Hedges is a Board of Trustees Professor of Statistics and Social Policy at Northwestern University and Faculty Fellow at the Institute for Policy Research (IRP). He is best known for his work to develop statistical methods for meta-analysis in the social, medical, and biological sciences. His books include *Statistical Methods for Meta-analysis* (with Ingram Olkin) and *The Handbook of Research Synthesis* (with Harris Cooper). He has been elected a member or fellow of numerous associations and professional organizations, is convener of the Campbell Collaboration's statistics group, and chairs the Technical Advisory Group of the U.S. Department of Education's What Works Clearinghouse.

Carolyn J. Hill is assistant professor of public policy at the Georgetown University Public Policy Institute. Her research focuses on the design, management, and performance of publicly supported programs, particularly those that serve poor families.

Paul Horwitz is a senior scientist at the Concord Consortium and a physicist with broad interests in the application of technology to education. As principal investigator on several projects sponsored by the National Science Foundation, he has created numerous computer-based learning environments, including ThinkerTools, which taught Newtonian mechanics to sixth graders, and GenScope, a multilevel model for teaching transmission genetics to middle- and high-school students. He designed RelLab, an open-ended tool for exploring special relativity that won two EDUCOM Educational Software Awards in 1992. Dr. Horwitz currently serves as PI for a project called Modeling Across the Curriculum, sponsored by the Interagency Education Research Initiative, which is using scripted computer models for teaching and assessing students' model-based reasoning and inquiry skills.

Carl Kesselman is fellow and director of the Center for Grid Technologies in the Information Sciences Institute at the University of Southern California and research professor of computer science at the University of Southern California. His research deals with distributed computing and its application in the sciences.

Michelle Llosa is the project coordinator for the Data Research and Development Center (DRDC) at Michigan State University and editorial assistant for *Sociology of Education*. Her research interests include educational policy as well as educational development and postsecondary aspirations of minority students. She received her B.A. in Human Development and Psychology at the University of Chicago in 2004. Her thesis project, which questioned the functional allocation of Spanish and English within a bilingual classroom, was published in the 2004 *TESOL Journal*.

Sarah-Kathryn McDonald is executive director of the Data Research and Development Center (DRDC) and a senior research scientist at NORC, at the University of Chicago. She received a Ph.D. from Northwestern University and an M.B.A. from the City University, London. She served as a member of the board of directors of EU government relations firm Counselors in Public Policy and joined the faculty of the Department of Management at Birkbeck College in the University of London in 1995, where she was elected to serve as a member of the college's Board of Governors. She joined the Consortium on Chicago School Research shortly after returning to the

United States and worked to promote the use of research findings for educational improvement.

Robert A. Moffitt is the Krieger-Eisenhower Professor of Economics at Johns Hopkins University and is affiliated with the University of Wisconsin Institute for Research on Poverty and the National Bureau of Economic Research. He is an expert on the economics of welfare reform and has conducted studies on causal modeling, econometric methods, female labor force participation, and the family.

Yvonne Randle is vice president of Management Systems Consulting Corporation and a lecturer at the Anderson School, UCLA. Her consulting and research focus on organizational transitions, strategic planning, management development, and corporate culture management. She is the coauthor of *Growing Pains, Changing the Game: Organizational Transformations of the First, Second, and Third Kinds,* and *The Inner Game of Management.*

Charles S. Reichardt is a professor in the Department of Psychology at the University of Denver. His research most often focuses on the logic and practice of assessing cause and effect. He is also the director of a project on quantitative literacy that introduces hands-on data analysis in college courses in the arts, humanities, and social sciences.

James A. Riccio is director of MDRC's Low-Wage Workers and Communities policy area. He has been a lead researcher on many MDRC evaluations, specializing in the study of work-related programs and policies for welfare recipients, public housing residents, and other disadvantaged groups. His current work includes directing a large-scale random assignment evaluation of a new employment retention and advancement program for low-income people in the United Kingdom.

Saskia Sassen (University of Chicago and London school of Economics) is the author, most recently, of *Territory, Authority, Rights: From Medieval to Global Assemblages.* She has completed a five-year project on sustainable human settlement for UNESCO, for which she set up a network of researchers and activists in more than thirty countries. It is published as a volume in the *Encyclopedia of Life Support Systems* (EOLSS), www.eolss.net. Her books have been translated into sixteen languages and her comments have appeared in publications such as *The Guardian, New York Times, Le Monde Diplomatique, International Herald Tribune, Vanguardia, Clarin,* and *Financial Times.*

Barbara Schneider is a John A. Hannah Distinguished University Professor in the College of Education and Department of Sociology at Michigan State

University. She is principal investigator of the Data Research and Development Center (DRDC) and codirector of the Alfred P. Sloan Center on Parents, Children, and Work at the University of Chicago. Her research interests focus on how the social contexts of schools and families influence the academic and social well-being of adolescents as they move into adulthood. Her most recent publications include *Being Together, Working Apart: Dual-Career Families and the Work-Life Balance*, with Linda Waite, *The Social Organization of Schooling*, with Larry Hedges, and *The Ambitious Generation: America's Teenagers, Motivated but Directionless*, with David Stevenson. She serves on a number of advisory boards, including the AERA Grants Board, and was selected by the American Sociological Association as the new editor of *Sociology of Education*.

Robert C. Wolcott, Ph.D., is a fellow and adjunct assistant professor of innovation and entrepreneurship at the Kellogg School of Management and a visiting professor with both Kellogg's executive MBA program with the HKUST (Hong Kong) and Keio Business School (Tokyo). He founded and directs the Kellogg Innovation Network (KIN), an exclusive group of innovation executives from global corporations including firms such as Motorola, PepsiCo, Cargill, DuPont, McDonald's, and Levi Strauss. He is also cofounder of Clareo Partners LLC, a boutique innovation strategy firm.